The Voices of Baseball

The Voices of Baseball

The Game's Greatest Broadcasters Reflect on America's Pastime

Kirk McKnight

ROWMAN & LITTLEFIELD
Lanham • Boulder • New York • London

Published by Rowman & Littlefield
A wholly owned subsidiary of The Rowman & Littlefield Publishing Group, Inc.
4501 Forbes Boulevard, Suite 200, Lanham, Maryland 20706
www.rowman.com

Unit A, Whitacre Mews, 26-34 Stannary Street, London SE11 4AB

British Library Cataloguing in Publication Information Available

Library of Congress Cataloging-in-Publication Data

McKnight, Kirk.
   The voices of baseball : the game's greatest broadcasters reflect on America's pastime /
Kirk McKnight.
      pages cm
   Includes bibliographical references and index.
   ISBN 978-1-4422-4447-4 (hardcover : alk. paper) — ISBN 978-1-4422-4448-1
(ebook)
   1. Baseball fields—United States—History. 2. Stadiums—United States—History.
3. Baseball—United States—History. 4. Baseball teams—United States—History. 5.
Sportscasters—United States. 6. Radio broadcasting of sports—United States—History.
7. Television broadcasting of sports—United States—History. I. Title.
   GV879.5.M35 2015
   796.35706873—dc23

2015008223

Printed in the United States of America

I dedicate this book to my wife, Collette, who, from kiss #1, has supported me on every level in my quest to become a professional writer. Every author should have one just like her.

A successful announcer is his own person and has his own personality. When you've listened to the great announcers—the Harwells, Scullys, Carneals, Bucks, and Carays—you can't help but, beyond your admiration for them, pick up on what it is they do well. In the cases of the gentlemen I just mentioned, they were in one town and one team for a long, long time, and, for broadcasting in particular, that's quite an accomplishment. Whether it's Chuck Thompson or Bob Murphy—all of the great voices we've heard so much of in the '50s, '60s, and '70s—the one thing they all had in common, I think, is wearability. They did their jobs. They covered the game. They injected their personality, but they never grew weary of their jobs or have fans get weary of how they did it. That's quite an accomplishment in this day and age.

—Dick Bremer, Minnesota Twins TV play-by-play broadcaster

Contents

Foreword

$\mathcal{W}$hen I was about six years old—which is as far back as I can go in the recesses of my mind to collect anything that resembles a memory—I watched my first baseball game on TV. This isn't one of those "we could only afford bunny ears" kind of stories. My family wasn't rich by any definition of the word, but we had cable TV and TBS. My favorite baseball team was the one showcased on TBS day in and day out: the Atlanta Braves. Living in Las Vegas, Nevada, I was always able to watch an Atlanta Braves broadcast at 4:05 p.m. local time.

Now, since the Atlanta Braves were my favorite team, I must have also had a favorite player, right? Well, you can ask anybody who remembers me around the age of six, and they'll tell you, Dale Murphy was my guy. I told Wayne Hagin during our interview, "There were 26 teams in baseball when I first started watching. That's 26 teams, 25 players each, which makes 650 professional players. To me, 649 of them didn't exist. There was Dale Murphy and no one else." To this day, I scratch my head in wonder about why Dale is not in the hall of fame. He had 398 performance-enhancing drug-free home runs in his career and back-to-back National League MVP awards in 1982 and 1983.

I'll never forget the first time I went to see Dale Murphy play in person. It was my first trip ever to Dodger Stadium. By this time "The Murph" was at the tail end of his career, and unbeknownst to me, his final year or so with the Braves. I remember they pulled Murphy from the game for either a pinch hitter or pinch runner. I was storming up and down my row like an angry manager. I did not quite understand the strategies of baseball at the time. Murphy, being in his advanced years as a player, was probably pulled for a speedier set of legs.

A couple of years later, my baseball world was turned upside down, as Dale Murphy was dealt to the Philadelphia Phillies. I remember seeing the Phillies games against the Atlanta Braves, and when the trade happened, I had the thought, "How's Dale Murphy going to play in those ugly uniforms?" I kept track of Dale a little when he played for the Phillies, but I didn't have that connection with him that I had had through TBS and Atlanta Braves broadcasts. Skip Caray was my connection to Dale Murphy. I remembered Skip, Pete Van Wieren, and Ernie Johnson Sr., but there was one name among that broadcast team that wouldn't surface until I met him face to face in May 2014.

When Murphy was cut from the Rockies, I went through another series of favorite players, beginning with Frank Thomas and ending with Cecil Fielder. I bought a Tigers baseball hat, and if you saw me from 1994 to 1996, I was wearing that Tigers hat. I named my dog "Cecil" and followed the real Cecil Fielder even more closely than I had followed Murphy. I became a Yankees fan the day Fielder was traded to New York back in late July 1996, which, any Yankees fan will know is the year Derek Jeter came onto the scene and helped the team to their first World Series title in almost 20 years.

As a Yankees fan, I could not get the broadcasts back in Las Vegas. The only time I got Yankees games were on the national broadcasts. John Sterling, Michael Kay, and, for a time Charley Steiner, were my link to the New York Yankees. Eventually Steiner would achieve his lifelong dream of broadcasting for the Dodgers alongside his childhood idol Vin Scully. There was something I couldn't quite register about Sterling, though. The familiarity of his name and voice kept telling me had I watched or listened to him at some other point in my life.

After about 18 years of being a Yankees fan and preparing for my interview with John Sterling, the chord was finally struck in my long-term memory. Atlanta! John Sterling had broadcast Atlanta Braves baseball during the '80s before moving over to the Yankees broadcast booth in 1989. There it was, like one of those moments in a movie that flashes through history and emerges out of the eye of the main character. John Sterling broadcast for Dale Murphy and the Atlanta Braves. Suddenly, my questions for Sterling had a twofold focus: Yankees baseball and Atlanta Braves baseball in the '80s. I had that link back to the team I had loved and followed right before my eyes. I've bled pinstripe blue for over half my life, and to speak with the lead voice of the Yankees face to face was a dream come true, yet I couldn't help trying to summon up those memories of me as a six-year-old boy watching Atlanta Braves baseball on TV.

Baseball does that to a person. It recalls so many of our memories because it's our link to the past. These memories and their origins all have a setting. As a matter of fact, they have 30 settings, and not one of them is exactly like the other. Not anymore, at least. I've always been fascinated with baseball's stadiums and ballparks. The design. The smell of the freshly cut and watered Bermuda grass mixed with peanut shell dust and a smoky grill. They all come at you full force once you make your way through the gates and into the concourses.

The first stadium I ever visited was Angel Stadium of Anaheim, or "The Big A" as it is better known, and not even *that* stadium is the same anymore. Dodger Stadium is my second baseball home and was where I took my (then) two-year-old daughter to see her first game: Dodgers versus Yankees, July 30, 2013. Pettitte vs. Greinke. That shouldn't come as a surprise to anyone who knows me. I hadn't even been married a year in 2008 when I told my wife, "Honey, Yankee Stadium is closing this year." The wonderful wife that she is, she merely responded, "Then I guess we'd better go." She could see in my eyes how much I wanted to see that stadium before it became a thing of the past. She knew that I would regret it the rest of my life if I didn't attend "the house that Ruth built," mainly because she understands my love for the game, and after taking a morning tour of Yankee Stadium, she, too, understood the mystique and importance of that cathedral. One of my favorite quotes from my wife is one she uses whenever somebody expresses to me their hatred for the Yankees. She merely replies, "How can you hate the Yankees? That's like saying you hate apple pie."

Yankee Stadium, Dodger Stadium, and Angel Stadium aren't the only parks I've had the privilege of visiting over my 30 plus years as a baseball fan. Others are Safeco Field, Petco Park, Chase Field, Tropicana Field, Coors Field, and perhaps my favorite, Globe Life Park in Arlington. Upon visiting these several baseball settings, I realized how much of an identity each park has. There is no uniformity of dimension in baseball. It's not like basketball, football, or hockey. No ballpark is the same on the field or in the seats. Hoping to visit all 30 ballparks, I thought to myself, "What if I were to write a book on the uniqueness of every stadium in baseball? How do they play differently? What are their quirks? What makes one different from the other 29?" Then I had the thought: "What if I were to get these answers from the broadcasters themselves? They outlast the players, managers, the *general* managers, team presidents, team owners, and, in the case of Vin Scully, the city itself. Why not get *their* perspective? After all, they broadcast in that booth 81 times a year for decades on end, so why not ask them?"

The following accounts are from 33 broadcasters whose accumulated experience in the booth is well over eight centuries. They have broadcast in both today's ballparks and yesterday's stadiums and have done so alongside those who have passed on, but whose voices still linger years later. Voices like Ernie Harwell, Mel Allen, Red Barber, Bob Murphy, and Jack Buck. The stories go back as far as a young Vin Scully growing up in the bleachers of the Polo Grounds in Manhattan, and as far forward as Rex "Hud" Hudler reflecting upon the Kansas City Royals' magical 2014 American League pennant-winning season. Made up mostly of what John Sterling himself would call "senior members of the firm," these storytellers live up to their name for the ballparks, teams, and cities they represent.

Introduction: In a Word, "Theatrical"

*W*hat would New York Giants outfielder Bobby Thomson's "shot heard 'round the world," walk-off home run to clinch the 1951 National League pennant have sounded like without Giants radio broadcaster Russ Hodges's immortal call of "And the Giants win the pennant. The Giants win the pennant!" there to provide the sound track as Thomson trotted around the bases? How would St. Louis Cardinals shortstop Ozzie Smith's National League pennant-clinching home run against the Los Angeles Dodgers appear without hall of fame broadcaster Jack Buck telling Cardinals fans to "Go crazy, folks! Go crazy!"? Finally, what would Los Angeles Dodgers outfielder Kirk Gibson's walk-off home run in game 1 of the 1988 World Series against Oakland A's closer Dennis Eckersley sound like without the vocal accompaniment of the Dodgers' own Vin Scully? Scully was often hired by NBC to broadcast World Series games even if his Dodgers weren't competing in them. The '88 season just happened to be magical enough that Scully and the Dodgers *both* found themselves in the fall classic. Before "turning the mic over" to Scully and Gibson's timeless shot, it's perhaps fitting to set the scene for this silver-screen-worthy moment.

Having already saved 45 regular season games and all four American League Championship Series wins for the Athletics, Dennis Eckersley came into the game having not surrendered a home run in almost two months. Eckersley's fastball slider lived up to its reputation, as shown by Los Angeles Dodgers catcher Mike Scioscia's infield pop-up to A's shortstop Walt Weiss and Jeff Hamilton's motionless bat as he watched Eckersley's patented pitch soar by for a called strike three. X-rays later revealed a bruised shoulder from the weight of Hamilton's resting bat. These two quick outs led some Dodgers fans to make their way up the aisles with slumped shoulders and hanging heads. Apparently, the price for being a part of World Series history is spending a half hour less in traffic on the California 101 Freeway. Now, let's turn the mic over to Vin Scully for a recap of the 1988 World Series game 1 some 26 years later: "It all began with the ninth inning. We had just gone into commercial before going to the bottom of the ninth and I asked the producer in the truck for NBC. I said, 'Do me a favor and follow me.' Now you rarely do that, but, at this instance, I felt that he was busy trying to get the time of whatever broadcast would follow the game. I asked him please to follow me and he said, 'Okay.' So when we came out of commercial, there was the overhead shot by the blimp looking down at Dodger Stadium and I said something to the effect 'If you were here with us tonight in person, the first thing you would do would be to look in the Dodger dugout,' and immediately, there was a shot of the dugout. Then the camera panned the length of the dugout and I said something to the effect of 'Obviously, Kirk Gibson is not in the dugout, and so, obviously, he will not be able to play tonight.' Well, as I was saying that, Kirk was in the clubhouse, sitting on the trainer's table, both legs encased in ice, watching on television like everybody else. For some reason, the way I said he's not going to appear struck a chord. You'd have to really ask him. All of a sudden, he jumped up and threw the ice off his leg and said to the clubhouse boy, 'Run down and tell Tommy (Lasorda) that I'll be there in a minute.' Now I'm totally unaware of all of that, and the clubhouse man ran down and told Lasorda that he was going to come in a minute.

Meanwhile, the Dodgers had an outfielder named Mike Davis, and Mike Davis, an aggressive, good outfielder and hitter, was getting a walk, so that consumed some time. After Mike got the walk, out of the corner of my eye, I saw Kirk starting to come up the steps in the dugout, using the bat as a cane, and I immediately reacted and said, 'Well, look who's here.' Well, as he came up off the steps, the crowd just went wild and he eventually went up to the plate to pinch hit. Mike Davis had also stolen second base, so the tying run was at second. In my mind, I knew they weren't going to walk Gibson. Gibson had bad legs and couldn't really do anything, so I hoped in my mind that he would not strike out because he had had such a tremendous year. He was such a courageous player and all banged up, so that was my silent prayer that he wouldn't strike out. He hit a couple of squirrelly little foul balls. Had they been fair, he never would have been able to run to first base. Then, out of the blue, he hits the home run, and I remember later, people asked me to kind of classify the home run. I thought that it was the most theatrical home run I had ever seen. I was very fortunate during the minute and a half that I let the crowd roar. I've always done that. That's when I had the thought 'In a year that was so improbable, the impossible has happened,' and that kind of stuck with the fans."

With Hollywood itself just over the hill, "theatrical" couldn't have been a better adjective. At the time Gibson's home run ball landed in the right-field bleachers, Scully had been in his 39th season as a Major League Baseball broadcaster. Some 26 years later, he could recall the event, down to the slightest detail, as if it had happened yesterday. Today's broadcasters, as well as those from yesterday, understand their responsibility as storytellers for the team. They received tutelage from voices whose names line the halls of Cooperstown, calling games for players who may someday grace those halls as well. Thanks to the example of veterans like Vin Scully, broadcasters know when to pause for the crowd and how to guide them through what they're seeing, or, in the case of a radio audience, hearing to the point that they actually *could* see it. Some 65 seasons after calling his first Dodgers game, Vin Scully still understands his and the other broadcasters' role in baseball, which is as everlasting as the game itself.

AT&T Park: San Francisco Giants

AT&T Park: "San Francisco, you could say, is renowned worldwide for its vistas, its beautiful and famous views, and this ballpark celebrates that aspect."—Jon Miller
©2014 S.F. Giants

The Giants are a "pitching first" ball club. That's the foundation of their success. I think the ballpark has worked very much in their favor.

—Jon Miller, San Francisco Giants
radio play-by-play broadcaster

ong before the Yankees took on the mantle (no pun intended) of New York's baseball team, the New York Giants had cemented themselves in baseball lore in the five-borough area of "The City That Never Sleeps." Known for their first two years of existence (1883–1884) as the New York Gothams, the Giants began sporting their current name midway through the team's third year in the majors. Playing with one of the greatest pitchers (Christy Mathewson), and arguably the greatest baseball manager in the history of the game (John McGraw), the Giants of the early 20th century ruled New York. In fact, under the stewardship of McGraw the Giants defeated Babe Ruth's Yankees in the 1921 World Series in the Polo Grounds home that the two teams shared for several years before McGraw had his pinstriped roommates kicked out, paving the way for Yankee Stadium to become the team's eventual home in 1923. The 1922 World Series would yield a similar result for the Yankees, who just could not beat McGraw's Giants. In McGraw's 30 years as the Giants' manager, he won three World Series titles (one in which he played and managed), 10 pennants, and 2,583 games. McGraw's 2,763 career wins as a manager are second only to Connie Mack's 3,731. In 1933, the year after "Little Napoleon" retired from baseball, the Giants won their fourth World Series title against the Washington Senators, thanks to the pitching of Carl Hubbell and the hitting of Mel Ott, who, in his 22-year career, would belt 511 home runs and knock in 1,860 runs. The crosstown tables turned over the next three World Series appearances for the Giants, in 1936, 1937, and 1951, as the Yankees, shaking McGraw's monkey off their backs, defeated the Giants in all three fall classics. In 1954 a young Willie Mays, who would prove to be a "Giant" contributor for the team, led the Giants to their fifth World Series title during his MVP season. In 1957 the fourth version of the Polo Grounds was slated to be demolished, and after much deliberation over the easily anticipated backlash from fans and residents of New York, "Say Hey" Willie Mays, the Giants, and their crosstown National League rival Brooklyn Dodgers packed up their teams and headed for the Golden State.

Now with the ocean on their left side, the Giants, likely used to being a transient team, played for two seasons in Seals Stadium before moving into their "poor venue" of Candlestick Park, where they would play for 40 seasons. While not the most suitable park for baseball, Candlestick Park housed two pennant-winning Giants teams, in '62 and '89, with hall of fame caliber players like Willie McCovey, Orlando Cepeda, and Juan Marichal, who would all be commemorated by the Giants community in a unique capacity a few years down the road. After the '92 season the Giants franchise already had the price tag "plucked" from the merchandise by Tampa Bay businessman Stuart Sternberg and appeared headed for central Florida, where Giants logoed T-shirts were already drawn up, pressed, and ready to sell. Thanks to eventual owner Peter Magowan, current team president/CEO Larry Baer, and enough red tape to physically reach Tampa Bay, the Giants not only stayed in the Bay Area but lured two-time National League MVP Barry Bonds from the Pittsburgh Pirates. With the Giants' proverbial suitcases tossed back into the closet to collect dust, the team was now in desperate need of a new venue, which wish was granted on April 11, 2000, as the Giants took the field of (then named) Pac Bell Park against their rival and "westward ho" travel buddies, the Los Angeles Dodgers.

JAM PACKED, INSIDE *AND* OUT

Considering the weight they carried not only of being one of the most storied franchises in baseball but also of being the fish that almost got away, the Giants needed a ballpark that spoke to the fans, and to do that they had to do their homework. Giants hall of fame radio broadcaster Jon Miller recalls the preparations that went into AT&T Park: "The Giants, when they built the park, did their research and said, 'Wrigley Field still exists in Chicago. The Cubs draw well whether they're good or bad. They have a history of not being good far more than being pennant contenders and yet the fans show up. They just love Wrigley Field. It seems like the affection for the Cubs is as much the affection for Wrigley Field. Can we create some of that same feeling here?' Wrigley Field was so apropos as a model because it was built on a very small piece of land in the inner city, as is Fenway Park and most of those old ballparks. It was a piece of land surrounded by neighborhoods and streets. AT&T Park is built on a smaller piece of land than any ballpark that's been built since Wrigley Field was opened in 1914. All of the ballparks since then have had more real estate. Most of them have had 35 acres or more, but AT&T Park is built on a 13-acre sliver of land. When you talk about a ballpark that is kind of a throwback to another era, the most authentic of all of them is AT&T Park, because it literally is built on a piece of land roughly the size of the land that Wrigley Field was built on, so they had to jam it in there." The obvious reason for this "jamming" was the expiration of real estate rather than its lineation, as AT&T Park practically sits on the waterfront of San Francisco.

Once enough negotiations had been concluded with the port authority to ensure the right-field dimensions weren't comparable to those of a "pee-wee league" team, the Giants organization, namely Peter Magowan and Larry Baer, got to work to make sure AT&T Park welcomed not only the fans but also the memories of the great Giants of the past. Miller notes: "When the park first opened, they dedicated the square right out by the home plate entrance of the ballpark to Willie Mays, and they unveiled a statue of Willie. I think most people, when they enter the ballpark, that's what they first see. Willie Mays, one of the greatest players who ever lived, and he was a Giant. A little bit further down Third Street, along the right-field line, there's a statue of Juan Marichal, another great Giants hall of famer of the San Francisco era, and if you go down the left-field line, there's Orlando Cepeda, another hall of famer. The Giants renamed the water behind right field 'McCovey Cove' for Willie McCovey, a great Giants hall of famer. So you get this big statement about the ballpark that you're going into as to whose home it is, and it's the historic franchise of the Giants." Of course, five months out of the year the park is devoid of baseball while situated in the heart of one of America's most beautiful cities. Miller adds, "There's this ballpark that has the look on the outside of a place that's been there for years. The brick facing the archways. Very 'California-ey' with all the palm trees. The day they dedicated the statue and announced the home address of AT&T Park would be 24 Willie Mays Plaza, Willie said, 'Everybody keeps talking to me about *Willie, have you been in the stands and seen the incredible views of the bay and the city*?' and Willie said, 'Views?! This isn't a *bleeping* condominium. This is a ballpark.' I think that's what's interesting about it. When you're a fan, it's just a great place to go. That great gathering place where people get together, tell stories, and enjoy each other's company. I think for San Franciscans—the baseball fans—it's become that place. They love it when the Giants are good and they win the World Series or are in a pennant race, but they also seem to love it when all those things aren't present. They just like to be there because it's a great spot and it celebrates the city. San Francisco, you could say, is renowned worldwide for its vistas, its beautiful and famous views, and this ballpark celebrates that aspect of San Francisco, maybe as much as any other ballpark celebrates and reflects on the great aspects of that city."

THE WINDY CITY . . . BY THE BAY

One-hit wonder Scott McKenzie was obviously 33 years removed from the opening of AT&T Park when he sang the words, "If you're going to San Francisco, be sure to wear some flowers in your hair." Much like its parent Wrigley Field, the genetically modified AT&T Park, located in, as the band Journey would sing, "that city by the bay," faces gusts that affect the players in a way that would make mom/dad Wrigley proud. Describing the park's nuances that result from the wind, Jon Miller says, "The players see that it's not easy to hit home runs or build a good batting average there. Candlestick Park was infamous for the winds often coming from two different directions that made playing there just a nightmare. I'm sure infielders and outfielders alike would wake up in a cold sweat, having a bad dream about trying to catch a pop-up which was sometimes impossible. With the new ballpark, they did wind tunnel studies. They originally wanted home plate to be where center-field is. They wanted the ballpark to open with the vistas of the downtown skyline. It's a city of hills like Rome, and they wanted to see all, but the wind tunnel study people came back to the Giants—after studying the prevailing winds for about a year—and said, 'If you do that, the wind is going to come right into the face of the batter and also the fans,' so they switched it around. They determined the prevailing winds would largely get blocked with the superstructure of the ballpark. What the architects wanted to do with not just the structure itself but the direction it faced was to block a lot of those winds, but they were not able to foresee how the winds seemed to come in from right field. Even sometimes, when the wind seems to be blowing in a different direction, the right fielder will tell you he almost always feels the wind at his back. So then you look at the flags above the centerfield scoreboard and you see something different than what the right fielder is feeling. On fly balls to center, high fly balls can get carried by the wind when it's blowing straight out like that, but if it's not a real high fly ball—on the same night with the same wind—that ball can get knocked down. I'm no expert, but I think it must be the scoreboard. That wind blowing straight out hits the scoreboard, curves back underneath, and comes back in. When the park was still new, Marvin Bernard played centerfield most of the time for the Giants, and he'd look up and see the winds blowing straight out to center. He'd grab some blades of grass, toss them into the air, and see them blow back toward the infield. He could feel that wind at his back. The other peculiarity of the ballpark is if there's no wind at all, it becomes a band box. You get ahold of one, it's go-ing to jump, so if there was no wind at all, this ballpark would be, just as you might expect, a great place to hit home runs."

Another accomplice to a starting pitcher's assassination of the home run ball is AT&T Park's unique dimensions and outfield walls themselves. Miller adds, "It's only 309 feet to the right-field foul pole. Then the wall angles out very quickly. It's a high wall, so balls will get hit well there and just get knocked down. J.T. Snow, a good left handed hitter with power who had as many as 28 home runs in a season, had years where he hit 12 or 13 home runs on the road and only one at home the whole year. If you hit the ball down the line, it's shallow but that wall angles out very quickly to that 421 spot in deep right center, and that's a graveyard; so, if you hit it out there, unless you really just annihilate it, that ball's not going to leave the yard. Left field can be an easier home run field in general because the wind generally blows out to left field. There's nothing to impede the flight of the ball in that direction, except that it's 338 feet down the lines and 382 to left center, not 370. There's a spot where the left-field wall meets the centerfield wall and it's 404 feet, so there's another little graveyard out there. It's actually a little bit deeper to that spot than it is to straightaway center." While a depth four times around the century mark is great for pitchers and their stats, the outfielders at AT&T Park certainly "put in a hard day's work" once they hang up their spikes in the clubhouse. Jon Miller notes, "There's a lot of room to cover out there for an outfielder, which can lead to doubles and triples. I think most years you'd find that the ballpark ranks very high in doubles and triples. Early on, Fernando Vina hit a ball out to the gap in right center and he ended up getting an inside-the-park home run. The Giants said, 'We can't let that happen,' and so they played the right fielder way off the line over into that gap. That's another peculiarity of the way the game is played there. Clockwise along the right-field line, balls that might get caught anywhere else often fall in for extra base hits because the right fielder's got such a long run to get over to the foul line. The theory is that a ball down the right-field corner is going to be a double one way or the other, so just go in and get it, but you want to see them cut off those triples and inside-the-park home runs into the gaps. I think it's a good park in which to hit triples except a lot of would-be triples end up getting caught. Aaron Rowand struggled every year he was with the Giants. He said, 'My power is to right center. Most of the well hit balls I have are hit there and they all get caught.' He was very frustrated by it, but I think most hitters come to realize it's the visiting hitters who really struggle and are unhappy about it. So, although it maybe hurts their home run total and batting average, the home guys see the overall effect works in their favor." In the early 2000s at AT&T Park, it didn't matter how far the right fielder was from the foul line, because the only place that ball was landing was McCovey Cove, at least when left fielder Barry Bonds was at the plate.

THE HOME RUN DERBY THAT LASTED EIGHT SEASONS

When we consider hitters like Ted Williams and his "Williamsburg" area in right center at Fenway Park or Babe Ruth and his short porch in right field at the "old" Yankee Stadium, we begin to see that some parks were designed for their stars. One could make such an argument for AT&T Park and Barry Bonds during the 2001 season. Jon Miller claims, "The other aspect of that ballpark that's easy to forget is when the ballpark was opened, the Giants hit very well. Still, if you look at the home/road splits for that year, they hit better on the road. It was just a real good hitting team. Bonds, Ellis Burks, and Jeff Kent. They had some real sluggers in the lineup. Bonds, in 2001, when he had 73 home runs, he had 37 at home. He hit 36 on the road. People who had not been to the ballpark just assumed he hit all those home runs at home because it's so shallow in right field. To those people, I pointed out he hit 37 homers here. The visiting teams, altogether in 81 games played, hit 49 home runs at the Giants' ballpark that year. Bonds was the exception to the rule that this was a hard place to hit home runs. In fact, when he passed Henry Aaron for the all-time home run leadership, he challenged that 421-foot barrier—the graveyard—and sent it two or three rows up in the seats past the deepest part of the ballpark. A lot of times, those epic home runs for guys late in their careers, that's not the kind of home run it is, but for Bonds, the toughest spot in any ballpark to hit a home run, that's where he hit it. He often did that in that ballpark. He often hit balls maybe even further out into the bay, but not many people hit a home run over that 421 sign. The night he hit 71 and 72 in 2001, number 71 went high over the 421 sign, up above the 20-foot-high wall. That whole area is a tough home run for anybody."

APRIL 17, 2001: BONDS FINALLY FEELS AT HOME INSIDE AT&T PARK

Looking back on the time line of the park's opening and Barry Bonds's record-breaking seasons, it's easy to assume the slugger took right to his "new digs" and exploded right out of the gates as soon as he got there. That was not the case. Jon Miller explains: "The first year they moved in there, they led the majors in wins, so they had a very fine season. When the season started, and everybody else was trying to figure out how this park was going to play, the hitters were not happy. They were losing home runs. Barry Bonds was losing home runs. Their first series, they got swept by the Dodgers, and then, in the next series, Bonds lost two home runs in one night against Randy Johnson. He hit them out to 421 and to center or the wind knocked them down. He always hit well against Johnson; maybe better than any other left-handed hitter in the game, so Bonds was a little frustrated and not too happy about this." Bonds's frustrations extended out into the field as well. Miller continues, "They were playing Arizona and Bonds was in left field. One of the catchers for the D'backs hit a ball to deep left, and Bonds goes back. He's getting ready to jump to catch it, and a fan reaches out and catches the ball inches above Bonds' glove. Bonds looks up and says, 'Are you kidding me?!' and the guy is wearing a Barry Bonds jersey. He's like Barry's biggest fan, and he felt so bad. He immediately realized what he'd done and he wanted to toss the ball back." Bonds would come into his element in the 2000 season and conclude the year six home runs shy of 500, which would set up a 2001 season for the ages for Bonds *and* baseball.

It's hard to imagine during Bonds's 73-home-run campaign in 2001 that he went more than 10 days without a round-tripper, but it happened three times. Considering that the two others occurred around the All-Star break and the weeklong furlough that baseball took after the September 11, 2001 attacks, it was the early season slump that affected Bonds the most. Miller notes, "He got into a slump. He hit a home run maybe opening day, and then he hardly had a hit at all for the next several days. He was in such a funk, and he admitted afterward getting a little overexcited. He's five home runs away from 500 for his career at the time, and he was really anxious to get it done. It took him entirely out of his game. They finally gave him a day off in San Diego at Qualcomm, where he terrorized the Padres his entire career. They could not get him out. For him to have a day off there, you know how screwed up he was. Dusty Baker said, 'Just take some batting practice, clear your head, and get your stroke back.' So the next day, they went to Milwaukee and he hit a home run there, and the next day, he hit another home run in Milwaukee, and the next day, he hit *another* home run. Now they come home to play the Dodgers. This was one of the great early moments of the ballpark because of the history of it. They were down 2–1 in the bottom of the eighth to the Dodgers, so that's always big. It's a very tight, tense, dramatic game. Terry Adams was the pitcher, and Bonds just crushed one. This was a spot where there was a runner at third and just a fly ball or a single would have been fine. I think the fans weren't even thinking home run. Just get that guy home and tie this game. Even with a single, Barry's well capable of stealing second and getting into scoring position, but, instead, 'Poom!' He just crushes this ball. It may have been the first really magnificent ball framed against a dark night, because, unlike any other ballpark, out beyond right field is just total darkness once the sun goes down. You knew the moment he hit it that it was headed for the water, and so, just like that, it was number 500 and he had knocked in the tying and go-ahead runs against the Dodgers in the eighth inning. It was a dramatic and huge clutch moment. They stopped the game, much to the chagrin of the Dodgers. Mays, McCovey, and Cepeda all came out. I was on television that night, and I remember we had a shot of all of them together. I made the comment, 'There's the history of the Giants. Mays, McCovey, and now Barry Bonds. All members of the 500 home run club.' That was a great early moment. As time went on, Bonds would hit 70, 71, 72, and 73, passing McGwire and then passing Aaron. All those were thrilling and memorable at the time."

A GIANT RETURN TO GLORY . . . FROM
THE MOUND, NOT BEHIND THE PLATE

In 2010 it had been a few years since Bonds's record-breaking 756th home run avoided the kayaks in McCovey Cove and even more since the Rally-Monkey-charged Anaheim Angels snatched the 2002 World Series title from the seven-time National League MVP. The team had not been to the post-season in six years, four of which the Giants ended with a record below .500. Depending on how far down one scrolled on the game's box score, one would never expect the 2010 Giants to be a playoff-worthy team, let alone a World Series winner. Jon Miller recalls: "In 2010, the team was very frustrating and broadcaster Duane Kuiper coined the phrase 'Giants baseball. It's torture.' It was a funny line and people picked up on it. That team didn't hit the ball well, and it just seemed like forever they'd have runners at second and third and nobody out. A guy would strikeout, pop out, and they couldn't get the runner home. Bases loaded and one out and they'd hit into a double play. Scoring runs was just like going to the dentist and having root canal surgery, yet the pitching was so good, they won more often than not. Then they signed Pat Burrell and they put together this group of people that were castoffs from other clubs that nobody seemed to want, and, somehow, it all came together." Where the team really came together in 2010 was from the mound and the dugout, as starting pitchers Tim Lincecum, Matt Cain, and Jonathan Sanchez and closer Brian Wilson, all under the stewardship of former Padres manager Bruce Bochy, brought the Giants back up the ladder to the top of the National League West. Miller describes the Giants hurlers who returned the team to World Series glory: "The ballpark has become sort of renowned for how the game is played because it's become a real pitcher's ballpark. The Giants have had a ball club that revolves around its pitching. The greatest memories I think the people have now about games and events at the ballpark have more to do with Tim Lincecum, Matt Cain, and Brian Wilson. The pitching was what brought them to the World Series, where they won two times in three years. Lincecum with the strikeouts and the Cy Young awards. This young guy, 'the freak,' that had this unorthodox and very cool looking delivery out of such a slight body and build. Matt Cain, whom we all followed in the minor leagues knowing he was a top prospect with a great arm. We couldn't wait to see him. Many of the great moments are aligned with the postseason. Facing Atlanta in his first postseason game, Lincecum pitches a shutout, striking out 14 guys. One of the greatest postseason performances ever turned in, and that was his first. Matt Cain, in that same postseason, not giving up a single earned run in all those games." Plowing through the Atlanta Braves, defending National League champion Philadelphia Phillies, and beating the American League pennant-winning Texas Rangers, the Giants won the team's first World Series title since moving to San Francisco, the franchise's sixth overall. Two years later, and with the added help of pitcher Madison Bumgarner, the Giants, having come back from a 1–3 deficit to the defending World Series champion St. Louis Cardinals in the 2012 National League Championship Series, reeled off seven straight postseason victories, including a four-game sweep of American League triple-crown winner Miguel Cabrera and his mighty Detroit Tigers, to capture the 2012 title, the franchise's seventh overall. Another two years later, practically on the shoulders of Madison Bumgarner's 21 innings allowing only one earned run in the 2014 fall classic, the Giants earned their third title in five years by beating the rejuvenated Kansas City Royals. With the rings on the fingers and the commemorative pennants painted into the left-field wall's padding, the San Francisco Giants, over five decades removed from exchanging their subway tickets for trolley car passes, embrace their history comprehensively. Jon Miller adds, "A unique aspect of the Giants that's unlike the Yankees, Red Sox, Cubs, and some of the other historic franchises is that the Giants were the 'New York Giants' and had a great club that was in many World Series—many pennants—and made that transcontinental move along with the Dodgers, but the Giants have very much embraced that New York aspect of their history. Some teams that have moved on ignore it. The Giants are one of the few exceptions that embrace their entire history. The Polo Grounds was the great early baseball park in the big city. Now AT&T Park is, I think, the cause of a renaissance of Giants baseball after this very poor venue, Candlestick Park. All those years and there wasn't a whole lot of success there. Now AT&T Park has brought that franchise back to those glory days in New York. The Giants embrace their history here. They don't ignore it, even though it has nothing to do with San Francisco. They're proud of it. It's possible that kind of karma has helped them to this great success in these days." Now that the champagne has thrice been soaked into the Kentucky bluegrass of AT&T Park and the confetti has reached the Tenderloin District and Alcatraz, don't expect makeshift Giants T-shirts from any region *not* within 1,000 miles of Silicon Valley anytime soon.

· 2 ·

Angel Stadium of Anaheim:
Los Angeles Angels

*You definitely know you're in a different climate when you're playing in
Southern Cal, especially in Angel Stadium."*

—Rex Hudler, former Los Angeles
Angels TV play-by-play broadcaster

*A*fter spending the franchise's first five seasons bouncing around the San Fernando Valley like a misplaced foster child, the Los Angeles Angels finally found a home in Anaheim, colorfully nicknamed the Big A. Just when the Angels felt situated in their own home, the Los Angeles Rams came into town and assumed roommate duties for 15 seasons. Sharing a stadium with an NFL team, however, can have its perks, as the seating capacity, once Anaheim Stadium had been renovated and remodeled, shot up from 43,250 to 65,000. In 1995 the great football exodus out of Los Angeles (Raiders, too) sent the Rams to St. Louis, and with an average attendance of 23,367 fans, left Angels fans with a great view of empty red seats over the next two seasons. Luckily, as in its movies, new team owner Disney came in and saved the day, returning the Big A to its original glory, a baseball-only facility named Edison International Field of Anaheim. The stadium would eventually be renamed Angel Stadium of Anaheim.

No one knows whether or not the success of the film *Angels in the Outfield* fueled Disney's decision to buy the team, but once the company did, there was no question who was signing the checks in the Angels organization, especially when arriving at the ballpark. Former Angels TV broadcaster Rex "Hud" Hudler notes, "You're going to come into the parking lot and you're going to see two big major league style hats. They're the same thing Major League players wear, but look like they would fit a giant. They also have some large baseball bats all congregated together in the front of the entrance way.

There's not any other place in the 30 teams and cities that have that." For fans, this touch of Disney continues through the gate. Beyond the center-field wall, where once was a sea of red bleachers unoccupied by Angels fans, lies the famous rock pile. Equipped with shooting fountains, the rock pile is an assembly of giant boulders, some of which are even arranged to form a large "A." Beyond the rock pile today, with the stadium once again unenclosed, while watching the game fans can observe traffic conditions on the Santa Ana Freeway, as well as the Amtrak trains passing through Anaheim on their way to Los Angeles. Opening the stadium back up, while allowing fans to see out, also allows for the weather to come in, which in Southern California can be known to change the game completely.

NO HAVING FUN WHEN
THERE'S NO WARM CALIFORNIA SUN

The word "California" evokes many images. Upright surfboards anchored to the bronzed sand by their fiberglass fins. A classic convertible seemingly parting the tall palm trees lining the sidewalks along streets like Rodeo Drive and Santa Monica Boulevard. A bikini-clad body scampering through the shallow waves of the Pacific Ocean. The common denominator in all three is, as '60s doo wop artists the Rivieras sang, that "Warm California Sun," and it's only natural the sun and its elements would find their way into Angel Stadium of Anaheim, making for quite a unique day game experience. A former player, Rex Hudler, recalls: "I remember being a young player. Coming to the 'Big A' when I was on visiting teams, stretching before games, looking into the stands at all the good looking California girls. Wow. I knew I was in the big leagues." Hudler would eventually play in an Angels uniform and go on to broadcast for the team for 10 years before calling games for the Kansas City Royals.

While the day games at the Big A may bring to life lyrics written by groups like the Beach Boys, night games—once the sun dips its spherical flame below the Pacific's blue horizon—give players from back East something they're not used to during the summer: cool weather. Hudler states, "Playing in California is different because there's no humidity. When you play in other parks from the Midwest on back, you start dealing with humid conditions, and it's totally different. You have to condition yourself a different way as far as hydration goes. At nighttime in California, it gets cool. In the 60s even. They're not used to that. Typically, I used some under garments to keep me warm because my legs would cramp up in the cool California evening. You have to find a different way to stay warm in California. You have to guard against not hurting your muscles by keeping some extra clothes on." With the coast just six miles away, Angel Stadium of Anaheim catches some of that ocean breeze, which at night can cause a fly ball to just die. It's no coincidence the Angels pitchers with the best stats in recent years (Jared Weaver, C. J. Wilson) have been those who left half the fielding to their teammates and the other half to the skies. Of course, in order to win, they need to battle that cold front as well.

Throughout the team's history, the Angels have sported a trend of acquiring big bats to help out-muscle that crisp southern California air. Free agent names like Pujols, Baylor, Guerrero, Jackson, Hamilton, and Teixeira have filled the lineup cards to accompany the products of the Angels' farm system, a system that would prove quite effective for the Angels throughout the early 2000s. Rex Hudler comments on an Angels roster unique to that of championship winners of the past: "In baseball, you can win a few different ways, but the main way to win is by homegrown talent. Having the fans be able to watch young players from when they were minor leaguers until they become major leaguers. To be able to watch Tim Salmon, Garret Anderson, Troy Glaus, Darrin Erstad, Benji Molina, John Lackey, and Francisco Rodriguez. There were so many homegrown guys, and that made it a warmer feeling. Even when you win with veterans or you win with free agents you go out and buy, winning is everything in professional sports, and there's still a happy fan base; but, there's even more happiness from a loyal fan base when you have your own players." Perhaps the member of the Angels roster providing the most happiness in the early 2000s was a two-foot-tall domestic primate.

THE "MONKEY RALLIED"
2002 WORLD CHAMPION ANAHEIM ANGELS

On June 6, 2000, the Angels were trailing the San Francisco Giants in a seemingly meaningless interleague game. Suddenly the stadium's Jumbotron screen in right field (a feature courtesy of Disney ownership) displayed a clip from the film *Ace Ventura: Pet Detective* showing a capuchin monkey jumping up and down above the superimposed words "Rally Monkey." The Angels would eventually "rally" in the ninth inning to win the game 6–5. The next night, with the Angels and Giants tied 9–9 in the bottom of the eighth, the scoreboard once again was alight with the jumping capuchin monkey. Three singles later, the Angels scored the go-ahead run, then held off the Giants in the top of the ninth to win, and the legend of this iconic pop culture mascot was born.

Flash forward two seasons to 2002 and we find a new-look Angels squad, starting with their uniforms. Rex Hudler says, "In 2002, they changed the color of the uniform to red, the favorite color of former team owner Gene Autry. That made the visual much better. They went from that ugly periwinkle blue—that looked more like a glorified softball uniform—to red, 'the cowboy's' favorite color. It was a beautiful uniform, and that made the fans feel real good. It turned out to be the last year the Autrys owned the Angels." Now dressed presentably enough to be taken seriously by visiting teams, the 2002 Angels "wore out the tape" on the Rally Monkey video en route to their first World Series title. Hudler adds, "The Halos had 43 come from behind wins that year. It was really a fresh baseball season, unlike any other I've ever participated in over 30 years of being in baseball as a player and a broadcaster. It was a very unique time, and to see and feel the excitement every day. I couldn't wait to come to the yard. I looked forward to engaging fans. They were so excited. They couldn't wait to see who was going to win." It just so happened that 61 percent of the time the Angels were the winning team, as their 99–63 record—although second in the division to an Oakland A's team that would become the subject of the Oscar-nominated film *Moneyball*—earned them a wild card spot in the playoffs against the defending American League champion New York Yankees.

Over the first 14 postseason games, six of the Angels' nine victories happened in come-from-behind fashion. With the 15th game being game 6 of the 2002 World Series, the Angels would reacquaint the Giants with the Jumbotron-hogging nemesis who had debuted against them back in the summer of 2000. Trailing 5–0 in the bottom of the seventh inning and in the World Series 3–2, the Angels, down to their last breaths, summoned the power of the Rally Monkey. Taking a cue from their unassuming mascot, the Angels scored six runs over the next two innings to take a 6–5 lead. Troy Percival closed out the game, and virtually the Giants, with his ninth inning save. Hudler notes, "Game 6 of the World Series was phenomenal. We came back and won from five runs down. That's one of the greatest games that I've ever seen. In game 7, they were just waiting to get beat because they knew they couldn't beat the Angels and the Rally Monkey." Hardly the five-run mountain of the night before, the Angels erased an early 1–0 deficit to go on to win game 7 and with it the 2002 World Series. The championship being the franchise's first, Rex Hudler describes how important the title was for the Angels organization: "Winning cures all. That's a term in baseball that you hear, and it really fits for that situation. The Angels had arrived, and they finally won a world championship. With that championship, it also erased all of the pain over the years of not making it. They had a lot of painful moments in Angels history, so part of the joy from that championship was the cleansing of the whole Angels nation."

HUD'S MOST MEMORABLE MOMENTS

As a TV broadcaster, Rex Hudler would turn his broadcasting duties over to the networks during all the Angels' postseason appearances; however, that didn't mean his presence wasn't still felt in the stadium. Hudler had nicknamed Angels shortstop David Eckstein "X Factor" because he "factors in on almost every play." Thanks to an adopted Japanese baseball tradition, that nickname was realized. Watching a playoff game with his wife, Hudler recollects, "My first experience with thunder sticks was when I was playing in Japan. They were loud and it was crazy. During the Angels 2002 World Series, the organization used those type of thunder sticks and passed them out to their fans. When David Eckstein came to the plate, they were crossing those thunder sticks, making an 'X' for 'X Factor.' I'll never forget my wife looked at me and said, 'See what you did? See what you started?' It was unlike any moment. I wasn't digging myself. I was just proud. I felt like a proud broadcaster that could bring that in and bring in a nickname the fans could relate to. It was really special to see that."

Perhaps some of Hud's most cherished memories of Angel Stadium of Anaheim come from outside the gates. Hudler notes, "Southern California fans—Angels fans in particular—get the bad rap around the league for not being as passionate. Coming late to the games and leaving early. Every fan base is different in different parts of the country, depending on the team and years of success they've had. Coming there to Angel Stadium as a broadcaster was so much fun. There was energy. There was passion. I would love to get out of my car and walk into the gates at 4:00, and there would be people out in front of the stadium underneath the red hats. They would yell, 'Hud, what are we gonna do tonight?' They would look at me like I was one of the players. They felt like I was a big part of their team and I was just a broadcaster."

From the booth, Rex Hudler's most memorable game at Angel Stadium of Anaheim took place on August 21, 2007, against the always well-traveled New York Yankees. The "homegrown" left fielder, Garret Anderson, went 4 for 6, knocking in a team record 10 RBIs and homering twice in an 18–9 route of the Yankees. Hudler comments: "That was a phenomenal individual feat. I couldn't believe it was happening. That's two or three weeks' production for most guys. That was really special. Whenever the Yankees are in town, it's always a sellout crowd. I remember looking at my broadcast partner, Steve Physioc, saying, 'He already has six RBI's. Can he get anymore?' And I'll be darned if—with three guys on—he didn't come up with a grand slam to get 10 RBI's. That was phenomenal." Being among the 44,000 plus witnesses to Anderson's feat, Hudler relinquished his duties to the sea of red, saying, "It was really special to hear the crowd. In moments like that, when you're a broadcaster, and the crowd cheers, and something like that happens, you just lay out. You don't have to say anything. You just let the crowd tell the story. It was neat to see that moment for Anderson, personally, as a broadcaster. To sit back and watch that." Anderson's 10 RBIs were just one short of the American League record, coincidentally set by the Yankees' Tony Lazzeri in 1936.

ANGEL STADIUM OF ANAHEIM TODAY

Though the organization has taken on more names than a CIA operative, and their home has undergone enough reconstructive surgery to make it eligible to star in *The Real Housewives of Orange County*, the Angels have not moved an inch in the team's 49 seasons in Anaheim. Granted, the Northridge earthquake of '94 gave the stadium a good shake, causing a Jumbotron screen and a scoreboard to collapse. Disney replaced the Jumbotron with an even bigger one, which today displays the Rally Monkey superimposed into the latest Hollywood movies every time the Angels trail or are looking to break a tie. As far as personnel, the homegrown talent of Rex Hudler's broadcasting days, and Hud himself, have moved on; however, the Angels' farm system continues to reel in the "big fish." Mike Trout, a 22-year-old hitting prodigy, exploded into the league in 2012, earning himself the Rookie of the Year award and coming in second (albeit narrowly) in AL MVP voting to triple-crown winner Miguel Cabrera and again in 2013, before receiving first place honors in 2014. Today, instead of "X"-shaped thunder sticks, red, trout-shaped hats swim throughout the stadium atop the heads of Angels fans, making The Big A look like a foam hatchery. More than a decade after the team's magical 2002 season, overly punctual fans still seek shade beneath the giant Angels hats outside the gate, waiting for the next familiar face to walk by so they can shout, "What are we gonna do tonight?"

· 3 ·

Busch Stadium: St. Louis Cardinals

It's not the stadium that dictates what managers want to do. It's their ball players. If you've got a fast team, you may want to bunt and run a little bit more. If you don't, maybe you sit back and wait for a home run. There's nothing unique in that aspect. It's as fair as it can get.

—Dan McLaughlin, St. Louis Cardinals
TV play-by-play broadcaster

St. Louis, Missouri, may be referred to as the Gateway to the West, but the city's flair lends more toward its eastern roots. Sold to the United States by France as part of the Louisiana Purchase, St. Louis, located right on the banks of the Mississippi River, has served as a significant geographic marker throughout its history. The city was the starting point for Lewis and Clark's westward expedition and became a destination for many European immigrants once it was established as an important center for trade during the 19th century. While the city was becoming a commercial powerhouse, due in part to a lasting trade relationship with New Orleans, a new sport was emerging east of the Mississippi. With baseball already taking states like Ohio, New Jersey, and Pennsylvania by storm, St. Louis soon wanted to join the party. In 1892 the St. Louis Browns, both the westernmost and southernmost team in all of baseball, joined the National League, and although known today by a different name (Cardinals), the team would never leave the city. Baseball took so quickly in Mound City that the Browns changed their name from the one-season-failed-experimental St. Louis "Perfectos" to the Cardinals. Up the river, the original Milwaukee Brewers moved to St. Louis after just one year (1901) and assumed the Browns name, making the league look like dead-goldfish-swapping parents. Unfortunately the Browns had a very ugly breakup with St. Louis, thanks in large part to former owner Bill Veeck, and moved to Baltimore in 1954.

With the city once again to themselves, the Cardinals have proven they're team enough to handle all the fandom and love St. Louis has to offer, a love that is as present today as it was more than 122 years ago.

BRINGING NEW MEANING TO THE TERM "FAN FRIENDLY"

If the New York Yankees and their 27 World Series titles and 40 league pennants were taken out of the equation, the St. Louis Cardinals' 11 championships and 19 pennants would be more than any other team in baseball. With the franchise being more than a century old, this trend has been sporadic; the team won eight championships from 1926 to 1967. The '70s were a quiet decade for St. Louis thanks to Cincinnati's Big Red Machine and the "family-oriented" Pittsburgh Pirates. The '80s showcased the Cardinals in three different World Series, with the team adding another title to their trophy case in 1982 against the Milwaukee Brewers. The Atlanta Braves and Pittsburgh Pirates were the bane of the Cardinals' existence during the '90s, but the team once again returned to pennant-chasing glory early this century, appearing in five National League Championship Series in seven years, including the team's 10th World Series title in 2006, defeating the Detroit Tigers. So far in the current decade, the Cardinals have made the last four National League Championship Series (2011–2014), going to two World Series (2011, 2013) and winning the team's 11th title in 2011. This success has not gone unnoticed by the city of St. Louis, as the Cardinals' home of "new" Busch Stadium, opened in April 2006, has broken the three million fan attendance mark in each of its first nine seasons. Cardinals play-by-play TV broadcaster Dan McLaughlin comments on the team's popularity: "I think the Cardinals, drawing 30,000 every single game, one of the reasons that they do is they've had a great tradition and history, but it's a recent history of winning and it just is the thing to do in St. Louis." A Busch Stadium experience being "the thing to do" extends beyond the 40,000 plus fans in their seats to the ones wearing name tags. McLaughlin adds, "People love their baseball and they get treated so well when they come to the ballpark. As a matter of fact, we have a waiting list for ushers because it's a fun job. Season ticket holders become lifelong friends with the ushers that are in their section." While the hospitality extends down the aisles of Busch Stadium, it is most certainly found outside the gates as well.

Busch Stadium's Ballpark Village, spanning over 10 acres and seven city blocks, is the league's first mixed-use development facility integrated into an actual ballpark. Including most of the amenities one would find inside Busch Stadium (as well as some not found), Ballpark Village provides pre- and postgame entertainment, and, more important, a way to hold over fans not wanting to be part of the unbearably slow procession of traffic flowing into and out of the stadium. Commenting on what Ballpark Village has to offer game attendees and nonattendees alike, McLaughlin says, "It stands out because it's got everything in one area. So, if you want to go to a bar, you can go to a bar. If you want to go to a nice restaurant, it's got a nice restaurant. It's got one of the biggest video boards in the country to watch games, so a lot of people congregate. They may not have a ticket to the game, but they can get into Ballpark Village right across the street because it's free and can sit there and watch a game. There are areas that have what would be the equivalent of rooftop seating at Wrigley Field. There's nice restaurants, there's bars, there's all kinds of stuff. It's also got the St. Louis Cardinals Hall of Fame. So, if you're a baseball fan, and you come through, you'd get pretty much everything you could possibly want from the St. Louis Cardinals in the vicinity of the ballpark in terms of the history, the Cardinals Hall of Fame Museum, fan stores, and all the restaurants. It's kinda got everything that you would want inside the ballpark there." Though an out-of-ballpark experience may be enjoyable, it doesn't replace the perspective fans get from their seats inside the stadium. When asked what features make Busch Stadium unique from the other ballparks in baseball, Dan McLaughlin responds, "The first thing would be the view. You've got the old courthouse in downtown St. Louis, which is visible to the fans. Also, a very clear view of the arch, which is obviously symbolic to St. Louis." With a view, a winning team both on the field and in the aisles, and a roster that has qualified for the postseason in 11 of the last 15 seasons, it's not likely those 40,000 plus numbers will be decreasing anytime soon.

FAIR DIMENSIONS, NOT SO FAIR CONDITIONS

Though built during the cookie-cutter era of stadiums, the "old" Busch Stadium would have rather not been considered one itself. The dimensions on the field were quite symmetrical, while the bowl of seats surrounding it stood four tiers high. However, the all-grass infield distinguished it from the others built at the time; that and hosting 10 League Championship Series and six World Series in 40 years. The "new" Busch Stadium, though not taking on exactly the same dimensions as its predecessor, plays quite symmetrically from foul pole to foul pole. The biggest difference in dimensions between the two structures lies in the power alleys, as right center and left center play 15 and 18 feet deeper, respectively, in "new" Busch Stadium than in "old" Busch Stadium. Commenting on how the field may strike an actual player, McLaughlin notes, "The way the ball plays in terms of if it's a pitcher's park or a hitter's park, it just plays fair. I know when they first did wind studies to try to figure out whether or not it was going to be a fair ballpark, there was concern, but you just don't know until you go in and play, and it plays as fair as any ballpark in the country." Though the ballpark may play fair, Mother Nature certainly doesn't. Of the five most humid months in the calendar year in St. Louis, four occur during baseball's regular season. In fact, throughout the month of July the humidity generally ranges from 49 to 94 percent, rarely dropping to 35 percent. Coupling this constant humidity with the high summer temperatures of the Midwest, Busch Stadium can be quite the torturous ballpark for players and fans alike. Still, according to McLaughlin, it doesn't seem to favor pitcher over batter or vice versa. McLaughlin adds, "When you're here at St. Louis, you can expect it to be hot. The ball may travel better when you get into the summer months because it gets steaming hot in St. Louis more times than not. You occasionally get the 95 to 100 degree heat, which stretches the games. Even when it's steaming outside, depending on the individual, I just don't see how the ballpark is really an advantage for one or the other, but it gets hot in the summer months. You can expect that in St. Louis." Reinforcing McLaughlin's comments regarding "the individual," Busch Stadium, as a park factor, has fallen as low as 25th for runs in 2009, 2011, and 2013, and risen as high as 4th midway through the 2014 season. In 2011 one individual in particular, David Freese, made Busch Stadium about as unfair a ballpark as any, at least for the American League pennant-winning Texas Rangers.

OCTOBER 27, 2011: BASEBALL
101 LECTURE SERIES—NO-DOUBLES DEPTH

Down three games to two in the 2011 World Series and 7–5 in the game, with two outs and two strikes in the bottom of the ninth inning, the Cardinals were just one pitch from handing the Texas Rangers their first-ever World Series title. With the tying run standing on first base and not in scoring position, perhaps the Rangers' best bet would have been to play their outfielders at "no-doubles depth," a baseball term that is another way for the manager to say, "The only way this ball gets past you better be over the fence." The Rangers' right fielder (and would-have-been series MVP) Nelson Cruz wasn't quite to no-doubles depth (or no triples for that matter), as the eventual series MVP David Freese lined a shot over Cruz's head and to the wall, scoring both Albert Pujols and Lance Berkman to tie the game, 7–7. The crowd, much like their beloved Redbirds, were once again alight with life, at least until Josh Hamilton's 406-foot home run scored both him and Elvis Andrus, giving the Rangers another two-run lead going into what seemed like yet another final frame for the Cardinals. After two quick singles and a sacrifice, the Cardinals had the tying runs in scoring position. A groundout brought the score to 9–8. Down to their last strike yet again, Cardinals veteran right fielder Lance Berkman knocked home Jon Jay, and the Cardinals lived to see yet another inning. By the top of the 11th inning, Busch Stadium seemed like a 40,000-seat whoopee cushion, expelling despair rather than feigned flatulence and expanding with hope and cheers rather than saliva-laced deep breaths. The prank pillow would have to tie a proverbial knot in itself on this night, as the already-heralded Freese would both lead off and walk off the 11th. The third baseman's second clutch hit in three innings—a solo home run—gave the Cardinals a 10–9 victory in one of the most dramatic games in World Series history. Signing off the broadcast, Fox TV's Joe Buck, son of the legendary Jack Buck, who spent nearly 47 years broadcasting for the Cardinals during his hall of fame career, channeled his late father with one of the icon's phrases: "We will see you tomorrow night." That next night, in the decisive game seven, the only two-run comeback the Cardinals had to mount came in the first inning, as they went on to win the game 6–2 and the series four games to three. The Cardinals got a well-earned 11th World Series title, and although the champagne bottles were uncorked and the pile of red-and-white bodies was stacked atop the pitcher's mound on *that* night, it's the celebration of the night before that will stand out among all those inside the "new" Busch Stadium. Dan McLaughlin notes, "Clearly the most historic game we've ever had in that ballpark was game 6 of the 2011 World Series."

As the 2011 season had begun, the team was unable to resign restricted free agent and face of the franchise Albert Pujols to a long-term contract and had lost team ace Adam Wainwright to Tommy John surgery, and it had seemed unlikely on opening day that these Cardinals would be the team standing triumphant at season's end on their own mound. Reflecting on the Cardinals' recent run of success inside their relatively new home—especially during their unexpectedly magical 2011 season—McLaughlin says, "It's the postseason moments that make it such a special place because you're defined by championships." With a continuous crop coming out of the farm system, which has produced pitchers like Shelby Miller and Michael Wacha and hitters like Matt Carpenter and Matt Adams, "new" Busch Stadium may become the default setting for the word "success"—at least in baseball's dictionary—for years to come.

Chase Field: Arizona Diamondbacks

Chase Field: "Chase Field does play differently. When the roof is open, the ball has a tendency to fly."—Greg Schulte
Photo courtesy of Jennifer Stewart/Arizona Diamondbacks

> *The fan friendly aspect of the Diamondbacks is a huge thing. The con-*
> *courses are spacious. The food is great. It's the cheapest ticket in all of*
> *baseball for fans to get in.*

> —Greg Schulte, Arizona Diamondbacks radio
> play-by-play broadcaster

$\mathcal{D}$eep in the US Sonoran Desert—and at the end of several cactus-lined, two-lane highways—lies the city of Phoenix, Arizona, part of the Valley of the Sun. As early as 1947, certain Major League teams had made the southwestward trip over the Mississippi River into Arizona for "spring training." Cleveland Indians owner Bill Veeck and New York Giants owner Horace Stoneham put down stakes in Phoenix and Tucson to give their players a more habitable environment in which to prepare for their upcoming baseball seasons. Soon enough more teams, like the New York Yankees and the Baltimore Orioles, had spring training sites in Arizona. By 1995 expansion baseball talks were on the table, and with several teams now calling Arizona their six-week seasonal home, Phoenix Suns (NBA) owner Jerry Colangelo was lobbying for yet another professional sporting team to bankroll, this one with Bermuda grass under the players' feet rather than hardwood. Granted, while an 80 degree climate is preferable to snow and sleet during the late winter/early spring, a four-month average rainfall of .54 inch and temperatures reaching as high as 117 don't exactly scream comfort for the players *or* the fans. Despite a daily red flag, courtesy of meteorological anchors on the greater Phoenix area's local newscasts, Colangelo got his wish in March 1995, and the Valley of the Sun was awarded an expansion team, 354 miles from the nearest Major League ballpark (San Diego). Of course the proper facilities would have to be erected to cope with the intense heat while contesting in three- to four-hour games 81 times a year. With the Toronto Blue Jays' Rogers Centre a somewhat recent technological breakthrough at the time, a ballpark with a retractable roof was on everybody's mind when architectural firm Ellerbe Becket was charged with the task of building the future home of Major League Baseball's newest team. Three years after the ground breaking, (then-named) Bank One Ballpark opened in downtown Phoenix on March 31, 1998, with a sold-out crowd of 50,000 plus, as their purple-and-white clad hosts, the Arizona Diamondbacks, took the field for the first time.

While sunset over a desert metropolis like Phoenix is a spectacular sight, it's unlikely Diamondbacks fans are privy to such an occurrence for over half of the regular season, as Chase Field really does allow Arizona to "take off her rainbow shades." Radio play-by-play Diamondbacks broadcaster Greg Schulte describes the unique structure of Chase Field: "Come summer time, the retractable roof usually closes for the heat, even for the night games; but, you also have to deal with dust storms. The humidity picks up in the summertime during the monsoons. We usually try to keep the roof open from April to June. If we're lucky, we get to open it maybe for the last couple weeks of September, so you're looking at July, August, and most of September where the roof is closed." While Chase Field was the second of the six current Major League ballparks to have a retractable roof, its unique panel system has never been copied by other teams' architects. Treating the downtown area of Phoenix as if it were a nosy next-door neighbor, Chase Field has panels beyond the outfield walls from foul pole to foul pole capable of opening and closing with the push of a button. Independent of the retractable roof, the panels at Chase Field refract the strong winds known to surface in a desert setting; however, much like the roof, they have a bearing on the offensive output of the games. Greg Schulte adds, "Chase Field does play differently. When the roof is open, the ball has a tendency to fly. When the roof is closed, the ball has a tendency not to fly as far. It's the second highest altitude in Major League Baseball. A lot of people don't know that. Denver's the highest and Arizona's second, so the ball's going to fly here a little bit more anyway. When the roof is open, left handed hitters will take the ball the other way and they can get it out of here. Adrian Gonzalez is one left-handed hitter who loves to take the ball the other way, and he's hit many home runs to left and left center at Chase Field over the years. The Diamondbacks' Miguel Montero is another lefty hitter who likes to drive the ball the other way. When Curt Schilling pitched at Chase Field, he liked the roof closed. In fact, he preferred it. As I recall, there was a bit of controversy about Schilling dictating the roof be closed when he pitched at home. I've always known it to be the team president who made the call—dictated solely on "fan comfort"—during the heat, and the threat of rain/dust. More was made out of it than really what should have been, but, at the same time, Schilling saw that difference." If Schilling were still playing in a Diamondbacks uniform today, the politics surrounding his strategy and fan comfort would perhaps be deemed irrelevant. Schulte notes, "The last couple of years or so, it's been really strange. There have been nights where the roof has been open and the ball has died in the outfield. There have been nights when the roof was closed and the ball has really carried, so it's all theory."

Perhaps playing a role in that "theory" has been the lack of Cy Young award-worthy pitchers over the past several seasons. Between 1999 and 2008, Randy Johnson, Curt Schilling, and Brandon Webb—collectively or individually—dominated the mound at Chase Field. Webb, with an average of 18.67 wins per year between 2006 and 2008, managed to win a Cy Young for the team ('06) before a shoulder injury ended his career early. Schilling, during his four years with the team, was a two-time Cy Young runner-up ('01, '02) to his teammate Randy Johnson, arguably the best left-handed pitcher in Major

League history. Johnson, in his eight years with the Diamondbacks, struck out 2,077 batters, won four National League Cy Young awards, pitched a perfect game, and sported a 2.83 ERA. Schulte continues, "It's always been a hitter friendly park unless you've got Randy Johnson and Curt Schilling in your rotation. Brandon Webb was great at Chase Field, and that was due to his terrific sinker. 'Webby' would go through some games throwing 80–90 percent sinkers. Got mostly ground balls. Very few home runs given up. Chase Field didn't faze him one bit. It has been more the norm for D'backs GM's to look to acquire sinker ball pitchers, but there have been fly ball pitchers who have had success at Chase Field. If a pitcher can keep the ball between the power alleys, the ballpark plays large."

Panels and roof open or closed, playing in the National League West against hitting tandems like Carlos Gonzalez and Troy Tulowitzki (Colorado), Buster Posey and Hunter Pence (San Francisco), Everth Cabrera and Jedd Gyorko (San Diego), and Adrian Gonzalez and Yasiel Puig (Los Angeles Dodgers), the ball is going to get hit, and far. With offense practically always a factor, the outfield configuration of Chase Field can toy with the fielders, making them look like cats chasing a baseball-shaped laser light. Schulte adds, "The center field overhang at Chase Field can give visiting outfielders fits. There are overhangs to the right and left of straightaway center. You'll see the yellow line up there. Anything over that line is obviously a home run. Anything that hits off that overhang is in play, and we've seen a lot of bad ricochets over the years. Many a ball has found that overhang and bounced towards right field or left field, or even straight back towards the infield. Center fielders can get too close to the wall and get burned. There was one time where the defender for the other team went back and got caught under the overhang. The ball hit the overhang and went over towards the pool. Easy inside-the-park home run. The corner outfielders must assist to try and prevent inside-the-park homers. Steve Finley was the absolute best. Rarely if ever did he get burned. He knew how far he could go back before he had to turn around and play it off the overhang. Chris Young played it well also. It took A.J. Pollock a little time, but he gives the impression he's going to be outstanding at playing the ricochets."

While the overhangs and right and left center field likely don't get proverbial good-bye hugs from visiting outfielders once the series is over, the same can't be said for the batter's eye beyond center field. A "batter's eye" is exactly that. It's what the batter looks out to when he's facing the pitcher. At Kauffman Stadium in Kansas City, a batter will see fountains. In Angel Stadium of Anaheim, a hitter will see giant boulders. As far as batters' eyes are concerned, for a hitter, less is more. Regarding Chase Field's batter's eye, Greg Schulte comments, "Jason Kubel said one of the reasons he signed a free agent contract with us is because of the batter's eye. He came in with Minnesota the previous year. The first year here, he hit 30 home runs. He had a lot of home runs the other way at Chase. Clint Hurdle was managing Pittsburgh, and they were slumping. He told his ball club, 'This is a great ballpark. You'll see the ball.' This was early in the season last year. They struggled in the first series of the season, and then they came in and played us three or four games. They either split or won two out of three. They weren't hitting at the time, but they came in and they raked it. Clint told them, having managed the Rockies all those years against the Diamondbacks, 'You're going to love hitting in this ballpark.' Most of them had played here before, but he said, 'Remember. You're going to see the ball perfectly coming out of the pitcher's hand.' The background is great. It's green. It's perfect." Considering the batter's eye, altitude, open roof, and an overhang better reserved for the 18th hole on a round of miniature golf, as hitter friendly as Chase Field is, it's even more friendly to Diamondbacks fans and baseball fans in general.

One area of professional sports that has been blemished by elements like agents and contract clauses courtesy of agents is player–fan interaction. Gone are the days of a baseball, daily program, scorecard, or baseball card signed by one's favorite player before or after a game; at least it seems that way everywhere *but* Chase Field. Schulte notes, "One of the great things about Chase Field is all the players are expected to and usually do sign autographs. We're affordable. Fans come early. They always use the term 'fan friendly,' and I think we're that. During batting practice, while the players are at the cage getting ready to go, there's a screened off area right behind home plate where the fans can come, and the players will go over there and mingle with the fans. Talk to them, sign autographs, get their pictures taken, which is a little unique. You'll see some teams do that but I don't think nearly as much as the Diamondbacks. They've been instructed to, but you know what, they'd do it regardless, because they realize the importance of the fans. I've talked to several and asked them, 'Does it bother you?' and they said, 'No. Not at all. We were kids once. We never had this opportunity where we could go on the field and basically have a chance to meet the players.' In that sense, that's one of the unique characteristics of Chase Field itself." Another unique feature of Chase Field, which is only fitting for a fan-friendly oasis out in the middle of the desert, is the Pool Pavilion beyond the right-field wall, where fans with special tickets can indulge themselves at poolside and in-spa treatments. Schulte adds, "You have to admit, the pool is unique. We've seen anything and everything there over the years. Balls that bounce into the pool we call 'ground POOL doubles.' Mark Grace hit the first home run ever into the pool when he was playing for the Chicago Cubs, and then, later on, came to play with us and went into the pool. It's different. It's fun. It's filled every night, sold out all the time. It's one of the highlights of Chase Field. You can go out, watch a baseball game, and, if you want a drink, you can have a drink and enjoy a dip in the pool." Even though their customer (fan) service exceeds most, in 2001, in just their fourth year of existence, the D'backs gave fans the greatest gift they could ever receive.

NOVEMBER 4, 2001: GRAVY ADDED
TO AN ALREADY DELICIOUS MEAL

If we were to look at specific stats of the 2001 World Series between the Arizona Diamondbacks and the New York Yankees, we would find it difficult to believe the series went the full seven games. Over the seven-game series, the Diamondbacks outhit the Yankees 65 to 42 and outscored them 37 to 14; however, the series would be decided by just one run in the bottom of the ninth in game 7, easily Greg Schulte's most memorable game in the booth at Chase Field. As the Diamondbacks storyteller since day one, Schulte describes the road that led up to the decisive game: "What transpired prior to that on 9/11 rocked everybody. We didn't play for a week. Major League Baseball came back, and we went to Colorado and resumed the season. The season pushed back a little bit because of the missed days and then we clinched in Milwaukee. Then we had a great series with St. Louis. It went five games. We won game 5 at Chase Field and then we won four out of five against Atlanta. They had Glavine, Smoltz, and Maddux, and they were no match for the Diamondbacks. On to the World Series. I think if you ask anybody who they wanted to play, everybody would have said the Yankees, which is what it ended up being." The phrase "be careful what you wish for" applied quite suitably, as the American League champions wrapped up their fourth straight pennant, beating a Seattle Mariners team that had won a record-tying 116 regular season games before heading to the Arizona desert for game 1 of the 2001 fall classic.

After games 1 and 2 in Arizona, one might have wanted to check the collective pulse of the Yankees, who mustered up only one run and six hits against Arizona's "two-headed snake," starting pitchers Curt Schilling and Randy Johnson. Games 3, 4, and 5, although low scoring as well, showed a more evenly matched set of teams. After 20-game winner and Cy Young recipient Roger Clemens outlasted Arizona pitcher Brian Anderson in the series' third game, games 4 and 5 instilled a sense of destiny in the hearts of New York fans, as two game-tying home runs with two outs in the bottom of the ninth off Diamondbacks closer Byung-Hyun Kim in back-to-back nights gave the Yankees not only hope, but eventually the series lead returning to the desert. The switch must have flipped back off for game 6, as the Yankees were beaten 15–2, thanks in part to a little reconnaissance by the Diamondbacks. Schulte adds, "The D'backs just obliterated them 15-2. Twenty some hits.

Andy Pettitte was tipping his pitches. The D'backs knew and had him out of there in the second inning, so that set up game 7." While 20 hits wouldn't be placed on the scoreboard for game 7, there were more fireworks than in the first six games combined when all was said and done.

The pinnacle of the Diamondbacks' glory is best described by Greg Schulte, the team's radio voice: "You couldn't ask for a better matchup. You had Roger Clemens and Curt Schilling, and they both dominated through seven. Come the eighth inning, Schilling's still in there. He gets ahead of Alfonso Soriano and throws a great pitch, and Soriano, a low ball hitter, hits it into the bleachers in left field. We're down 3-2. Torre had two pitchers in the bullpen. If they get the lead, it's a no brainer. They're going to use Mariano Rivera for two innings. Mariano comes in the eighth, gives up one hit, but he strikes out the side. Now we go to the ninth inning. Randy Johnson's come on. He threw over 100 pitches the night before. He came on in the eighth inning and got the final out. He pitches the ninth inning, gets the three outs, and the place is going crazy. All the pom pons are going. Bottom of the ninth inning, but you're still thinking to yourself, 'There's no way we're going to beat Rivera.' This is the greatest closer. At that time, still young enough in his career, but everything he had done during the seasons and during the postseason, your possibilities didn't look good. Mark Grace gets him on the second pitch and lines a single to center field, so the crowd gets into it. He gets the tying run on base."

Before continuing with Schulte's account of game 7, it is important to set up Rivera's second batter of the ninth, Damian Miller, with a Chase Field feature, which may or may not have fazed the Yankees closer. Schulte notes, "One unique feature we have at Chase Field is a dirt path to the mound. The Tigers at Comerica Park might be the only other team in baseball to have instituted it. There was a theory in the 2001 World Series game 7. I don't think Mariano ever confirmed or denied it. Damian Miller's up at the plate and he's bunting. The bunt goes back, on the dirt portion, to the mound. Rivera comes in, picks it up, and throws it wild to second. There's a theory that path bothered him. When he went to pick it up, he also picked up a pebble. It was right on the cut of the grass. That's the only time I ever saw that come into play." Schulte continues his account of game 7: "Now you've got two on and nobody out. Jay Bell comes up. He bunts. Rivera throws to third base. A lot was not made of this, but Scott Brosius caught the ball at third and never looked to first. Rivera got the ball to third base so fast, had Brosius looked to first base instead of second, he'd have had Bell by 10 feet. He did not throw the ball, so they get one out instead of possibly two. You've got runners at first and second, and Tony Womack comes to the plate. Tony got the game winning hit in game 5 against the Cardinals that sent us to the National League

Championship Series. He comes up and takes ball one, takes ball two, takes a strike, and fouls one back. He's got a 2–2 count, and Rivera throws a pretty good pitch in on him. He lines a single to right field down the line. Midre Cummings, in to pinch run at second base, comes in to score. Bell, the runner at first base, goes in to third. Womack goes in to second with a double. So now you've got runners at second and third. The ballpark's going berserk. We're going berserk up in the booth. Craig Counsell comes up. The irony about Counsell is he had scored the winning run in the '97 World Series for the Marlins on the base hit by Edgar Renteria. Now he's got a chance to win it. Rivera's pitch hits him on the wrist. That loads them up. A brief conversation by Joe Torre. 'You've gotta play the infield in/you've gotta play the infield back.' Torre opts to play the infield in. Luis Gonzalez is at the plate, and I'll never forget this. I heard it later on. Tim McCarver, on Fox, made mention of the fact the problem with playing the infield in with Rivera on the mound is hitters get jammed a lot and they get little pop flies on the grass just over the infield. Well I'll be darned if Gonzalez didn't hit a little bloop that just hit onto the grass. Jeter was up. He had no chance to go back. The winning run came in. The place goes bananas. Everybody's celebrating. We're high fiving each other up here, but it started with Clemens and it started with Schilling. They were outstanding. Just the atmosphere of going to a game 7. Having it decided in the ninth inning. The home team down a run. The greatest closer in the history of the game, Mariano Rivera; but, the Diamondbacks had the will to win it." Since 1960, only four World Series have ended with a walk-off hit in the seventh and deciding game. Having such an elite opportunity as a broadcaster at the time didn't quite occur to Greg Schulte as one would expect. Schulte explains, "Everybody asks, 'Did you have something rehearsed?' No. I had nothing rehearsed. You can't plan for something like that. Number one, you've got Mariano Rivera on the mound. He's not going to lose, right? What had gone through my mind—I believe—at the time Torre went to the mound, was there were a lot of people out front. They had a big screen out there. I thought of the people driving around the valley probably listening to the ball game. I thought, 'We've got a tremendous audience,' so that's where the 'honk the horn' came in. Everybody was just going nuts."

While Diamondback fans didn't ever have the long-suffering "wait 'til next year" mantra of those in the Brooklyn, New York, area code, the team has not returned to the World Series since 2001. However, with free agent signings like Bronson Arroyo and Mark Trumbo, a farm system springing up hitters like Paul Goldschmidt and Miguel Montero, and a summer wind "giving" unlike Sinatra's "taking," the Diamondbacks may one day return to baseball glory and once again give the fall classic a warm setting.

Citi Field: New York Mets

Citi Field: "Where home runs come to die."—Wayne Hagin
Photo courtesy of the New York Mets

Citi Field is a ballpark as opposed to a stadium and an intimate one at that. I think that's what they wanted to achieve and that's what they did.

—Howie Rose, New York Mets radio play-by-play broadcaster

The obvious thing that a fan would feel about Citi Field is that you're coming off the "7" subway train that stops right there at Flushing in Queens. There are very few places that you can take a subway and actually end up right at the ballpark.

—Wayne Hagin, former New York Mets radio
play-by-play broadcaster

$\mathcal{I}$n 1957, the "other two teams" in New York were having two distinct seasons on the field and in the stands, but both ended with the same result *off* the field. The Brooklyn Dodgers were just two years away from finally beating the Yankees and were packing Ebbets Field on a daily basis. The Giants, however, only three years removed from their Willie Mays–led World Series championship in 1954, were not having such luck at the Polo Grounds. Understandably, the Giants, led by owner Horace Stoneham, made their westward trek to San Francisco, where they have remained ever since. The Brooklyn Dodgers, although filling Ebbets Field to capacity and playing past the final day of the regular season seemingly on an annual basis, were not granted a new stadium. Team owner Walter O'Malley finally decided to, like his crosstown rival Giants, make his way to the Golden State, leaving fans from Brooklyn, Queens, and two other boroughs outside the Bronx with "them damn Yankees," at least for the time being. It wouldn't take long for the collective grumblings of abandoned fans to get the ball rolling for a new club in New York. William A. Shea, with the help of other lawyers, was able to establish an expansion team in New York, which would emerge in 1962 as the Mets. Interestingly, one of the motivations leading the New York Giants out of New York—the failure to build a ballpark to replace the Polo Grounds—became the binding factor keeping the new team around. For their first two seasons, the New York Mets, under the wing of seven-time World Series–winning manager Casey Stengel, battled their opponents inside the historic Polo Grounds, while their future home—which would be named after the lawyer who got them to Queens—was being built in Flushing. On April 17, 1964, the Mets opened Shea Stadium, which would remain their home for another 44 years. While at Shea Stadium the Mets, playing under former great New York players like Gil Hodges and Yogi Berra, eventually obtained the team's first taste of glory, in their eighth year of existence, as the 1969 "Amazing" Mets defeated the Baltimore Orioles in what current Mets broadcaster Howie Rose refers to as "the greatest New York sports story ever told." Another 17 years later, and at the cost of Red Sox first baseman Bill Buckner's safety in "bean town," the Mets again reclaimed baseball glory thanks to players like Dwight "Doc" Gooden, Mookie Wilson, Darryl Strawberry, and Keith Hernandez. The Mets returned to the fall classic in 2000 for the city's first ever "Subway Series" against the Yankees, where they lost in five games. With their interleague/intracity rival Yankees announcing construction of a new ballpark over in the Bronx, the Mets, too, eventually did a little ground breaking in 2006. Later that year the team came within one swing of the World Series, but watched those hopes fall right into Yadier Molina's catcher's mitt in the form of a lollipop curveball from St. Louis pitcher Adam Wainwright, freezing Mets outfielder Carlos Beltran, who probably kept the bat on his shoulder all the way home, either because it was obviously too heavy to lift or to protect himself from the angry Mets fans on the subway. The Cardinals went on to win the 2006 World Series, leaving the Mets community to stew for the winter. Over the next couple of seasons the Mets' future home was being built right before the eyes of fans attending Shea, as what would eventually become Citi Field arose in perfect view beyond the center-field bleachers. On April 13, 2009, the Mets completed the move next door and took the field of their new home before a crowd that was 45,000 strong.

While over in the Bronx the Yankees were coming in over half a billion dollars over budget for the stadium originally dreamed of by former New York City mayor Rudy Giuliani but eventually announced—albeit grudgingly—by then mayor Michael Bloomberg, the Mets "played ball" and got Citi Field built almost exactly at the cost of the proposed budget. Although both edifices in the Big Apple were being built at the same time and replacing historic "cathedrals," Citi Field's intended design differed greatly from that of the "new" Yankee Stadium. Mets radio broadcaster Howie Rose explains: "I think in New York, what you do at Citi Field is compared to what they do at Yankee Stadium and vice versa. I know that the Mets sought to achieve an intimate feel to their ballpark, which puts it on a somewhat different plane than what the Yankees did. They sort of envisioned this grandiose, five-star hotel that just happened to have a baseball field in it. The Mets wanted a more intimate experience, which would hearken back to the '50s when the Dodgers and Giants played here, specifically because of the outside design of the ballpark, Ebbets Field. I think that both teams achieved their objectives." Speaking about the park's nostalgic outside design, former Mets broadcaster Wayne Hagin says, "Before you get into the stadium, it's an interesting perspective because of what the Mets ownership wanted. People have to understand 'Why is it the Metropolitans?' It's because it's the first National League team since two left with the Brooklyn Dodgers and the New York Giants. I would say, because Fred Wilpon was the owner and grew up a Brooklyn fan, it certainly was not a combination of the Giants and the Brooklyn Dodgers. It was truly Brooklyn because he did the Jackie Robinson Rotunda, which is right out in front. When you come off the subway or you park your car, you walk right into the Robinson Rotunda and that is magnificent. That is very unique and it does look like Ebbets Field from that side." Distinguishing Citi Field from the Bronx's "five-star experience," Hagin continues, "From a fan's perspective, as opposed to the 'new' Yankee Stadium, at Citi Field, you're right on top of the field. They built it beautifully from that standpoint. You felt like you were on top of the field instead of recessed so far back that you felt like the game might have been a rumor."

For the players, the fan proximity can be a cause for comfort or discomfort, depending on the state of mind of these New Yorkers. Reflecting on an experience that he claims typifies New York, Wayne Hagin recalls opening day of the 2010 season: "In 2009, it was a rough season with injuries for the New York Mets, so when they have the home opener in 2010, they line up everybody; the trainers, the strength and conditioning coaches, the equipment manager. They all stand. One player was booed unmercifully and that was Oliver Perez. The fans couldn't stand him, and they booed him, but, when it came to Ray Ramirez, the trainer—a really sweet, humble guy from Texas— the stadium announcer says, 'And the head trainer of the New York Mets, Ray Ramirez.' The crowd reacted, 'Boo!' They booed him worse than Oliver Perez. Then they booed his assistant trainer. They booed the two strength and conditioning coaches. I felt bad for them because you could see in their faces 'I wish I'd never been introduced,' but, to see the fans, to hear the fans react to those injuries, that's how much they love or hate their team. I laughed so hard because it just gave me an inkling of what this city was all about."

RIP HOME RUN BALL

Citi Field is regarded as one of the pitcher friendliest ballparks in the majors. Describing what a player or fan might see when visiting Citi Field for the first time, Wayne Hagin says, "As you walk into Citi Field, the first thing you say is 'My goodness. This is where home runs come to die.' It was so big and the walls were so high, you knew it was a pitcher's park. That was the idea of Jeff Wilpon—the son of owner Fred Wilpon—to make it as tough a home run ballpark as he possibly could. Much to the delight of his pitchers, it was great, but not to the hitters. They were very, very upset, and they looked at Citi Field with a great deal of disdain. The first time we broke spring training, we came back and were going to play a two game exhibition series with the Red

Sox. The hitters were mumbling and the pitchers were rejoicing." Taking a year to "settle in," the Mets pitching staff, thanks to starters R. A. Dickey, Johan Santana, and Mike Pelfrey, as well as record-breaking closer Francisco Rodgriguez, jumped from 20th to 7th in team ERA between the 2009 and 2010 regular seasons. While the Mets hurlers were disposing of their Shea Stadium homesickness, it's safe to assume many of the "mumblings" mentioned by Wayne Hagin came from the mouth of All-Star third baseman David Wright. Hagin adds, "The emphasis became defense, and that's what the Mets needed to do to win. Of course, they had to have some offense. Every single day that I was there—every one of those 81 home games—I heard nothing but mumbling from the players at batting practice. They would tattoo a ball, and it would go nowhere. The fences were so high that it really bothered the hitters. David Wright, who I think in a normal ballpark would hit 30 home runs a year, was hitting 18 or less, and it frustrated him. He's the team leader, the face of the franchise, and it just drove him batty that he could not put up those numbers. Then it became the doubles game for him and trying to drive in the runs. I know one thing. He was a significantly different hitter. If you're the face of the franchise, that's who you look at, and that's who you compare everything to, especially when he had been at Shea, where he could hit the ball out of any part of that ballpark. A lot of his power was to straightaway center and to right center. He could really hit it the opposite way, and, at Citi Field, it was absolutely, humanly impossible to hit home runs. He became much more of a pull hitter and his average dipped because of it. If you're going to look at Citi Field from an offensive standpoint, there's nobody better to look at than David Wright. Just examine the numbers. I think you'd be astonished at how different a player he was at Shea as opposed to Citi and he was in the prime of his career." Unfortunately, it appeared that for a power hitter like David Wright, the easier way to get a home run at Citi Field was by watching the first and third base coaches, not the baseball. Hagin adds, "There were some crazy angles, especially in that first year, into right centerfield. You had no idea just how far a ball would travel. You never had an idea that it was going to go over the fence. Whenever anything was hit significantly to right centerfield, you knew it was going to be in the ballpark and there was a chance for a triple, and there was certainly the chance for an inside-the-park home run. It was very similar—as it got hit in the gap in right center field—as it is at AT&T Park, even though it was different in structure. I saw a lot of inside-the-park home runs and a lot of triples in that ballpark."

After the 2011 season Citi Field, much like the hitter-prejudiced Safeco Field and Petco Park, brought in its fences as much as 12 feet in certain areas and trimmed the outfield walls from 12 to 8 feet, the "home run robbing" standard. The change didn't go unnoticed in the long ball department, as the

Mets, as a team, hit 31 more home runs in 2012 than the adjustment-inspiring 108 of the 2011 season, which at Shea Stadium would have left the home run apple rotting in its barrel. Still, at 408 and 398 feet to straightaway and right center field, Citi Field continues to be one of the toughest ballparks for hitters. The one exception, if left-handed batters could pull their swings, would be Citi Field's "Pepsi Porch" in right field, which has a bit of a flair for baseball's past. Hagin notes, "The thing that visually captures you is the Pepsi Porch in right, which is a very unique thing that they've established for that ballpark. The Pepsi Porch actually comes out over the field itself. It's kind of like the upper deck at Tiger Stadium. Anything above that fence in right is a home run. Above all places, that could be the cheapest home run that you hit at Citi Field. It certainly would favor left-handed hitters way above any right-handed batters." Pepsi Porch or not, in 2012 Johan Santana reestablished Citi Field's reputation for being pitcher biased, at least against the defending world champion St. Louis Cardinals.

JUNE 1, 2012: JOHAN SANTANA "RESETS" THE COUNTER

Since the New York Mets first took the field in 1962, 10 teams have been added to Major League Baseball. Minus the San Diego Padres, every one of these expansion teams recorded a no-hitter prior to June 1, 2012, which likely rubbed salt into the wound of the Mets, who, through 8,019 regular season games, had still not put up a nine-frame goose egg in the column marked "H" on the scoreboard. Johan Santana, on that first day of June 2012, left the San Diego Padres alone in that no-hitter-less nest. Summing up the box score portion of Santana's masterpiece, the left-hander struck out eight and walked five over nine innings. With the aid of Citi Field's home-run-killing depths, not one of the 16 fly balls hit off of Santana made it over the fence. Almost in a reversal of game 7 of the 2006 National League Championship Series, this time it was a Met on the mound and a Cardinal at the plate striking out, as third baseman David Freese's "K" on Santana's 134th pitch of the night sealed the gem and the Mets' place in baseball history. Having been in the booth to broadcast what was clearly the most memorable game in the young Citi Field's history, Howie Rose recalls the event: "It was one of the most surreal nights of my broadcasting career, because I had just essentially adopted the thought along the way over a number of years—for whatever esoteric reason—it was fated never to be. I don't know that a no-hitter has ever been thrown under less likely circumstances. You have to understand the backstory of that night. Santana had been coming back from major shoulder surgery and Terry Collins, the Mets manager, was asked before the game what his pitch limit was going to be that night, because Santana pitched a complete game the start before the no-hitter. He went a long way, so Terry was adamant before the game that he was going to hold Johan to about 110, 115 pitches with 115 being the absolute outside limit. So, as the game progressed, and Johan was walking people here and there, I even remember saying on the air, even though he had been hitless through five, 'If you think tonight is going to be the night, forget it, because he's on a tight pitch count. He's going to hit that somewhere around the seventh inning the way things are going, so this is not going to be the night,' and, yet, there we go through the sixth and now into the seventh. That's the point—given the Mets history, Johan's determination, and his status as an elite pitcher in the game—Terry was in no-man's-land. He had no choice, and he knew he had no choice. Johan basically said as much to him along the way, saying, 'I'm not coming out of this game while this is happening.' It ate Terry up inside, and, in some ways, it still does because of the ramifications of that game. Whether you want to ascribe them specifically to being allowed to throw 134 pitches, he was never the same after that night. He got lit up his next start, which was the following week at Yankee Stadium. I mean absolutely smoked. He went on to need another shoulder surgery and was trying to come back from that last year, and he blew out his Achilles, so there's no telling if he's ever going to pitch again. He'd certainly be a serious underdog—at this point—to pitch again, and you'd have to ask him whether or not he would trade the ensuing few years for that one night, but, my suspicion is he just might have. It was *that* wild of a night." While the San Diego Padres have yet to throw a no-hitter, their tally is still way less than that in Flushing, New York, the morning of June 1, 2012. Howie Rose adds, "As we got to the year or two, ironically, just before that night, I started to keep track just in case it ever was coming into focus. It might happen on this particular day or night. I just started scribbling the game number—the all-time Mets regular season game number—in the corner of my scorecard, and, as we went into it that night, the number on my scorecard said, '8,019.' So it was very easy for me, upon the final out being made, that I was able to look right up to that scorecard and go, 'In the 8,020th game in the history of the New York Mets, they finally have a no-hitter." No one knows if it'll be 50 years and 8,020 games before the Mets throw another no-hitter, but when we consider the mumblings of hitters; a New York general manager's propensity to consume—in this case—a pricey, free agent pitcher; and a home-run-killing outfield, it's highly doubtful.

· 6 ·

Citizens Bank Park: Philadelphia Phillies

Citizens Bank Park: "The way the sun splashes off the glass buildings down in Center City, those kinds of things catch your eye and cause you to daydream a little bit." — Tom McCarthy
Photo courtesy of Miles Kennedy/Philadelphia Phillies

> *The city of Philadelphia itself is a beautiful setting, and the way they built this ballpark is that if you're basically sitting behind home plate from the third base bag to the first base bag—or even down the right-field line—you basically have a view of the city. The skyline on a beautiful night is something to behold.*

> —Tom McCarthy, Philadelphia Phillies TV
> play-by-play broadcaster

For a town nicknamed the City of Brotherly Love, Philadelphia has been known to prove itself otherwise from time to time. The most famous of these occurrences was on December 15, 1968, when Philadelphian Frank Olivo wore a Santa Claus outfit to an Eagles game in their temporary home of Penn's Franklin Field. With the Eagles at the tail end of an abysmal 2–12 season, Olivo was invited to come down and walk the length of the field; it was hoped the sight of the jolly icon might bring some life back into the crowd. Unfortunately for Olivo, the crowd's concept of restored life came in the form of flying snowballs aimed at a red-and-white, waving target. Olivo was pelted with snowballs and booed during his procession across Franklin Field, giving Philadelphia sports fans the reputation for being "the worst in the country." In defense of the snowball-hurling, disgruntled Philadelphians, the only team, by that time, to have won a championship for the city, the Athletics (A's), had been shipped westward to Kansas City 14 years earlier. The NHL's relatively young Philadelphia Flyers would pacify the Keystone State in '74 and '75 with back-to-back Stanley Cups, but the "brotherly love" wouldn't be fully restored until the 1980 World Series, when baseball's Philadelphia Phillies, led by all-time hit king Pete Rose and slugger Mike Schmidt, beat the Kansas City Royals four games to two. The city was once again able to parade a World Series winner past the Liberty Bell.

Formed in 1883, the Philadelphia Phillies are the longest-running "one-name, one-city" franchise in Major League history. Not only did they arrive 18 years before their cross-city neighbor Athletics, but they have stayed 62 years after that team took their gothic script "A" logo with them to the Show Me State. Much like their inter-sport cousins the Eagles, the Phillies have bounced around many homes in their 131-year history. In fact, the Phillies and Eagles even shared three different venues (Baker Bowl/National League Park 1933–1935; Shibe Park/Connie Mack Stadium 1940–1942, 1944–1957; and Veterans Stadium 1971–2003) for the better part of the 20th century. The last of these, Veterans Stadium, otherwise known as "the Vet," is one of the famed "cookie-cutter" multisports facilities that were so popular during the early '70s. The Vet, in its 33-year history, housed two NFC Champion Eagles teams ('80, '04) and three World Series–worthy Phillies teams ('80, '83,

'93). With the champagne of hall of famers Mike Schmidt and Steve Carlton's 1980 title all but dried up by the likes of Baltimore's Rick Dempsey in '83 and Toronto's Joe Carter in '93, the Phillies, in '04, resumed their 15-year journey back to the fall classic in their new home, a mere 100 feet from their old one.

A "PHAN"-FRIENDLY ENVIRONMENT

On April 12, 2004, the Phillies introduced their fans to Citizens Bank Park, a new-look baseball facility with a flair for baseball's past in "The Quaker City." Hoping to prevent the proverbial snowball pelting from Philadelphians, the organization had the fans well in mind when it came to building the park's amenities, starting with the ever-so-welcoming Ashburn Alley. Named after Phillies all-time great Richie "Whitey" Ashburn, this fan-friendly section, according to Phillies TV broadcaster Tom McCarthy, is one thing that "really stands out" at Citizens Bank Park. McCarthy adds, "Ashburn Alley is this sort of ode to the Jersey Shore, where they have food stands and this nice open area for folks to walk around and sort of take in the sights of the ballpark." Along with good food and a direct window to the action on the field, Ashburn Alley includes the All Star Walk, Memory Lane, and Phillies Wall of Fame, all paying tribute to the finest the city of Philadelphia has offered the game for over a century.

Though too big to fit into a standard Phillies uniform, one featured member of this Wall of Fame belongs not only to Baseball's Hall of Fame but to one for which he is "better suited," the Mascot Hall of Fame. Born in 1978, the Phillie Phanatic revolutionized baseball's mascot/fan interactivity for decades. Arguably the most recognizable mascot in sports history, the Phanatic, upon his introduction, proved himself an opponent not only to visiting players but to Philadelphia players as well. Tom McCarthy adds, "Mike Schmidt told me when the Phanatic was first introduced in Philadelphia in the '70s, the players didn't like it because they didn't want the attention being taken away from them. It was pretty soon after that, they realized it was an uphill battle. He was indeed more popular than most of the players." Though the Phanatic's modus operandi is not to invoke jealousy from the boys in red pinstripes, one would be hard pressed to find anything else that has garnered the attention of mythical-figure-assaulting sports fans for 36 years and counting. Praising the Phanatic's long tenure, McCarthy says, "He's just an added bonus. He is the most talented mascot in all of baseball. The way he moves. The way he is able to use his body language in that costume and sort of dictate the moment. He's flexible, and it's a big costume. He's in tune with the Phillies fans, so he understands what gets them going and when he should or shouldn't slide into the moment. If you watch his antics before the game—when he's imitating the other teams, or even imitating Phillies players, or wandering up to the plate to have a discussion with the umpires—it's one of the funniest things you'll ever watch, and it never gets old. That's the cool thing about him. It's always fresh. Even some of the dances that he puts together that I've seen a million times, I still can't get enough of it." With all due respect to the Phillie Phanatic, he, too, would not have been exempt from the ire of the snowball-throwing assailants at Franklin Field that wintry Sunday in 1968.

DAYDREAM BELIEVERS

The uniqueness of Citizens Bank Park does not stop at the concourses and the six-foot-six, jersey-wearing shag carpet with a horn for a nose. Tom McCarthy explains the design process for the Phillies current home: "There were several things they wanted to do. They did not want 'cookie cutter'—which is what the Vet was for all those years—so they wanted something that was not symmetrical all the way around. There's nothing that's the same in left center or right center field." One area that is definitely not symmetrical by any definition of the term is "the Angle" out in left center field. Looking more like a lie-induced spike on a polygraph test, the Angle starts when straightaway center field drops back from 401 feet to 409 feet in left center, the deepest part of the ballpark. The wall slopes down to 387 feet and then Angles back another few feet into the left-field power alleys, where it's smooth sailing all the way down to the left-field foul pole. Commenting on the Angle and its purpose, McCarthy says, "The one area that is different than the others is out in left center field. The wall kinda goes up on an angle, and I have seen balls that have hit there and kind of shot back toward right center field, so if you're gonna have an inside-the-park home run, that's probably the area the ball has to hit first to elude the center fielder." While the Angle may toy with the outfielders' emotions, the horizon beyond the park's perimeter may do the same for the fans, but in a good way. Built facing downtown Philadelphia's skyline, Citizens Bank Park provides a view unlike any other, especially during those rare late afternoon games. Tom McCarthy adds, "We had a five o'clock start, and the way the sun was splashing off the glass buildings down in Center City, it was just a marvelous, marvelous landscape, and that's something, whether it be the capitol in Washington or the water in San Francisco, those kinds of things catch your eye and cause you to daydream a little bit. Daydreaming and baseball, when you're a fan, kind of go hand in hand because you think back to when you were a kid playing or when your dad took you to a game. That type of thing. I think daydreaming is a huge part of it and that center field look sort of soaks you in."

While daydreaming and baseball may go hand in hand, the dimensions at Citizens Bank Park preclude any such reverie from those in the field of play, especially during warmer months, when the ball has the tendency to jump. McCarthy notes, "The dimensions are probably a little shorter in some places in left center field and in right center field, so the outfielders generally look like they're right on top of you compared to Marlins Park or some of the other bigger ballparks. The biggest test, to me, is the third base coach because he has to gauge whether a ball to left field or right field is easy to score on. It's easier for them to wave a runner home from second base on a ball hit to left field at Marlins Park or Citi Field. There's a little deeper thinking that goes into it at Citizens Bank Park." Of course a team's success doesn't always hinge on the windmilling arm of the third base coach. From 2007 to 2011 the Philadelphia Phillies qualified for the postseason all five years, including three straight trips to the National League Championship Series, two World Series appearances, and a World Series title in 2008.

FAMILIAR FACES IN NEW UNIFORMS AND OLD DEMONS TO EXORCISE

Winning the National League East division for five straight seasons, the Phillies certainly tested a young Citizens Bank Park's endurance beyond game 162. Commenting on the playoff atmosphere inside Citizens Bank Park, Tom McCarthy says, "We always say that the greatest thing in the world in a baseball season is getting to the postseason. It's the greatest time of the year. One of the things that really sets Citizens Bank Park away from any other stadium in the National League—it doesn't matter how many times the Atlanta Braves or any other team has been in the postseason—the energy at a sold-out Citizens Bank Park is unmatched in any spot around baseball. You can't even see. You can just hear in the field, and that's what Citizens Bank Park was like in all those years. They sold it out every time."

In 2008 the Phillies, thanks to a crop of homegrown all-stars that included hitters like Chase Utley, Jimmy Rollins, Ryan Howard, and Shane Victorino, as well as ace pitchers like Cole Hamels and Brett Myers, returned to the fall classic. Mixed into this bunch were noteworthy free agents Pedro Feliz (Giants), Jamie Moyer (Mariners), and Geoff Jenkins (Brewers); however, the free agent who would arguably count for the most in this magical season for the Phillies, Brad Lidge (Astros), had his own season for the ages. On October 17, 2005, with the Houston Astros one out from clinching their first pennant in franchise history, Lidge served up a slider to Cardinals first baseman Albert Pujols, which caromed off the hurricane-proof glass encompassing Houston's Minute Maid Park. The Astros eventually made it to the fall classic later that week, but Lidge served up yet another game-winning home run, this time to the White Sox's Scott Podsednik, closing out the worst week of his career. In 2008 Lidge rebounded in perfect fashion, converting all 48 of his save opportunities, including seven in the postseason. With number 48 being the World Series clincher (and the tying run in scoring position, no less), Lidge fell to his knees at the base of the pitcher's mound and threw his arms up in unforgettable praise, as catcher Carlos Ruiz was the first of the Phillies teammates to swarm their closer. Tom McCarthy reflects on the moment: "It was the greatest moment that this ballpark, at a very young time, has absorbed. You're not gonna get anything that will top that on so many levels because there's nothing greater than a world championship. Just the way the city reacted. The double by Geoff Jenkins that eventually led to the Phillies taking the lead. Although the Rays tied it back up again, the Phillies were able to pull ahead and walk away with the championship. That celebration is a picture that will always be in the mind of everybody." For the second time in the franchise's one-city, one-name, 125-year history, the Phillies were once again kings of the baseball world. No snowballs were thrown that late October night.

Comerica Park: Detroit Tigers

Comerica Park: "Walking into Comerica Park, people see the city skyline. It's a great view that just sets the whole feel and atmosphere of the ballpark." — Dan Dickerson
Photo courtesy of the Detroit Tigers

*From a fan's standpoint, the thing that I like is you can see the game
from anywhere you are in the ballpark if you're walking around the concourse. The concourses are open so you can always see the game. I don't
think many ballparks have that where you never lose sight of the game
as you walk all the way around it.*

—Dan Dickerson, Detroit Tigers radio broadcaster

*E*ddie Cicotte, a right-handed pitcher who once threw 346.2 innings in a
single season and recorded 29 wins in another, may best be remembered in
the Chicago White Sox community as one of the "Eight Men Out," but in
Detroit, he may be remembered as "The Tiger who disappeared into Cobb's
shadow."

In 1905 the Tigers acquired Tyrus Raymond Cobb, and 3,900 hits,
2,088 runs, and 869 stolen bases in a Tigers uniform later, Cobb's name alone
was bought for $70,000 by Connie Mack, owner of the Philadelphia Athlet-
ics, where Cobb spent the last two seasons of his career padding records that
would take three-quarters of a century to break. Despite 13 batting titles, a
triple crown, an American League MVP award, and all-time records in more
than 90 offensive categories, Cobb was never able to capture a World Series
title. Seven years after Cobb joined the team, Tiger Stadium opened where it
would stand for a remarkable 88 seasons. While Cobb never rode the victory
parade float down Michigan Avenue, other great Tigers players, like "Hammerin'" Hank Greenberg ('35, '45), Al Kaline ('68), and "Trammellandwhita-
ker" ('84), helped Detroit to its four respective World Series titles. Had Tiger
Stadium remained open past the '99 season up 'til today, it would have stood
alongside Boston's Fenway Park as the two oldest ballparks in the majors, and
as a centenarian, have received a complimentary jar of Smuckers jelly courtesy
of NBC's Willard Scott. Instead, on April 11, 2000, downtown Detroit's latest
addition, Comerica Park, opened its bronze-statue-guarded gates.

Unlike Tiger Stadium, which was famous for its center-field bleachers,
the Tigers' new home of Comerica Park opened the outfield up to views, fan
friendliness, and a flair for Tigers' past. Lead radio play-by-play broadcaster
and former Tiger Stadium parishioner Dan Dickerson reflects on the old feeling Comerica offers: "Having kind of grown up in the center field bleachers
at Tiger Stadium, there is that similar view in straightaway center field because
the field is set down a little bit. You can go out to those statues in left center,
which, to me, is a true feature of the ballpark. Then, if you turn around and
look at the field, you're on the railing. If you go to a game, you'll notice
there's always somebody on those railings looking in because that's kind of
the old Tiger Stadium view. It's a great view. I've been out there just to look
at it and remind myself what that view was like. I've always liked that feature
of Comerica Park."

It's arguable that the view looking back *in* to Comerica Park doesn't hold a candle to the view looking *out*. Dickerson adds, "Another unique feature is you walk in and you see a city landscape out beyond center field. They aligned this ballpark to have home plate in the northeast corner to take advantage of the view of looking downtown. Say what you will about the abandoned buildings, but there really are some beautiful buildings downtown. I think there's a certain feeling you get when you walk into a ballpark. Like Safeco Field—the first time I walked in, I thought, 'Wow! This is something.' I think a lot of people get that same feeling walking into Comerica Park and they see the city skyline. It's a great view, and it just sets the whole feel and atmosphere of the ballpark." While government bailouts of the GM Corporation have helped ensure the GM Renaissance Center isn't added to the list of abandoned buildings in the Motor City, the no-man's-land which is Comerica Park's straightaway center field could probably house an abandoned building within *its* depths. Dickerson adds, "The size of the outfield is probably the biggest thing players have talked about. From a hitter's perspective, the gaps are big. It's actually not a bad ballpark for a hitter. It's not a big home run park like a couple of ballparks. If you're an outfielder, left field is huge; 340 down the line, and the gaps are large in left center and right center." At a staggering 420 feet to straightaway center, very few in baseball can lay claim to as much real estate as those patrolling Comerica Park's outfield. Austin Jackson, who delved into the park's abyss for four and a half seasons before being traded to Seattle and its almost-as-expansive Safeco Field, may find his new surroundings a little less taxing on both the legs and the mind. Dickerson notes, "I talked to Austin Jackson about the ground he has to cover. It's a lot and I'm sure players admit to that right away. I've walked out there enough times, and when I look in, those gaps *are* big. Right field angles out to right center, and the wall gets higher."

Adding to the cardiovascular overkill that is Comerica Park's outfield is the way the stadium was built. Dickerson notes, "The upper deck is set back a little further. It's a little more open behind home plate than at other ballparks. You'll hear outfielders comment about how, because of that, the perspective is different when a ball comes off the bat. It's pretty tricky to read sometimes. I think day games are a little tougher than night games to read the ball off the bat than it might be at other ballparks where the upper deck is a little closer to the field. It's a unique dynamic. The gap between the lower and upper deck also plays into it because of the wind. The wind goes between the two decks and it can create some problems for the outfielders. That can be a little tricky as well." While outfielders may have to relax their eyes when guessing a fly ball—like staring into a stereogram image trying to find a sailboat, a bunny, or a bunny riding a sailboat—Comerica Park is a multi-acre science experiment for pitchers. Detroit Tigers aces Justin Verlander and Max Scherzer, over a combined 15 pitching seasons, accumulated 234 wins, two Cy Young awards, a Rookie of the Year, and an American League MVP with the aid of Comerica Park. Dickerson explains the two pitchers' heightened sense of security: "Power pitchers tend to be more fly ball pitchers than ground ball pitchers, and I do think Tigers pitchers know how to take advantage of that. They know when they're facing a power hitter, and they pitch him away, it'll be hard to hit it out. You'd have to miss your spot badly, or they would have to put an incredible swing on the ball to get it out. I'm not sure they change their pitching style a ton at home, but I also think, in key situations, there's probably some comfort knowing you can pitch to the big part of the field and that there's room for your outfielders to go make a play." Whether or not the outfielders get an extra nice Christmas card from Verlander and Scherzer remains to be seen, but there's no question that if some mistletoe hung from the batter's eye in center field beyond the 420 mark, Verlander and Scherzer would be kissing it after each start.

WELCOME BACK TO THE POSTSEASON

While Verlander and Scherzer have brought the Motor City to a World Series (2012) and three straight American League Championship Series appearances (2011–2013), it was another "ace" in 2006 who helped bring to fruition what Dan Dickerson calls "one of the greatest turnarounds in baseball history," starting with game 3 of the American League Division Series against the New York Yankees. Dickerson comments, "In 2006, it was the first time the Tigers had been to the playoffs in 19 years. They were playing the mighty Yankees. The Yankees had won 97 games, and the Tigers won 95, but, if you go back, it's amazing how heavy a favorite most people considered the Yankees to be in that series. But the Tigers split the first two in New York, and then headed back home for game 3. It was Kenny Rogers against the Yankees and it was one of the greatest pitching performances you will ever see." Kenny Rogers, then in the 18th season of his 20-year career, had his fair share of memorable moments, such as pitching a perfect game during the strike-shortened '94 season as a Texas Ranger and winning a World Series in 1996 during a two-year stint with a "core four" of these '06 Yankees. For 18 seasons as a "non-Yankee" in the American League, Rogers likely wished *not* to see the pinstripes staring back at him on the mound. Dickerson continues, "He didn't have good numbers in his career against the Yankees with an ERA around 9.00. He didn't have good numbers against *anybody* in that lineup the Yankees were throwing at him, so you could tell the Yankees weren't too concerned about going back to Detroit 1–1 with Kenny Rogers on the mound for game 3. But Kenny completely changed his pitching style for that game. He was a crafty lefty at that point in his career, but he geared it up and it may have been the last big game of his career. It was like he left everything on the table. He powered up into the low '90s with his fastball and completely dominated the Yankee lineup, and the place was just electric. He would come off in the half inning pumping his fist. The emotion was written on his face. When he came off the mound in the eighth inning, they were done. It was just an incredible moment. He was fired up. The crowd was fired up. That wasn't the clinching game, but they won that game because of him and then clinched it the next day in game 4. That was a great series win, but in terms of an individual performance, that's one of the best games I've seen since the ballpark opened. The Tigers were back in the postseason for the first time in 19 years, and he rose to the occasion—changing his game plan and his style for one game because he *knew* he had to do something different. It was a remarkable performance. I always think of that game." While Rogers had two more gems in him that postseason, it was another traveled veteran who would return the Tigers to their first World Series in 22 years, in game 4 of the American League Championship Series.

Magglio Ordonez spent eight years in a Chicago White Sox uniform playing outfield for "the Good Guys," batting .307 with 187 homers. Coming over to the Tigers before the White Sox's magical '05 championship season, Ordonez had only been to the playoffs once, back in 2000, when his team was swept by the Seattle Mariners. In 2006, with his Tigers just one win from the World Series, Ordonez hadn't exactly been the long ball type recently, hitting just one home run in his first 32 plate appearances against the Yankees and the Oakland Athletics. Leading off the bottom of the sixth in game 4 of the American League Championship Series, with the Tigers up 3–0 in the series but trailing 3–2 in the game, Ordonez lined a home run off A's starter Dan Haren to tie the game. Turning the ball over to both teams' bullpens, the score remained 3–3 until the bottom of the ninth. Two quick outs by Marcus Thames and Curtis Granderson suggested the game would go to extras and the Tigers' celebratory champagne would have to temporarily be put on ice, but two straight singles by Craig Monroe and Placido Polanco had the winning run in scoring position for Ordonez. When another single would have sufficed, especially to the "Motown Abyss," Ordonez launched a walk-off three-run home run to left field that would have likely "left" old Tiger Stadium. The Tigers were back in the World Series, and Comerica was literally rocking. Looking back on the moment, Dickerson notes, "I think a lot of people remember the ALCS clinching game against the A's because of the way it ended. Not many series have ended on a walk-off home run. It's amazing how many people still talk about that home run and hearing the call. It was a very fun moment. Unexpected? Absolutely. It was completely unexpected to me, and I think you can hear the surprise in my voice when I call that home run. There were two men on and two men out and Ordonez' specialty seemed to be that opposite field single to get a run home. He made that an art form. His power was down at that point in his career, and he just didn't hit many home runs. He hit an absolute no doubter. You plan for that clinching moment—that call—but you can't plan *that*. That was truly a great moment because they were going to the World Series for the first time since '84. I still remember when he hit that, where we were sitting in our booth, you literally could feel the stadium shaking. I'm getting goosebumps just thinking about how loud it was when he got to home plate." Though the Tigers would eventually lose the World Series in five games to the St. Louis Cardinals, the "edit button" on many Tiger fans' memories arguably stops on Ordonez's walk-off moment.

FROM "MAGS" TO "MIGGY"

There are six "Han Solo-esque" statues beyond left center field of Tigers' greats from the past, including the already mentioned Ty Cobb, Hank Greenberg, and Al Kaline, as well as Charlie Gehringer, Willie Horton, and Hal Newhouser. Should the league ever protest the unfair treatment of non-pull hitters and demand the 420-foot wall be brought in to a more practical depth, there just may be enough room to add statues for Tigers like Verlander, Ordonez, and, most important, two-time American League MVP, Miguel "Miggy" Cabrera. In what was hardly a Cicotte/Cobb balanced trade, after the '07 season the Tigers acquired Cabrera and pitcher Dontrelle Willis as part of a (then) Florida Marlins biennial fire sale. In his seven years with the Tigers, Cabrera has hit 252 home runs, averaged nearly 200 hits, and become the first triple-crown-winning hitter since Carl "Yaz" Yastrzemski in 1967. Despite having to play a corner infielder's version of musical chairs over the past few seasons, Cabrera continues to chalk up MVP-worthy stats, which, coupled with the starting pitching of Verlander, Anibal Sanchez, and David Price; the hitting of J. D. and Victor Martinez; and the defense of Rajai Davis, may bring that elusive fifth world championship to Detroit.

· *8* ·

Coors Field: Colorado Rockies

Coors Field: "Some of the greatest sunsets in the world."—Jack Corrigan
Photo courtesy of Clarkson Creative/Colorado Rockies

I think it's the best ballpark in baseball to watch a night game. The weather's good. There's no humidity. There aren't any bugs, and, if you're sitting on the right side of the ballpark, especially if you're in the upper deck, you see some of the greatest sunsets in the world over the Rocky Mountains. You won't find that at any other ballpark in baseball.

—Jack Corrigan, Colorado Rockies radio
play-by-play broadcaster

$\mathscr{B}$efore 1993, of the 26 ballparks in Major League Baseball, Atlanta Fulton County Stadium stood the highest, at an elevation of 1,057 feet. Thanks to its slight advantage with respect to thinness of air, Atlanta Fulton County Stadium was referred to as the "launching pad." On April 9, 1993, at an altitude five times that of Atlanta, the Colorado Rockies played their first game in Mile High Stadium, before a record opening-day crowd of 80,227 fans. Taking advantage of their shared quarters with the Denver Broncos, the Rockies drew football-like numbers and topped the four million attendance mark their opening year. Even with the '94 players' strike shortening the season by six weeks, the Rockies still broke the three million mark in their second and final year at Mile High Stadium. On April 26, 1995, after an extended fall/winter break, the Rockies moved out of Mile High and began playing in their very own home of Coors Field.

Even while Coors Field was being built in 1993 and 1994, the team's attendance at Mile High Stadium showed that the original plan of 43,000 seats wouldn't be enough. The proverbial eraser on the original blueprints was worn out, and an additional 7,000 plus seats were added, making the future home of the Rockies one of those with the greatest capacity in the league. Though Coors Field's 50,000 plus seats pale in comparison to Mile High's 80,000, the new ballpark's design helps it have practically the same effect. Colorado Rockies radio play-by-play broadcaster Jack Corrigan describes the setting: "The ballpark is built wonderfully well to create noise. Coors Field— to keep people closer to the field—is a little steeper; a little more upright so the sound stays." Speaking about the Rockies' walk-off win in their playoff game of the '07 season, Corrigan continues, "I've gotta tell you the sound on the field with 50,000 people was better than any football stadium that had 30,000 more people. It was incredible." Even with the term "nosebleeds" literally a plausible outcome at Coors Field, it seems even the cheap seats have their own special place in Rockies lore. Around the stadium's entire upper deck, at 5,280 feet above sea level, is a row of purple seats to indicate the fruition of the city's nickname. Out in right field, even beyond the binocular-necessitating purple stripe, lies the "Rooftop," a concourse area with bars, restaurants, and a view of the Rockies both on the field and across Colorado. The Rooftop, replacing seldom-used upper-deck seating, has become one of the hottest tickets in baseball. A section of "cheap seats" that has existed since day one at Coors Field is "the Rock Pile," a 2,300-seat section beyond center field, which, when looking out from home plate, appears more like a misplayed piece in a life-sized game of Tetris. Though the Rock Pile has yet to see a home run ball reach its borders, nothing is impossible at 5,280 feet.

ENTER THE HUMIDOR

Having surpassed Atlanta Fulton County Stadium's elevation by some 4,123 feet, it's only natural Coors Field would become baseball's new "launching pad." Jack Corrigan comments, "I think the uniqueness of Coors Field starts with the fact that it's a mile above sea level, so the game itself is always going to be a little different than anywhere else. The air is a little lighter. There's a little less humidity. The ball has a tendency to travel more." In 1999 the balls traveling out of Coors Field would have gathered enough frequent flyer miles to finance an encore season for John Elway and the Broncos, as the Rockies and visitors combined for 303 home runs, a single-season record for any venue. While the thin air and high altitude were the obvious reasons for the season-spanning home run derbies, baseball scientists turned their attention to the dryness of the game balls reserved for and used inside Coors Field. Hypothesizing that adding moisture to the balls before they were used in the game would slow them down, Major League Baseball ordered that they be placed in a room-sized humidor, which was installed inside the stadium prior to the 2002 season. The humidor had an immediate impact, especially for the Rockies, who went from 4th in the league in home runs in 2001 to 23rd in 2002. Coupling the humidor effect with the opening of Citizens Bank Park in Philadelphia and Great American Ball Park in Cincinnati, the high home run numbers inside Coors Field have become, at least for the time being, a thing of the past. However, just because the ball stays in the park a bit more doesn't mean runs stay off the scoreboard. Corrigan notes, "You come to Coors Field expecting more offense than you might get at Dodger Stadium or Petco Park, which are, especially at night, heavy pitchers parks. A way they attempted to counter the thinner air was to make the ballpark bigger. Since they've added the humidor, it's not so much that there's home runs all the time. It's that there's a lot of space for balls to find green grass. There's a lot of offense as a rule."

Since half of this expected offense comes from visiting players, the Rockies have worked on strengthening their defense, starting with the outfielders. Corrigan explains: "One aspect of Coors Field is it has a very large left center field. In the Rockies' case with Carlos Gonzalez, you're taking a guy that would be a Gold Glove center fielder and you make him a Gold Glove left fielder because you need two center fielders, essentially, to cover all the territory. Many times with other teams, the left fielder might be their least effective defender. Not meaning that he's not a good defender, but of their outfielders, he's their third best and so they have to play differently. If he's not as good going back on the ball, it seems like he's always on the warning track. If he doesn't run exceedingly well, maybe he's going to cheat a little bit towards left center, hopefully, to keep a double from being a triple. The result is more space for a Rockies hitter to find down the left-field line or in shallower left." Of course, whether or not the ball travels to these adapting left and center fielders depends on the guy standing on the mound and his pitch selection. Corrigan adds, "The humidor has helped a great deal, but there's no question, as much from the dry conditions as the elevation, a breaking ball doesn't always break quite as much. The pitchers may change their target point to compensate. The old big twelve to six curveball is going to be more like two to four. It's not quite the same, so you're going to adjust how you throw that pitch. I think pitchers will tell you that you have to get less concerned when you miss a spot with a breaking ball and it gets hit. That's just the nature of pitching there. I think you see from a philosophical perspective, from the Rockies point of view, you want sinker pitchers, but, more often than not, you want a power sinker guy. If he's a sinker/slider guy, that usually means all of his pitches are like 87 to 91 (MPH). Those guys have to be very sharp to succeed long term at Coors Field." Two of the Rockies' better pitchers in recent years have been Ubaldo Jimenez, now with the Baltimore Orioles, and Jorge De La Rosa. In 2010 Jimenez, finishing third in the National League Cy Young award voting, won 19 games and had an astonishing-for-Coors-Field 2.88 ERA. Though not quite as staggering as Jimenez's numbers, De La Rosa's 16 wins in '09 and '13 still help him qualify for third all-time in Rockies history. Speaking about the feats of these two pitchers, not normally found in a setting like Coors Field, Corrigan explains, "When Ubaldo had his great year, and when De La Rosa has had the numbers he's had in the ballpark, it's an understanding of having a good fastball, and, in De La Rosa's case, also having a great change up. With Jimenez in that phenomenal year he had in 2010, he was just throwing gas and hitting his spots all the time. I don't think it would have made any difference where he was pitching. Jorge De La Rosa has been better at Coors Field than he has on the road. In fact, he is 30 games above .500 at Coors Field. Who would've guessed that?"

Though the humidor has kept baseballs from bursting into flames upon entering the atmosphere above Coors Field, the same can't be said for the effect the mile-high altitude has on the players themselves. Corrigan notes, "Because of the elevation and lack of humidity, guys really have to be concerned about hydration. If they don't—for a visiting guy at the end of a three or four game stand—he's bone tired. Our guys, if we're in an eight to ten game home stand, they've gotta be real careful that they don't burn a guy out; maybe not so much in that series, but when a road trip follows and he's got nothing in the tank." Going into the last two weeks of the season, the '07 Rockies were anything but bone tired, having enough gas in their tanks for a postseason run.

OCTOBER 1, 2007: ROCKTOBER ARRIVES IN COLORADO

Having won 13 of their last 14 games to end the 2007 regular season, the Rockies hosted the San Diego Padres in a one-game playoff, a game that was, in Jack Corrigan's opinion, "the greatest game ever at Coors Field." His claim could actually be condensed to "greatest *inning* ever at Coors Field," as the regulation frames hosted only two lead changes and a blown save by Brian Fuentes in the top of the eighth inning, hardly "greatest game ever" caliber. Fuentes's save was not the only one of the night to be blown, as Scott Hairston's 13th-inning home run off Jorge Julio left the Rockies three outs from missing the postseason. The Padres called on their closer—and soon to be all-time saves leader (at the time)—Trevor Hoffman to secure their spot in the National League Division Series against the Philadelphia Phillies. Three Rockies extra base hits later, the game was tied with nobody out and Matt Holliday on third. Backup third baseman Jamey Carroll, who was called into the game earlier as a pinch runner, hit a fly to right field, deep enough to prompt Holliday to tag up from third, but close enough to make the play at the plate one of the most unusual game winners of recent years. While Holliday slid, literally, face first past Padres backup catcher Michael Barrett and into home, a debate ensued—mainly among the millions of Padres fans watching at home—about whether or not Holliday actually touched the plate. The ball having squeaked free of Barrett's grasp, home plate umpire Tim McClelland ruled Holliday safe, and the Rockies would pack their bags for Philadelphia. Having had his own unique experience during the thrilling marathon game, Jack Corrigan recalls, "Jeff Kingery was my partner at the time. One of us would go down and be right behind home plate for the final half inning to be in place for a live postgame interview. We'd have a wireless microphone so that guy could do color and/or analysis from that unique vantage point. We finished the ninth inning still tied. I ran upstairs because I would be doing the play-by-play for the 10th inning, and Jeff came downstairs. In the 11th inning, we switched again. In the 12th inning, we switched again because it was still tied, and it was the same way for the 13th inning. I was right by the door to the field when Matt Holliday came to the plate. He has the collision with Michael Barrett and the home plate umpire Tim McClelland hasn't made a sign yet. 'Did he touch the plate or not?' I saw the ball rolling away from Barrett and I made my move. I had one foot through the door as McClelland gave the safe sign because I saw the ball. I screamed on the broadcast, 'He scored!' I wasn't going to worry whether he touched the plate or not. He was going to get called safe." Though it's unlikely anyone would have deferred to Corrigan's amateur expertise as a Major League umpire, the broadcaster signs off on the birth of "Rocktober," saying, "Outside of when we see the team win a World Series clinching game, we'll never be able to top the play in game 163 that got them to the 2007 playoffs."

COORS FIELD TODAY

Coming into its 20th season in 2014, Coors Field has kept its youth. Corrigan adds, "Another thing I think you'd notice about the park is its beauty. The fact that Coors Field is now in its 20th year, you have to give the people who run the stadium side of things for the ball club all the credit in the world. You walk in and you think it's a new ballpark. They've done a remarkable job staying on top of things so it has a very fresh feel to it." Another "fresh feel" to Coors Field has been the addition of young and imported infielders to help increase the ground-ball pitching necessary to thrive in Colorado's thin air. Second-year players D. J. LeMahieu and 2013 gold glove winner Nolan Arenado, along with team leader Troy Tulowitzki and former American League MVP Justin Morneau, have helped keep the balls from escaping into the abyss of Coors's outfield. While the team haven't celebrated Rocktober since their run to the 2007 World Series, the Rockies continue to chip away at that mile-high summit, hoping for another shot.

· 9 ·

Dodger Stadium: Los Angeles Dodgers

*It's home sweet home. It's a beautiful ballpark. You don't really think
that you're in the city because you're surrounded by mountains.*

—Vin Scully, Los Angeles Dodgers TV/radio
play-by-play broadcaster

*In terms of weather, in terms of view, Dodger Stadium is about as good
as it gets. It really is home field advantage in every sense of the word.*

—Charley Steiner, Los Angeles Dodgers TV/radio
play-by-play broadcaster

$\mathscr{F}$or seven decades the Brooklyn Dodgers staked their baseball claim among
the New York City boroughs, playing their intraleague rival Giants and interleague nemesis Yankees—often—in a postseason setting. In fact, over a
13-season span, the Yankees defeated the Dodgers in the World Series five
times. However, on October 4, 1955, Brooklyn finally beat the Yankees in
their own home in game 7 of the World Series, bringing the championship
glory to Brooklyn for the first time in the team's 66-year history. Two years
after this pivotal moment for the Dodgers came another, as team owner Walter O'Malley announced the team would be moving west to Los Angeles the
following season. Despite appearing in nine World Series and hosting perhaps
the most iconic moment in sports history—Jackie Robinson breaking the
color barrier—just 10 years before, the Dodgers began their pilgrimage westward, leaving in their dust legions of broken hearted Brooklynites. Though in
a new city, the Los Angeles Dodgers weren't quite in a new home. The team
played in the Los Angeles Coliseum for four years, waiting for a permanent
residence. On April 10, 1962, 2,800 miles from their old home of Ebbets
Field, the Dodgers took the field atop Chavez Ravine in their new home

61

of Dodger Stadium, which stands today as the third oldest ballpark in Major League Baseball.

A PLACE AMONG THE PALMS AND THE TRAFFIC

Dodger Stadium's geographic location is among the most unique of any ballpark in baseball and allows fans to soak in elements specific to the Golden State. When asked what features made Dodger Stadium unique from the other 29 ballparks in baseball, Charley Steiner simply responded, "You mean the sunsets, the palm trees, and the San Gabriel Mountains? Oh, and did I mention it never rains?" Located just minutes (depending on traffic) from downtown LA in one direction and the Hollywood Hills in the other, Dodger Stadium is cemented into the hillside of Chavez Ravine, an area once relegated to the lower income families of Los Angeles. While the slanting foundation and clay surface weren't the most ideal for building a residential home back in 1962, a $23 million (roughly $181 million today, adjusted for inflation) stadium didn't seem that implausible. With the high-rising buildings of downtown LA at its back, Dodger Stadium sits with an amazing view of the nearby San Gabriel Mountains, and where there are mountains, there's bound to be a beautiful sunset. Around the time the second inning would be coming to a close on a summer evening, the three natural elements described by Charley Steiner all culminate in what many would consider to be the most beautiful landscape in all of baseball. Longtime Los Angeles Dodgers play-by-play broadcaster Vin Scully gives his own, more personal description of the surroundings of Dodger Stadium: "The biggest thing about Dodger Stadium—certainly in July, August, September—when the air is clear and you are looking out beyond the pavilions, you would see the mountains, and you would remember the words from the song and the words 'the purple mountains' majesty' and that's out there for all the world to see. It's a beautiful ballpark. They spent a lot of money building it. They've spent even more money maintaining it. There's also been a lot of careful planting, which was done by Walter O'Malley, who designed it and built it. Mr. O'Malley loved the earth. He loved flowers, and so we have a lot of that as well. The current ownership has not just taken it over, they've taken it over and tried to add considerably to the fans' experience. So when you look at this great sprawling acreage with a lot of parking, you have a beautiful, clean, modern stadium even though it was built and opened up in 1962. They spent a lot of money to make sure it remains the edifice that it is. It's a great tribute to the game, it's a great tribute to baseball, and it's a great tribute to Walter O'Malley, so, all in all, it's a rather sacred place for me."

The nature of Dodger Stadium isn't just found in the palm trees planted by Walter O'Malley or the shrubbery landscaping the San Gabriel Mountains. Downtown LA's "other nature" slows to a crawl in the form of a steel-framed, exhaust-emitting species, many of which migrate to their colony alongside Chavez Ravine on a nightly basis. Just a few miles south of Dodger Stadium, the California freeway system converges on itself again and again, making it look, from above, like a tangled-up string of Christmas lights fresh from the box the day after Thanksgiving. The eastward/westward US 10 meets up with northbound/southbound I-5, only to merge onto California 101 for a brief moment before connecting to the 110, and three right turns and a circle or two around Chavez Ravine later, you're at your parking spot just in time for the bottom of the second inning. If you're the earliest bird of the bunch type, the view from your seat at Dodger Stadium will likely include the sight of red brake lights blinking lethargically on and off as drivers perform an exercise in futility searching for that perfect parking spot. This usually takes place during the first and second innings and resumes during the eighth and ninth, with the cars facing the opposite direction. Though this tardiness is often criticized by fans across the country, Charley Steiner defends the blue-and-white latecomers, saying, "The reality is Dodger Stadium is located off a freeway. Games begin at 7:10. Fans arrive right at the height of rush hour. That's one of those deals where that ain't gonna change. They're not going to pack up and move Dodger Stadium 50 miles away out of Los Angeles where there's less traffic. These are the cards we're dealt. All I know is that when the Dodgers are on the road and people are trying to arrive and leave at whatever the stadium at roughly the same time, when you've got 20, 30, 40, 50,000 people all in one place at one time, guess what; there's going to be traffic there, too. It is certainly an easy criticism that's aimed at Dodger Stadium, but that's the way it is. I don't see how that's going to change. As long as the Dodgers are popular and lead the league in home attendance, there is going to be traffic." Reinforcing Steiner's words, the Dodgers have led the league in total attendance for the past two seasons ('13, '14). Referring again to LA traffic, Steiner adds, "I suppose if there's any upside, from a perfectly selfish point of view, I've got a captive audience if they're stuck in traffic, coming or going."

DODGER STADIUM PLAYED FAIR BUT PLAYS FAIRER

In 1968 right-hander Don Drysdale was only one of the two remaining Dodgers from the Brooklyn days at Ebbets Field (the other was Ron Fairly). Already having won three World Series titles and a Cy Young award, Drysdale made history in his second to last year as a player. Starting May 14 against the

Chicago Cubs, the right-hander delivered 58 consecutive innings of scoreless baseball, breaking Washington Senator Walter Johnson's record streak of 55⅔ innings, which was set 55 years earlier. The following season, in order to increase fan stimulation, the diamond at Dodger Stadium was shifted a full 10 feet closer to the fences, making the park slightly more hitter friendly. In 1988, 20 plus years after Drysdale's feat, another "boy in blue," Dodgers right-hander and soon to be Cy Young winner Orel Hershiser, not only broke Drysdale's scoreless inning streak, but did so with a 10-foot disadvantage.

Today, Dodger Stadium is one of the only symmetrically designed outfields left in all of baseball. There are no angled walls, deepening triangles, or ascending hills to torment the outfielders. Steiner comments, "In terms of the perfection of the ballpark—the layout itself—you'd be hard pressed to have any sort of complaint. There are no weird hops off the walls. It plays fair, but it plays long." The "long" he refers to has more to do with what takes place *above* the field than on it. Situated relatively close to the Pacific Ocean, Dodger Stadium tends to attract much of the cool air the coast has to offer once the sun sets, and for a hitter, cold air equals heavy air. Steiner continues, "The numbers are misleading because of the heaviness of the air. You would think if you look strictly at the dimensions (330 feet down the line, 395 in straightaway center) that it would be an easy home run hitter's park. Au contraire. The numbers are painted on the walls because they've got to put them somewhere." Perhaps the consolation, if there is any, for the batter is the vantage point for such a "loud out." Steiner points out, "It's a pristine setting. The grass is always immaculate. The weather is always perfect, so it plays fair except if you're a hitter. You can smash it and mash it and hit it about as hard as you possibly can, and, sometimes, it doesn't go as far as you think it would or should. Blame it on the moist, heavy air and the marine layer." Dodger Stadium is constantly in the bottom third of the league for home runs allowed by either team, which is good if you're a pitcher but not if you're a long-ball-craving ticket holder. Fortunately for the fans, on September 18, 2006, the Dodger Stadium air went on a temporary diet.

MELEE ON THE FIELD AND IN THE PARKING LOT

In a town where brevity in storytelling is practically mandatory, Charley Steiner excels as a broadcaster. Having wanted to be a broadcaster for the Dodgers since he was seven years old, Steiner recalls the most memorable game he has called for the boys in blue—which took place in only his second year with the team—in a way only he could describe it: "The Dodgers were trailing the Padres by four runs in the bottom of the ninth. It's the middle of

September, and it's a battle for first place at the time. The Dodgers are trailing 9–5, and fans are beginning to leave. It was Jeff Kent who led off the inning in the bottom of the ninth against Jon Adkins. He hits a home run. All right, 9–6. J. D. Drew comes up. Back to back homers. Now it's 9–7. I'm thinking, 'Well, this is getting interesting, isn't it?' The first home run, my voice is kind of matter of fact. 'Okay, home run. The Dodgers trail by three.' Drew hits a homer, makes it 9–7. So, it's out with Adkins and in with Trevor Hoffman, and the first pitch from Hoffman to Russell Martin, a home run to left center. Three home runs in a row! Now it's 9–8. Well, *this* is getting really interesting. Still nobody out. Up comes Marlon Anderson. *Marlon Anderson* of all people—a journeyman utility player acquired by the club down the stretch— damned if he doesn't hit a home run to right center. It's now 9–9. Four home runs in a row. The crowd is going crazy. I am looking out beyond the walls and you see the traffic leaving. You see all the red, brake lights. Now, all of a sudden, the brake lights are illuminated, and the fans are making u-turns coming back. Now the remaining crowd is just going berserk. The next batter, Rafael Furcal, people forget that he hit one right to the wall in left center that was about two feet from being five home runs in a row. So the Dodgers tie the score in the bottom of the ninth, but in the top of the 10th inning, the Padres score a run. Now, it's 10–9 San Diego. So, all the people who made the trek back—(the next day, I think they said it was about 5,000 people who made a 'B line' back into the ballpark)—they get back inside and no doubt are thinking 'We turned around for this?!' In the bottom of the 10th, Kenny Lofton led off the inning with a walk and Nomar Garciaparra hits a two-run, walk-off home run to win it. Damndest finish I ever saw."

Interestingly, Garciaparra is now one of Steiner's broadcasting partners. Steiner adds, "Nomar and I have known each other a long time, back with my days with the Yankees and he was with the Red Sox. He, of course, played and I announced. He will often say that is the craziest moment of his career, and it certainly was for me watching. It was one of those moments where you go, 'Whoa!' Back to back home runs are nice. Three in a row are sweet. Four? You know, it happens once in a blue moon, but four in the bottom of the ninth trailing by four to tie the score was historic. That was one of those special nights I will always remember." Providing another simple yet sound perspective on his night at "the Ravine," Steiner signs off, "That game was so wonderful and unpredictable and for all of the reasons why we do what we do. Why players play, and fans come out, and writers write, and broadcasters broadcast."

Fenway Park: Boston Red Sox

Fenway Park's Green Monster: "You notice how tall it is, how green it is, and how close it is."—Joe Castiglione
Photo courtesy of Amanda Sabga/Boston Red Sox

*Coming home from a road trip at three or four in the morning and wait-
ing for the buses, we'd go out and sit by the first base stands and just look
at the park and the quiet of Fenway when it's dark. That's always been
a cool thing to do. There are so many things about it that are charming.
What they've done with Fenway is absolutely incredible. The way it's
been rebuilt is amazing. Who knew you could keep the old charm with
the modern amenities?*

—Joe Castiglione, Boston Red Sox radio
play-by-play broadcaster

$\mathcal{O}$pened on April 20, 1912, just five days after the *Titanic* sank into the
depths of the Atlantic Ocean, Fenway Park, home of the history-rich Boston
Red Sox, is the oldest stadium in the majors, beating Chicago's Wrigley Field
by over two years. Fenway's first year in Boston proved to be a fruitful one,
as the team won the first of four World Series championships they would take
home in a seven-year span. Perhaps the greatest contributor to three of those
championships was Red Sox left-hander George Herman Ruth, otherwise
known as "the Babe." In his six seasons with the Red Sox, Ruth, arguably
the greatest slugger in baseball history, was better known for his feats from
the mound. The southpaw won 89 games, not including the three he won in
the 1916 and 1918 World Series, and struck out 483 batters, while sporting a
Red Sox uniform. After the 1919 season, Red Sox owner Harry Frazee sold
Babe Ruth to the New York Yankees for $125,000, which Frazee, in turn,
invested in his Broadway ventures. While the title of Frazee's play escapes the
memories of virtually every Bostonian, Ruth's 659 home runs, 1,978 RBIs,
and four World Series titles over the next 15 seasons with the Yankees haven't
been so forgettable for New Yorkers.

THE CURSE OF THE BABE: JANUARY 5, 1920–OCTOBER 20, 2004

Although the number that hung over the heads of Red Sox fans and players
alike was 86 seasons without a championship, what the sporting world came
to refer to as "the Curse of the Babe" actually began 14 months after Boston's
1918 World Series championship, when Frazee sold Ruth to the Yankees.
Over the next 85 years, Red Sox fans would have more heartbreaking moments than a low budget telenovela. In the 1946 World Series, the heavily
favored Red Sox lost game 7 to the St. Louis Cardinals when Enos Slaughter
scored from first unexpectedly in the top of the 9th. Many believe Red Sox
shortstop Johnny Pesky held the ball too long, and it cost them the title.
Pesky's name would eventually be cemented in a different way at Fenway

Park. Although fruitless in their next two World Series appearances in 1967 and 1975, the manifestation of the curse was at its peak in game 6 of the 1986 World Series against the New York Mets. With the Red Sox leading by two going into the bottom of the 10th and leading the series 3–2, the team relinquished the lead. The collapsing of the Red Sox's hopes of breaking the curse culminated in Boston's all-star first baseman Bill Buckner's misplay of a ground ball hit by the Mets' Mookie Wilson, which scored the winning run and forced a game 7 that the Mets won 8–5. Buckner's gaffe, which is arguably the most famous in baseball history, plagued the Red Sox for another 18 years. Perhaps the last great run of the curse took place during the 2003 American League Championship Series against (who else but) the New York Yankees. With the visiting Red Sox leading by three runs as late as the eighth inning of game 7, manager Grady Little left starter Pedro Martinez in the game arguably too long. The Yankees tied the game to force extra innings. After two and a half innings of scoreless ball courtesy of Yankees closer Mariano Rivera, New York's third baseman Aaron Boone led off the bottom of the 11th with a walk-off home run off knuckleballer Tim Wakefield. The Yankees won their 39th American League pennant, and the last image before the broadcast went dark was that of Babe Ruth winking.

Almost a full year later, the Yankees and Red Sox met again for the pennant. After being bludgeoned 19–8 on October 16, 2004, the Red Sox trailed the Yankees a seemingly insurmountable 3–0 in the best of seven series. The following night the Red Sox found themselves down 4–3 and one inning from their season ending, once again, without a championship. Then in his 22nd year as a Red Sox broadcaster, Joe Castiglione looks back on game 4 of the 2004 ALCS as one of his most memorable, saying, "We're on the verge of elimination and Dave Roberts steals, Bill Mueller singles him home, and Big Papi (David Ortiz) wins it with a walk off in extra innings and then again the next night." Beginning that night, the Red Sox won an unprecedented four straight games facing elimination and broke the 85-season-spanning curse. Practically opposite to what had happened just one year before, the 2004 ALCS broadcast ended with the Babe, as Joe Castiglione, channeling his mentor, Detroit Tigers play-by-play broadcaster Ernie Harwell, signed off, saying, "Move over Babe," a lyric written years before by Harwell.

FENWAY PROVERB: PESKY'S POLE GIVETH, BUT THE GREEN MONSTER TAKETH AWAY

Having provided some background to the mystique and lore one can only find in a sports venue nicknamed "the Chapel," we turn our attention to the playing field itself, which is among the most unique in baseball in dimensions. Without question, the most recognizable landmark in any of the league's 30 ballparks is Fenway's "Green Monster." The fame of this feature is so prominent, the Red Sox organization probably receives royalty checks from campfire storytellers from time to time just for use of the name. When asked what a newcomer would notice while walking up Fenway's aisles for the first time ever, Joe Castiglione, a man who has called more than 5,000 games, including 112 in the postseason and three World Series championships, simply answers, "the Wall." After a brief chuckle, Castiglione continues, "Definitely the left-field wall. You notice how tall it is, how green it is, and how close it is." The adjective "close" is a huge understatement; the base of the 37-foot-high Green Monster lies just 310 feet from home plate, a mere 50 feet farther than most regulation little league fields. The proximity of this famed (and often copied) Fenway feature to the batter does not necessarily guarantee a home run. A "laser shot" that may land deep into the bleachers of other ballparks wouldn't have enough time or distance to lift before caroming off the Green Monster some 25 feet up, falling back onto the field for a very loud "wallball single." Of course, a moon raker that may linger high in the air and fall on the warning track in pitcher-friendly stadiums like Petco Park in San Diego could find its way over the Green Monster and deposit itself on Boston's famous Lansdowne Street. While the hitters inside Fenway make swings usually reserved for a game of "three flies up," the left fielders drop anchor in relatively shallow territory, playing balls hit off the wall on a regular basis. Any outfielder coming to Boston knows he had better hit the squash courts at his local recreational center before boarding that plane; still, as Joe Castiglione would reassure the Fenway skeptical should a fresh face don the red and white, "It's really not that difficult for a major leaguer to adapt defensively. These guys play all over. There's 30 ballparks in baseball. They adapt very quickly." One distinct feature of Fenway's Green Monster to which "these guys" must quickly adapt is the manually operated scoreboard. With the word "BOSTON" always displayed in the home half and dozens more slots on the wall doing Massachusetts's version of the "hanging chad," left fielders tend to find playing off the Green Monster a bit tricky. Castiglione comments, "It's not that tough unless it hits one of the slots where the score numbers are placed, one of the ledges, or the ladder; but, generally, the bounces are fairly true."

Aside from making the outfielders chase down bad bounces like a junior high school gym class running ladder drills, the Green Monster has been host to some of Boston's most famous (and infamous) home runs. On October 2, 1978, in the 163rd game of the season, the Yankees and Red Sox squared off in a one-game, winner-take-all playoff at Fenway Park. With the Red Sox leading 2–0 in the top of the seventh, Yankees shortstop Bucky Dent, having only hit four home runs in the season's previous 162 games, hit a fly ball to left, just barely clearing the top of the Green Monster, scoring Dent, Chris Chambliss, and Roy White to give the Yankees a lead they would never relinquish. Although Bucky Dent has probably never been on the receiving end of a free drink in Boston watering holes, the same *cannot* be said for former Red Sox catcher Carlton "Pudge" Fisk. On October 21, 1975, with game 6 of the World Series between Boston and Cincinnati's "Big Red Machine" tied 6–6 in the bottom of the 12th, Fisk was at the plate facing Reds reliever Pat Darcy. On Darcy's second pitch of the night, Fisk launched a fly ball so close to the left-field foul pole, he had to wave it back inside. Fisk's home run over the Green Monster to send the series to a decisive game 7 is arguably the greatest in postseason history.

The Green Monster has had its fair share of "upgrades" over the park's 103 seasons. Originally 25 feet tall and made of wood, the wall was extended 12 feet in 1934 to the height it is recognized by today. In 1947, Fenway's feature earned its nickname as a result of owner Tom Yawkey having the advertisements draping the wall's facade painted over with the color green. The wall was rebuilt in 1976 with added safety features like padding and a relocated yet still manual scoreboard. The Red Sox organization made the Green Monster a fan-inclusive experience in 2003, adding 274 seats atop the wall, making it look, from the batter's perspective, like an overfilled dam about to burst red-and-white-colored debris all over the field.

As close as the Green Monster is to home plate, its right-field counterpart, complete with its own nickname and legend, is a full eight feet closer. In 1940, after the arrival of arguably baseball's greatest hitter ever, Ted Williams, the year before, the Red Sox installed bullpens in right field, which brought the fences in 23 feet. A left-handed hitter, Williams pulled so many balls over to right field and beyond the fences that they nicknamed the bullpen area "Williamsburg." While the Green Monster in left field is known to take away many would-be home runs, the foul pole in right field, nicknamed "Pesky's Pole" by former Red Sox player and broadcaster Mel Parnell, has been known to hand out a few of them. Former Red Sox shortstop Johnny Pesky, a teammate of Ted Williams, was not a slugger by any definition of the term. In fact, he only hit 17 home runs over his 10-year career, and just six of those were at Fenway Park. Today, well over half a century later, "Pedroia's Pole" just wouldn't sound as right to the "Red Sox Nation."

In between Pesky's Pole and the Green Monster lies another of Fenway's famous features, "the Triangle," in straightaway center. Some 420 feet from home plate and standing 17 feet in the air, the Triangle is one of the toughest home runs to hit in baseball. Though sluggers may tend to scratch their heads at the futility of a 400-plus-foot "loud out," base runners bring new meaning to the term "love triangle." While fly balls caroming off the Green Monster tend to slow the wide-rounding base runner, limiting him to the notorious wallball single, a shot to center over the outfielder's head, especially one that pinballs around in that confounding crevice, is a surefire triple for even the slowest of legs and a potential inside-the-park home run for the speediest.

As far as Fenway's stance on pitcher versus hitter, Joe Castiglione says, "It depends on the wind and time of the year. It can be forgiving in right center and right in April and May when balls don't travel, but, in the summertime, it's definitely more of a hitter's park. Not a home run park but a doubles park. When it's cold the first couple of months, I think it's really more of a pitcher's park." Regardless of the time of year, no hitter felt befriended by Fenway when Pedro Martinez pitched in a Red Sox uniform. Aside from the obvious game 4 of the 2004 American League Championship Series, when asked which was his most memorable game announcing at Fenway Park, Castiglione replied, "Anytime Pedro Martinez pitched. He was so electric and dominant. The best I've ever seen." Considering that the list includes names like Curt Schilling, Josh Beckett, and Roger Clemens, Pedro Martinez's slot at the top is no small feat. In fact, Martinez's Cy Young performance during the '99 season (23 wins, 2.07 ERA, 313 Ks) is considered arguably the greatest pitching performance of the modern era.

FENWAY PARK TODAY: GOOD LUCK FINDING A TICKET

As a testament to the "Fenway faithful," former Red Sox outfielder and current lead TV play-by-play voice for the Chicago White Sox Ken "Hawk" Harrelson looks back on his most memorable days in his Fenway red and white, saying, "Anytime anybody asked me about Fenway Park, it was the fans because you'd go out and have a tough evening where you don't get much sleep. You come to the ballpark the next day. Maybe the night before, you had a couple too many beers and you don't feel good. All of a sudden you put that uniform on and you walk out that dugout, and there's 38,000 right there going, 'Hawk, Hawk,' and all of a sudden, poof. You feel good again. That's what I will always remember about that ballpark. You have those moments that are so memorable. I played against Mickey Mantle in his last game at Fenway Park in '68. We knew it was gonna be his last game when (Ralph) Houk sent him up to pinch hit, and I was standing out there in right field crying. I looked over to Yaz in left field and he's crying. I couldn't see our infielders but I'll guarantee you Rico (Petrocelli), Mike Andrews, and those guys were crying, too, because Mickey Mantle was a symbol of baseball. Mickey Mantle was loved by all of his peers. Mickey really never knew how much he was loved by us. We loved that guy because he was a great guy, and maybe the greatest talent that God ever put on the face of the earth. Mickey was something special, and playing against him his last game was something special, too. I played against him for six years and I was almost crying like a baby out there in right field."

While over time the chants may have changed from "Hawk" or "Yaz" to "Pudge," and then to "Papi" or "Muddy Chicken," the one constant has been the standing-room service taking place in "the Chapel." On May 15, 2003, still a year and a half from ending the Curse of the Babe, the Red Sox fans started a decade-spanning run of their own, selling out a major sports record-breaking 820 straight home games. Baseball's previous record of 455 was held by the 1995–2001 Cleveland Indians at (then) Jacobs Field, while the major sports record of 814 was held by the 1977–1995 Portland TrailBlazers. During the streak, which included play-off games as well, the Red Sox made the postseason six times, including four American League Championship Series and two World Series titles (2004, 2007). One portion of the streak—a rather forgettable one for the 36,000 plus fans in attendance—was the historic collapse of September 2011. Leading the Tampa Bay Rays by nine games for the Wild Card on September 3, the Red Sox finished the season 6–18, the 18th loss being a blown ninth-inning save by then-Boston closer Jonathan Papelbon. Coupled with a walk-off, seven-run-deficit-erasing win by the Rays over the Yankees, the Red Sox's play-off hopes went out the door, soon to be followed by once-beloved manager Terry Francona, general manager Theo Epstein, and eventually a few of the Red Sox's priciest players. Castiglione describes the off-field events of the following year, in which the team dealt Josh Beckett, Adrian Gonzalez, and Carl Crawford to the Los Angeles Dodgers: "It was more of a purge to get rid of a lot of money and bad contracts. Probably bought about eight years of financial recovery by getting rid of those people." The spring after "the purge" marked the end of Boston's record-shattering home sellout streak, on April 10, 2013, one month short of a full decade. Although the streak was over, Boston's 2013 season still had plenty of room for history, as the team became the 11th ever to go from worst to first in one season. Winning their first division title in six years, the Red Sox mowed through Tampa Bay and Detroit in dramatic fashion to represent the American League in the 2013 fall classic. Interestingly enough, on the National League side, the Los Angeles Dodgers fell two wins short of the World Series, which would have pitted the Red Sox against a 2011 version of themselves, like a virtual matchup on EA Sports' video game *MLB: The Show*. Instead, the Sox bested the St. Louis Cardinals for the second time in 10 seasons on baseball's biggest stage, restoring the balance, and with it, the love from the Fenway faithful.

Globe Life Park in Arlington: Texas Rangers

Globe Life Park in Arlington: "It's very different out in center. Those railings and balconies give it a very different look from anyplace else." —Eric Nadel
Photo courtesy of Kelly Gavin, Texas Rangers

There are days in our ballpark when the wind is blowing where there could not possibly be a harder place to pitch.

—Eric Nadel, Texas Rangers radio play-by-play broadcaster

$\mathcal{I}$magine walking up to a classic American ballpark. The warm summer air sears your nostrils, causing them to beg for the scent of freshly cut Bermuda grass. You enter through the gate behind home plate, and you can already see the field. Just a few more steps and you're greeted by a four-story ironwork façade behind centerfield and a home run porch towering over right field. You think to yourself, "What year is this?" If you were in Arlington, Texas, and you answered "anytime before 2013," you would have been wrong. Opened in 1994, Globe Life Park in Arlington, home to MLB's Texas Rangers, had to undergo a different kind of "opening" after the '12 season.

When visiting Texas, perhaps the second thing one notices (the first, of course, being the Alamo) is the south Texas winds. When the $191 million Globe Life Park was being built in the early '90's, many meteorological studies were done to determine the effect the wind would eventually have on the field of play. Strangely, none of the studies revealed what would become known by Rangers fans as the *jet stream* once the park was built. The jet stream effect is when the wind blows not only into Globe Life Park, but out of it as well. Known to occasionally document the event when it happens, Texas Rangers radio play-by-play broadcaster Eric Nadel describes the jet stream, saying, "It actually blows in from right field, hits the building, and then shoots back out. The flags are pointing in, but when you're standing at home plate, the wind's at your back." Of course wind alone shouldn't have too great an impact on the game's outcome, but when we add the humid summer heat of Texas, we get what baseball's Sigmund Freud would refer to as a pitcher's nightmare. Providing a player's insight into these wind-tossed games, Eric Nadel comments, "Somebody asked Brian Bannister what it was like pitching out there, and he said 'it was like pitching on the moon.'" Eventually, enough bad press circulated to warrant changing the physical makeup of Globe Life Park. After the '12 season, the private area behind home plate known as the Capital One Club was moved to give entering fans a direct window into the playing field, and more important, to allow the jet stream winds to exit and not circulate back out along a visiting hitter's home run ball. Interestingly, a recent climate change has caused the winds to become, according to Nadel, "much less prevalent." Nadel adds, "The last two years, there have been very few really windy nights, so our ballpark has been totally different and much easier to pitch in." Seeing that a cosmetic adjustment of Globe Life Park wouldn't affect mother nature, perhaps it was just the baseball gods' attempt at critiquing architectural design.

Since Rangers ownership didn't "let the air out" of Globe Life Park until late 2012, that left 19 seasons of hitter-friendly baseball 81 times a year. Considered "an extreme hitter's park," Globe Life Park's playing dimensions lend to the fortuity of both home and visiting batters. Along the first and third base lines, the player dugouts are eight feet closer to the field of play than the Major League average. This feature gives hitters many second chances, fouling away pitches until they get one they can hit. These long at bats run up the pitch count, and as a result, cause an early exit from the starters. Since Globe Life Park opened, Rangers starting pitchers have finished 11th or worse in innings pitched during all but one of their non-playoff seasons. The allure was obviously not resonating from Arlington for free agent starting pitchers. Nadel adds, "For a long time, pitchers didn't want to come to the Rangers. Once the Rangers started winning, though, pitchers realized they can win there if they just pitched okay." Perhaps the best example of this "okay" pitching was Rangers starter Bobby Witt, who won 16 games during the '96 season with a highly inflated ERA of 5.41, and, more important, the hitting support of MVP caliber players like Juan Gonzalez, Will Clark, Rusty Greer, and Ivan "Pudge" Rodriguez.

DESIGN WITH PURPOSE

When it opened as "the ballpark in Arlington" 20 years ago, Globe Life Park was among the first of the post "cookie cutter" ballparks. One adjective you won't find in any of the Wikipedia descriptions of Globe Life Park is "symmetrical." From foul pole to foul pole, the outfield walls contain eight different angles, as if someone cut open a stop sign, disfigured it, dropped it onto the doorstep of David M. Schwarz Architectural Services, and said, "Here. Something like this." The reason behind the nonlinear wall configuration, other than to increase the chance of Rangers outfielders making the blooper reel, is to induce more triples, arguably the most fan-friendly play in baseball. Another fan-friendly design of the outfield wall is its height from left center to the right-field foul pole. Dwarfed by Fenway's "Green Monster," Globe Life Park's eight-foot wall is intended to lure outfielders into making a home-run-stealing catch. On July 1, 2006, Gary Matthews Jr. brought the architect's vision to fruition, not only climbing up but reaching well over the center-field wall to rob Houston Astros first baseman Mike Lamb of both a home run and a chance of completing the cycle. Nadel calls Matthews's catch "the best I've ever seen."

Several feet behind the center-field wall lies a large, rectangular incline of beautifully cut grass. Situated right between two economically priced seating sections, this Globe Life Park feature was nicknamed "The Grassy Knoll" by fans when the park opened in 1994. Considering the proximity to a negatively associated Dallas landmark of the same name, the Rangers quickly changed the grassy area's name to "Greene's Hill" after former mayor Richard Greene, who was quite instrumental in getting the park funded and built. Beyond Greene's Hill lies Budweiser Bowtie at Vandergriff Plaza, a strategically placed concession area that just happens to lie at the foot of Globe Life Park's most unique structure, the office building in the center. Standing four stories tall, this southern-designed business center's realty is leased to the baseball and non-baseball alike, with an amazing and elevated view of the field. Describing the office building from the opposite view inside the broadcast booth, Eric Nadel says, "It's very different out in center. The fact that it's enclosed in center field with that ironwork, which looks almost like New Orleans. Those railings and balconies give it a very different look from anyplace else." Also, part of the office building area is the Texas Rangers Hall of Fame, a two-level, 30,000-square-foot facility complete with a hall of plaques, great field views, and a 235-seat theater.

AN ALL STAR CAST OF A FIELD

Taking the nonlinear, pinball-machine-like dimensions of Globe Life Park's playing field out of the equation, one could easily say the ballpark's architect had a flair for the past. The clearest example of this architectural nostalgia is the home run porch in right field. Looking more like an open fishing bait and tackle box, the right-field seats resemble the Tigers and Yankees stadiums of the past, inducing left-handed batters to swing away. Drifting from right center to straightaway center, the dimensions delve deeper, giving the ballpark the "triangle" effect found most famously in Boston's Fenway Park. Another adopted Fenway feature (although only to 5/12 scale) is the 15-foot left-field wall. Considering the looming home run porch in right field—towering over the fielders like a baseball-gobbling sentinel—the high left-field wall is the more preferred target for starting pitchers. Eric Nadel notes, "There are so many opposite field home runs there. A lot of pitchers probably adjust to that. They might pitch inside more to righties because it's so hard to hit a home run to left." As is vital in any hitter-friendly ballpark, the best way for a pitcher to mitigate damage is to keep the ball down. Nadel adds, "You wanna be a ground ball pitcher there more than anything. The Rangers have tried over the years to get ground ball pitchers." Perhaps not found in Yogi Berra's archive of "Yogi-isms" is the phrase, "If you can't buy ground ball pitchers, forge them."

JULY 28, 1994: KENNY ROGERS'S
PERFECTLY SIZED STRIKE ZONE BLANKS THE HALOS

Texas Rangers starting pitcher Kenny Rogers quickly learned the formula for being a successful pitcher in Arlington. Describing Rogers's transformation, Eric Nadel says, "Kenny Rogers, when he came up, was a high fastball/curveball pitcher, and he became a sinker ball pitcher. He's probably the best example of a guy who adapted to the ballpark." Before mastering his craft as a sinker ball pitcher—and playing before a (then) record regular season crowd of 46,581 fans in the park's first year—Rogers took to the mound against the (then) California Angels, not realizing he would make a "friend" in the process. The home plate umpire, Ed Bean, was a rookie, just up from the minors. From the onset of the game, Bean generously called some of Rogers's outside pitches strikes, thus widening both Kenny's target and his comfort level. In his broadcast Eric Nadel commented, "If the plate remains this wide, Rogers will have a field day." Nadel's words proved true, as Angels hitters found themselves facing two opponents: Rogers's fastball and Bean's literal "wide berth." Nadel notes, "The Angels started swinging at everything early in the game once the strike zone was established as huge." Giving credit to Rogers and not just Bean's strike zone, the game *did* occur on a midsummer's night, more conducive to a hitter than a pitcher. The Rangers' designated hitter Jose Canseco didn't have any problem with Bean's strike zone, belting two home runs in support of Rogers. The Angels, however, had no such luck. Leading up to the ninth inning, the Angels had nothing even close to a hit; that is, until second baseman Rex Hudler came up to bat. Hudler lined a looper to center field, which, being the deepest area of the park, would normally spell disaster for a perfect game bid. The Rangers' rookie center fielder Rusty Greer came in and made a diving, backhanded catch to rob Hudler of a base hit and preserve Rogers's perfect game. After the game, Rogers said, "When Rusty did that, I thought, 'Somebody wants me to do this.'" Two batters after Greer's diving catch, Angels shortstop Gary DiSarcina gave the center fielder a much simpler, routine pop-up to end the game and seal Rogers's masterpiece, the 14th perfect game in major league history.

Unfortunately, Kenny Rogers's perfect outing came about two weeks before the players strike of 1994, and the mystique of his accomplishment faded into the looming mist of contention between the owners and the players. On August 11, 1994, Major League Baseball shut down, and an important question was left unanswered: "Will there still be playoff baseball this year?" When the previous players strike had occurred, during the '81 season, the season was split in two, and the teams with the best records during each portion qualified for the postseason. This format left the Cincinnati Reds, the team with baseball's best overall record percentage wise, watching the playoffs at home. When the '94 season strike occurred, everyone assumed the division leaders would compete to go to the World Series. The Texas Rangers, although 10 games below .500, were the American League West division leaders on August 11. As it turned out, there were no playoffs during the '94 season, and baseball wouldn't resume until April 25 of the following year. When asked about the strike and its effect on the Rangers, Eric Nadel responds, "It was disheartening because it was the first year of the ballpark. There was so much excitement. We were on our way to obliterating our attendance record. It was so exciting to come out there every night and have big crowds, and then, all of a sudden, it's over." Luckily for the Rangers, they were able to recover from the strike, reaching the postseason in three of the next five years. Other clubs from the '94 season, however, weren't as fortunate. The Montreal Expos were 74–40 on August 11, sporting the league's best record. The voiding of the postseason in 1994 began a 10-year downward spiral for baseball in Montreal, culminating in the team's move to Washington, D.C., after the '04 season. Interestingly, it was the Washington Senators version 2.0 (the original Senators became the Minnesota Twins in 1961) that endured a similar pilgrimage when attendance was low and price tags were high. The team moved to Dallas/Fort Worth in 1972 and became (who else but) the Texas Rangers. Perhaps a players' strike will take place in 2019 and return baseball to Montreal's devoted fans in the year 2029, thus completing expansion baseball's circle of life.

WELCOME, RANGERS, TO THE POSTSEASON: Y'ALL COME BACK NOW, YA HEAR?

While not drawing the dismal attendance numbers that drove the Washington Senators out of the nation's capital, the Rangers did show similar results in the standings to their former identity, failing to qualify for the playoffs in their first 24 seasons in Arlington. On October 4, 1996, playoff baseball was born in Arlington, Texas, via game 3 of the American League Division Series against the eventual World Series champion New York Yankees. Though the Rangers would lose both the lead and the game in the ninth inning, Eric Nadel recalls the crowd of Rangers faithful: "The first playoff game we ever had at home, the crowd stood for the entire game. They roared. I didn't believe our crowd could ever make that much noise, and then, at noon the next day, they did it again. It was the first thing that showed me we could be a baseball town. That we had a winning team and it was going to be really special." After a one-year hiatus, the Rangers returned to the postseason in back-to-back seasons in '98 and '99, but were swept, once again, by the eventual World Series champion Yankees. The Rangers did not return to the postseason for another 11 years, but in 2010, against the reigning World Series champion Yankees, the team was finally "not plum but pert near" en route to their first American League pennant since "coming down from Washington." Looking back on the Yankees' final out, which came at the expense of former Ranger Alex Rodriguez, Eric Nadel reminisces, "The game in 2010 where they clinched the pennant—where Neftali (Feliz) struck out A-Rod for the final out—that's the most exciting call I ever made. Probably the most emotional I've ever been in my life about anything." The Rangers eventually lost the 2010 World Series to the pitching arms of the San Francisco Giants, but came back the next year to the same stage against the St. Louis Cardinals, where they came within one strike of winning the team's first-ever World Series. Acquisition of the players Prince Fielder, Shin Soo Choo, and Alex Rios—as well as an already established hitting lineup of Adrian Beltre and Elvis Andrus and the overwhelming power of pitcher Yu Darvish—make it very unlikely another decade of playoff-less baseball will take place in "these here parts" of the Lone Star State.

· *12* ·

Great American Ball Park: Cincinnati Reds

Power Stacks at Great American Ball Park: "A great part of the history of that city being right on the Ohio River."—Marty Brennaman
Photo courtesy of the Cincinnati Reds

Like so many of the new parks, it's very pleasing to the eye. There are things in the ballpark that are particular to the area and to the history.

—Marty Brennaman, Cincinnati Reds radio
play-by-play broadcaster

There are many debates about when the first-ever Major League game was played. Some argue that it was between the New York Nine and New York Knickerbockers on June 19, 1846, in Hoboken, New Jersey, which in all fairness was the first *organized* baseball game ever to be played. However, to qualify as a professional team in Major League Baseball, payrolls have to be established and contracts drawn up. On June 1, 1869, the Cincinnati Red Stockings met that prerequisite and emerged as baseball's first professional ball club, mauling the Mansfield Independents 48–14. It's arguable that June 2, 1869, was the day the first sports agent was hired, by those same Mansfield Independents.

Even once the Cincinnati Red Stockings were able to "quit their day jobs," it was still another 34 years before the first World Series was played, and 16 more years until Cincinnati itself competed in the fall classic. In 1919 the Reds took on the Chicago White Sox, featuring eight soon-to-be banished "Black Sox." Aided by organized crime, a fall-taking opponent, and a roster whose names are reserved for the $2,000 slot on Baseball Jeopardy's home edition, the '19 Reds took home the first of the club's five world championships and were the innocent party to perhaps the sporting world's all-time greatest scandal. Although 50 years as a franchise is considered a long time to wait for a World Series championship anywhere outside of Chicago or Boston, the Reds had to wait another 21 years before "earning" what many consider to be the team's first legitimate title, besting the Hank Greenberg–led Detroit Tigers in the 1940 World Series.

If the 1940 title left any doubt of the club's worthiness to bear the name "champion," the '75–'76 back-to-back World Series–winning Reds, also known as "the Big Red Machine," would most certainly erase it. Having begun his hall of fame career during the '74 season, Reds radio play-by-play broadcaster Marty Brennaman describes the early years of his career as being "without question, the most fruitful period in the history of the franchise." Brennaman further comments, "We had a ball club in '75 and '76 that, quite honestly, many people feel may well be the greatest team in the history of baseball; if not, then in the top two or three."

Arguably the biggest cog in that Big Red Machine was all-time hit king Pete "Charlie Hustle" Rose. After accumulating 4,256 hits, shattering Ty Cobb's all-time record, Rose went on to manage the ball club during the '80s, when someone in a Reds uniform would be the *guilty* party to another of the sporting world's greatest scandals. As team manager, Rose was found guilty of betting on baseball games—specifically his own teams—and received a lifetime ban from baseball on August 23, 1989, at the hands of then commissioner A. Bartlett Giamatti. To this day Rose, along with his 4,256 career hits, is ineligible for induction into the Baseball Hall of Fame. A little over 13 months after Rose's lifetime ban was issued, the '90 Reds—with a bullpen nicknamed the "Nasty Boys"—won the organization's fifth championship.

Today, 145 years after the team's inception, the Cincinnati Reds pay homage to their history-rich franchise in their relatively new home of Great American Ball Park. Although claiming that "anybody who says their ballpark is unique among all other ballparks is full of crap," Marty Brennaman does concede one distinguishing feature of Great American Ball Park: "If you want to include the whole area, the one thing that makes this park unique among all parks—and this is indisputable—is their Hall of Fame Museum. Nobody in baseball has what they have. They were the first. In fact, it's so good that other clubs are now coming to Cincinnati in their off season to see the Hall of Fame Museum because they have an idea of doing the same thing." Bearing the weight of 145 years, five World Series championships, and a Big Red Machine, the Reds' Hall of Fame Museum, as large as it already is, finds itself in a perpetual state of expansion, welcoming new members every two years. One member the museum still has not welcomed is Pete Rose, as his ineligibility for baseball enshrinement precludes him from that of the Cincinnati Reds as well. This flair for history at Great American Ball Park does not confine itself to the walls of the Hall of Fame Museum or the Reds organization itself. Some of the ballpark's unique features are specific to the city of Cincinnati and its industrial contribution to this nation over the past two centuries.

The stadium sits right on the banks of the Ohio River, and fans who enter Great American Ball Park are immediately met with a taste of the Queen City's history beyond the outfield walls. In right center, two large replica power stacks, which light up after every Reds home run, stand behind the bleachers, representing the riverboats common to the city and the Ohio River. Just to the left of those power stacks and in straightaway center sits the Cincinnati Bell Riverboat Deck, with a maximum capacity of 300 people, which serves as a private section reserved for big groups and parties. Whether they be private "riverboat deckers" or nosebleed sufferers way up in section 509 behind home plate, the one constant at Great American Ball Park is fan friendliness. Brennaman adds, "I think the one thing that you would find about Great American Ball Park is that it's as friendly a park as there is in baseball, and it's got to do with the close proximity of the fans to the actual playing field. That's not by accident. That's the way it was constructed. It's a message that's been delivered to everyone who walks in since the park opened. All the years they played at Riverfront, you were so far away and the walls were so high where the stands were located. I don't think there was ever a feeling of closeness to the team, and this ballpark is the antithesis of that. You will rarely find a fan who leaves our ballpark and said they didn't have a great experience, whether they were a Reds fan, a Dodgers fan, or whoever they might have been a fan of. That's the one thing that would make our park stand out." Unfortunately, Major League pitchers may not make the same resounding endorsement fans do when leaving Great American Ball Park.

THE LAUNCHING PAD

The distance to the seats in straightaway left and right field are, respectively, 328 and 325 feet. Take out of the equation a Green Monster–sized wall, an air-thickening, cold marine layer, and a foul territory upon which one could open a flea market, and we have the dimensions of Great American Ball Park. Playing in arguably the hitter-friendliest ballpark in the National League, Reds batters display no shortage of output. Sluggers like Joey Votto, Jay Bruce, Adam Dunn, and Ken Griffey Jr. have been known to light up the smokestacks on many occasions with their home run power. No stranger to witnessing the long ball, Marty Brennaman describes the nature of batting in a Reds uniform: "I think every player on our club—whether he's a guy who's come up in the system or someone who they've traded for or signed as a free agent—knows that when they come to the ballpark, this is a launching pad. They've got a chance to hit the ball out if they have the reputation of being a long ball hitter; more so than maybe in parks like Petco Park in San Diego or AT&T Park in San Francisco. Our guys love to hit in this ballpark. The ball jumps out; I think more so than anybody ever envisioned when the park was built, and there's really not a whole lot they can do about it. Wind is rarely ever a factor. It's simply the way the ball carries. I don't think our hitters tailor make their swings to take advantage of the areas in which the ball jumps out because the ball pretty much jumps out everywhere. Quite honestly, it was the same way at Riverfront. The ball jumped out of that place, too." Although Reds hitters would probably never want to alter such gratuitous circumstances, the pitchers may one day find themselves lobbying up and down the Ohio River for team owners to "raise that wall." Coming in as the top four or five in home runs allowed each year—a category in which they would probably rather stay near the bottom—Reds pitchers still manage to adapt, finishing fourth in the league in ERA over the '12 and '13 seasons. Marty Brennaman notes, "I think the pitchers are cognizant of how it is. They all have a tendency to give up more home runs in our ballpark than they do on the road, but that's a way of life. It's not going to change. Nothing's going to go away. The biggest thing about our ballpark is just simply do not be intimidated by the numbers. Obviously, the need is greater to try and keep the ball down as opposed to pitching in other parks, but that's a tenet of being a successful pitcher anyway. You pitch down in the strike zone. The guys on this pitching staff have done rather well and not gotten overly destroyed by pitching in our ballpark as opposed to the way they pitch on the road. They don't do anything differently. They approach their craft with the same basic principles, whether it be at Great American Ball Park or somewhere else." Perhaps the incarnation of Brennaman's words is 28-year-old right-hander Homer Bailey.

JULY 2, 2013: HOMER DOES IT AGAIN

In the team's final series of the '12 season, the Reds' Homer Bailey no-hit the Pittsburgh Pirates 1–0 en route to their playoff series against the eventual World Series champion San Francisco Giants. Although Bailey's gem was the seventh "no-no" of the season, from September 28, 2012, to July 2 of the following year, no other pitcher in baseball pitched a no-hitter. Facing virtually the same Giants team that had bested the Reds in the playoffs the year before, Bailey allowed just one walk while striking out nine, passing baseball's no-hit torch back to himself. An interesting note about Bailey's performance is that it was against Giants "freak" Tim Lincecum, who has also thrown two no-hitters. Pitching to just one batter over the minimum in nine innings, Bailey had all the run support he needed in the first frame, when Joey Votto's sacrifice fly scored Shin-Soo Choo. Brandon Phillips's two-run blast in the sixth was more than enough cushion for Bailey, who, after a Gregor Blanco walk in the seventh spoiled his perfect game, retired the final eight Giants batters he faced to complete his second no-hitter in just over nine months. Having announced for more than 41 years in his hall of fame career, Marty Brennaman has called five no-hitters, including Tom Browning's perfect game against the Los Angeles Dodgers during the team's "improbable" '88 season. Commenting on the fifth, Bailey's gem, Brennaman says, "It was a big crowd, and the guy had already had a history of pitching one no-hitter. He was just dominant. In the two no-hitters that he's pitched, I don't know that the '75 Reds or the '27 Yankees could have hit him." Considering the second was at the "launching pad" known as Great American Ball Park, Brennaman's words undoubtedly carry with them considerable weight. The broadcaster describes his role as a storyteller on such occasions: "I've often said a good game makes you a better broadcaster than you really are. You reach a certain point in the game, where, all of a sudden, it becomes a real probability, or a heck of a possibility. I know

I've never really paid a lot of attention until the game got through the seventh inning. Once it gets through the seventh, now he's got six outs to go. Now it makes a difference, and you get on top of your game."

GREAT AMERICAN BALL PARK TODAY

Along with Homer Bailey, several other noteworthy pitchers, such as Johnny Cueto, Aroldis Chapman, and Alfredo Simon, have helped mitigate the damages of the launching pad. Chapman's 105-mile-per-hour fastball is the fastest ever recorded in baseball history. It's likely the Reds' Hall of Fame Museum has construction contractors on retainer for the closer's innumerable contributions once he is eligible for enshrinement. Another young specimen of speed is 23-year-old Billy Hamilton, whose 155 stolen bases for the Reds' Triple A affiliate Louisville Bats set a professional record. It's likely a few dusty and removed base bags with Hamilton's signature will don the museum walls alongside Chapman's radar gun and its overused third digit light. Couple the arm and leg speed of Chapman and Hamilton with the precision of Bailey, the longevity of Cueto, and the hitting of Joey Votto, Brandon Phillips, and Todd Frazier, and the Reds have a team that has qualified for game number 163 and beyond in two of the past three seasons and likely will do so in the foreseeable future, perhaps prompting another team nickname to make its way down the Ohio River.

• *13* •

Kauffman Stadium: Kansas City Royals

Kauffman Stadium Fountains: "When I started with the Royals, it was all grass, the water fountains, the scoreboard and that was it. It was just a very peaceful sight."—Ryan Lefebvre
Photo courtesy of the Kansas City Royals

I think you'll find it to be fan friendly for beginners. People working there are very accommodating and very helpful, so that's a good start because that'll be your first impression.

—Denny Matthews, Kansas City Royals radio
play-by-play broadcaster

They've done such a great job working with the landscape. It blends in so nicely. It's the anti Soldiers Field in Chicago, where they put a newer stadium inside an older stadium, and the two just don't look good together at all. With Kauffman Stadium, there are times when you really have to look at an old picture to remember what it looked like because it fits so perfectly.

—Ryan Lefebvre, Kansas City Royals TV
play-by-play broadcaster

If you were to look at the United States through a planet-sized scope, the crosshairs would probably fall right on Kansas City, a town so coveted, it had to be shared by two states. Aside from the occasional jurisdictional battle between local and federal law enforcement, Kansas City resides on the western border of the Show Me State, which has been booming with baseball since the late 19th century. Not wanting its eastern counterpart, St. Louis, to have all the baseball fun, Kansas City received Philadelphia's Athletics in 1955. With the Philadelphia import resuming their division cellar-residing duties for the majority of their 13 seasons in Kansas City, owner Charlie Finley eventually packed up the team after the '67 season and paraded it westward into Oakland, California. A year later expansion baseball touched down in west Missouri, as the Kansas City Royals were unveiled to the American League. For the first four years of their existence the Royals played in Kansas City Municipal Stadium, the former home of the Athletics and, more famously, of the Negro League's Kansas City Monarchs for more than 25 seasons. The Royals themselves were just barely getting situated when a new ballpark was announced. On April 10, 1973, Royals Stadium opened with three tiers of 40,000 plus tricolored seats, all filled with grateful fans. In 1993, the team changed the stadium's name to Kauffman Stadium after owner Ewing Kauffman, a name that remains today for the sixth-oldest ballpark in Major League Baseball.

Though its construction took place during the "cookie-cutter" era, Kauffman Stadium adopted its design from a different model. Kansas City Royals hall of fame play-by-play broadcaster Denny Matthews, a man who has called games for the team since day one, explains Kauffman's original design: "You'll find that every seat is facing towards second base and the pitcher's mound, so if you're way down the left-field line, you are facing straightaway, like the old parks used to be. Kauffman Stadium was designed by the same architect, Nobel Herzberg, who designed Dodger Stadium and Angel Stadium. They took the best of Dodger Stadium and incorporated that into Anaheim Stadium, so you really could see how similar those three were to each other right after they were built. The 'cookie cutters,' the round stadiums that were so prevalent in the '60s and '70s, which, you figure a baseball diamond isn't round. The way those stadiums fit into the context of the game wasn't that good." Kauffman Stadium's most distinguishing feature, though they probably don't fit into the context of the game the way Matthews describes, are the fountains beyond the outfield walls, which pay tribute to Kansas City's nickname, the City of Fountains. Extending 322 feet along right center field, they are the largest privately funded fountains of their kind in the world. In the mid-2000s, plans surfaced for a stadium renovation, which would eventually take away another of Kauffman Stadium's distinguishing features. Ryan Lefebvre, TV play-by-play broadcaster for the Royals, explains: "Walking into the stadium when I first started with the Royals was very unique in that there was no seating in the outfield. The seating basically ended in both corners. It may have gone a little past the foul poles, but most of straightaway left field to straightaway right field, there was nobody out there. It was all grass, the water fountains, and the scoreboard, and that was it. Fans couldn't even walk out there, and it was a very peaceful sight just looking at the grass and the water. The grass hills extended even beyond the stadium, so that was a very unique setting. When they wanted to renovate and put something out there, it made sense, but, for some of us who would describe one another as Kauffman Stadium purists, we were concerned we would lose that, but they did a wonderful job. I think when you walk in now, you will notice it's almost like walking into an arena because you're surrounded 360 degrees by something that's going on." Once the renovation took place after the '08 season, those most affected were the visiting outfielders. Lefebvre continues, "I think the visiting players still like to come to Kansas City because of the upgrades, but once they get on the field during the game, it's not as peaceful as it once was. It was very strange to not see any fans in the outfield at all. You always heard Kauffman Stadium was just a comfortable place to play, but, when they added the seats in the outfield, it really gave the ballpark a new dimension. One of the downsides to having just the grass berm and the fountains out there was there was never any sound coming from the outfield. There was nobody sitting out there. We could have a big crowd—a sellout crowd—and the sound would go off into the outfield and just kind of fade away. Now that we have seats in the outfield, we have sound coming back towards home plate. Even when we have a smaller crowd, if the outfield is well filled up, it's still a pretty loud ballpark. It's made it a lot less comfortable for visiting players because you've got some of our rowdier fans in the outfield."

Aside from adding new seats, the $250 million renovation of "the K" also included a merry-go-round for the kids and a new Jumbotron screen beyond the center-field wall. Prior to the opening of the Dallas Cowboys' AT&T Stadium in '09, Kauffman Stadium's Jumbotron had the biggest high-definition screen in the world. Describing the majesty of the Royals' new couch potato nirvana, Lefebvre adds, "The first year or so, it was hard to keep your eyes off it. In between innings, it was just so big and so clear that when the inning came to an end, you'd just be mesmerized. If you've never been to Kauffman Stadium, and you're just used to seeing a regular sized Jumbotron, it really jumps out in your lap when you see it for the first time." With new seats, a carnival, and a screen a Cessna plane could land on engulfing the quarter-billion-dollar budget, it's a good thing adjustments on the playing field itself had been made 14 years earlier.

KAUFFMAN STADIUM: PITCHER FRIENDLY/HOME RUN HITTER *NOT* FRIENDLY

Even with the "cookie-cutter" phase drawing to a close and the trend toward natural grass increasing, the artificial turf at Kauffman Stadium wasn't removed until the '95 season. Regardless of the texture of the grass, Kauffman Stadium's 410 feet to straightaway center and 390 feet to the power alleys in left and right center field predated Citi Field, Marlins Park, and Petco Park, making it one of, if not *the*, pitcher friendliest ballparks in all of baseball for many years. Denny Matthews explains: "Over the years, the trend has been bigger players, smaller ballparks, smaller strike zones, and a little livelier baseball, and none of that's going to help a pitcher very much. Busch Stadium in St. Louis and Kauffman Stadium were the two most difficult ballparks in which to hit home runs. They were the biggest pitcher friendly/home run hitter not friendly, and there were just acres and acres of ground to cover in both ballparks. Then we went to the natural grass, and it was still a big ballpark, so you needed fast outfielders. Whitey Herzog, who managed in both places, incorporated speed. The first thing he did was get athletes who could run, especially in the outfield." Though Herzog has been retired from the game of baseball for over 24 years, his style still resonates in Kauffman, as Royals outfielder Alex Gordon has won four straight gold gloves and has the most outfield assists of any major leaguer since the start of the 2011 season. Perhaps the most appreciative of both Alex Gordon and Kauffman Stadium itself during the 2013 season was Royals pitcher Ervin Santana. Between his '12 season with the Los Angeles Angels and '13 with the Royals, Santana's ERA went from an inflamed 5.16 to an impressive 3.24. Speaking about Kauffman's generosity toward Santana,

Matthews adds, "Santana always gave up a lot of home runs and he always will. 2013 was a perfect storm for him. He was pitching in one of the biggest ballparks in the league. He had the best defense in baseball behind him and they scored a lot of runs for him. That's a pitcher's dream come true, and he had a nice year." Reinforcing Matthews's words, Santana's home runs given up decreased 33 percent from 2012 to 2013. Santana's pitching and Gordon's fielding weren't the only thing going for the Royals during their unexpectedly successful '13 season. First baseman Eric Hosmer and catcher Salvador Perez joined Gordon in bringing three good gloves to Kansas City, the most in team history. The team matched that number in 2014. Joining Santana from the mound were James Shields with his 196 strikeouts and 3.15 ERA and reliever Greg Holland, whose 47 saves in 2013 were just three behind Baltimore's Jim Johnson and Atlanta's Craig Kimbrel for most in the majors. With decent pitching, stellar defense, and a friendly ballpark, the Royals had more to lose than usual going into the 2013 home finale.

SEPTEMBER 22, 2013: MAXWELL KEEPS THE FANS IN THE PARK, NOT THE BALL

At 81 wins for the final home game of their '13 season, the Royals had already assured themselves of their first nonlosing season in 10 years, but they, like their fans, were hungry for more. On September 22 against the visiting Rangers, who also were vying for an American League wild card spot, the Royals sent their ace James Shields to the mound against the Rangers' Alexi Ogando. At arguably his most memorable game as a Royals broadcaster, Ryan Lefebvre was overtaken even before the first pitch. He recalls, "The last home game of the year ended, first of all, with a sellout. That was the first time for me in 15 years because, normally, the Royals were out of it and people would turn their attention to the Chiefs or Kansas State, Kansas, and Missouri football. So, our last game every year, if we had 12, 13, 14,000, that was pretty good, but we had a sellout because the Royals were still in playoff contention and the fans were excited about the team." For nine innings before the sold-out crowd, both the pitchers and the stadium itself were taunting each team's hitters, as starters Ogando and Shields combined to pitch 15 innings of shutout baseball. The Royals only had two hits through the first nine frames. Finally, in the bottom of the 10th inning, the Royals got their third hit on a double by Eric Hosmer, which opened the bullpen doors to Texas reliever and former Royals closer Joakim Soria. Setting up the home season ending drama, Lefebvre continues, "For years, we had Joakim Soria as our All-Star closer. He had never faced the Royals as an opponent. It's a tie game in the 10th inning, and, with the bases loaded and nobody out, Soria got the first two outs without a run scoring. We had seen him do *that* many times. Then it went to 3–2 on Justin Maxwell. We're hoping single, ball four—any way to get the run in—and Maxwell hits a walk-off grand slam. The place just went nuts. The fans didn't want to leave when the game was over. It must have been 10 or 15 minutes after the game and two-thirds of the people were still there just excited and talking about the game. We didn't see Soria come up short in many games like that as a Royal, and, of course, the first time he faces the Royals, he gives up the game winning hit." Though the Royals ended up not playing past game 162, their win against the Rangers eventually forced a one-game playoff between Texas and the Tampa Bay Rays to decide who would play in the one-game playoff against the Cleveland Indians. The Rangers lost the play-in-to-play-in-a-play-in-playoff game to Tampa Bay 5–2.

"MULLET" WAS IN STYLE BACK IN 1985

Without question, the greatest player in Kansas City Royals history is George Brett. Nicknamed "Mullet," Brett played every single position inside Kauffman Stadium except catcher over his 21-season career, which included 3,154 hits, 13 All-Star appearances, three silver sluggers, a gold glove, and the American League Most Valuable Player award in 1980. Perhaps outside of Kansas City, Brett is best known for his tantrum-laced standoff with home plate umpire Tim McClelland on July 23, 1983, after Brett's go-ahead ninth inning home run was nullified thanks to Yankees manager Billy Martin protesting the excessive use of pine tar on Mullet's bat. The incident was all for naught, as a Royals protest was later upheld, and the game resumed 25 days later with Brett's home run counting and the Yankees eventually losing to the Royals 5–4.

Inside Kauffman Stadium, Brett may be best known for his performance on October 11, 1985, in game 3 of the American League Championship Series. Going 4–4 with two home runs and a double, George had three RBI's and scored four of the team's six runs, including the go-ahead run in the bottom of the eighth. This was his most memorable game at Kauffman, and Matthews recalls Brett's contribution: "We played the Blue Jays before the Cardinals, and Toronto was good. They had a better record than we did, and they won the first two games in Toronto. So we come back to Kansas City down two games to none. In game 3, it was a night George Brett had, in my opinion, the best game of his career. He dominated the game offensively, and he had four or five chances at third on balls hit to him. He really willed the Royals to win that game, and now we're back in the playoffs. If we lose that game, we never see the Cardinals. That, to me, was the most exciting, most important game in Kansas City Royals history. Without that, we wouldn't have a World Series ring." After Brett's all-around effort on both asides of the ball in game 3, the Royals went on to beat the Toronto Blue Jays in seven games, setting up a matchup with the St. Louis Cardinals. Though the series was marred by first base umpire Don Denkinger's controversial call in the ninth inning of game 6, which awarded Kansas City's Jorge Orta first base on a play in which he was arguably and visibly out, the Royals destroyed St. Louis 11–0 in game 7, and the team won their first and only World Series championship.

TODAY'S NEW LOOK ROYALS LOOK TO END THE DROUGHT

Since the team's magical title run in 1985, the Royals had only finished over .500 five times in the 24 seasons leading up to 2014. Having had experience announcing for a similar team back in Anaheim in 2002, former Angels broadcaster and current Royals TV play-by-play broadcaster Rex Hudler described the '14 Royals on March 10, 2014 (three weeks before Opening Day): "This team is very similar to the 2002 Angels. They've got five, six, seven, eight stars on the team that are all homegrown. They're young, they're energetic and they're on their way to win. They were 10 games over .500 last year, and the people here are starting to come unglued and getting excited. Everything that happened in '02 is going to happen here, minus the Rally Monkey. They don't have a monkey here, but they have Billy's Barbecue Sauce."

A "ROYAL" RETURN TO THE POSTSEASON

At the time Rex Hudler was perhaps unaware of how prescient his words were about what would happen 233 days down the road, but it's debatable. Experiencing deja vu from 12 years prior, Hudler describes the Royals '14 postseason run: "I believed the Royals would win it all in 2014. I was two runs shy of that prediction. I didn't feel like I was any kind of special baseball fortune-teller just because I'd been to the World Series. Unfortunately, I didn't get to go as a player, I got to witness it as the Angels broadcaster and how they did it in 2002. My experience of 21 years of playing professional baseball has also given me good insight as to what it takes to get there. Yes, in 2012, my first year broadcasting for the Royals, they lost 90 games but I knew it didn't matter. I could see the nucleus of talent that General Manager Dayton Moore and the Glass family had assembled. Dayton had a vision and he shared that vision with me in 2012 when I accepted the job. They were going to get to the playoffs in '14. They had a plan and they didn't waver from it. Dayton had only been with the club for eight years before they got to the 'Big Dance.' That's a very short time in baseball life to build a championship team. Being a broadcaster, one of my jobs is to sell their baseball club. In seeing what they put together and becoming more educated about the organization, it made for an easy sell. It was clear which direction they were going. They had young talent, premium position players, and they acquired many number one picks because of all of the losing years in KC. It was time to change from a losing environment to a winning environment. They traded Wil Myers, and they got James Shields and Wade Davis. Two big pieces of their championship team. They were able to add more pitching by trading for Jeremy Guthrie. Duffy and Ventura were developed by their outstanding Minor League department. I could see it was going to be a special season."

The right moves and prospects for this "special season" were key to the Royals' success in 2014, but it takes a special kind of general to lead his troops into battle. Hudler continues, "They started the year in '14 just like they did the last couple of years. Up and down, up and down; .500. They had some moments where we thought they would never make the postseason, even until the last month. However, manager and leader Ned Yost had them believing in themselves. They were all pulling on the same end of the rope. Ned made very few mistakes in the postseason. Up to that point, there were a lot of people in KC that weren't happy with his decision making. He seemed to be more relaxed in the postseason. The players felt it and the fans saw it, too. His personality changed along the way. He had more energy. More life. He became more cordial and flexible. He deserves a ton of credit. He got 'em there and the fans embraced him. There were all kinds of signs in the stands supporting him. The best one was 'In Yost We Trust!' His guidance and leadership got them to the playoffs."

The Royals kicked off the '14 postseason in a "wild" way against the deflating Oakland A's, who at one point in the season were 28 games over .500 and looking to run away from the American League. The A's settled for the road slot in the wild card game in a stadium full of blue-and-white fans excited to be in game 163. Jumping on top quickly, the A's looked as if they were shaking off their seven-week downward spiral to end the regular season. Hudler describes the wild card game: "In that one game playoff against Oakland, they were down four runs to John Lester, a guy who, up to that point, owned the Royals and was deep inside their heads. They came back and beat him and beat the Oakland A's in a one game, extra inning, gut-wrenching, wild card that was truly wild. Once they captured a playoff spot, that was it. That game really propelled them on to win eight straight postseason games.

That had never been done in the history of Major League Baseball. Kansas City was in the national spotlight. The team captured America's attention and they were behind us. America's Royals team was here and baseball was now relevant in Kansas City. It was an incredible run."

Though they fell a Salvador Perez home run shy of fulfilling Hudler's spring prediction, the Royals shocked everybody in baseball except themselves. Hudler signs off on the Royals unprecedented playoff run, saying, "It was time the Royals fans got there due, too; 29 years was a long wait to make the playoffs. Almost every game had you on the edge of your seat. The month of October was very emotional and we heard from many fans that it took several weeks to get back to their normal routine. It was a beautiful thing to see the joy on the fans' faces and to see the energy it brought to the entire city. The fans were happy even though they didn't win the World Series championship. The players were happy, too, but they want a world title. They aren't satisfied with second place. With talent like theirs, how can you lose? It was a heart-warming season. One for the ages. People will never forget it and the Royals organization can be proud."

Marlins Park: Miami Marlins

I think the first impression anybody has coming into that ballpark for the first time is the fact that it just says Miami. It speaks to Miami. It's bright, it's colorful, and it's very unique in the color patterns inside the ballpark as well as the design outside.

—Dave Van Horne, Miami Marlins radio
play-by-play broadcaster

The University of Miami, otherwise known as "the U," has a team whose name is quite suited for the city it represents: the Hurricanes. Situated on the nation's Eastern seaboard like a lemming suspended in animation, Miami is no stranger to Atlantic Coast hurricanes reaching as high as category 5, meaning "buy used and always send your insurance agent a Christmas card." While open air sports like football tend to "dig in" and play through conditions like rain—though perhaps not an actual hurricane itself—baseball umpires raise their arms and let the fans in the seats endure the conditions they paid for while the players work out in rain-free clubhouses, sharpening the skills they may or may not get to exhibit that day. Sound like something one fan, let alone tens of thousands, would want to pay to do 81 times a year? In 1990, thanks in part to business developer H. Wayne Huizenga's investment in both the Miami Dolphins and their home of Joe Robbie Stadium, the expansion talks about baseball started to focus around south Florida. The following year, in a marketing experiment, a two-game spring training series between the New York Yankees and the Baltimore Orioles, which averaged nearly 63,000 fans in attendance, all but put the ink on the paper to invite Major League Baseball's 28th team to Miami, where the Florida Marlins played their first-ever game on April 5, 1993, in front of 42,334 fans. The Marlins' home, which took on so many names that corporate finally stopped ordering letterhead stamps, was one they shared with the NFL's Miami Dolphins for 19 seasons. During that time the Marlins won two World Series championships (1997 and 2003) and hosted just as many fire sales that relinquished players like Kevin Brown, Hanley Ramirez, and Miguel Cabrera. As could be expected from fans who paid an average of $19 a ticket to crane their necks for three hours in Miami's intense humidity to watch a player whose name appears on his jersey in stitched lettering but who is referred to as "the guy we traded Miggy for," the attendance at Marlins games dropped considerably from the team's opening season average of 38,000. The overall season attendance was over one million less than Major League Baseball's average, but with the team having announced in December 2000 that a new stadium would be built, the question from Marlins fans—most of whose viewership of Marlins games took place in their living rooms—understandably was "When?" Finally, in July 2009, ground breaking took place in Miami's Little Havana for the team's new ballpark, and on April 4, 2012, under their new identity, color scheme, and on-field management, the Miami Marlins took the field at Marlins Park.

The newest ballpark in Major League Baseball, Marlins Park brings with it many of the baseball-compatible amenities overlooked and unseen at the team's original home of Dolphins Stadium/Joe Robbie Stadium/Pro Player Stadium/Pro Player Park/Dolphins Stadium(again)/Dolphin (singular) Stadium/Land Shark Stadium/Sun Life Stadium. The first and obviously most important issue addressed by Marlins Park was the weather. A retractable roof and built-in air conditioning system, likely sporting the highest energy bill in Miami-Dade County, gives Marlins fans the cool feeling they never had for 19 seasons watching the team in a stadium "awkwardly reconfigured for baseball." Hall of fame Marlins radio play-by-play broadcaster Dave Van Horne describes the park's welcoming climate: "A retractable roof makes for a wonderful facility in the heat of Miami. If the Marlins were to survive in south Florida, they had to get the fans not only out of the rain but out of the searing heat and humidity of those midsummer days, and that's what Marlins Park does for the fans. It takes them away from the heat, humidity, and the rain. The biggest complaint the first year from Marlins fans—believe it or not—over the course of the first home stand was that the air conditioning was set too high. It was too cold in there. Here they had designed an indoor, retractable roof facility to get the fans out of the heat and humidity, and the number one complaint was that it was too cold. They had to make some modifications in the way the air conditioning units were directed down onto the fans, and now it's really comfortable. They couldn't ask for more. We don't hear any more complaints about fans being too cold in Marlins Park."

In addition to a thermostat needle resting just on the right spot, the Marlins' new home offers many of the amenities baseball's newest ballparks are practically mandated to include in order to draw fans from their sofas, including an angle ideal for baseball viewing. Van Horne continues, "Every seat in the ballpark is angled towards the middle of the diamond. You're really looking from any seat at the pitcher. No more having to sit forward in your seat, as you did at the football stadium, crane your neck, and turn—to your left if you were on the right-field side or to your right if you were on the left-field side—to look down and see home plate, the pitcher, and to follow the game. At Marlins Park, everyone can sit back, relax, and enjoy a baseball game with their seat properly angled towards the middle of the inner diamond." While the comfortably angled seats may give the "popcorn, peanuts, beer" vendors backaches supplying greater demands from settled and unmoving spectators, the stadium concourses accommodate transient, specialty food seekers, as well as the short attention span of adolescents in attendance. Van Horne adds, "It's a wonderful facility for the fans. The concourse above the lower seating bowl goes all the way around the field. You can walk around the entire ballpark on that concourse and never lose sight of the field of play. It's wide for the food services, the art displays, and everything else that's in that ballpark. A lot of the work around the concourse and the walls that back the lower bowl seating areas are a variety of colored tiles. The colors correspond with the section of seats for which you hold a ticket and the tiles blend from one section to another. Some use ballpark green for the color of their seats, but the seats forming that sea of blue that looks like the ocean certainly attract attention when fans walk in there. Straight back from home plate—to the left and to the right—there are two large aquariums stocked with all kinds of tropical fish that are *topical* to the waters of the Atlantic in the south. It wouldn't fit in in Denver, Seattle, Boston, Pittsburgh, or even Atlanta, but it fits right into the Miami landscape." This "Miami landscape" extends to all walls at Marlins Park, including the ones between the two foul poles on the field of play. Van Horne continues, "The first thing that catches everyone's eyes is the ballpark looks different. For example, in most ballparks, they've used the standard ballpark green for the outfield walls and for the padding on the railings around certain parts of the field. There's no ballpark green in that ballpark. The green is a color that the owner Jeff Loria came up with that he calls 'vibrant green.' Some people have referred to it as a lime green. It's actually got a little more green in it than lime green. It also has a little touch of yellow in there that creates the vibrant, high-visibility green color. That's very unique about the ballpark."

While the kids are out enjoying "real life Nemos" and the spicy food aficionados savor meals for which every menu item contains the word "Goya," it's arguable that the pitchers are the ones having the most fun at Marlins Park. Van Horne notes, "To use a baseball term, the park plays big. The dimensions are big. It's a pitcher's park. The outfield fence is 11-feet high, and it goes from 11 feet to 13 and a half feet from right center all the way to straightaway center field. I think, from a baseball standpoint, that's the first thing the players see, and, of course, word gets around quickly that Marlins Park is a pitcher's park, but it makes for some exciting baseball because it's a great triples and extra-base-hits park." When advocating Marlins Park from a pitcher's perspective, Cuban right-hander Jose Fernandez is as expert of a witness as the court will allow. The 2013 National League Rookie of the Year, who also came in third in Cy Young voting, is the incarnation of home-field advantage while on the mound at Marlins Park. Van Horne relates, "Jose has responded not just to the ballpark, the dimensions, and the fact that it's a pitcher's park, but also to the fact that the fans have taken to him and he to them. He has excelled at Marlins Park. Here's a young man who's had just a touch over a full season in the Major Leagues, and he has already established this is certainly his home park. He hasn't been beaten. He has 11 wins, no losses, and an ERA of 1.07 after 18 starts in his home park, and that's in sharp contrast to his 3–7 record on the road and an ERA of 4 after 14 starts. Not to use just statistics to describe what Jose has done. I think they underscore the fact that he is really comfortable there, and, obviously, so far, tough to beat there." Luckily for Fernandez, he never has to face his own teammate, Giancarlo Stanton, who has been credited in some circles with having the most natural home run swing in all of baseball, which he has proven even in pitcher havens like Marlins Park. Van Horne adds, "Some of the more exceptional hitters like the Marlins own Giancarlo Stanton, can make any park look small, and, sometimes, he makes Marlins Park look small." Since 2012 balls off Stanton's bat have left Marlins Park faster than former club manager Ozzie Guillen's job security after his infamous "I love Castro" comment. The slugging outfielder has 98 home runs in only two and a half seasons' worth of games since Marlins Park opened in 2012, earning him two All-Star game appearances. With Stanton at the plate and Fernandez on the mound, that sea of blue seats may eventually be blanketed daily with fans wearing Miami's "vibrant" colors. Van Horne comments, "Now the Marlins, as an organization, just have to put a winning product on the field. I'm sure we'll see attendance figures climb, but it's a challenge in Miami. It's an event city, and, even the ballpark itself doesn't attract all that many people. I think there are a lot who go to see it one time, but, as far as locals who purchase season ticket packages, the ballpark itself, while new, is not an attraction. The team on the field will be the attraction, and the Marlins appear headed in the right direction now, but, until they win on the field, the ballpark is half empty on most nights." Definitely more than half empty during the final home game of the 2013 regular season, Marlins Park sent fans home for the winter with a going away present courtesy of starting pitcher Henderson Alvarez.

SEPTEMBER 29, 2013: ALVAREZ THROWS A WILD NO-HITTER

A total of 287 no-hitters have been thrown in baseball history through the '14 season. For some teams, like the Florida Marlins, the fans had to wait only a few years before someone like Al Leiter or Kevin Brown came in and broke the "drought." For teams like the Mets, who endured 8,019 games before Johan Santana brought them a goose egg under the "H" slot on the scoreboard, or the San Diego Padres, Major League Baseball's sole no-hitter-less franchise, whose tally is up to 7,328 and counting, a pitching gem of that caliber seems downright implausible. Through these 287 no-hitters, which include combined pitching efforts, a losing decision, and a fill-in for an ejected Babe Ruth, Marlins pitcher Henderson Alvarez's feat is unmatched in a most peculiar way. Announcing up in the broadcast booth, Dave Van Horne recalls the contest between the Marlins and the defending American League champion Detroit Tigers: "It was a very strange weekend. First of all, the Tigers were getting ready for postseason play, so their game was being handled and managed very differently than the Marlins game. The Marlins were winding up a season in which they had lost an even 100 games. They wound up, in the final weekend, sweeping three games from the Detroit Tigers, one of baseball's most powerful teams and headed to the playoffs, so it was a different kind of situation for the Marlins to end the season than for the Tigers. The Tigers were playing for their playoffs, so none of the starters stayed in the games very long. Justin Verlander started that final game and went the first six innings. That was his tune-up for the playoffs. Jim Leyland had this plan in mind even before the game had started. Then Doug Fister pitched an inning, and then Rick Porcello pitched an inning. Three of their starters pitched in that game and Luke Putkonen went out there and pitched the bottom of the ninth inning. So you had all three of those Tigers starters, Verlander, Fister, and Porcello, appearing in the game, and the Tigers hitters failed to score a run for any of their pitchers." While the three Tigers were combining for 13 strikeouts and no runs on 103 pitches, Alvarez was "hanging" with them, striking out four and walking one in his impressively economic 99 pitches over nine innings. The big difference between Alvarez and three-fifths of the Tigers rotation was the numbers displayed on the scoreboard's hit column: Marlins 4, Tigers 0. Van Horne adds, "There was no score when the Marlins came to bat in the bottom of the ninth inning. Alvarez is sitting on a no-hitter, but he only gets the no-hitter if the Marlins win the game while he's still the pitcher of record. Putkonen gave up a couple of hits and a couple of wild pitches in that inning. The wild pitch that decided the game brought home Giancarlo Stanton to score the only run of the day. It was the first no-hitter that was decided by a walk-off wild pitch in the bottom of the ninth inning. Ironically, instead of being on the mound to finish the no-hitter—which is usually the case—Alvarez was in the on deck circle. He would have come up next to bat. There have been walk-off home runs, walk-off singles, etc., so that made for certainly the most memorable of our games to date at Marlins Park. It would have been memorable in *any* ballpark." Though Henderson Alvarez's '14 season ended on the opposite end of a no-hitter pitched by the Washington Nationals' Jordan Zimmermann, the Marlins were relevant as a playoff contender much further into the season than they were in 2013 thanks to MVP-candidate-caliber numbers from hitters like Stanton and Marcell Ozuna and a stellar ERA of 2.65 from Alvarez, who, due to a season-ending injury to team ace Jose Fernandez, "shouldered" the rotation's load. Though the 15-win improvement from 2013 to 2014 resulted in only a one-slot improvement on Major League Baseball's total attendance list, the new look Marlins improved almost 2,000 fans a game, which in baseball's ballpark with the smallest capacity is 5 percent; hopefully good enough to keep the "fire sale" signs shelved away in management's proverbial garage for the time being, keeping Giancarlo Stanton and Jose Fernandez "playing with the fishes" for at least a few more seasons.

• *15* •

Miller Park: Milwaukee Brewers

Miller Park: "It's a nice, solid, well-built facility you know you're going to play games in."—Brian Anderson
Photo courtesy of Milwaukee Brewers Baseball Club

*Nobody doesn't enjoy coming to Milwaukee to play. Not the broadcast-
ers, fans, or opposing players. It's a nice, solid, well-built facility you
know you're going to play games in.*

—Brian Anderson, Milwaukee Brewers TV
play-by-play broadcaster

*W*hen visiting the Badger State, Wisconsin, one does not have to look far
to find a sports fan. With the NFL's Green Bay Packers and college football's
Wisconsin Badgers occupying practically every bumper sticker, T-shirt, and
local business façade throughout the state, it's indisputable that football reigns
supreme in America's Dairyland. However, on April 6, 2001, Major League
Baseball's Milwaukee Brewers made a case for Wisconsin fan allegiance
with the opening of the state-of-the-art Miller Park. Although not built in
the heart of the city like so many facilities in baseball, Miller Park, with its
magnificent retractable roof, is still able to pull in big attendance numbers, as
fans are guaranteed uninterrupted baseball 81 days of the year. Brewers play-
by-play broadcaster Brian Anderson describes Miller Park's attraction from
a fan's perspective: "Miller Park excels in its functionality. It has a uniquely
configured retractable roof. There's not another like it in Major League Baseball or any other sport. The way it stands—opened and closed—it's the best
of both worlds. Because there's bad weather in Milwaukee in April and May,
it becomes the instant fan favorite venue because you know you're going to
play. It offers the opportunity for the ball club to sell a lot of pre-advanced
group sales. Folks who would travel from all over Wisconsin and Illinois come
because they know there's not going to be a rainout or delay. It's the primary
selling point of the park." Perhaps it's not the park's invitation *inside* that's so
alluring to fans as the one *outside*.

     With the precedent of hunter-green-and-gold-clad fans with foam hats
in the shape of incomplete cheese wheels idling beside mobile grills and open
truck beds in Green Bay, and cardinal-red-and-white-flashing college students
and alumni alike doing the same thing in Madison, the Brewers managers
have proven themselves not only tolerant but enabling of metallic-gold-and-
navy-blue-sporting tailgaters in the stadium parking lot. Brian Anderson describes the pregame festivities outside Miller Park: "Most fans treat a Brewers
game like you would see in a Saturday college football setting. Even in poor
weather, the fans just love to tailgate in Milwaukee and all over Wisconsin.
Of course, tailgating for a Packers game in Green Bay is legendary and so is it
with the Brewers. So much so that the Brewers front office, every year, packs
port-o-johns and garbage cans out in the parking lots. I don't know a ballpark
or stadium in the country that allows their fans to basically fill up on food and
drinks before they come in, but that's what the Brewers do. With a huge lot all

the way around, there's plenty of parking for everyone." Of course, in a setting where seven-foot-tall sausages run around the park's perimeter on a daily basis, one can only expect the food inside Miller Park to be just as appetizing as that blistering atop the circular iron grates throughout the parking lot. With massive concourses spanning 360 degrees on each of the park's four levels, fans can walk around the entire stadium and still catch all the action. In fact, as Brian Anderson explains, even the vendors accommodate the fans' experience: "All the concession stands throughout the stadium and around the concourses are perpendicular to the field. When you're standing in line, you still have a view of the ballpark, so you can look to your left or your right. Your back is not to it. You never feel like you're disconnected from the game." While it's commendable to accommodate the 35,000 in attendance, Miller Park is known to pamper the men in uniforms as well.

While the assurance of rainout-free baseball helps a visiting manager fill his lineup card more easily at Miller Park, the team facilities—both home and away—do everything for the players short of putting the bat to ball. Commenting on Miller Park's hospitality, Brian Anderson says, "It's a comfortable place where players can work. There's a full, state-of-the-art workout facility with a lot of room. Multiple batting cages underneath on each side, both home and road. There's really no excuse for not being able to get your preparations. The facilities really allow you to give your best as a player." Regardless of how much of their "best" the players give, Miller Park's clubhouses provide incentive for the next day, or in the case of visiting players, perhaps another day down the road. Anderson adds, "One area I like a lot is the visiting clubhouse. It's so sizable. So spacious. It's such a great place for players to hang out and get that good feeling. Players love coming to Miller Park. They love consistency. Baseball is a game of consistency, and Miller Park allows players to have that. I think our owner Mark Attanasio feels that every player who comes to our ballpark is a potential employee at some point. You just want to make the best impression you can, and you hope they'll come back as a Brewer one day."

Anderson's words ring much truer than they would have at the old Milwaukee County Stadium. The broadcaster continues, "It's becoming a destination for free agent players. The Brewers still don't have the payroll where they can pay top dollar, but those players who are on the fringe—if it comes down to making a slightly larger salary somewhere else—Milwaukee seems to be the place where free agents are now starting to sign. You're starting to see waves of players like Aramis Ramirez, Kyle Lohse, and Matt Garza. They want to be in Milwaukee and they want to play where they're guaranteed to have 30–35,000 fans a night in that stadium."

A HALL OF FAME TOUCH

Having played his entire 20-year career in a Brewers uniform, Robin Yount is arguably the greatest player in the team's 45-season history. During his tenure, Yount had 3,142 hits, 1,406 RBIs, three silver slugger awards, a gold glove, and two American League MVPs, in 1982 and 1989. As such an integral part of the Brewers' past, three years after his retirement Yount began to play his role in the team's future, helping to break ground on Miller Park. However, unlike a suit-wearing assemblyman, Yount's participation in the park extended way beyond the ceremonial shovel. Having patrolled the outfield at Milwaukee County Stadium for 9 of his 20 years as a Brewer, Yount was very present in the design of the playing field at the future Miller Park, beginning with the dimensions themselves. Though straightaway left and right field—as well as left and right center field—seem rather standard, Miller Park then takes a unique dip into straightaway center, which, although it looks more like an anvil-induced welt on Elmer Fudd's head in a Looney Tunes cartoon, was designed with purpose. Brian Anderson relates, "The specific area that Robin Yount had influence on was the right and left center field gaps. The walls going into center field sort of create an angle and it's a pretty sizable difference. The most exciting play in baseball is a triple in Robin's mind. You can create some opportunities for triples and inside-the-park home runs because of those angles. A fly ball will go into left center or right center and hit that angled wall, and it will just dart all the way across center field. There's some skill level involved. As an outfielder, you have to prepare for that. Play that. Typically, the home center fielder is the guy who really needs to know that, and, in our case now, it's Carlos Gomez, who won a gold glove last year (2013)." Another area in which Gomez has brought Robin Yount's design to fruition is above the center-field wall. Like many of today's ballparks, Miller Park's outfield walls stand just eight feet high, allowing fielders the opportunity to go up and bring back a would-be home run ball. Anderson adds, "It allows the home-run robbing catches, which, I think, is a tremendous element to the game of baseball when a skilled outfielder can get to the ball, leap in the air, and pull one back from being a home run. It happens all the time throughout the course of a season. I think Carlos Gomez had four of them last year."

Thanks to a group-party section called the ATI Club just beyond right field, center field isn't the only spot with a fielder-plaguing angle. Anderson notes, "The porch in right field is a little bit shorter. It wasn't originally designed that way, but they moved those fences in about 15 feet. The element about that is it's a hospitable VIP area. The fans come there in a group setting (75 people), and it's always sold out every night. There's a brick wall that are the bricks from Milwaukee County Stadium, so it's a nice way to use something from the old stadium and bring it into the ballpark. That's an area where you can get some tricky bounces because of the angle of that wall and it's a chain-link fence. Matter of fact, Prince Fielder had an inside-the-park home run down that right field line because the ball got stuck under the padding. What makes baseball great is the nuances of each stadium and the home team can actually have an advantage in that regard. They know how to play. It puts a little more pressure on the visiting team when they have to come in and learn how to play the certain angles of the wall."

One would think a field whose dimensions torment outfielders with tricky bounces, baseball-vanishing padding, and elongating walls would throw the pitchers a proverbial bone. Such is not the case with Miller Park. Brian Anderson adds, "There's not a whole lot of foul room down the lines. It's a hitter-friendly park. A lot of home runs there every year. There's some potentially high-scoring games and exciting comebacks." Although in the early years at Miller Park the pants on team mascot Bernie Brewer may have collected some dust on the way down the ceremonial home run slide beyond the center-field wall, the '07 Brewers led the majors with 231 home runs, setting up '08, one of the franchise's most magical seasons to date.

THE '08 BREWERS RETURN PLAYOFF BASEBALL TO MILWAUKEE

Known as the City of Festivals, Milwaukee did not have many festive nights, baseball wise, beyond game 162 on the season schedule. Prior to 2008, the team's only playoff appearances occurred in '81 and '82, with the Brewers— then members of the American League—losing the 1982 World Series to the St. Louis Cardinals four games to three. With the help of what Brian Anderson calls "one of the most significant trades in franchise history," the '08 Brewers acquired left-hander C. C. Sabathia from the Cleveland Indians in exchange for four of the Brewers' prospects, one of them better known by sportswriters as "a player to be named later." Over his 17 starts in a Brewers uniform throughout the second half of the '08 regular season, Sabathia went 11–2 with a 1.65 ERA and 128 strikeouts. Anderson comments on Sabathia's presence: "He was at the top of his game. The Indians were miserably out of the pennant race and he was in the final year of his contract. He got traded before the All-Star break and was rejuvenated by the energy in the stadium. The Brewers had not been to the postseason in 26 years prior to that. C.C. came in and the Brewers just caught lightning in a bottle with him. He really enjoyed Miller Park. He always comments on how great Miller Park is for a pitcher. The great crowds and the energy in the building." Some of that "lightning in a bottle" included the likes of then-reigning National League Rookie of the Year, outfielder Ryan Braun.

With the Brewers going 4–15 in their first 19 games in September 2008, the team, despite the remarkable pitching run of C. C. Sabathia, seemed poised to end yet another season without a playoff appearance. Three straight wins against the Reds and Pirates would set up a potential sweep of Pittsburgh on September 25. Anderson recalls, "For me, as an announcer, probably the best moment at Miller Park was a moment that ended up on an iPod commercial. Ryan Braun hit a game-wining grand slam to beat the Pirates in a walk off." Braun's 10th-inning slam was the first of two game-winning round-trippers he hit during that final week of the regular season. On September 28, in the season's final game, Braun hit a go-ahead home run in the eighth inning against the Chicago Cubs that proved to be the game winner. Coupled with (who else but) Sabathia's complete game and a loss by the Brewers wild card race partner New York Mets, the Brewers secured the National League's final playoff spot.

Although the Brewers fell short in the Division Series to the eventual World Series champion Philadelphia Phillies three games to one, that one victory proved to be a "loud" one. Anderson adds, "I've been a lot of places. Yankee Stadium. Fenway Park. I've been to every Major League ballpark, and, for my money, there's no better place or more electric atmosphere in all of baseball than Miller Park when they're in a pennant race. The community is starving for a winner. I've never heard or seen anything like it. The passion of the fans there. That's what's so great about Milwaukee being a big city but a small town. Milwaukee is their own team and it really shows inside the stadium." Referred to by Anderson as "the Mount Rushmore of moments at Miller Park," C. C. Sabathia and the Brewers' playoff run of 2008, coupled with Brewers outfielder Nyjer Morgan's Division Series–clinching single in 2011 against the Arizona Diamondbacks—giving the Brewers their first play-off series win since 1982—are proof of how "electric" players, as well as fans, can make this fall-weather-comfortable ballpark in October. Rounding out the "Lincoln and Roosevelt" of Anderson's Miller Park memories are former closer Trevor Hoffman's 600th career save in 2010 and former first baseman Prince Fielder's 50-home-run season in 2007. This relatively recent string of successes in Miller Park has definitely had the tailgates open and the foam cheese wheels resting on Wisconsin fans' shelves, if only for a brief period, to show the world there's still room in the Badger State for baseball.

Minute Maid Park: Houston Astros

Crawford Boxes and Hand Operated Scoreboard At Minute Maid Park: "Quite charming to people who have been baseball fans for a long time." — Bill Brown
Photo courtesy of the Houston Astros

> *There is so much more energy in this ballpark when the roof is open and it's an outdoor park. You can really feel it.*
>
> —Bill Brown, Houston Astros TV play-by-play broadcaster

$\mathcal{D}$eep in the heart of the Lone Star State, the historic Union Station stood for many decades as a railroad hub in downtown Houston. Today this Texas landmark's "hub" duties are reserved for the Houston Astros and baseball fans alike. Opened on April 7, 2000, Minute Maid Park (formerly named Enron Field) was actually built into Union Station's lobby, which today serves as the most frequently used entrance for attending fans. Houston Astros broadcaster Bill Brown describes this unique feature: "It's a fairly wide open passageway into the ballpark. They wanted to make it a pretty brisk walk right through Union Station into the turnstiles. Fans who come in through that entrance are coming through a different experience than they would have anywhere else." Once through those turnstiles, fans can still experience the train theme just by looking at the façade beyond the left-field wall. An 800-foot train track, equipped with its own coal-cart-toting locomotive, provides the fans with a one-of-a-kind home run celebration. As much a fan favorite as the locomotive is, it still must share its track with perhaps Minute Maid Park's most customized feature, an eight-million-pound, hurricane-proof, retractable roof.

With the city of Houston being right on the Gulf of Mexico, many preparations were necessary to make Minute Maid Park suitable and safe for both the fans and the players. While the team's former home, the world-renowned Houston Astrodome, could probably host a day/night doubleheader in the eye of a level five hurricane, the 50,000 square feet of glass scaling Minute Maid Park's retractable roof was tested to withstand winds up to 250 miles per hour and still provide fans with a clear view of downtown Houston's skyline. Hurricanes aren't the only element from which the roof protects the fans. In a city famous for its monsoon season, Minute Maid Park, without the aid of a retractable roof, would be very humid and unpleasant for the fans. When this heat would become the most unbearable, the roof at Minute Maid Park is generally closed. Bill Brown adds, "Because it would be hot, the air conditioning would be on for maybe the first five innings of the game, and, by then, the sun would be down, and it would have been—maybe—ten degrees cooler than it was at the beginning of the game. They would deem it to be more comfortable, so the roof could be rolled back and that would create an entirely different experience for the fans." Whether the roof is open or closed inside Minute Maid Park, it's not likely the fielders will *ever* deem the park comfortable.

FIELD OF ~~DREAMS~~ NIGHTMARES

When it opened in 2000, Minute Maid Park was originally named "Enron Field" after the energy-based company whose wealth reached well into 12 figures before its infamous collapse in the early part of the century. During the company's scandal and the investigation into its activities, the running joke at Enron's headquarters in Houston was, "What do you think they'll rename the stadium?" Today, long after the stadium's name change, the running joke inside Minute Maid Park is the on-field feature most ridiculed and reviled by the players: Tal's Hill. Named after former Astros team president Tal Smith, Tal's Hill is a 90-foot-wide area of grass in deep center field with a 30 degree uphill grade and its own flagpole planted right in the field of play. With an advisory count that would rival that of a Cialis commercial, center fielders know what to expect when coming to Minute Maid Park. Regarding Tal's Hill, Bill Brown says, "Center fielders really detest it because they're running back on a ball difficult to catch anyway. Then, all of a sudden, they're running uphill. It's very easy to fall on that hill." With the threat of injury already an issue, the flagpole seems to add gravy to this fielder's recipe for disaster; however, it is not always the fielders who are affected by this aesthetic abnormality. On July 1, 2003, Milwaukee first baseman Richie Sexson hit perhaps the loudest triple in Major League history. Bill Brown recalls the event: "Richie was with Milwaukee. He hit a ball and absolutely crushed it. It hit the flagpole near the top and caromed back down onto the field. It would have been out of any ballpark, but the rule is if a ball caroms off the flagpole onto the field of play, it's still in play, so he got a triple. I remember him standing there—hands on hips—at third base, looking out and wondering how that could possibly *not* be a home run." Had the play been ruled a home run, Sexson's run may have made the difference for the Brewers, as the Astros won the game 6–5 in extra innings.

At Minute Maid Park, center field isn't the only position that requires free agents to sign a proverbial waiver before coming to town. The uniquely situated Crawford Boxes in left field create not only a short porch but a potential adventure for both the left fielder and the shortstop. Sitting relatively high atop a manually operated league scoreboard, the Crawford Boxes lie just 315 feet from home plate. Since left center is almost a full 50 feet farther back, the left fielder must place himself strategically to prevent an extra base hit. Bill Brown notes, "There are challenges to the left fielder who plays the carom off that wall. If he's going to do it correctly, he needs to be over where that wall ends in left center and jumps back toward the visitor's bullpen. If he plays a straight up left field, and the ball's hit to left center, he would have to go towards center and then back, but if he plays to the corner of the wall, he can

just head straight back and make the catch in front of the visitor's bullpen."
On the opposite end of the outfield right fielders at Minute Maid Park have
their own challenges as well. The ball travels well to right field, and although
the leap up the fence isn't as daunting for a visiting right fielder, the same
can't be said for his inevitable encounter with the crowd. With a proximity one foot closer than average outfield walls, fans have a one foot greater
chance of plaguing outfielders, robbing *them* of their home run robbing duties.
If that isn't enough, the right-field line is narrow and lined with an iron railing, threatening fast-charging fielders with injury. Not to be excluded from
the outfielders and their list of idiosyncratic tasks, the shortstops, aside from
running the infield, also have to play backup in case things get ugly. Brown
adds, "The shortstop has to go out to left field when the ball hits over the left
fielder's head because it may carom off that scoreboard wall past him on its
way back to the infield and the shortstop would have to play it. Otherwise,
the ball would just be there in shallow left field and someone could be circling
the bases." Adding to the "caroming" theme expected in a setting so rich with
brick façades is the backstop behind home plate, which unlike the flagpole
and Crawford Boxes, has been known to aid the defense rather than toy with
it. Bill Brown notes, "The seats behind home plate are close, and it's a brick
wall, so it's possible on a wild pitch for that ball to carom right back to the
catcher, and the runner at third trying to score could be out." Finally! Some
good news for the guys with the gloves.

PITCHER FRIENDLY TO HITTER FRIENDLY JUST LIKE *THAT*

The Houston Astros moved from the Astrodome to Enron Field with virtually
the same roster for both hitters and pitchers. As could reasonably be expected
during a transition from the behemoth, pitcher-friendly Astrodome to short
porches and an outfield *literally* suited for a game of "capture the flag," the stats
for each department shifted dramatically between the '99 and '00 seasons. Hit-
tingwise, the Astros adapted quite well to their new home, setting a National
League record for home runs in a season. The team's overall total of 249 was
81 better than their 168 in '99, which ranked 20th in the league. Taking a
pessimistic approach, one's gain is another's loss, and in the case of Minute
Maid Park, the losers quickly became the pitchers. Bill Brown cites the Astros
pitchers' woes of the '00 season, saying, "The pitchers just could not adapt
that first year of Enron. They gave up 234 home runs in 2000. 131 of those
were at home. The year before, Houston pitchers had allowed 128, so they
went from 128 to 234 in one year, and went from an E.R.A. of 3.83 in '99
to 5.42 in 2000." Perhaps a foreboding feat, Astros starting pitcher Jose Lima

hit a home run during the team's first batting practice in their new home. Brown comments, "That just blew his mind because he was a terrible hitter. The fact that he could hit a home run had an impact on him. He said, 'I'm a fly ball pitcher. How many of these am I gonna give up?' He gave up a ton. He was the perfect example of a guy who benefitted from the Astrodome." Luckily enough for Astros pitching, a different breed of "Killer Bs" than the ones found on the National Geographic Channel was about to swarm its way through east Texas.

THE ORIGINAL "KILLER B"

In 1988, at the age of 22, New York native Craig Biggio began his 20-year tenure with the Houston Astros, which would include nine trips to the postseason, seven All-Star game appearances, five silver slugger awards, and four gold gloves. Although better known for getting hit (285 HBP, second all-time), Biggio was known to make a few of them as well. On June 28, 2007, with the Astros returning home for an 11-game home stand starting with the Colorado Rockies, the second baseman sat on 2,997 career hits. Ranking very high on his list of favorite games over 28 seasons as a broadcaster, Bill Brown recalls about this game, "Biggio had five hits that night. He needed three to get to 3,000. There was a big crowd, and the team was actually hoping it would take a while because they knew they'd be packing the stadium until he got his 3,000th hit, and it happened the first day back." Interestingly enough, Biggio's 3,000th hit quickly became an out, as he was thrown out at second trying to stretch his single into a double. The crowd proved to be more speedy with their forgiveness than Biggio was with his legs, giving the slugger a standing ovation that lasted over five minutes. Among the first to congratulate "Mr. 3,000" on his feat were Brad Ausmus and Jeff Bagwell, two of Houston's famous "Killer Bs."

OCTOBER 9, 2005: THE "BS" WERE BUZZING THAT DAY

Having earned the National League wild card spot for the second straight year, the '05 Houston Astros roster had one interesting commonality: the letter "B." With a hitting lineup that included names like Biggio, Bagwell, Berkman, Brad Ausmus, and Burke, and pitchers named Brandon Backe and Brad Lidge, the house speakers at Minute Maid Park were always bursting with the sound of buzzing bees. Even the opponent Braves' name started with a B. On

October 9, 2005, in game 4 of the National League Division Series, thanks to a grand slam from Adam LaRoche off Astros starter Brandon Backe, the Braves would eventually jump out to a 5–0 lead. Trailing 6–1 in the bottom of the eighth inning, Lance Berkman hit a grand slam into the Crawford Boxes, a ball that was caught by Shaun Dean, the same fan, coincidentally, who had caught LaRoche's grand slam a few innings before. Eight runs, two balls, one fan. In the bottom of the ninth, Brad Ausmus hit a game-tying home run, sending the game into extras. Astros closer Brad Lidge kept the Braves' bats at bay for two innings. By the time Roger Clemens came out of the bullpen in the bottom of the 15th to pinch hit, he was probably due for his next start anyway. The seven-time Cy Young Award winner even laid down a bunt to advance Craig Biggio. After Clemens struck out in his second at bat in the bottom of the 18th, the stage was set for Chris Burke. With the count two balls and no strikes, Braves reliever Joey Devine left a fast ball over the plate, which Burke belted into the Crawford Boxes, sending the Braves home and the Astros to St. Louis for a rematch of the 2004 National League Championship Series against the Cardinals. Bill Brown, whose duties as a TV broadcaster are turned over to the networks during the playoffs, watched the marathon game from the press box. Brown states, "The 18 inning game, just for the sheer drama, the impact that happened on that day, for me, had to rank number one in the history of the team. That was blazoned into the memories of Astros fans. I think anybody who saw that game who's been around for a long time would say, 'Yeah. That's at the top of the chart.'" The Killer Bs eventually went on to their first World Series in team history against the Chicago White Sox. Even though the "Good Guy" Sox would sweep the Astros in four games and win their first World Series in 88 years, it's inarguable that baseball had never taken the Space City by storm quite like it did during that magical '05 season.

• *17* •

Nationals Park: Washington Nationals

The one thing about Nationals Park—with all the modern amenities and everything—you walk in on a sunny day and it has that classic Major League ballpark feel to it.

—Charlie Slowes, Washington Nationals radio
play-by-play broadcaster

$\mathcal{T}$he concept of baseball in the nation's capital, Washington, D.C., has taken on a unique connotation, especially when it comes to expansion. The original Washington baseball team was known as the Statesmen, who would then change their name to the Senators. Along with three other disposable teams in the league in 1899, they had their players "contracted" out to the rest of baseball. Predating baseball's first amateur draft by 66 years, this particular contraction left D.C. fans in what would be a short-lived state of abandonment. In 1901 the city acquired the Kansas City Blues, who changed their name to the familiar-to-D.C. "Senators," a name that would stick for another 60 seasons. During their second tenure in Washington, the Senators called Griffith Stadium their home for 50 years, during which the team won a World Series in 1924 and three American League pennants (1924, 1925, 1933), thanks, in great part, to 417-game winner and two-time MVP Walter "the Big Train" Johnson, who, had the Cy Young award existed prior to 1956, would have likely won 10 of them. After the '60 season, baseball packed up and left the District once again, this time for Minneapolis, where the Minnesota Twins would begin their storied franchise. Although the team left, no merchandise recall was necessary on Senator paraphernalia, because in the spring of 1961, expansion baseball reached the Potomac River shores on the D.C. side and give the city its third round of Washington Senators baseball. During the team's third campaign, which ended up being only 11 seasons, the Senators

117

had three owners, five managers (including Ted Williams), and only one winning record. With the numbers in the seats reflecting those in the win column, team owner Bob Short shipped the Senators off to Arlington, Texas, where they became the Rangers. Seeing as how "fourth time's the charm" never really caught fire in any of life's circles, the same went for baseball in the District of Columbia, at least for 33 years.

At the turn of the century and north of the border, the Montreal Expos were doing their impression of the Senators during the late '60s, and eventually, in 2005, baseball made its historic return on through the Springfield Interchange and back into the City of Monuments. This time the team took on a not-quite-as-legislative name, the Nationals. While baseball played the role of the proverbial parents who were away from home for a weekend lasting 33 years, RFK Stadium, the home of the Senators version 3.0, was a multi-use facility, which unlike many similar ones, was a baseball stadium retrofitted for football, not vice versa. After the NFL's Washington Redskins moved into their own home of FedEx Field after the '96 season, all the necessary measures were taken to welcome both a franchise and 46,000 plus fans back into RFK, and on April 15, 2005, the Nationals took the field. Three seasons that did not resemble their final days in Montreal later, the Nationals were granted a new home just blocks from the Capitol, and on March 30, 2008, before a crowd of more than 41,000, the team opened their eponymously named Nationals Park.

The fifth-youngest ballpark in the majors, Nationals Park provides fans with a baseball experience even blocks before they reach the park's entrance. Nationals play-by-play radio broadcaster Charlie Slowes describes the experience: "You come in the main entrance gate from left center field. It's about a half a block from the Metro system in Washington, D.C. From the entrance, you come in with a view from left center field, and you see the entire ballpark that way. It's different than say a main gate behind home plate where you come into the park under the stands and then walk out through the grandstands. You're half a block away and you're looking into the ballpark, so it's quite a presence." Providing the ballpark entry experience one should have—especially if going to a baseball game for the first time—Nationals Park strives to make sure the next three hours are just as memorable for the fans. Slowes continues, "Being opened in 2008, they had the advantage of seeing a lot of the other new ballparks; retro-type ballparks to open over the recent years. Nationals Park is a combination of all those things. The outside is a more modern one. They didn't go with an old brick, retro look. They tried to make it look a lot like other buildings in D.C. They have some steel and a lot of stone involved, so it's a different kind of look. One of the great advantages of it is when you're on the main concourse, it's totally open. The concourse is huge, so there's room for a lot of people to walk. There are places for you to stand or sit and eat, and, anywhere you are, you can still have a view of the game. You're not going through a tunnel where you're far from a game and you have to see it on a monitor. If you're in line for food and something happens, you can literally just move a few feet and see the field. The view of the field is great from anywhere. There's not a bad seat in the park. The video board is one of the best and biggest in baseball. You've got state of the art, crystal clear HD replay videos. The sound system is phenomenal, and, depending on how high up you are in the park, you can get a view of the Capitol at the same time you're watching the game. When you get to some of the upper levels from the main concourse, you've got a club level that's really nice and air conditioned. If it's a cold, rainy night, you can get warmth. It's a real top flight amenity. Friends come and visit me, and they come to Nationals Park and they're like 'Wow! Wow!' Maybe Nationals Park doesn't have the view of the bay at AT&T or of downtown Pittsburgh, but, just the park itself—the amenities, the scoreboard, the feel of it—is pretty spectacular. Almost everybody I know that's come to D.C. with the kids for a summer vacation, they like to go to a baseball game at Nationals Park, too."

While fans might not argue with Slowes's sentiment about "not a bad seat in the park," visiting broadcasters may beg to differ. Slowes explains, "The broadcaster's view is unique to any other park. We are at the very top of the park behind home plate. The only thing higher than us is the lights and barely. We're about at the height of the lights. It's hard for visiting broadcasters coming in to get used to the depth perception. Balls hit back to the mound are sometimes hard to tell if they're a line drive or a one hopper because you can't see the bounce in front of the plate. An old 'Baltimore chop' out in front of the plate versus a bloop pop up can freeze you for a split second. The trajectory of the ball to the outfield. We can see the whole park. There's virtually no out of view for us anywhere. Maybe part of the corner in left field and right field; but, otherwise, we have a tremendous view. We're high enough that we can tell if a ball hit over the fence and came back in kind of thing that the umpires can't and have to go to replay. We always know before they do. For Dave Jageler and I, doing 81 games there, it really doesn't faze us anymore. We love the size of our booth, the amenities, that sort of thing, but I imagine it's extremely difficult for someone else coming in for a three game series. They probably get used to it by the final game of a series. You've got to watch the outfielders on fly balls. If you watch the ball hit in the air, it will fool you. The ball goes up in the air, you think it's in the outfield and it's an infield pop-up. In our place, you can watch the ball, because the ball, at the height of the arc of the pop-up, will most likely still not be as high as we are. We see a few that go up and we actually have to crane our necks to look up but very few. If a helicopter flies over, we call it a 'fly under.' We have tried to match up our height to one of the office buildings straight across from us, and I would say we're 10 stories high. When you look out from our booth, you can see the whole Capitol Hill area. If you go to the right end of the broadcast level, you can almost see the Washington Monument."

While the broadcasters are waving to the helicopter pilots in their sniper-level booths, the outfielders at Nationals Park have a six-angle wall to patrol. Looking like the ballpark's architect sneezed while tracing out the left-field portion of Nationals Park, the dimensions accommodate the visitor's bullpen and fans sitting in the "Red Porch," an all-red section of seats leading up to the Red Porch Restaurant and a three-tiered standing-room bar called the Red Loft, which according to Slowes "looks a little like Fenway." With the trend of new ballparks opting for eight-foot walls in order to increase home run thievery, a visiting outfielder, on many occasions, has the added burden of battling the fans just beyond the walls. At Nationals Park, however, really only the left fielder—while he's playing the line—and a jurisdiction-toeing center fielder will ever face that problem, especially when nearing the Red Porch. Jutting out of the left center-field wall like a ballpark-green-colored polyp, the Red Porch itself can cause more havoc to the outfielders than the fans who have been drinking, as a ball caroming off of that "protrusion" may shoot back toward left field and create a triple or inside-the-park home run. The right fielders at Nationals Park, although nestled in the sanctuary of the home team bullpen, have their own game of wall ball to prepare for when hitters "get ahold of one." Slowes notes, "When you get from right center field almost to straightaway right, you've got the out-of-town video scoreboard built into the wall and it's 14 and a half feet high, so visiting teams would have to come in and deal with how the ball caroms off that wall. Typical of all high fences, you're going to go back and have a play. If you don't make the play, there's a chance it's going to carom past you and your outfielder has to come back and play the carom of the ball coming back in towards the infield. Then, in straightaway right, the fence drops down to a lower height again in front of the Nationals bullpen. The ball carries pretty well to right center field. You'll have some hit the wall, but, if you hit it well, they'll hit it over that wall. When the weather's warm, right center field is probably the area where the ball carries best in our park." As in many East Coast, open-air ballparks, the adjudication on the case of "Hitter Friendly vs. Pitcher Friendly" need not go to an appellate court, which is likely visible from the broadcast booth as well. The earlier it is in the season, the tighter your fantasy baseball grip will be on Nationals pitchers. Slowes adds, "Early in the year, when it's cold, the ball doesn't carry well. When the weather's warm, the ball carries better and there are a lot more home runs. Temperatures get into the '80s, and you'll see the park play a lot more differently. Through the first couple months of the season, I think Nationals Park was near the bottom of baseball in total home runs hit. In the cold weather, without question, it's a pitcher's park. In hot weather, it's going to leave balls up. They're going to carry. It'll play much bigger, so it really depends on the time of year. If you're a fly ball pitcher, you love pitching there early in the year." What goes for some doesn't go for all, and in the case of Nationals outfielder and 2012 Rookie of the Year Bryce Harper, it goes far. Opening at home in 2013, Harper became the youngest player in history to homer in his first two at bats of the season, the closest day to winter for which an opposing pitcher could ask. In hindsight, had the pitcher really been granted a request, it would probably have been not to face Harper at all.

Throughout the year, regardless of the season both meteorologically and electorally, a presidential race is run within the "halls" of Nationals Park. Inspired by the Racing Sausages at Miller Park in Milwaukee and Pierogi Races at PNC Park in Pittsburgh, the Nationals have a more historical approach to between-inning "edutainment," the "President's Race." Describing the event itself in the detail that only someone who witnesses the event more than 81 times a year can provide, Charlie Slowes says, "Milwaukee had it all first with sausage races, but I think the presidents are kind of becoming the most well known for this sort of thing. For the longest time, hundreds of races, you had George Washington, Teddy Roosevelt, Abe Lincoln, and Thomas Jefferson, and Teddy would never win. He won on the final day of the 2012 season. The last game of the year. They'd have these different story lines or scripts of how Teddy would break down, be distracted, or have something where someone would come out of the stands or have a picture of himself that somebody holds up and then he stops. Some of it was pretty funny. They had some really good scripts. So now you have Teddy finally win. Then before last year (2013), they introduced a fifth running president, William Howard Taft, the first president to throw out an opening pitch. When the Pirates come in, they'll bring the Pierogies. When we were in Pittsburgh, our presidents were there and, usually, they get to beat up on us in Pittsburgh, and we get to beat up on them in our place. The presidents are pretty popular. The kids run the bases after Sunday games. The presidents will be at each base. It's pretty cool. They travel around town and do all kinds of appearances and have become pretty popular with the kids." As popular as the presidents are in Washington, it's unlikely one of them would be the incumbent racing against outfielder Jayson Werth in game 4 of the 2012 National League Division Series.

OCTOBER 11, 2012: THE
"NATS" LIVE TO SEE ANOTHER "TERM"

In their former identity as the Montreal Expos, the Nationals got as far as the National League Championship Series only once in their 36 seasons in French Canada, losing to the eventual World Series champion Los Angeles Dodgers in a best of five series. While it took about half as long for the Nationals to qualify for the playoffs in their new uniforms as opposed to their old ones, the fans in the nation's capital had already suffered through back-to-back, 100-loss seasons, and the postseason was long overdue. After a 98-*win* season in 2012, the Nationals captured the National League East from the "token-division-winning" Atlanta Braves and faced the defending World Series champion St. Louis Cardinals in the Division Series. Falling down two games to one, the Nationals sent pitcher Ross Detwiler to the mound against Kyle Lohse in a must-win for the Nats. With both starters collectively giving up just five hits over a combined 13 innings, each pitcher had surrendered just one run, with Detwiler's being unearned. After they turned the ball over to the bullpens to do the rest, the results on the scoreboard showed the same, especially for Nationals relievers, who pitched three hitless innings, striking out eight along the way. In the bottom of the ninth, Cardinals pitcher Lance Lynn threw an inning's worth of pitches yet faced only one batter, Jayson Werth. Charlie Slowes describes the experience as arguably his most memorable game as a broadcaster for the Nationals: "The game ended on Jayson Werth's home run in the bottom of the ninth inning on the 13th pitch of the at bat. It was a pitcher's duel. The Nationals won the game 2–1. They were facing elimination and down to their last strike. The noise was unbelievable." The Nationals lost the next game, and with it, the series, sending the team home a few days earlier than they would have liked, but still, thanks to Jayson Werth, one day later than they expected.

While the Nationals added only two to their 98-win season total in 2012, they again showed signs of life in 2014, a season that would end not only with the team having secured home-field advantage through the playoffs but also with the team's first no-hitter, courtesy of Jordan Zimmermann, on the final day of the regular season. Coupled with the home run power of Bryce Harper; the walk-off proneness of third baseman Ryan Zimmerman (nine career walk-off home runs); and the pitching arms of Jordan Zimmermann, Stephen Strasburg, Rafael Soriano, and recent import Max Scherzer, the young and harvested talent of this Washington Nationals team is bound to fill the "Red Porch" until a World Series parade makes its way up Capitol Hill, around the monument, down 1600 Pennsylvania Avenue, and past all the memorials of presidents immortalized inside Nationals Park with giant heads, speedy legs, and schtick comedy.

• 18 •

O.co Coliseum: Oakland Athletics

O.co Colisem: "You could drop the Coliseum into the middle of Ohio and you wouldn't even know where you were." —Ken Korach
Photo courtesy of the Oakland Athletics

I think you almost have to separate the Coliseum from the standpoint
that there have been, in a sense, two Coliseums. In other words, the
Coliseum, before the Raiders returned, was a different ballpark than it is
now because of the building of what they now call Mount Davis.

—Ken Korach, Oakland Athletics radio
play-by-play broadcaster

In 1962, in the Alameda County of northern California, ground broke on
what would four years later become the Oakland Coliseum, home to the
NFL's Oakland Raiders. About 1,500 miles east of Oakland, in the City of
Fountains, Kansas City Athletics owner Charlie "O" Finley became quite interested in the possibility of his division cellar-dwelling A's (formerly of Philadelphia) completing their coast-to-coast trip in just under 13 years. After the
'67 season Finley, appearing much like the Wizard of Oz himself, paraded his
hunter-green and California-gold-clad Athletics into "Oaktown," where the
team's proverbial Greyhound bus has remained in park for the last 46 years.
Quite contrary to their records in both Philadelphia and Kansas City, the
Athletics took well to their new habitat, winning three straight World Series
titles by their seventh season in Oakland. After 14 seasons of cohabitation with
the Raiders, the Athletics became the sole occupants of what is now known
as the O.co Coliseum after the '81 season. After just one Super Bowl win in
the team's 14-year residence in Los Angeles, Raiders (then) owner Al Davis
began talks with Alameda County representatives to bring his team back up
the coast. Part of this agreement included the concession to add a 22,000-seat
grandstand beyond center field, replacing both the bleachers and the view so
many A's fans had enjoyed for almost 30 years. This concrete marvel, known
in the sports world as "Mount Davis," has been a target for much criticism
since the Raiders returned home to Oakland, especially in the baseball community, as its only contribution is doubling as an umbrella shade for deep-
fly-ball-chasing outfielders on the warning track. Of course, per the litigated
agreement among the law firm of "Yours, Mine, and Ours," much of Mount
Davis was to be tarped off, reducing the once-envied 50,000-seat capacity
of the Coliseum to a mere 35,000. Ironically enough, most of Mount Davis
today is tarped off for Raiders games as well in order to finagle sell-outs and
increase the ratings of local networks airing the games. Either the tarp outbid
15,000 would-be season ticket holders, or Alameda County simply does *not*
need that extra $13 million a year. Perhaps the term "break-even point" was
never discussed with Mr. Davis during the negotiation phase of the Raiders'
return to Oakland. Commenting on the change Mount Davis brought to the
O.co Coliseum, Oakland A's radio play-by-play broadcaster Ken Korach says,
"The Coliseum, before the Raiders returned, was a different ballpark than

it is now because of the building of Mount Davis. There was an editorial in the *San Francisco Chronicle* which called the Coliseum awkward because of the renovations, but since I've been with the A's, that's all I've known as far as working here. As a fan, I was there in the old days where you had a beautiful view of the East Bay Hills, and you had the bleachers, and it was a wonderful setting. Now, you could drop the Coliseum into the middle of Ohio and you wouldn't even know where you were because you're looking at a lot of concrete." While that concrete may be draped in the hunter-green tarp brandishing the team name and retired numbers of former A's greats, the only real excitement Mount Davis has to offer a spectator looking on from outside the foul poles is the potential pinball game the walls and their now asymmetrical dimensions create. Thanks a lot, Al.

CAMPING OUT UNDER THE CANOPY

Since the O.co Coliseum was built two years before the A's came over from KC, one can't reasonably blame Al Davis for perhaps the park's most distinguishing feature: its copious amount of foul territory. Ken Korach adds, "One of the great things about baseball is that there's really no necessary uniformity. Some ballparks have symmetrical dimensions, and some have all kinds of quirks and nooks and crannies. I think the one thing that people would always point to that would make the Coliseum unique would be the foul territory. There's no question that, by far, it's the largest foul territory in baseball. Hitters hate it, and pitchers love it. I think it's been a contributor to the A's success over the years because it's created this environment where the pitchers have a lot of confidence when they work there. They know they can throw a pitch over the plate and oftentimes get an out. Foul balls that land in the seats in every other ballpark are caught at the Coliseum. I think that's really helped pitchers get deeper into games, pitch deeper into a season, throw more innings, get outs where you wouldn't normally get outs. Hitters have not enjoyed that aspect of it." While skeptical fans could just chalk up the extra foul territory to another squandered use of valuable East Bay real estate, Oakland's starting pitchers have taken advantage of it. At the O.co Coliseum in 2013, A's starting pitchers were third in the American League in ERA (3.86) and complete games (6). Of course, a pitcher's confidence isn't the only thing recording outs at the O.co Coliseum. Korach notes, "You need to have good corner infielders who are really adept to going after foul balls. Eric Chavez and Josh Donaldson were phenomenal at learning the nuances of the foul territory at the Coliseum and being able to chase down balls there. You'll see some visiting players give up on a ball because they're not used to running. You feel like you could run forever. Maybe you get towards the warning track and you think, 'There's no way that ball could still be in play,' or it'll look like it's going to land in the stands and it'll come back on an angle, so you can't give up on it. Having people that can do that is important." To reinforce Korach's praise of Chavez, the All-Star third baseman won six straight gold gloves from 2001 to 2006 while policing the Coliseum's third base line in an A's uniform. Donaldson is trading in his foul territory for artificial turf, as his third base skills will now be tested north of the border in Toronto's Rogers Centre.

In the case of the Oakland Athletics, a gold glove could also justifiably be awarded to mother nature and geography. Being situated so close to the Pacific Ocean, the O.co Coliseum receives a cool helping hand during night games from an entity more suited to a Stephen King novel: the marine layer. Korach explains, "The marine layer comes in at night, and it cools down. So many of the night games are played under the canopy of the marine layer as it moves its way across the coast over to the East Bay. The ball isn't carrying as well, so you have a real difference at the Coliseum. You see this at a lot of parks, but it's dramatic at the Coliseum. You're going to see maybe a different game played to a certain degree at night because the ball just dies when it's hit to the alleys." Considering that not all games are played under this pitcher-aiding canopy, a visiting player might expect some sort of reprieve playing a day game at the Coliseum, but in the words of Dodgers broadcaster Charley Steiner, "Au contraire." The sun, another of Mother Nature's cohorts plotting against visiting players at the O.co Coliseum, rears its head and brings a whole other challenge to the fielders. Korach adds, "You would think the sun would be a factor in every ballpark. I'm not sure I can fully explain why the sun is such an issue playing at the Coliseum, but we've seen numerous fielders, especially visiting players, have a really hard time with the sun at the Coliseum. Dropped fly balls, dropped pop-ups, and it's not configured in an unusual way. It's configured in the traditional way where when you have a night game at 7:00, right field is the sun field, and the sun is setting over the left-field stands to the west. The right fielder looks toward the west, but, in the daytime at the Coliseum, there is a very tough sun." Unfortunately, the perfect storm of limited sun distraction and marine layer interference would only take place during the 5:00 p.m. starts reserved for Sunday night baseball and playoff games, the latter being more common for the Oakland A's.

MAY 9, 2010: DALLAS BRADEN'S PERFECT MOTHER'S DAY GIFT

Having completed his 19th season ('14) in the broadcast booth, Ken Korach's most memorable game at the O.co Coliseum has been and still is Dallas

Braden's perfect game against the Tampa Bay Rays in May 2010. Perhaps even more amazing than the pitching performance itself is the backstory that sets up Braden's monumental feat. Korach recalls, "I can say that the most intense I think I have ever been—maybe my stomach was churning—and where there was the most drama in one single game was Dallas Braden's perfect game. When you're a broadcaster, you think that you'll never have that opportunity because they're so infrequent. That was the 19th in history. In terms of the confluence of story lines, people always say, 'Hollywood would never write a script like that. Nobody would believe it.' Well, that's why you have Hollywood, and that's why you have wonderful scripts, because there are these remarkable human stories, and that was the story of Braden's perfect game. Braden's mom died when he was in high school and his grandmother became even more instrumental in his life, raising him in a hard scrabble neighborhood in Stockton, California. Tough background. So now he's pitching to try to accomplish something that really puts you in almost a baseball immortality on Mother's Day with his grandmother there watching the game. All that he had gone through with his mother passing away. He, by his own admission, had gone off the tracks a couple of times in his own life. Searching for direction, which his grandmother gave him, and now it's Mother's Day, and he's pitching a perfect game. I'm not sure you're ever going to find a better story than that." One of the downsides—if there ever really could *be* any—to a perfect game is the speed with which they occur. Korach explains what it was like in the booth when the game was closing in on the final three outs: "Of course, he accomplished it in a rapid fire ninth inning. It was extremely quick. I barely had the time to do the things I had set out to do. I didn't have a script. I didn't know what I was going to say when the game ended. That really was an amazing day." Ironically, in what would be only the second perfect game in the Athletics' 114-year history, the attendance was a paltry 12,228 fans. Not even Mount Davis's tarp could be blamed for that low number. The game started at 1:05 p.m. local time, hours before the marine layer would ever become a factor, and only 9 of the 27 recorded outs ever made their way out of the infield, so take *that*, warm California air. On Braden's last out, Gabe Kapler grounded out to shortstop Cliff Pennington, sealing the victory and reserving wall space in Cooperstown for Braden's jersey, hat, and shoe polish shavings; however, it was the young hurler's mind-set going into his 109th and final pitch that really made for such an interesting end to Braden's day. Korach comments, "There's an interesting sidebar story to it. The last batter was Gabe Kapler, who hit a ground ball to shortstop Cliff Pennington on a 3–1 pitch, which was a fastball. As soon as the game ended, there was this incredible celebration. Braden leaps into the arms of the catcher Landon Powell. The A's explode out of the dugout. There's this wild celebration, and they play my call on the stadium

P.A. up in the Diamond Vision. They replay it, and you hear my call of the last out, and they asked Braden about the pitch he threw to Kapler, which was a 3–1 fastball, and he said, 'I thought the count was 2–2. I didn't realize it was 3–1 until I heard Ken Korach's call on the highlight. If I had known it was 3–1, I would have thrown him a changeup.' That was my only real link to Braden's perfect game. He didn't know the count. He was so involved in the moment that he thought the previous 2–1 pitch, in his own mind, was a strike, but it was a ball, so it turned the count to 3–1 instead of 2–2. That was a pretty amazing afternoon, and to have it happen on Mother's Day, too." With the changeup being Braden's signature pitch, it's only fitting this Hollywood script ended with a twist.

THE COLISEUM YESTERDAY, TODAY, AND TOMORROW

The O.co Coliseum, approaching its 50th anniversary in 2016, has seen its fair share of history. Along with being home to two Super Bowl–winning Raiders teams ('76 and '80), as well as four Oakland A's World Series titles (1972, 1973, 1974, 1989), the Coliseum was the birthplace of world-famous super fan Krazy George's spectator-inclusive invention, "the wave," during the 1981 American League Championship Series between the A's and the eventual pennant winner New York Yankees. Interestingly, Krazy George was "dealt" to the NFL's Chiefs, giving back to Kansas City "with interest" from the city's franchise relinquishment two decades before. Of course some of the nuances of the Coliseum's construction and cohabitation have raised the question of whether or not a new home should be built. The O.co Coliseum is the last of the shared facilities for NFL and MLB teams. Though nothing really changes from the A's perspective in this regard, Korach comments on the roommate situation come fall: "It does create an unusual set of circumstances for the Raiders in September and October if the A's are in the playoffs, because they're playing on the dirt infield. Sebastian Janikowski made some comments this year about having to kick a field goal in the dirt." While on-the-field circumstances annoy the Raiders, it's the below-the-field circumstances that have perhaps inspired the discussion of a new stadium. To allow for a facilitated entry into the stadium's upper deck, the O.co Coliseum was built deep into the ground back in 1966. The error of this decision became apparent in July 2013, when an overworked and backed-up sewer system forced the A's and visiting Mariners to integrate clubhouses like at the end of the film *West Side Story*. Recent talks among A's owner Lew Wolff, the city of San Jose, and Major League Baseball once had the A's searching for a possible new home. Unfortunately, San Jose fandom is apparently reserved for the neighboring San

Francisco Giants, precluding A's fans from having to "know the way" to home games. Wolff and Alameda County came to an agreement in July 2014 that will keep the A's inside O.co Coliseum for another 10 years. While part of the agreement includes upgrades like ribbon boards and HD video boards, the best upgrade of all—should the Raiders come through on their threat to once again leave Oakland—would be to pack up Mount Davis and take it with them, allowing outfielders to once again live without fear of a jutting wall or an overhanging concrete community collapsing on top of them.

· 19 ·

Oriole Park at Camden Yards: Baltimore Orioles

Oriole Park at Camden Yards: "I'll never forget the first real look at the actual ballpark. It was finished and there was that warehouse looming over everything. The size of it made the ballpark its own little world." —Jon Miller
Photo courtesy of Todd Olszewski/©Baltimore Orioles

This ballpark was not built to be a copy of Wrigley Field or Ebbets Field.
It was built for the same reasons that those ballparks were built the way
they were built. I think that's a very important distinction.

—Jon Miller, former Baltimore Orioles radio
play-by-play broadcaster

*A*rt Modell's moving Cleveland's NFL franchise to Baltimore was not the first time Monument City was handed a team named the Browns. Back in 1953, with the attendance in the seats resembling what a 100-loss team would be expected to draw, St. Louis quickly became the gateway to the *East*, as the city's "other" major league team, the Browns, announced their move to Baltimore; like Modell's team 40 years down the road, they would change their name, becoming the Orioles. Having already hosted a team named the Orioles in a minor league capacity a decade before, Memorial Stadium in Baltimore became the home to the major league version of the Orioles. The inaugural '54 season of the Orioles ended with the exact 100-loss record of the Browns the year before; however, attendance was over the one million mark, which was a far cry from the team's numbers at Sportsman's Park in St. Louis. Unfortunately for Baltimore, the ensuing years of increased success occurred in the same league as the New York Yankees, who dominated the '50s and early '60s and were unwilling to share the glory with their new neighbors. In 1966, however, the Orioles emerged from the Yankees' shadow and won the team's first World Series title. The team returned to the fall classic three years later to not only face the New York Mets but fate as well, and the Orioles lost to the "Amazings" four games to one. The following year, thanks to players such as pitcher Jim Palmer and slugger Frank Robinson, the Orioles defeated the soon-to-be-known-as "the Big Red Machine" Cincinnati Reds in the 1970 World Series. The Orioles returned to the World Series twice more in the '70s but lost both times, to the Pittsburgh Pirates and Roberto Clemente in 1971 and Willie Stargell in 1979. Four years later, the team won their third World Series title, as Pete Rose and Joe Morgan, wearing a different shade of "Red" in Philadelphia, fell to Storm Davis, Rick Dempsey, and the "O's" four games to one. The following few years were not promising ones for a Baltimore return to the World Series, as the '88 team began their season 1–23; however, despite their cellar-dwelling placement in the division, history did not repeat itself for these "Browns"-blooded Orioles. During the team's horrendous 54–107 season in 1988, a ballpark was announced for downtown Baltimore, which would tentatively open for the '92 season. Enter the two most influential individuals in what would soon become the new evolution of baseball stadium construction and development: Orioles president and CEO Larry Lucchino and (at the time) unknown architect Janet Marie Smith, who broke away from the "cookie-cutter" mold with the Orioles' future home of Camden Yards.

~~THERE GOES~~ HERE COMES THE NEIGHBORHOOD

Before taking his broadcasting talents to a Giants team he had loved and followed ever since he was a young boy, Jon Miller spent 14 years in the Orioles booth. Having been with the club since well before construction began on the new stadium, Miller describes the events that led to Camden Yards' literal and metaphorical ground breaking: "What happened with Camden Yards was new. The ballparks that had been built in close proximity to the time frame like Toronto, who had built something totally new. A retractable dome that was huge. The Blue Jays had the 21st century seeming ballpark and something that had never been done before. Then the White Sox built a new ballpark, calling it the 'new' Comiskey Park at that time. They broke ground for that park about a month before the Orioles broke ground for Camden Yards. They had the same architectural firm. It was called H.O.K. at the time. A guy from H.O.K. explained to me years later the White Sox had the oldest ballpark in the game, and they wanted their new ballpark opened as quickly as possible. They looked at it as a good revenue producer. They wanted luxury suites and a big stadium club where the lawyers, and stockbrokers, and what not would want to hang out, whereas, with Camden Yards, the Orioles people said, 'We want to do something that's going to be great, and we want to do it right. Maybe it will take a little bit longer.' They hired Janet Marie Smith to be the architect from their standpoint. They said to Janet, 'People remember Ebbets Field so fondly 40 years after it's ceased to exist. They love Fenway Park and they love Wrigley Field. We want you to find out, specifically, why those ballparks were built the way they were built.' If they asked me, as a baseball person, 'Why are Fenway Park and Ebbets Field so fondly thought of,' I would have told them. I felt like I already knew, but Janet Marie Smith was sort of a blank canvas in that regard. If they had told her, 'Three Rivers Stadium in Pittsburgh is the most beloved park in baseball. Find out why,' she would have just gone with that and assumed that was right. She didn't take anything for granted. She didn't assume anything."

Smith's unassuming approach eventually gave birth to the genius her mind had been harboring and took her from a "blank canvas" to a pioneer. Miller continues, "She went to the architectural firms that designed all those ballparks 90 years before, and she found out why they were built the way they were built. She came back and said, 'They were built according to the architectural attitudes in that city and in that neighborhood at that time.' For her, the old 19th-century B&O Warehouse, where the ballpark was going to be, was a key to getting that feel. If they could duplicate the brickwork and some of the architectural features like the archways design, then the two would look like they had been side by side for 100 years. The Orioles liked that idea. It also kept the idea of Eutaw St., which bordered the warehouse. You had the ballpark, then you had Eutaw St., and then the warehouse. There was a lot of sentiment to tear down the old warehouse. It was just a big brick monstrosity, and that would open up the ballpark to the downtown inner harbor. You'd have these views of the skyline and inner harbor, and it would just be a show-case for the city. Smith said they could do that as well, but if they wanted these odd dimensions and the kinds of things to replicate the feeling they have at Fenway, Wrigley, and the old Ebbets Field, the warehouse was the key to all of that, so they kept it. That truly gave an authenticity to everything else. The outside of the ballpark had the brickwork just like the brickwork on the old warehouse. They truly did blend together like they had been built at the same time, even though one was built more than 100 years before the other."

Once the footprint was cast, and before Camden Yards went out "on the market," it was time for baseball's version of a "focus group." Miller notes, "People were excited about seeing this new ballpark. The players the same thing. I remember we flew in from spring training. We got in after a day game down in Miami, and everybody immediately walked through the clubhouse and out into the dugout to see the field. Everybody was so excited, and they turned the lights on so we could all see it, and the first thing that struck you—I'll never forget the first real look at the actual ballpark—it was finished and there was that warehouse looming over everything. It was so dramatic. The size of it made the ballpark its own little world." It should come as no surprise that the buzz about Camden Yards made its way to the Big Apple. Miller adds, "Before opening day, the *New York Times* architectural critic had come down and wrote a review of the ballpark and was just effusive with praise. Something totally unique. He thought it was the most important new baseball-stadium building since probably the '20s, maybe even Yankee Stadium itself. He pre-dicted that this would revolutionize baseball-stadium building from that point onward. That this would be sort of the idea that every new stadium would follow."

Camden Yards inspired not only the ballparks to be built after it but also the ones that had been built just before it. Miller notes, "Subsequent ballparks took things from Camden Yards, but, also, they said, 'Maybe we can improve on this or improve on that.' The new ballpark in Chicago—which had great attendance the whole first year—after Camden Yards opened, people said, 'We did it the wrong way. The Sox park is nothing compared to that.' That hurt the White Sox and it hurt Toronto. I remember people in Toronto specifically saying to me, 'We really screwed up. We should have built like a Camden Yards park,' even though what they had done was state of the art. Suddenly, the fans themselves were not satisfied. That became a big thing up there that they had *not* done the right thing. Chicago did a major renovation to their ballpark eight or nine years ago when they cut off the top few rows of seats in their upper deck and then put sort of an 'old timey' looking rooftop with supporting poles that had more the look of the 'old' Comiskey Park. That ultimately was brought about because of Camden Yards."

ENOUGH! JUST PLAY BALL ALREADY, WOULD YA?

After the biggest commotion to set up a ballpark perhaps since Fenway Park or Wrigley Field 80 years before, Camden Yards opened its gates to the fans and other media outlets on April 6, 1992, and the Orioles christened their new home with a 2–0 win over Charles Nagy and the Cleveland Indians. If there was any doubt about whether the new ballpark would attract enough attendance to live up to its hype, it was quelled before April 7. Miller notes, "The people of Baltimore got very excited—first off—because they thought they had a good team. They won that opening day game, and the *Today* show from New York came down and originated its show from the ballpark for a couple of days. They were on the field, showing the ballpark to a national audience, and Baltimore people got very excited about that. They were excited about the ball club. They were excited the *New York Times* said their ballpark was a groundbreaker. A beacon of the future. Because of that, the ticket office was flooded with people wanting tickets. They were finding out the next game that had tickets available was the next month. It was just an incredible phenomenon, and they started selling out all these games in advance. Ultimately, it was just the place to be seen in Baltimore." Relatively close to Baltimore, the nation's capital was catching wind of the park as well. Miller continues, "It was much easier for people from Washington to come to the ballpark. I remember the old writer Mo Siegel from Washington made the drive himself for a column for the paper. He drove from the White House to Camden Yards. He said it took him 45 minutes. It was like a 40-mile drive, so it looked like it was a fairly easy task. The Orioles research showed that maybe 20 to 25 percent of their total attendance came from the Washington, D.C. area, so this became a real attraction all by itself."

Regardless of the *Today* show, Mo Siegel, and a *New York Times* architectural critic's praise of the young Camden Yards, it was all for naught if the boys in orange and white couldn't find a way to play inside it. At the time, that "if" didn't seem so unreasonable. Prior to Camden Yards, the trend in stadium construction over the previous few decades had been "cookie-cutter," multipurpose edifices. Three Rivers Stadium, Atlanta Fulton County Stadium, Veterans Stadium, and Riverfront Stadium were all ballparks in which a batter would literally have to check the logo in the on-deck circle to know where he was playing. The dimensions of the fields all seemed the same, the bowl of the bleachers all rose up like an above-ground coliseum, and whatever scenery there was beyond the stadium gates was better seen *after* the game. While Toronto's Rogers Centre and Chicago's "new" Comiskey Park were not considered "cookie-cutter" facilities, their outfield design was still quite standard. Fenway Park and Wrigley Field, the two settings from which Janet Marie Smith sought inspiration for Camden Yards, had their own idiosyncratic dimensions and angles in the outfield because their proverbial "cookie-cutter" tins were pushed in by the inner-city neighborhoods of both Boston and Chicago. Flash-forward to opening day, 1992, at Camden Yards and a "cookie-cutter" tin pushed in by Eutaw St. and the B&O Warehouse; the unanswered question on everybody's mind was: Hitter's haven or pitcher's paradise? Jon Miller describes Camden Yards' uniquely designed field: "We all thought right field—where they had a higher wall—would be sort of a reverse image of Fenway Park, but what happened was the winds would come in from left across to right. Apparently, that wind would hit the warehouse and be deflected back in towards the batter, so when you hit a ball to right field, it was actually getting knocked down by the winds. Not many balls were clearing that wall, much less scraping off it. At Fenway, the effect was always to left field. High fly balls that were going to be an easy catch in most ballparks would scrape off that wall and guys would get doubles on them. At Camden Yards, that was not happening. At first, we thought, because of that, it might end up becoming a pitcher's park, but it became evident, especially when the weather heated up, that it was going to be a very good home run ballpark. I think, to this day, it's still one of the best hitter's ballparks in the league."

While the reverse image of Fenway in Camden's right field is great for hitters, it can also be a good assignment for the not-so-fleet-footed fielders. Miller continues, "Right field is a shallow field. You could put a guy who doesn't necessarily cover a lot of ground and get away with it in right field because there's not a whole lot of ground to cover. The center field is still pretty big. The deepest part of the ballpark is not in straightaway center. It's a little bit off to the side. Guys can go up and make catches above the plane of the wall other than in right field. It's not until you get out to right center, where the scoreboard ends, that the wall is just a normal, 8-foot height." Considering that the "cookie-cutter" molds also included high outfield walls separating the players from the fans, the eight-foot, fan-inviting wall of Camden Yards was new territory for Orioles outfielders, and, for that matter, the fans. Miller adds,

"Brady Anderson was the left fielder, and he actually practiced making catches where he brought the ball back into the park. Brady would practice vaulting himself up on the padded wall—digging his cleats into the padding—and he was good at it. The third game that first year, he goes all the way back to the wall on this fly ball, and a fan reached out of the stands, caught it, and kept him from catching it. Brady was so upset and he came down from his leap and took his glove off and threw it on the ground. He was swearing, so we, on the air, used that video to admonish the fans, 'Don't do that. Brady's good at that. Let him go in and make that catch. Don't let the other team get a home run if Brady can catch it.' It never happened again the whole time I was there."

One truly unique feature of Camden Yards, which never really had a chance in Wrigley or Fenway due to space constraints, is the home and visiting bullpen area of the ballpark. Miller notes, "They wanted both bullpens to be in complete sight for everybody in the ballpark. This had never been done before. The Orioles bullpen was raised up a little bit behind the center field wall so as not to be hidden. The visiting bullpen was raised up still further. It was like a terraced effect. You could see both bullpens from just about anywhere in the ballpark. They were very forward thinking in that regard." Though many would argue that as groundbreaking as Camden Yards was when it opened, it still was not perfect. Miller describes the team's exercise in customer service: "There were some complaints by people who were sitting down the lines—especially in the lower deck—that the seats were facing the outfield and people would have to turn in their seats and crane their necks to look back to the infield and home plate. A company had come up with a different idea for the seats where they could actually be turned inward so that you could just sit and—straight on—look at the pitcher's mound and home plate. They replaced all those seats where that had been a problem with seats that had a little twist in them. They still fit perfectly in the rows." With the seats adjusted to their desired comfort level, the fans had the perfect view for one of the most-anticipated moments in baseball history, which would occur in 1995 at a still-young Camden Yards.

SEPTEMBER 6, 1995: THE IRON MAN TROTS CAMDEN LIKE THE IRON HORSE

Before retiring from the game because of the illness that would not only end his life but eventually be named after him, Lou Gehrig played in 2,130 straight games, a streak that by today's scheduling standard spans 13 seasons. Beginning in 1981, a new face with a familiar name in baseball began his own road to Gehrig's record in an Orioles uniform. Cal Ripken Jr. won the American

League Rookie of the Year award in 1982 and during the team's world championship campaign the following year won the league's Most Valuable Player award as well. Ripken won another MVP during the '91 season. Eventually, as the years piled on and Ripken stayed healthy, Gehrig's 2,130-game mark began to show on the horizon. Finally it came down to 1995, when history, foreseeably, would be made late in that baseball season. Having the advantage of being able to plan around a record, the Orioles had their own way of recognizing Ripken's feat. Miller explains, "When Cal Ripken was approaching Lou Gehrig, there was the question about 'How will we mark this historic moment?' because basically, before the season even starts, assuming there were no rainouts that changed the schedule, we already know what night he's going to break the record. It's not like the big home run to break 'the Babe's' home run record for Henry Aaron. We don't know when that's going to happen. With Cal, we know exactly when, and we can make sure the schedule makers give us a home game for that event. I think it was Charles Steinberg who came up with the idea. Charles was a local Baltimore guy who became a dentist, but he always kept this nighttime job with the Orioles. They put him in charge of Oriole productions when they got their first big Jumbotron colored screen at the old Memorial Stadium. Charles was also a huge music fan, and so he was always taking actual songs and tying them into baseball themes. Charles came up with this idea that the record only becomes official in baseball once the game becomes official. It's not that Cal takes the field at the beginning of the game and there's the record. According to baseball rule, it becomes an official game and everything counts after four and a half innings—if the Orioles are ahead—or five innings if the Orioles are behind or tied. A couple of home stands before, they put numbers up on the warehouse wall as banners. Either at the top of the fifth inning or whenever the game became official, they would put that rule up on the board so all the fans could read it. Meanwhile, they had this rousing, emotional music built to a crescendo, and right at the ultimate crescendo, the banner fell for the new number. Cal hated it because he was always all business on the field. That's the way he was raised with the game. He didn't want to be spotlighted or brought out like that. Now they're putting his picture on the screen and the fans would cheer. I didn't understand. I just thought, 'They're overdoing this,' until we got real close, and then I saw the genius of it. This is how it's going to be commemorated. This is when it actually happened. This is the home run moment. This is Pete Rose getting the base hit that put him ahead of Ty Cobb. This is how it's going to be enacted, and Steinberg got the fans used to it. We all saw what was going on. Now it's two nights away and now it's the night that he ties the record. There's the banner coming down and that was the moment." Now that the party was planned, all that remained was the guest of honor, a guest who—unbeknownst to anybody at the time—almost didn't even RSVP.

On September 6, 1995, with the numbers spread across the B&O Warehouse windows reading "2,130," baseball's "Iron Man," on the inside, was showing his rust. Miller recalls, "The night that he actually broke the record—we didn't know it until afterward—Cal was sick. He was running a fever because he was getting no sleep. For several weeks leading up to the breaking of the record, Cal would come out of the clubhouse back into the ballpark, and he'd start signing autographs. People started lining up for this. Not just Camden Yards but all the cities we were in because his wife said, 'Cal, I hope you can enjoy this experience, and I hope that you can celebrate it and not just look at it as an annoyance and something you have to get through.' It was a beautiful sentiment, so he embraced it. Everybody wanted a piece of him because he was going for this record. He didn't charge any money for it. He just stood there and he would sign hundreds—maybe even a thousand—autographs every night. To me, it was unprecedented, but it was Cal's personal, private thing with the fans. Cal was running a fever by that last night because he hadn't gotten any sleep. He was trying to live a normal life. He was getting up with his kids and taking them to school. He was getting maybe an hour or two of sleep during the night—because of all the excitement and things going on—and got some kind of a bug, so he was really tired and he was run down. He told the Orioles, 'There will be no celebration during the game. I know Charles has figured out this thing of when it becomes official, but I will not tolerate any kind of stoppage of the game for any kind of ceremonies. After the game, you can do whatever you want, and I'll definitely be a part of it,' because Cal had that respect for the game. Nobody is bigger than the game. That had been instilled in him by his dad growing up in the game."

One particular attendee at Ripken's big game was the commander in chief himself, President Bill Clinton, who took his seat beside Jon Miller in the broadcast booth. Miller describes his presidential encounter behind the microphone: "I remember President Clinton came on the air with me in the fourth inning, and Cal came up while the president was on and went to three balls and no strikes. The pitch came in and boom! He hit it. He hit it a long way, and I knew it was going to be a home run the moment he hit it. I started getting real excited with my call, but the president had his own microphone, and he shouted me down. He's like, 'Go! Go! Yesss! Ha Ha!' and he started clapping and laughing. I remember hearing the highlight afterward and I was just sort of a disembodied voice. I sounded like I was in the back of the booth somewhere, and I was a little irritated by it because I thought this is an historic game and that's a home run that the guy hit himself and I'm basically not even on the call. Then I thought, 'No. That was perfect because the president of the United States is leading the cheering for Cal's big moment in his historic game.' I also thought, 'What am I going to do? Call the White House and say, 'Tell the president that I will never work with him again. He's got no booth etiquette?' That's probably not going to happen, so I just better allow myself to realize it made the call. In effect, the president of the United States led the cheering and made the call on Cal's home run."

Orchestrated by Charles Steinberg, the fans of Baltimore, and the iron man himself, Cal Ripken Jr., took his seat in baseball immortality. In a way only a hall of fame broadcaster could relive a hall of fame moment, Jon Miller relates, "The night of, the Orioles were ahead after four and a half innings. The music played and they put the rule up on the screen, and, at the moment of crescendo, the banner fell. It's official. It's an official game, and he actually has the record now. The fans would not stop cheering. Cal kept coming out of the dugout, waving to them and touching his heart. It was really kind of an impromptu celebration between the fans and Cal. The fans themselves stopped the game to celebrate with Cal. Nothing that was planned or put in motion by the club or anybody else. It just happened at that moment. Rafael Palmeiro and Bobby Bonilla were in the dugout and they kept telling Cal, 'You have to go out and make a lap around the field or we're never going to get this game started again.' Cal kept telling them, 'I can't do it. I'm exhausted. I would not make it around the field,' which is the ultimate irony, right? On the night he breaks the Iron Horse's record, he's exhausted and he can hardly move. They had said this to Cal a couple of times, and Cal kept waving them off, and then they just pushed him out of the dugout. 'You've got to go. We're never going to get the game restarted. You've got to go. You're the Iron Man. You can do it,' and that's what he did. I still kind of get emotional just remembering it. It was very beautiful. He just trotted around the field. When Cal got to the bullpen, Elrod Hendricks was the bullpen coach and a former catcher who had known Cal since he was a little kid when his dad was a minor league manager. They had a moment where Elrod reached over to shake his hand and congratulate him. Cal stopped his little trot at that point. It was very poignant, I thought. That's the way it all came down. The ceremony in the middle of the game that Cal refused to let happen, it happened anyway."

CAMDEN YARDS AFTER THE IRON MAN

Not long after Ripken's cementing himself in the halls of Cooperstown, Jon Miller assumed broadcasting duties with the San Francisco Giants, where he has called four World Series with the team (2002, 2010, 2012, 2014), which won three of them. Speaking about the team's 15-year absence from the postseason, which began years before the Iron Man hung up his cleats, Miller notes, "The sad part of Camden Yards, the team went downhill and people were not happy with ownership. All of a sudden, attendance went way down, and it was really sad because the Orioles were a leader in the game in terms of how it's done. How to build a ballpark and then how to fill a ballpark. To see the ballpark half empty or even two-thirds empty night after night was just really kind of a downer." Of course, just as streaks are meant to be broken, so are droughts. In 2012, thanks to the slugging power of Adam Jones and Chris Davis and 51 saves from team closer Jim Johnson, the Orioles returned to the postseason and defeated the Texas Rangers in the one-game wild card play-off. Although the O's lost to the Yankees in the deciding game of the Division Series, the Orioles came back in 2014 to capture their first American League East title since '97, and after sweeping the Detroit Tigers in the Division Series, were in turn swept by the Kansas City Royals in the ALCS. Having led the majors in home runs as a team for the past two seasons, the Orioles seem to have readapted to their confines and, with a winner on the field, the fans seem to have rediscovered their place as well. Miller signs off, once again, on Camden Yards, saying, "It's been exciting, to me, to see the ball club kind of rise up, especially this year (2014) or even two years ago when they got good and then stayed good until the very end. The crowds started coming back. I don't think it's still anything like what it was, but I think it's still one of the best parks in baseball and the fans still enjoy going there. With Buck Showalter and Dan Duquette, they've done some great things. Hopefully, they'll be able to keep that up for a while." With a starting rotation that includes Wei-Yin Chen, Bud Norris, and Chris Tillman, as well as a bullpen with set-up man Darren O'Day and closer Zach Britton, the Orioles have some arms to go with their bats, making another 15-year postseason absence as unlikely as a young rookie starting out today breaking Cal Ripken Jr.'s 2,632-game streak sometime during the 2032 season, with a (then) "over-the-hill" Camden Yards being used as a prototype for the newest Major League ballpark, to be built in downtown Nashville. Stay tuned.

PNC Park: Pittsburgh Pirates

PNC Park: "Without question, the most beautiful ballpark in the country."—Greg Brown
Photo courtesy of Dave Arrigo, Pittsburgh Pirates

When you walk up into that press box and into your broadcast booth and open the windows, whether it's for an afternoon game or an evening game, you look across to that skyline, river, and those bridges, and still have to pinch yourself because it's, without question, the most beautiful ballpark in the country.

—Greg Brown, Pittsburgh Pirates TV/radio
play-by-play broadcaster

$\mathcal{K}$nown throughout the world as the Steel City, Pittsburgh, Pennsylvania, is host to three U.S. rivers: the Ohio, the Monongahela, and the Allegheny. The latter two merge into the Ohio, leaving downtown Pittsburgh on one side of its banks, and for 30 years, the multisports facility Three Rivers Stadium on the other. Known as one of the "cookie-cutter" stadiums, Three Rivers hosted two World Series champions ('71 and '79 Pirates) and four Super Bowl champions ('74, '75, '78, and '79 Steelers). Although the '80s was a forgettable decade in the Steel City, in the early '90s the Pirates returned to baseball's postseason spotlight. The team reached the National League Championship Series thrice, during the '90, '91, and '92 seasons. When free agent Barry Bonds exited for San Francisco after the '92 season, a 21-year play-off drought began for Pirates fans. In fact, the franchise was in danger of relocating to another city before being bought out by Kevin McClatchy in 1996. With an "extended lease" on baseball life, a new stadium was announced, and the ground was broken for the Pirates' future home on April 7, 1999. Two playoff-less seasons later, Three Rivers Stadium was imploded on February 11, 2001, and the club's new home, the baseball-specific PNC Park, took its seat on the banks of the Allegheny. Providing a visual that couldn't be outdone by the best advertising agency, Pirates play-by-play broadcaster Greg Brown recalls his first impression of the team's new home: "I will never forget, in Spring of 2001, we left our last Grapefruit League game in Bradenton, Florida, and headed to Pittsburgh with the team. It was just about sunset when the other announcers, the players, and I arrived at PNC Park. We took a fairly long walk from the clubhouses to the dugouts and walked out for the first time. I don't know that a lot was being said. We all looked around, and all I could see were literally jaws dropped just in complete awe of what they saw. They couldn't believe in that moment what a jewel they had built."

With the press boxes located at the top of this "jewel," the broadcasters have the highest vantage point of anyone and a view better reserved for marriage proposals and political ads. Greg Brown reflects, "Most every time when a sponsor or fan walks into our TV booth, they look at the skyline, the Clemente bridges, and the river and say, 'Wow! What a view! This must be the greatest ballpark for you.' Please understand I don't mean this derogatory to the ballpark.

It should be the greatest ballpark for fans—and it is—but, from a broadcaster's perspective, it's one of the worst ballparks. We're so high up and so far back, to call a game is quite difficult." Soft infield fly balls can be mistaken for balls grounded off the plate, causing the broadcasters to glare over at first base rather than at the umpire with his fist already raised. While the fans are watching the game at home on their TVs, the broadcasters are watching the game on their own monitors, making the process seem more like a Pink Floyd album cover. Brown adds, "There's a fly ball to—what I believe off the bat is—deep left center field, and I see the left fielder camped out under, 10 steps in front of the warning track. It really throws off your depth perception. No matter how many games you've done as a play-by-play guy, it's still quite a challenge."

A GOLDEN TRIBUTE TO NUMBER 21

Undoubtedly one of the greatest players to ever put on a Pirates uniform, Roberto Clemente, a native Puerto Rican, played 18 seasons for Pittsburgh, leading them to two World Series titles, in 1960 and 1971. Over his hall of fame career, Clemente had 3,000 hits and won the National League MVP award in 1966, but he is perhaps better known for his defense than his bat, winning 12 straight gold gloves in right field. Sadly, Clemente perished in a plane crash in 1972 while attempting to deliver emergency aid to Nicaraguans suffering from a recent earthquake. Clemente's humanitarian efforts are recognized to this day by Major League Baseball, with an award in his name given every year to the player in the league with the greatest display of altruism outside the playing field.

At PNC Park, you don't have to look far to see the tribute the team pays to their beloved hero, as the bridge beyond the outfield walls bears his name. In fact, before home games, the Clemente Bridge is closed to vehicular traffic so fans can make their way across the Allegheny and into the park. The architects of PNC had Clemente on their mind when they designed the field's dimensions as well, building the right-field wall up to a height of 21 feet, the number the gold glover wore during his 18 years of patrolling the outfield. Although the porch in right field is a mere 320 feet from home plate, a home run isn't all but guaranteed to lefties. Greg Brown notes, "I remember saying to Brian Giles, the left-handed power hitter, 'That's gotta be fairly routine for you to try and pull that ball and hit home runs over the right-field wall.' He said, '320 sounds cheap, but you don't know how difficult it is to get lift and 21 feet high. It's not easy." Another area where a home run is not easy is "the north field notch" in left center field. At 389 feet, this nook in the left-field power alley is just 10 feet shy of straightaway center for the deepest part of the park honors. The broadcasters may not be the only ones with their depth perception tested by the park, as left center to straightaway left comes in a full 64 feet, culminating in a "literal" short porch. Though the left-field wall's six-foot height isn't in honor of former Pirate number 6, Smoky Burgess, Orlando Merced, or Rennie Stennett, it does allow the fans to interact with the outfielders, especially of the visiting team. The bleachers in left appear to be what Greg Brown refers to as a "band box," and the broadcaster describes the difficulty visiting left fielders face: "Fans have played a role because they can reach out and touch a player as they go back and try to catch a home run ball. They've battled left fielders who have tried to leap over that wall and rob home runs. The fielders have had to fight Pirates fans for those balls." All black-and-gold-wearing pillagers aside, PNC Park's asymmetrical dimensions help make it what Brown refers to as "the fairest ballpark in the National League."

WEATHER AND NATURE PLAYING THEIR PART

As can be expected in a city east of the Mississippi, baseball tends to play differently in summer than in the introductory months of April and May at PNC Park. With the thin, warm air in place, it becomes the pitcher's task to keep the ball down, especially to right-handed hitters. Greg Brown explains, "The weather comes into play at PNC Park unlike any other yard at different parts of the year. You just never know how that ball is going to play. There comes a stretch, for whatever reason, the ball seems to jump out in right center field. It has to do with the time of year, the climate, and density of the air. If you look at it from home plate or the press box, you say to yourself, 'There's no way that's ever going to happen. That's a fluke,' but it does. There are times when you see a right-hander poke that ball over the right-field wall. It's so unpredictable and that's another reason why it's such a great yard."

The placement of PNC Park with respect to the Allegheny River gives the hitters a target for which to display their power. Although a splashdown into the water may not be as commonplace as in San Francisco's McCovey Cove, the atmosphere in Pittsburgh is quite similar. Greg Brown notes, "There have been dozens of home runs hit on the fly in the bay in San Francisco, but the Allegheny is the most difficult poke of all. There have been maybe a dozen that have bounced in off the river walks, but only twice in the history of the ballpark (Darryl Ward, Garrett Jones) has a player hit it on the fly. We have people in boats out there—as they do in the bay in San Francisco—ready to catch home run balls, especially during batting practice." Though Barry Bonds himself would have hit a few into the Allegheny had he not departed for San Francisco, his playoff torch was finally passed some 21 seasons later to 2013 National League MVP Andrew McCutchen, who, Greg Brown says, is "the antithesis of Bonds."

HOISTING THE JOLLY ROGER

In a sport of traditions dating back to the 19th century, a relatively new and winning one has started to catch fire in Pittsburgh thanks to broadcaster Greg Brown, who relates: "About 15 years ago, Bob Walk suggested I come up with a signature phrase after a Pirates victory in the traditions of Lanny Frattare with his, 'There was Nooooo doubt about it', and Bob Prince before him with his iconic, 'We had 'em all the way.' I told Bob that when I was a young man working in the Pirates front office back in the early '80s, I had suggested to our Stadium Operations VP that we take a page out of the Cubs playbook and fly a flag over the stadium after each win. My thought was since pirates fly the skull and crossbones after capturing a ship, we should fly those colors after a Pirates victory so that everyone would know—throughout the following day—the Buccos had won just by looking toward the sky above the stadium. The response I got from that VP was 'get out of my office, kid.' When I relayed that story to Bob, he suggested something like, 'Hoist the flag!' I played with that awhile and finally decided on 'Raise the Jolly Roger!' They have a small flagpole by the batter's eye in center field, where, after each win, a fan would be selected to hoist the skull and crossbones and raise the Jolly Roger. They leave it up overnight, and take it down the next day before batting practice. It got little attention for about a decade as the team continued its struggles and didn't win a whole lot of games, but, over the last few seasons, it's caught on beyond my wildest dreams. Flags, T-shirts, banners, signs proclaiming, 'RTJR,' 'Raise It,' 'Stay calm and Raise it,' 'Raise the Jolly Roger!' are everywhere! It has become a Pirates fan's rallying cry all over the country. Other fans and I have tried to campaign to convince Pirates management to get a gigantic flagpole out in right field, so people who go to work the following morning in Pittsburgh and didn't know whether the team won or lost the night before, if they look across the river, they could easily see if the colors were flying."

THINGS GET "WILD" AT PNC PARK

On October 1, 2013, after 21 years of early vacations, the Pirates played past game 162, hosting the Cincinnati Reds in a one-game, wild card playoff.

Arriving well before the game's opening pitch, Greg Brown found he wasn't the only early bird at PNC Park. Describing the atmosphere, Brown says, "It was almost tribal. I took a walk around the circumference inside the park before the gates opened and looked down at this sea of black. Andrew McCutchen, Michael McKenry, and A. J. Burnett had tweeted out to the fans to wear black and they responded like nothing I've ever seen in my life. They're out there chanting, 'Let's go Bucs' an hour and a half before the gates even opened. You couldn't move on the sidewalks or in the streets outside the ballpark. It was a mob scene. Then, as the introductions started, Andrew McCutchen got announced. He made his way from the dugout to the third base foul line, and he was hopping around. He pointed a 360-degree point and beat his chest, telling the fans how much he loved them as much as they loved him. I couldn't control my emotions. I had tears. It was unbelievable." Although it seemed as if a baseball lifetime had already passed, there was still the actual game to be played.

Known in more recent years as a football and hockey town, the city of Pittsburgh made it clear what sport reigned supreme that night. Brown adds, "I've had hardcore Pittsburgh fans tell me it was the single greatest event that they've ever been to, and they've been to Super Bowls, AFC Championships, and Stanley Cups. My broadcast partner John Wehner, who grew up a Pittsburgh sports fan, said the same thing. He said, 'I've been to playoff games for all the sports, and nothing compared to that night.' For those that were there, they understand it. For those that weren't, they think they understood it by watching or listening to it, but, unless you were there, that was a surreal moment that will probably never be duplicated. It was unlike anything anybody in that ballpark had been a part of in their entire lives, and that's pretty special."

As could be expected from a sea of black-shirt-wearing Pirates fans, the crowd had an impact on the game's outcome. Out past left field are the "left-field loonies," a group of 2,000 fans who wear wild hats and *Looney Tunes* shirts to Pirates games. During the bottom of the second inning of the wild card game, the left-field loonies contributed to Cincinnati starter Johnny Cueto's unraveling. Having already given up a home run to Marlon Byrd, Cueto faced Pirates catcher Russell Martin. Greg Brown relates the events that took place next: "In unison, they started chanting, 'Cueto, Cueto.' Just then, he drops the ball on the return toss from the catcher, and it was probably coincidental. There are those who believe it had nothing to do with what happened next, but when he dropped the ball, the chants started louder and louder. Russell Martin stepped out of the batter's box, looked toward his dugout, and actually laughed. I don't believe what happened next was coincidental. I believe that Cueto wanted to quickly throw a strike to stop the chant, and what he did was throw a quick strike to Russell Martin that he could hit out of the ballpark." Martin's home run was the first of two he hit that night, as the Pirates went on to win the game 6–2, earning them a spot in the Division Series against the eventual National League champion St. Louis Cardinals. Looking back on that historic day, on which playoff baseball returned to Pittsburgh, Greg Brown concludes, "The fans played a big role in that ball game. That'll live on in Pirates lore for the rest of our lives."

PNC PARK TODAY

Although it didn't take another 21 years for the team to play past game 162, the '14 Pirates—thanks to the MVP-caliber numbers of Andrew McCutchen, the speed of fellow outfielder Starling Marte, and the starting pitching of Edinson Volquez—made it back to the wild card game at PNC Park against the San Francisco Giants. Although the stands were "blacked out" once again, Giants starter Madison Bumgarner began his phenomenal 2014 postseason pitching run with a complete game shutout of the Bucs. Bumgarner won three more games that postseason, including two in the 2014 World Series, to cement his MVP honors. With two straight playoff appearances and a black-clad fan base standing with arms open to any and every free agent and current player, the glory of Pirates baseball has returned to the Steel City.

Petco Park: San Diego Padres

Psychologically at least, especially for the guys who play there 81 times, it has been more fair. It's not an easy home run park. It's not a hitter's park, but it's a fair park.

—Ted Leitner, San Diego Padres radio play-by-play broadcaster

$\mathcal{O}$ver the years, the city of San Diego, California, has practically been symbolized by the arcing image of a killer whale named Shamu. Considering that San Diego's Sea World has been around for 50 years, coupled with the fact that killer whales only live an average of nine years in captivity, the original Shamu has probably been replaced enough times to make even the producers of *Lassie* scratch their heads. In recent years, a documentary film titled *Blackfish* has shed a very negative spotlight on what has been San Diego's most famous attraction for the past half century, causing its stock to lose great value and redirecting would-be tourists to other local attractions. Unfortunately (except for the animals, whose life spans will multiply by an average of six times), this long-standing symbol of the San Diego community may eventually wash away with the tide, leaving an aqua blue hole in what is known as America's Finest City. Throughout most of this 50-year love roller coaster between San Diego and Sea World, Major League Baseball's San Diego Padres, along with their beloved hall of fame mascot the San Diego Chicken, have entertained the city both on and off the field. Arriving in the "corridor to Mexico" as an expansion team in 1969, the San Diego Padres played 35 seasons inside Qualcomm Stadium, which to this day still hosts the NFL's San Diego Chargers. During their Qualcomm years, the Padres qualified for two World Series, losing to Sparky Anderson's Detroit Tigers in 1984 and to the 125-game-winning New York Yankees in 1998. In fact, thanks to postseason qualifications in 1996 and 1998, plans for a new ballpark in the downtown area were solidified. Finally, on April 8, 2004, after an almost decade-long dispute between the team and what San Diego Padres play-by-play broadcaster Ted Leitner refers to as "the committee on no for everything," the San Diego Padres took the field in their new stadium with an old feel, Petco Park.

APRIL 8, 2004: MOST MEMORABLE RIGHT OUT OF THE GATES

Currently in its 11th season ('14), Petco Park has been host to some of baseball's biggest milestones, including San Francisco Giants' Barry Bonds's record-tying 755th home run on August 4, 2007, and fellow Giant Tim Lincecum's first career no-hitter on July 13, 2013. Petco Park has seen some feats by the boys in white as well. Former Cubs/Braves/Dodgers/Padres and hall of fame pitcher Greg Maddux earned career win 350 on May 10, 2008, in Petco, and Padres reliever Trevor Hoffman passed all-time saves leader Lee Smith with career save 479 on September 24, 2006. Hoffman was later dethroned by New York Yankees closer Mariano Rivera, on September 19, 2011. All these achievements took place on his watch as the voice of the Padres, but Ted Leitner would still say not one of them compares to game 1 at Petco.

With the defending 2003 National League West division champion San Francisco Giants coming in to christen the new park, the Padres sent their ace, David Wells, to the mound against Dustin Hermanson. Both starters excelled, allowing only one earned run over a combined 13 innings. As was the case so many hundreds of times with a ninth-inning lead, Trevor Hoffman was called in from the Padres bullpen to secure the victory. With two outs, Giants second baseman Ray Durham doubled to what the Padres found to be a much more expansive left center field, and San Francisco took a 2–1 lead going into the bottom of the ninth. With one out in the Padres' ninth, third baseman Sean Burroughs singled home Khalil Greene to tie it up and send it to bonus baseball in Petco's grand opening. A go-ahead home run by the Giants' Marquis Grissom in the 10th left the Padres, once again, with just three outs. After spending two of those outs on a Jay Payton strikeout and a Ramon Hernandez fly out, the Padres, with two men on, sent pinch hitter Miguel Ojeda to the plate. Ojeda's ground rule double to what must have seemed to Marquis Grissom an endless center field plated Kerry Robinson and left Khalil Greene on third as the potential winning run. Though Greene's positioning on third as opposed to second precludes any suggestion of deja vu, Sean Burroughs once again singled home the Padres shortstop, this time for the game winner, making the "Friars" 1–0 in their new home.

Though the third act of this inaugural game had a Hollywood ending, it was the setting and backstory that made April 8, 2004, so special for Leitner, who comments, "It wasn't so much the impact and the import of the game. It was the fact that we'd gone through years of delay; 14 to 16 lawsuits by those in San Diego fighting against having a ballpark, if you can imagine. This went on for years and years to where the metal frame—the skeleton—sat there rotting, and it cost the ballpark millions. It cost the owner John Moores millions. We had a time where we thought this may never get done. Maybe the money's not there, this thing is scrapped, and that big frame looks like the Worlds Fair in 1964, where you could see the old exhibits rotting around Shea Stadium for the next 40 years. Finally, not one of these lawsuits was found to have merit by a lower or appellate court and they started construction again. So this thing was finally there. It was gorgeous. It was gleaming. We had the ballpark, and I really believe there's no other game that I remember where I sat there thinking, 'Pinch me. Pinch me. This is incredible.' All those delays and now here we are. Capacity crowd, the Giants, and I really believe no other game is in my mind more than that one. Nobody in baseball history—that I know of—has ever gone through that. I was so happy to be doing a game in that place. That will always be my number one."

LARRY LUCCHINO THROWS IT BACK ONCE AGAIN

Before coming over to Boston in 2001, Red Sox president and CEO Larry Lucchino helped to revolutionize baseball's ballparks and the way we see them today. Working alongside Janet Marie Smith, the "go-to human being at construction and reconstruction of ballparks," Lucchino, as owner/president of the Baltimore Orioles, helped bring to fruition Oriole Park at Camden Yards in 1992. Built alongside a giant warehouse building that ran the length of right field and then some, Camden Yards was the first of several ballparks to take a longstanding piece of the community and incorporate it into the park itself. Ted Leitner adds, "Larry Lucchino should be in the hall of fame someday. He's the one that put Camden Yards online and built that ballpark when he was an executive with the Orioles, and the idea was to make it look like it has history on its very first day of existence and it worked. Larry would say, 'It's not a stadium. It's a ballpark,' and there's a difference." In 1994 Lucchino took his ballpark expertise to the opposite coast and became owner/president of the San Diego Padres, where his first order of business was to bring the city a new "ballpark." By the time Sean Burroughs's two clutch singles on April 8, 2004, brought the Padres a win on day one, Lucchino was already "silencing his r's" back in bean town. However, the former owner/president's dream for downtown San Diego still had his signature stamped all over left field in the form of the Western Metal Supply Company. Speaking about this feature and its incorporation into the ballpark, Leitner notes, "The Western Metal Supply Company was this building from the early part of the 20th century that was sitting there on this land, and they basically built the ballpark around it, which may be cart before the horse, but it just makes it different from any ballpark in America. The only thing close is Camden Yards. It seems to fit so well. It looks like they put the Western Metal building in *after* they built the ballpark to give it that old flavor. There's nothing else like that. Not that that makes a ballpark better or greater than the others. It's just different." Jutting out over the left-field corner like Juliet's balcony, Western Metal Supply, while providing Petco Park with a feel of early 20th-century San Diego, includes three tiers of seats along its façade and another atop its roof, which gives pull hitters somewhat of a target. Leitner comments, "It's not just the building and its age being there and fitting so well. It's the idea of hitting in the first row, second row, third row, on to the roof. That's a pretty fair poke for a home run." When considering Petco's dimensions, the Western Metal Supply area probably seems like the *only* fair poke from a hitter's perspective.

"BRINGING THEM IN" TO MAKE IT "FAIR"

Prior to the '13 season, Petco's dimensions were among the deepest in baseball, with the right and left center power alleys extending as far as 402 feet. Adding the Pacific Ocean's marine layer to the mix, Petco Park is arguably the hitter-unfriendliest ballpark in baseball during night games. Leitner adds, "The prior planning and due diligence to build a ballpark like that is amazing, but I don't think they thought the marine layer would be so extreme that you hit a ball, and it would just bring it down. It would hold it and bring it down to the point that the ballpark played like 'old' Yankee Stadium with 457, 461 feet in centerfield. Before players adapted to it, they were affected by it. The home run hitters the Padres had—Ryan Klesko and Phil Nevin—those guys would just kill the ball and couldn't get it out. Maybe on a Sunday afternoon where it was warmer, but at night, even during batting practice, you could tell around 5:00, and then at 7:00, you had no chance. I asked if it was home-run proof, and one player said, 'It's baseball proof.' From a management standpoint, they finally decided it should play fair. If a guy really hits the hell out of the ball, it should be a home run, and it's not in this ballpark, so they adjusted that by bringing the fences in." So as not to make the outfield walls look like the world's largest furrowed eyebrow, Petco Park's power alleys were brought in from 402 to 390 feet, making straightaway center's 396 the park's new summit. Though the Padres couldn't get the city's approval to remove the ocean, and with it the marine layer, to begin the '13 season, Petco went from 29th in the league in combined home runs per game (1.35) in the '12 season to 22nd (1.80).

Perhaps if Sea World's tanks were as expansive as Petco Park's outfield, *Blackfish* would have never been filmed. Still, as one of the National League West's pitcher-friendly ballparks, Petco doesn't give the Padres nearly the advantage it would in divisions like the American League East. Ted Leitner notes, "In our division, you have Colorado—which is a huge outfield to cover defensively—and Petco was obviously the same way. Dodger Stadium is a pitcher's park. That whole division, except for Arizona, which is a launching pad with that altitude, was a pitcher's division. The Padres literally had to start drafting, developing, trading, and signing free agents to play to their ballpark. When they played Tampa in the first couple of years of the ballpark, Carl Crawford came in, and they saw him patrolling in the outfield. They thought, 'That's what we need. We've gotta get faster guys like that to cover this outfield and to play in Colorado,' and they did. The ballpark changed their entire approach to how to build a baseball team." In 2011 the Padres called up Cameron Maybin from Tucson, who, in four seasons in Petco's outfield, has fielded .986 or better. Having gloves like that to cover the greater part of their outfield, pitchers have found a comfort level in Petco Park they likely wouldn't find elsewhere. Leitner adds, "We've had pitchers. There's no question about it. In '05 and '06, we won the division with pitching. You'd pick up a guy, and he'd lower his ERA at least a half a point, knowing if a guy hits the hell out of a ball, it ain't going out here." Padre pitchers like Jake Peavy—who won the National League Cy Young Award in 2007 with a 2.54 ERA, 19 wins, and 240 strikeouts—have seen their numbers swell when retreating from under the marine layer and going off to other teams. During his four years in hitter-friendly U.S. Cellular Field and Fenway Park, Peavy's ERA dipped below 4.00 once ('12). Peavy, starting 2014 with the defending World Series champion Boston Red Sox and playing with the eventual World Series champion San Francisco Giants the second half of the season, deflated his ballooned 4.72 ERA from Boston down to an astonishing 2.17 over 12 games in the City by the Bay.

A DAY AT THE BEACH

While San Diego has not played game 163 since the Colorado Rockies' "Rocktober" back in '07, Petco Park has quickly become one of San Diego's most popular venues. From the Western Metal Supply roots to the beach-sand area behind the center-field wall, the planning, lobbying, litigating, and approval-gathering that have gone into this $456 million "ballpark" has brought fans and Larry Lucchino the happy ending they sought for nearly a decade. While Sea World may one day resemble the "Worlds Fair–like" skeleton that once occupied downtown San Diego, Petco Park, as well as its Chicken, will stand for non-captive-killer-whale lifetimes to come.

· 22 ·

Progressive Field: Cleveland Indians

Progressive Field's Left Field Wall: "It's not the Green Monster, but it'll take away some home runs, no question." — Jim Rosenhaus
Photo courtesy of the Cleveland Indians

It's just amazing to think that they sold out that many games in a row (455) for a stadium that seats over 40,000.

—Jim Rosenhaus, Cleveland Indians radio broadcaster

$\mathcal{T}$he last time the city of Cleveland, Ohio, won a championship in any of its three major sports was 1964, when the Cleveland Browns shut out Johnny Unitas's Baltimore Colts 27–0 in the NFL Championship Game. Going back even further, on the baseball side of Cleveland there hasn't been a championship since 1948, when the Indians beat the Boston Braves 4–2 in the World Series. Since then the Indians have been to and lost three World Series; Cleveland Browns owner Art Modell moved the team to Baltimore; and Cleveland Cavaliers forward LeBron James took his talents to South Beach, Florida, only to come back home four years later. Needless to say, many faithful hearts have been tortured—if not broken—in the Forest City. Back in the days at their old home of Cleveland Municipal Stadium, the Indians were mired in their own mediocrity, finishing fifth or worse in the division 13 straight seasons. Things were so bad for "the Tribe" that Oscar-winning screenwriter David S. Ward selected the team as the protagonists for his sports satire film *Major League*. Though the film didn't inspire the real-life Cleveland Indians—at least for a few more years—plans were made to give the team and the fans a new home. Opened on April 4, 1994, with the name Jacobs Field, Cleveland's Progressive Field turned the baseball world's attention back to the Indians, who wrote their own script worthy of the silver screen.

Between June 12, 1995, and April 4, 2001, the Indians, thanks to a booming Cleveland economy and the departure of their inter-sport cousin to Baltimore, sold out 455 games in a row, a record that would eventually be overtaken by the Boston Red Sox and their 6,000-seat-quicker-to-capacity Fenway Park. Over that stretch, the Indians appeared in all but one postseason, making the World Series twice in a three-year span. Cleveland Indians radio broadcaster Jim Rosenhaus describes the tribe's formula for continued success: "The teams were great. There was one year where it was all stars at every position. You're looking at Thome, Alomar, Vizquel, Lofton, Albert Belle, another Alomar behind the plate. You had some of the best players in the game. Teams that, offensively, were just tremendous and scored runs like crazy, so it was a perfect storm." Contributing on the other side of the ball during the Indians' heyday was a pitching rotation that included Orel Hershiser, Charles Nagy, "Black" Jack McDowell, Bartolo Colon, Dwight "Doc" Gooden, and Dennis "El Presidente" Martinez. Hershiser, better known for his '88 season with the Los Angeles Dodgers, during which he won the National League Cy Young and World Series MVP and broke Don Drysdale's scoreless inning streak, managed to pitch the Indians to two American League pennants, in 1995 and 1997, the latter bringing the Tribe within two outs of their first World Series championship in 50 years. The Tribe qualified for the postseason five straight years during their 455 straight standing-room-only contests, something they had never done before and haven't done since. In honor of the Indians' once record sellout streak, the team unveiled the number "455" with the word "Fans" beneath it to accompany the other numbers of Indian greats whose names are immortalized above the stadium's second level beyond right field.

THE FOREST CITY EVEN HAS A LAKE

Built within blocks of the mammoth Lake Erie, Progressive Field attracts the weather of Cleveland, which at the onset of the regular season proves quite different than most any other ballpark. Jim Rosenhaus adds, "Clearly weather, early in the season, is a factor. My first year in 2007, our home opener was against Seattle, and we had gotten to the fifth inning. It had snowed intermittently throughout. Mike Hargrove came out to argue that the conditions were unplayable, and the game was called one out from being official. It didn't stop snowing for three days. The whole series was postponed. Then the next series with the Angels had to be moved to Milwaukee to the indoor Miller Park to get the series in." Even without there being actual snow on the ground, Cleveland's cold front affects the games that make it beyond the postponement barrier and are actually played. Often the Indians will return from spring training in Arizona and the lake will still be frozen. Discussing the effects of a chilled Lake Erie, Jim Rosenhaus says, "In the early season, when it's cold, that wind's blowing in off the lake and that'll kill hitters." *That* is the invisible canopy of icy air, which, when it meets a towering fly ball, slows its momentum like an arresting wire on a jet landing on an aircraft carrier, and that's only if the batter even *wants* to hit the ball. Rosenhaus explains, "If Justin Masterson has his sinker running and it's a cold day, hitters don't want any part of that. If they don't get the sweet spot on it, it's going to hurt." Of course, baseball's regular season trespasses onto three calendar ones, so Lake Erie tends to have an opposite effect once the weather gets warm. Rosenhaus adds, "Overall, it's a better pitcher's than hitter's park, but there's times, when the summer finally gets there, that the wind blows out." Luckily for the pitchers, left field to left center, with depths ranging from 325 to 370 feet, also includes a 19-foot wall. Rosenhaus claims, "It's not the Green Monster, but it'll take away some home runs, no question." Indians pitchers since 2000 have ranked in the top third of the American League for home runs allowed in all but three seasons, so Lake Erie doesn't seem to factor in as much over the summer as it does in April. In October 2007, however, the lake, along with a few of its transient residents, factored in much more than the visiting New York Yankees would have wanted.

OCTOBER 5, 2007: THE "BUG GAME"

After throttling their opponent 12–3 in the opening game of the 2007 American League Division Series, the Indians trailed the Yankees and starting pitcher Andy Pettitte 1–0 late in game 2. Though he was not yet a play-by-play broadcaster, Rosenhaus recalls the "eerie" events that were about to take place at Progressive Field: "We're sitting in the booth, and here it is. Game 2 of the series with a chance to go up 2–0 going back to New York. It was a real tight game. They brought in Joba Chamberlain and these midges (bugs) started coming in off the lake because it was unusually warm that night. Bug spray doesn't bother them. It attracted them almost, and the Yankees are out there spraying bug spray on themselves and it wasn't working. Chamberlain, really struggling, wild pitched in the tying run, and the Indians won in extra innings. I'll never forget it because it was just so bizarre." Adding to the bizarreness of the situation was the bugs' bias toward the players, as Indians starter Fausto Carmona (now known as Roberto Hernandez) played right through the madness, pitching nine full innings and allowing just one earned run. Perhaps one of Rosenhaus's favorite moments related to the game occurred the next morning in New York, as he read the local papers' collectively perplexed take on nature's untimely intervention the night before. The Indians went on to win the Division Series 3–1, but then lost three straight series–clinching games (including game 7) in the 2007 American League Championship Series to the eventual World Series champion Boston Red Sox. The tribe did not return to the postseason for another six seasons.

TODAY'S "NEW LOOK" BALL CLUB

Perhaps feeling their sleeve being tugged by the ongoing grudge match between litigious Native Americans and the NFL's Washington Redskins, the Cleveland Indians have gradually strayed from their 53-year-old, feather-sporting "Chief Wahoo" logo, opting for the simple yet throwback "block C" formerly used in team batting practice. During the '13 season, the logo wasn't the only throwback-themed element of this mixed-generation Indians squad. Having been thrown under the biggest bus the Massachusetts Bay Transportation Authority had to offer following the Red Sox collapse of 2011, two-time World Series-winning manager Terry Francona was relieved from his one-year stint as an ESPN television analyst and hired as the new Indians manager. On the players' side of the personnel makeover came the team's newest designated hitter, 42-year-old journeyman and former American League MVP Jason Giambi. Together, Giambi and Francona gave Indians fans something to "Wahoo" about, helping the team to an astonishing 21–6 over the final month of the regular season.

In the second year of the new playoff format implemented by (then) MLB commissioner Bud Selig, the two non-division-winning teams with the best records from each league qualified for a one-game playoff to determine who would move on to play in the Division Series. With 10 games to go, the Indians found themselves implausible candidates for game 163; however, their resilience in game 157 proved the contrary. The game was his most memorable inside Progressive Field as a broadcaster, and Jim Rosenhaus recalls the experience: "Last year, on September 24th, the Indians are going down the stretch, trying to make the playoffs. The Tribe won 10 straight to end the season and needed every one of them. In the middle of that, they are playing the White Sox in a three-game series. On the 24th, the Indians were leading most of the game. The White Sox had a pair of solo home runs in the top of the ninth to take the lead. They did it off Chris Perez, who developed a love/hate relationship with the fans. The booing when he left the game was unbelievable. It looked like that game, and, potentially, Cleveland's playoff hopes had been lost. The team was down by a run in the bottom of the ninth, and Michael Brantley gets on base to keep the game going. Jason Giambi pinch hits a two-run home run to win the game. It's because it was Giambi. He meant everything to this team from a morale standpoint throughout the year and came up with many huge base hits, but never like this. It was unbelievable. Here's this 42-year-old guy—still going—who hits the biggest home run of the season, and it was just pandemonium. I'll never forget it. The air was out of the balloon after the top of the ninth, and he hits a home run and it just changed everything." Punching the 10th "W" on their wild card ticket five days later, the Indians hosted the Tampa Bay Rays for Progressive Field's 82nd home game of the '13 season. The Rays shut out the Tribe 4–0 and moved on to face the eventual World Series champion Boston Red Sox. Despite the team's playoff run ending just as quickly as it began, Francona was named American League Manager of the Year for the first time in his storied career.

20 YEARS AND COUNTING

In the follow-up season to their brief playoff run of 2013, the Indians celebrated 20 years at Progressive Field. Since the park opened back in 1994,

19 other Major League teams have christened new homes; however, many would argue that the Indians cut the ribbon just yesterday. Considering the place was sold out for nearly six seasons in a row, one wouldn't expect such an immaculate setting, especially in a facility two decades old. Praising the park's maintenance in its relatively old age, Jim Rosenhaus comments, "What you hear most from other broadcasters who come in from out of town, fans who maybe see it for the first time, or fans who come all the time, they're surprised it's 20 years old because it's held up so well." Something else that has held up very well in Cleveland is the dedication of Indians fan John Adams, also known as "Big Chief Boom Boom." Since 1973 the Cleveland resident has hauled his bass drum into the bleachers of both Progressive Field and Cleveland Municipal Stadium and rallied the fans during Indians games more than 3,300 times. Even though one could spot a fan from the opposite side of Cleveland Municipal Stadium as long as his shirt didn't match the color of the wooden seats back in the *Major League* film-inspiring days, Adams still stands out among the Tribe's faithful, even at the high-capacity Progressive Field. While it's more likely his bass drum will make it into the hall of fame in Cooperstown than into the Rock and Roll one just a few blocks down the road, it's safe to say that Adams, along with the biblical midges of Pharaoh Joba Chamberlain's downfall in 2007, have a standing invitation among the faithful in Cleveland, whatever the setting.

· 23 ·

Rogers Centre: Toronto Blue Jays

You'll see a different sort of look from visiting teams on a pretty routine basis when they're in Toronto because they don't want their older players or their star players out there on the turf that much.

—Mike Wilner, Toronto Blue Jays radio
play-by-play broadcaster

*N*orth of the Canadian border, the Montreal Expos were Major League Baseball's lone representative for eight years. Predating interleague play, this meant only the National League players had the unfair disadvantage of having to adjust for the exchange rate on hotel room service and gratuity, convert the playing depth from meters to feet, and get two minutes less sleep after a 7:07 local time start. After years of "wooing" Major League Baseball, Toronto was awarded its own franchise, the Blue Jays, thus forcing American League players to update their passport photos and metric conversion charts as well. Perhaps surprised by being granted an expansion team, Toronto was unprepared in 1977 when the Blue Jays began playing baseball, as there was no new stadium built or even talk about development. For 12 seasons the Blue Jays played their home games inside the retrofitted-for-baseball Exhibition Stadium, which from a batter's perspective looked more like an unfinished, turf-lined NASCAR track than a ballpark. Inside their temporary home, the Blue Jays made the playoffs once, in 1985, where they lost to the underdog and eventual World Series champion Kansas City Royals. A year later ground was broken in downtown Toronto for the future home of the team, a dome that proved to be a baseball pioneer in the field of engineering and architecture. Three years and $500 million later, the (then named) Skydome opened, on June 5, 1989, with more than 50,000 in attendance.

163

U.S. Cellular Field in Chicago had taught the world that a stadium can be erected in 711 days for $150 million, as long as the owners don't mind shelling out another $100 million to fill in the gaps over the next 6,570 days. Perhaps foreseeing that the exchange rate would shift in their favor two decades later, Toronto chose to take its time and "splurge" by including the world's first "functioning" retractable roof. Covering eight acres and rising 282 feet, Rogers Centre's roof introduced the world to "convertible facility" baseball. Blue Jays radio play-by-play broadcaster Mike Wilner, who grew up in Toronto, describes the retractable roof: "For its time, it was revolutionary. I remember being in there on June 5, 1989—when we were getting ready for the first game ever there—and being blown away by it. You still catch visiting players who have never been there before checking it out and seeing how it works when it opens and closes during the game. It is a really cool thing to see. Here in Toronto, we forget how revolutionary it is."

Made up of four panels—three of which move—the roof takes 20 minutes to close, which in its 26-season history has only delayed the Blue Jays twice. Mike Wilner notes, "There are never any weather issues. There have been—I think—two delays in the history of the building. There was a five minute rain delay in the first series ever played at Skydome in 1989 when the Brewers were in there. It started to rain, and they started to close the roof. I guess they were a little late starting, and there was a moment in time, where, because of the configuration of the roof, it was only raining on home plate. The entire building was dry, but the batter, catcher, and umpire were getting soaked, so Richie Garcia called the delay. There was another delay because they closed the roof late, and it was a crazy, humid night. All the humidity got trapped in the building, and there was a crazy insect infestation on the field. They couldn't get the air conditioning going to get the building cooled down enough, so the building was full of bugs. They had to delay the game so they could open the roof up and let all the bugs out. I believe it's the only insect infestation delay in Major League Baseball history."

Since Rogers Centre opened, five other teams have built similar stadiums based on that prototype, improving and evolving the design. Chase Field includes opening and closing window panels; at Safeco Field, when the roof is fully extended the park is still unenclosed. Milner adds, "In those ballparks, even when the roof is closed, it feels like more of an outdoor experience. In the Rogers Centre, when the roof is closed, it feels like THE ROOF IS CLOSED, and it feels a little bit darker even though it really isn't." Regardless of whose idea it was first in this Ivy League–caliber science fair, the goal of uninterrupted baseball is achieved inside the Rogers Centre. Wilner notes, "You know you're going to play a game. You don't have to make a decision where, 'It looks like it's going to rain at 8:15. What am I going to do with my starting pitcher? I don't want to waste him for two and a half innings.' That helps out a lot."

IT "SEAMS" THE TURF'S UP

All of Major League Baseball's teams, except the Toronto Blue Jays and the Tampa Bay Rays, have now opted for natural grass rather than artificial turf. The Blue Jays have a better excuse than the Rays for declining their annual invitation from the North American Union of Sod Layers: cohabitation with the Canadian Football League's Argonauts. The turf inside the Rogers Centre provides an interesting experience for *any* visiting team. When asked what makes the Rogers Centre unique from the other 29 ballparks in baseball, Wilner responds, "The turf. It's one of only two Major League ballparks left that has artificial turf. They use AstroTurf, and it's different from the turf at Tropicana Field because at 'The Trop,' they have a dirt infield, and, at Rogers Centre, they don't. They're just dirt cutouts on the infield. A retractable roof kind of plays with that, too, because when the roof's open and the sun's shining and it's hot, the turf gets really springy; more so than usual. Even in a neutral environment, it's bouncier than natural grass is, and that means there'll be a lot more ground rule doubles, infield choppers, and balls bouncing out of play or over the outfielder's head. It's the only park where the ball's going to hit a seam and take a crazy hop. With natural grass, there aren't any seams, so nobody has to worry about that. That's not in play anywhere else in the major leagues." While the retractable roof leaves the Blue Jays' rescheduling calendar blank 81 times a year, the turf's presence leaves a proverbial red mark all over visiting managers' schedules where the letters "TOR" appear. When asked how visiting players and managers adapt to Rogers Centre as opposed to other ballparks, Mike Wilner responds, "I'm not sure they do. The San Francisco Giants came in for interleague play last year and were just eaten alive by the turf. The middle infielders could not time the ground balls. Stuff was flying by them. It was crazy. The Blue Jays blew them out in consecutive games. I think the Blue Jays scored six or seven runs in the first inning of the first game because the Giants were just lost, and, a lot of times, you just can't get used to it. The speed. The bounces. Outfielders, you'll see, will back off a lot more balls on the turf than they would on natural grass. They're not going to try for that great diving catch, because you know that if it squirts by you, nothing is going to stop it, and it'll roll all the way to the wall. A little dying quail Texas leaguer that's falling in, you're going to sprint, but then you're going to pull up well before you would on grass, because, if you don't and you don't get it, it bounces over your head for a triple, at least. Those are things they have to get used to, and it's managers, too. Visiting managers manage around the turf a lot. You'll see a visiting team pull its guys off the turf every once in a while. When the Texas Rangers were in town this year, Adrian Beltre DH'd all three games because they didn't want to get him on the turf. Mike Trout DH'd a game for the Angels in a four game series because they didn't want him on the turf the whole time."

Unfortunately for the outfielders inside Rogers Centre, their "pulling up" duties include running *out* on a fly ball as well. Wilner adds, "The warning track really isn't a warning track. It's just a different color of the same stuff. It sits apart from what a warning track is supposed to be. In footing, it's supposed to change, right? You go from grass to dirt. All an outfielder at Rogers Centre does is go from green artificial turf to orange artificial turf, and there's really no way for him to know where he is without looking down." While nobody really knows whether it was a shortage of crushed red brick or turf-cutting utility knives in the Toronto area that led to the omission of a dirt warning track, the outfield walls themselves add to the park's uniqueness, as well as its advisory count. Wilner notes, "There are video boards in left and right center, and it hurts a lot more to try to make a jump or leaping catch into those video boards than it does into the fence. There are chain link fences in left and right field so a lot of the fans can see into the bullpen, and that's a little bit different, too. We saw Josh Reddick climb up the chain link and take a home run away, so that's an aspect that doesn't play in a lot of ballparks." Although its construction preceded the ballpark boom of the early '90s, Rogers Centre still includes the high-wall standard, which, coupled with the eight-foot "norm" of the newer parks, reduces its appearance on the "Web Gem" portion of ESPN's *Baseball Tonight*. However, on August 12, 2012, the Blue Jays' Rajai Davis, in addition to his five RBIs that made the offensive difference against the Yankees, used his defense to take a couple away as well. Wilner recalls, "In my memory, there's only been one player to ever go over the wall to make a leaping catch without using that chain link fence and that was Rajai Davis. It was awesome. It was a high fly ball, so he was able to time it, and he actually ran back to a point about eight feet away from the wall, stopped, and then took a running leap up and made a spectacular catch." While no longer having to time his leaps on 10-foot walls, Rajai Davis, currently in a Detroit Tigers uniform, is now charged with the center fielder's task of patrolling Comerica Park's 420-foot depth.

WILNER'S BEST BEHIND THE MIC AND IN THE SEATS

Having grown up in Toronto, Mike Wilner has seen the team through their peak as a fan and their dregs as a broadcaster. He has many memories from

Rogers Centre, one of which doesn't even include *live* baseball. Wilner states, "The most memorable game I saw at Rogers Centre was a game that wasn't even played there. I was in attendance for game 6 of the '92 World Series on the Jumbotron from Atlanta with 20 or 30,000 of my closest friends. I was in attendance live for game 1 of 1993 when we played the Phillies, but game 6 of 1992—the extra inning game—just watching it on the scoreboard at the dome was just amazing. The Blue Jays won the World Series for the very first time, and that was just an incredible moment. An incredible night. Going out and just parading through the streets of downtown Toronto afterwards. It was unbelievable, and, yet, very strange that that's the greatest game I've ever witnessed as a fan at Rogers Centre." The following year, the Blue Jays won their second consecutive World Series title, defeating the Philadelphia Phillies, thanks to the pitching of Jack Morris and Dave Stewart and the hitting of Paul Molitor, Ed Sprague, and John Olerud. One hit in particular, Joe Carter's walk-off home run in game 6, was only the second World Series–clinching home run in baseball history.

Along with regular season games for the Blue Jays, Mike Wilner has also been in the broadcast booth for other great contests hosted by Rogers Centre, including the 2009 World Baseball Classic. Wilner states, "The greatest game I ever *called* at Rogers Centre actually wasn't a Major League Baseball game. It was the 2009 World Baseball Classic. Canada and the United States. I was the play-by-play guy for the game all nine innings. The atmosphere in the dome. It was a sellout. It was an unbelievable game that went back and forth, and Canada was down 6-4 going into the ninth. Russ Martin hit a home run, and then Joey Votto doubled and got the tying run to second base for Justin Morneau and Jason Bay. They couldn't seal the deal, but, just being there and getting a chance to call that game. That excitement. That's how I felt in there when the Blue Jays were winning World Series. When there were 50,000 fans in there every night. When it was routine to have a sellout. It had brought it all back for that one game."

While not behind the mic doing the play-by-play, Wilner has been in the Blue Jays' broadcast booth for some memorable pitching performances, including a Brandon Morrow near no-hitter. With a struck-out batter being almost as synchronized as the crowd's performance of "Okay, Blue Jays" during the seventh-inning stretch, Morrow's 17 Ks helped him to what Wilner regards as "one of the greatest games ever pitched in baseball history." Going eight and two-thirds innings without giving up a hit, Morrow's no-hitter was lost in the ninth on an infield single. Recovering, Morrow struck out the final batter to defeat the Tampa Bay Rays. Wilner adds, "That was a pretty amazing game. One of the best I've ever seen."

Though neither dons the maple-leaf-eared uniform today, Roy Halladay and A. J. Burnett were a tandem igniting hope in Blue Jays fans for three seasons. Speaking about Burnett, Wilner says, "He and Halladay were supposed to team up to give the Blue Jays their return to the playoffs. A. J. was sort of Halladay's protégé. Halladay took him under his wing, and then Burnett left." While Halladay stuck around one more season in 2009, he and his "protégé" faced each other early in the season, with the Blue Jays leading the division and the Yankees taking water in their lungs at 15–16. Wilner notes, "The Blue Jays were, at the time in 2009, off to one of the best starts in club history. That was the year they would go 27–14 to start the season. It was near the end of that the Yankees came in, and Burnett pitched against Halladay." Living up to the mentor/apprentice dynamic, Halladay out-pitched Burnett, going the distance and winning the game 5–1. Though the game took place on May 12, hardly one-fifth into the season, Wilner regarded the contest as a "phenomenal game" and "a great playoff atmosphere." The roles eventually reversed for the two teams, and the Yankees finished both the regular and postseason on top, winning an unprecedented 27th World Series title.

While the Halladays and Burnetts have moved on to other mounds, imports like knuckleballer R. A. Dickey and former "good guy" Mark Buehrle have helped the Blue Jays back over the .500 mark. Coupled with sluggers like Jose Bautista and Edwin Encarnacion—who have helped Toronto finish in baseball's top five in home runs for five of the last six seasons—hitting imports Colby Rasmus and Jose Reyes kept Toronto a legitimate playoff contender for virtually the entire '14 season. Though they may have run out of runway before taking off in 2014, it wouldn't be too surprising to soon see the Rogers Centre roof open, once again, over a playoff-qualifying Blue Jays squad.

• *24* •

Safeco Field: Seattle Mariners

Safeco Field's Supreme Court: "There were about 34,000 people with yellow T-shirts. To see this from my vantage point in our radio booth was just an overwhelming sight." —Rick Rizzs
Photo courtesy of Ben VanHouten

I think the first thing you're going to notice about Safeco Field is that it's a ballpark. It has all the elements of a great ballpark. It's fan friendly. It's fair for the players. It's great for the fans, and, yet, it also incorporates what it's like to live and be a part of the Pacific Northwest, which is one of the most beautiful parts of this country, so I think it's the best ballpark in baseball. They did it right, and there's a great feel and look to it.

—Rick Rizzs, Seattle Mariners radio play-by-play broadcaster

In the Pacific Northwest, there's so much moisture even a rolling stone gathers moss. Seattle, the metropolitan epicenter of this region, although it pales by comparison to its rural neighbors, catches much of that moisture all year. Since a baseball player's contract does not include the postman's oath of "neither rain nor sleet nor dark of night . . . ," something had to be done to not only invite baseball to the Emerald City but have it endure there as well. The Kingdome, a rain/sleet/dark-free Seattle landmark, hosted both MLB's Seattle Mariners and the NFL's Seattle Seahawks for years. Four fallen ceiling tiles, a player's strike, and $517 million later, Seattle achieved the improbable, moving the Mariners into Safeco Field, an open-air ballpark with a state-of-the-art, 22-million pound umbrella.

Opened on July 15, 1999, Safeco Field features a very unique, nine-acre, retractable roof that shields the fans and field of play from the falling rain while still keeping the park unenclosed. Seattle Mariners play-by-play radio broadcaster Rick Rizzs describes the park's unique feature: "I think that's one of the greatest features of Safeco Field. We needed a roof. For years, we played indoors and had to because of all of the rain in April and May and later on in the year in September. So they had to have something, but, when the roof is extended and comes across the field, it's still open. It's still an open-air ballpark because there's trusses that hold up the roof on the railroad tracks, so the elements are still there. The wind. The cold. The heat. It's still an outdoor stadium that's covered, so it's very unique in that way." While Safeco's unenclosed, unsealed structure would probably not pass in the field of water filtration or as a potential site for the Washington State Center for Disease Control, you won't hear Mariners fans complaining about the "elements" this configuration allows them to absorb. Rick Rizzs continues, "You're gonna notice downtown off to your left. One of the other things that you're gonna notice—you're not gonna see it, but you're gonna hear it—you're gonna hear the sounds of the train beyond the right-field stands; of the commuter trains going in and out of the King Street Station, and that's a very unique sound. It brings back great memories for me because of where I grew up on the south side of Chicago. There was a train track not too far away, and you could still hear the wail of the whistle of the engine, so you're gonna hear that.

You're gonna hear seagulls. You're gonna *see* seagulls come in off of Elliott Bay, where the wind will come in. You're gonna smell the fact that we're pretty much right on the water there." Although not a fishmonger's throw from world-famous Pike Place Market, Safeco Field's proximity to the water helps it haul in the ever-so-fresh smell of the Pacific Ocean and its former residents, many of which will likely be found on the menu at the Ricenroll sushi and sake stand in section 137. One rainy city feature Safeco's unenclosed canopy *doesn't* completely detain is the fog. Luckily for the fans, in the event an untimely fog rolls in off Elliott Bay during a game, the 11,425-square-foot LED screen (largest in the majors) above the right-field bleachers, which could probably stop a tsunami, refracts these prodigal cumuli like a pocky pier and stays the hand of the umpire calling for a stoppage of play. With all these technological marvels keeping things from coming *in* to the ballpark, Mariners management, after the '12 season, began to make changes to help things (like a home run ball) go *out* of it.

While Petco Park, Citi Field, and Marlins Park have outpurchased Safeco as far as sod is concerned, it's the quality—not the quantity—that matters. Rizzs comments, "It's one of the best playing surfaces in the game. Bob Christofferson is our head groundskeeper, and his crew—Leo, Tim, and all the guys—they do a great job, so if you're a player at Safeco Field, you've gotta appreciate the surface that you're playing on." In its inaugural season, Safeco Field was considered one of the pitcher-friendliest ballparks in the majors. Its left center depth of 390 feet and counting was one of the largest in baseball. Adding to the equation, the foul territory down the base lines, although not nearly as expansive as that of the O.co Coliseum, allowed corner infielders to chase down a considerable number of foul balls, depriving hitters of would-have-been second chances in Globe Life Park in Arlington or Yankee Stadium. At the end of the '12 season, the fences were brought in from right center all the way to left field just before the foul pole. Although not too dramatic in right or straightaway center field, the changes in left center were the biggest, bringing the fences in as much as 17 feet. Since the areas behind the sections with the greatest change are occupied by bullpens and an eating concourse, no additional seats were added to Safeco's capacity. In defense of Seattle Mariners management, who seem more like baseball-hoarding, crotchety next-door neighbors, this alteration was for the benefit of the fans, making Safeco Field a more hitter-friendly ballpark. Rizzs adds, "It's your home park, and you've gotta make it feel at home. It's a fair ballpark. It was a pretty good pitcher's ballpark, and now the fences have come in, but you've still gotta hit it out for a home run. It's still fair. If you hit it in the gaps, a line drive is a base hit, whether it's Safeco Field, or Yankee Stadium, or the old Metrodome, or wherever. A left-handed hitter will get it out to right field.

Right-handed hitters, if they hit the ball the other way, it's gonna go out, so it's fair for the pitchers. It's fair for the hitters. I think it just plays well for the players and especially for the fans who come watch these guys play." The results of the changes in field depth were almost instantaneous; in the following season ('13), the Mariners were second only to the Camden Yards–aided Baltimore Orioles for most home runs in all of baseball. With the addition of Seattle's third "C" (Cobain, Coffee, and) Robinson Cano, the Mariners may just unseat the O's for the long-ball title. "Rounding out the field," Safeco is best described by Rick Rizzs as a *fair* ballpark; however, from a visiting player's standpoint, one could bring the fences in to Little League regulation, and it still wouldn't impede Safeco Field's feature that is most *un*fair to hitters: "King" Felix Hernandez.

THE KING'S COURT IS IN SESSION

Currently in his ninth season ('14) as a starter, Felix Hernandez has surpassed the 200-strikeout plateau in each of the last six years, and though averaging only 13.33 wins a season, has a career ERA of just 3.08. In fact, since 2010 Hernandez has had 45 starts of eight innings or more allowing one earned run or less, more than any other pitcher in all of baseball. Rizzs notes, "Every time that Felix Hernandez pitches, this guy just turns up the crowd. He turns up the electricity at the ballpark. He's a treasure for us. We love the kid. He's the king." As a king will have his subjects, one of Safeco Field's most unique elements is "the King's Court," an entire section located near the left-field foul pole dedicated to the Venezuelan right-hander. To obtain a seat in the King's Court, a fan buys a specially priced ticket, which includes a yellow "King's Court" T-shirt and a giant yellow "K" card, representing the pitcher's propensity to strike out hitters. Living up to his title, on August 15, 2012, King Felix pitched the first perfect game in Mariners' history, striking out 12 batters and out-dueling Tampa Bay starter Jeremy Hellickson for a 1–0 victory. Rick Rizzs calls Hernandez's perfect game "one of the most phenomenal pitching performances that I have ever seen." In honor of King Felix's gem, the Mariners and their fans held a special session for their ace's next start, calling it the "Supreme Court." Everyone in attendance was given a yellow T-shirt that read, "King of Perfection" with a silhouette of Fernandez's arms raised in celebration. Rick Rizzs describes what was easily one of his most memorable moments as a broadcaster: "I think there were about 34,000 people with yellow T-shirts, and just to see this site from my vantage point up in our radio booth; to see this sea of yellow honoring this young man who has accomplished so much in a Mariner's uniform. It was just an overwhelming site to see the city, the organization, and the fans give this kid the hug they gave him on that day. It was a beautiful site." Hernandez pitched 7⅔ innings, giving up only one run and striking out five in a 5–1 victory over the Cleveland Indians. Serving as the proverbial bailiff in King Felix's Supreme Court, Seattle manager Eric Wedge took the ball from the right-hander, causing the 39,204 fans in attendance to "all rise" as court was adjourned.

ALL ALONE UP THERE IN THE PACIFIC NORTHWEST

Since Major League Baseball hasn't made its way up the Oregon Trail from Silicon Valley or through the badlands of South Dakota, Seattle stands as baseball's hub for the Pacific Northwest and sometimes finds itself with the unlikeliest of fans. Rick Rizzs relates how far his broadcasting voice echoes: "There's always a lot of people that come up to us. People that are shut in. The elderly folks that have no chance of getting out to the ballpark and we're their one connection. We can take 'em to the ballpark, wherever they are listening to the ballgame. I'll never forget many years ago, I got a letter from these two elderly ladies from Montana. They said, 'We really enjoy listening to your broadcast, but the only way we can get it in Montana is if we get in our pickup truck, drive up to the top of the mountain, turn the radio on, and then we can get reception and listen to the games.' Every night, from that point on for the rest of the year, I thought about these two elderly women sitting in a pickup truck at the top of a mountain somewhere in Montana. We were the connection to them and Mariners baseball." It's likely that pickup truck made its way up the mountain many more times during the '01 season.

SEPTEMBER 19, 2001: A DIVISION WIN FOR THE AGES

Although a year to forget for America, 2001 was one to remember for the Mariners, whose lineup consisted of hitters like Edgar Martinez, John Olerud, MVP runner-up Bret Boone, and MVP and Rookie of the Year winner Ichiro Suzuki. On September 10 the Mariners were an astonishing 64 games over .500 and 17 games ahead of an Oakland A's team that would still end up winning 102 games. With Seattle on its way to breaking the American League record for most wins in a season, 9/11 occurred, and baseball shut down for a week. As soon as play resumed, the Mariners shut out the Anaheim Angels 4–0 on September 19, clinching the American League West Division for the first time in four years. Considering the division title was practically inevitable by the All-Star break, the Mariners' postgame celebration was one for the country more than for themselves. Rizzs notes, "When the Mariners clinched, it wasn't a wild, raucous celebration. We had a great crowd at Safeco Field. They were on their way to winning a record 116 games to tie the 1906 Chicago Cubs. It was a celebration on the field that was respectful to what was going on in the country. The guys went out to the mound led by Lou Piniella. I'll never forget it. Mark McLemore and Mike Cameron had the American flag. It was just a celebration of our resolve as a country, as a people; to come back from these terrible events, and it was a way for baseball to galvanize the country. It was a time for the people of Seattle to, at the time, rally around the ball club and the success they had, but also be very respectful to the lives that had been lost in the World Trade Center and those brave firemen and policemen who tried to go in and help those people. It was just one of the most incredible days that I've ever seen at a ballpark." Two weeks later, the Mariners won their 116th regular season game, tying the '06 Chicago Cubs.

THERE'S NO PLACE LIKE HOME . . . IN THE EMERALD CITY

Safeco Field opened nearly five years (to the day) after four tiles fell from the Kingdome ceiling onto seats that would have been occupied by fans only hours later. With the '94 season players' strike occurring just a month after, Mariners ownership had the fall and winter to assess the situation. While a bandage was applied to the Kingdome, the state legislature got to work on finding ways to fund a new stadium, which included a surcharge on rental cars. Why not, right? If the voters don't want to be taxed, syphon money from tourists, who will probably never go to a game because they're too busy hiking Mount Rainier. Even though restaurant patrons in the Seattle area had to scratch their heads over the added "food and beverage" tax on their bills, and Mariners ticket holders found a fourth added charge (after the LET, online purchasing fee, and "just for the hell of it" fee) to their price of admission, the owners have been gracious hosts in this new ballpark. Since their magical 2001 season, the Mariners have not returned to the playoffs, and attendance numbers have gradually decreased, yet the team continues to supply the fans with the best and most enjoyable amenities they can. Despite the team finishing last in the AL West and attendance being the fourth lowest in the American League, a $15 million renovation took place after the '12 season, which included the addition of the "fog bouncing" MarinersVision, the second-largest scoreboard in all of sports (first is AT&T Stadium, Dallas). Although it's unlikely low attendance numbers will be rewarded after *every* season, it's clear baseball is here to stay in the Emerald City. The Ichi-roll may be a thing of the past in Safeco

Field, but Edgar's Tacos are as much a stadium fixture as its indoor plumbing. Sounding off on Safeco Field—from its inception to today—Rick Rizzs adds, "I love it there. I really do. It's a great ballpark. They did such a great job of going to all the other ballparks—the old ones and the newer ones—and to incorporate what they wanted in Seattle, and they built a ballpark. Great sight lines and it just feels like baseball, and I'm so glad they did that because we shared the Kingdome, but now we have the best of both worlds. We've got the best ballpark in the country, and, right across the street is Century Link Field, home of the (2013) Super Bowl Champion Seahawks. It's going to be a monument to the game up there in the Northwest for a long time."

Target Field: Minnesota Twins

Target Field: "A 12-acre ballpark on an 8-acre site."—Dick Bremer
Photo courtesy of Brace Hemmelgarn, Minnesota Twins

I think to fully appreciate Target Field, you have to have been to a Twins game at the Metrodome. Everything that Target Field is, the Metrodome was not in terms of a fan experience at a baseball game.

—Dick Bremer, Minnesota Twins TV play-by-play broadcaster

 eparated by the mighty Mississippi River, Minnesota's twin cities of Minneapolis and St. Paul, although fraternal at best, have a sibling rivalry. Whether it be culture, food, or nightlife, the citizens of one always state their case against those of the other about which is better. Though the result may be a "push" across the boards in most categories, sports reign supreme in Minneapolis. With the exception of the NHL's Minnesota Wild, all of Minnesota's representing sports teams reside on the Minneapolis side of the Mississippi. Two of these, Major League Baseball's Minnesota Twins and the NFL's Minnesota Vikings, even shared a home in the colossal Hubert H. Humphrey Metrodome for nearly three decades. A close proximity to Canada, coupled with the many lakes that have given it the nickname Land of 10,000 Lakes, has given Minnesota its fair share of unfriendly weather over time, a large reason the Twins and Vikings played their games in the "comfort" of the Metrodome for so many years. In May 2006, plans for an outdoor ballpark in the Minneapolis area were approved, causing a collective "scratching of the head" for baseball enthusiasts across the country, as well as in the Gopher State.

Many likely argued the need for a retractable roof, which has been the recent trend for baseball in areas known to have harsher climates. Unfortunately, the area designated for Minnesota's new ballpark wouldn't allow for such a venture, unless the league agreed to shrink the dimensions to little-league regulation just for Twins home games and balloon the American League's offensive stats even more. Longtime Twins TV play-by-play broadcaster Dick Bremer comments, "It would have created an architectural dilemma if they had tried to have a retractable roof because there was really no place for it to retract. You still have to have some place to support the roof when it's not over the field, and there really wasn't much of a place to do that." Nearly four years after the stadium was announced—and despite the harsh yet reasonably anticipated conditions for holding a baseball contest—the Twins opened their new home of Target Field on a cloudy April 12, 2010, with 38,000 plus fans in attendance enjoying the warm (at least by Minnesota's spring standards) 65-degree weather. To a Minneapolis pilot doing a flyby before touching down, the sight from above may have looked like a giant removed the seal from an 8.5-acre can of navy blue, red, and white peanuts, because open-air professional baseball was once again taking place in Minnesota. The first "thumbs-up" may have been given by Dick Bremer himself, who says, "Personally, I'm glad they didn't put a roof on it. I don't mind the rain delays and I sat through a lot of them last year (2013), but I spent 28 years in an indoor ballpark. I enjoy the fresh air." Bremer's sentiments have been shared by many in Minnesota, but not all.

A COMFORTABLE PLACE TO PLAY *AND* WATCH

Though some may argue that building a $545 million, open-air ballpark in Minnesota ranks up there with Euro-Disney and the XFL (X-treme Football League), attendance at Twins games was over three million in the first two years of play at Target Field. A major reason for this, aside from the Twins winning the division in the park's inaugural year, is team management's going to great lengths to provide both the fans and the players with as comfortable an atmosphere as they had experienced in 28 seasons at the Metrodome. Dick Bremer comments on the stadium amenities specific to the fans of Minnesota; "What the Twins have done is allow for the fact that it's going to be cold in Minnesota, and so, for the players, they had a heating element put under the playing surface to improve the playing conditions, and, to some degree, the playing temperature. There are radiant heaters throughout the ballpark, so, in those times when it's pretty cold outside, for the fans, they have an area where they can retreat and get warm. There's a lot of protected areas for fans to go if it does rain. The first couple of years, the Twins were very fortunate. They didn't have many weather problems. Last year (2013), there was a little bit of everything. Rain, snow, sleet. In some ways, the fans appreciated Target Field *more* last year." Much of the fans' appreciation stems from being transitioned out of a dome setting, whose only benefit, according to Dick Bremer, was that "it had a roof on it and was relatively stable temperature wise." Bremer adds, "The Twins had some success in the Metrodome, but at Target Field, it's very fan friendly in terms of proximity to the field. You experience the game on a much more intimate level at Target Field, I think, than at most ballparks. Certainly a lot more so than you did at the Metrodome." Sequestering the subterranean field heaters from the discussion, when asking Twins hitters versus Twins pitchers, Target Field may be a little one-sided when it comes to player approval.

As already mentioned in an article in "Obvious Weekly," the weather in Minnesota is colder during the first couple of months of the regular season. Cooler air slows down the balls hit in the air: a luxury for pitchers, a nightmare for hitters. Without the thick, cool outside air, the Metrodome yielded many more home runs than Target Field ever will. Now, considering baseball is played throughout the warm summer months, one might think the ball will start to travel better once short sleeves and sunglasses are back in fashion;

however, Target Field's structure brings with it a whole different element of nature. Bremer comments, "One thing that's unique about Target Field is they put a 12-acre ballpark on an 8-acre site. It really is an architectural marvel. They had a very small parcel of land to work with, and, as a result, it's a very vertical ballpark. Because of that, when the wind gets in there, it sometimes has a hard time getting out. It's one of the adjustments the players have had to make in the ballpark." As if the wind needed any help garnering would-have-been-a-home-run-in-the-Metrodome balls, the outfield wall beyond right center to the right-field foul pole stands a daunting 23 feet high. Needless to say, player stats changed noticeably when the Twins took their game outdoors. Bremer continues, "I think for the players, in terms of baseball, it was a tremendous adjustment. Target Field is much more of a pitcher's ballpark. Within the stable environment of the Metrodome, the ball carried pretty consistently to all areas of the field, and, now, Target Field is much more like a conventional ballpark. There are areas where the ball travels well, and there are other areas where it doesn't seem to travel well at all." This "adjustment" proved to be difficult for even the best Twins hitters.

AN MVP WITHOUT MVP NUMBERS ANYMORE

Without question, catcher/first baseman Joe Mauer has been the face of the Twins franchise for several years. The six-time all-star has won five silver sluggers, three gold gloves, and, in his final year at the Metrodome, batted an astonishing .365 to earn the American League Most Valuable Player award in 2009. Though his numbers inside Target Field haven't been poor by Major League standards, they certainly haven't been the .365 with an on-base percentage of .444 and slugging percentage of .587 he trophied during his MVP campaign. About Joe's decline in stats, Bremer notes, "Mauer has dealt with the transition more than anybody else. When he won the AL MVP in 2009, he only played five months and he had 28 homers, which were a career high; 20 of them went to center and left field—the opposite field—and it is very rare at Target Field anyone will hit an opposite field home run. That's how much of a pitcher's ballpark it is, and, as a result, the balls Joe hit that cleared the fence by maybe two or three rows at the Metrodome have gone to the warning track and that's it. He's the same hitter that he was. There's no decrease in power so much as the dimensions in the ballpark are different." Currently in his 11th season, Mauer's behind-the-plate duties have been turned over to Kurt Suzuki, as the former MVP has "transitioned" over

to first base and DH. Luckily for Mauer, the team added some power going into the inaugural season at Target Field that *no* ballpark could contain.

AUGUST 17, 2010: JIM THOME
CHRISTENS TARGET FIELD'S WALK-OFF TROT

Over his 22-year career, Jim Thome accumulated 612 home runs with six
teams, two of which he played for in an encore setting (Phillies, Indians).
Ranking seventh all time in round-trippers, Thome came over to the Twins
after a one-year stint with the Dodgers. On August 17, 2010, with the division
rival (and Thome's former team) Chicago White Sox in town and a 23-foot
right-field wall practically screaming for the left-hander to pull one, Target
Field was primed for its first taste of dramatics courtesy of the "Thomenator."
Dick Bremer gives his account of the contest, the most memorable game at
the young Target Field to that point: "It was the first year of the ballpark, and
the Twins and White Sox were involved in a big American League Central
pennant race. The White Sox were in town, and, in extra innings, they got
a run in the top of the 10th. It was late enough in the season where it would
have been a big, big win for whoever won the ballgame. Jim Thome stepped
up and hit one of the longest home runs at Target Field. It was the first walk-
off home run of the new ballpark, and it really turned the American League
Central race around. It took a game that was lost for the Twins and turned it
into a win. The Twins never looked back and the White Sox never really recovered from that loss." Thome's "big fly" resume includes home runs off 30
different teams, 403 different pitchers, and in 38 different ballparks. Although
he would eventually hit another 31 home runs in a career well worthy of the
hall of fame, including one more walk-off in 2012 with Philadelphia, Thome's
blast-off of Chicago's Matt Thornton in August 2010 was, according to him,
"one of the big moments of his career." Bremer adds, "It really crystallized
his place in Twins history. I can't think of anybody who played for the Twins
for such a short period of time—in Jim's case, it was a year and a half—who
was so universally admired and revered by Twins fans. I think, in some way,
Jim's presence on the team, though very short, reminded Twins fans a lot of
Harmon Killebrew. Both were very genuine people. Gentlemanly kind to
fans. Wonderful to be around. Twins fans hadn't really had someone like that
since Harmon Killebrew. Jim kind of reminded them of what Harmon was
like during his heyday in the '60s and '70s." Though the Twins won't likely
be unveiling any statue of Jim Thome to go along with the bronze parade
outside Target Field, ranging from Kirby Puckett to "T.C. The Bear," career
home run 580 will resonate within the ballpark for many years to come.

TARGET FIELD TODAY

The only division race between the Twins and White Sox today is to see which one doesn't end up in the American League Central's "cellar spot," yet Target Field still provides Twins fans with all the amenities they could ask for. Several high-quality restaurants throughout the stadium, named after former Twins like Rod Carew, Kirby Puckett, and Kent Hrbek—as well as rooftop-deck seating—give the fans plenty of options for watching the game besides the torn-ticket approach. Another of Target Field's links to the past lies just beyond the center-field wall in the form of a 46-foot-high display of "Minnie and Paul," the team's first logo when they came over from the Washington Senators in 1961. With the caricatured giants representing the cities of Minneapolis and St. Paul on their respective sides of the Mississippi, the display comes to life electronically with the two shaking hands every time a Twins player hits a home run. Although the bulbs may have burned out with greater frequency inside the Metrodome, current hitters like Brian Dozier and Oswaldo Arcia are known to wear out Minnie and Paul's wrists on occasion. On the opposite side of the ball, pitchers coming to Minnesota are seeing the favorable circumstances Target Field offers them. Current team ace and former New York Yankee Phil Hughes has seen his ERA shrink from 2013's 5.19 with the Yankees to 3.52, as well as surpassing his innings pitched by 64 (209.2) and strikeouts by 65 (186). The reviews may be mixed when asking pitchers like Hughes or hitters like Mauer about Target Field, but Dick Bremer's endorsement after 28 years spent recycling oxygen in an 8-by-10 box says it all for outdoor baseball in the Twin Cities: "They did a lot of things right there. I'll tell you that."

· 26 ·

Tropicana Field: Tampa Bay Rays

Tropicana Field Catwalk (Ring) System: "You shouldn't be playing Major League Baseball popping things up and hitting things."—Dave Wills
Photo courtesy of Steven Kovich/Tampa Bay Rays

The speed of the game is a little quicker with the Astroturf infield. The ball takes more of a skip off the dirt after the hop off the Astroturf, so you have to be ready to react to that.

—Dave Wills, Tampa Bay Rays radio broadcaster

You're always inside, the ball can hit the catwalks, and the lights are not where they would normally be in an outdoor ballpark; those are the things you deal with that are different than anywhere else. Otherwise, it plays like a baseball field.

—Charlie Slowes, former Tampa Bay "Devil" Rays
radio broadcaster

$\mathcal{B}$aseball has been played on a professional level in the Tampa Bay/St. Petersburg area of west central Florida for over 100 years, when teams like the Chicago Cubs and St. Louis Browns would conduct their spring training operations prior to the regular season.

Today, half of Major League Baseball calls Tampa and its surrounding towns home from mid-February through opening day. With so much of a presence in Cigar City, it's baffling that representation by an actual Major League team itself eluded the area for so long. In fact, the city of St. Petersburg, in poker terms, "showed its hand" in 1990 by building the Suncoast Dome. In 1992 Tampa came as close as it ever had to acquiring a team when San Francisco Giants owner Bob Lurie agreed to sell the team to a Florida group when the city wouldn't agree to help fund the construction of a new stadium. For the Tampa Bay and San Francisco sides of the country, it really was "A Tale of Two Cities." Current Washington Nationals and former Tampa Bay "Devil" Rays broadcaster Charlie Slowes describes the team that never was: "To get a team, a ball needed to be in place. It (Suncoast Dome) was designed by HOK but not necessarily with people of a Major League Baseball team because it was built in the hopes of getting the Giants or another team to move. It looked like they almost had San Francisco moving, when, at the last minute, Peter Magowan, one of the Giants owners, stepped in and they eventually built AT&T Park and that team didn't come. They were printing T-shirts and sweatshirts that said, 'Tampa Bay Giants.' Vince Naimoli was going to be the owner. MLB stepped in and this was back when they still had individual league presidents. Former big league first baseman and later a Yankees broadcaster Bill White was the National League president. He told Magowan, 'One of the owners needs to step up. We don't want to lose San Francisco.' They didn't, and then the next expansion, it was the Marlins and Rockies in 1993. They thought they were going to get the team in Tampa Bay and they gave the other team to Wayne Huizenga and the Marlins, so they had this empty ballpark sitting there. It was used for other events, including the Tampa Bay Lightning playing hockey there for several years." As if getting passed over in 1991 for a town just as prone to hurricanes and *not* under the cover of a dome wasn't enough, a city full of Salvation Army and Goodwill stores overstocked with fan apparel for a ghost team really had to rub salt into the wounds of would-be baseball fans in Tampa. Finally, two and a half years after Lurie's near sale, another announcement was made by Major League Baseball, in March 1995, this one making Tampa Bay the proverbial prettiest girl in the room. Finally, on March 31, 1998, after an open house lasting eight years, Tropicana Field opened its doors to 45,000 plus fans, as the (then named) Devil Rays took the field for the first time ever against the Detroit Tigers.

When it comes to uniqueness, Tropicana Field stands out from the other 29 ballparks in Major League Baseball in two areas: what stands above and what lies below. For a fan approaching to take in a game of baseball, Tropicana Field looks more like the world's largest indoor pool, as its fixed roof—the only one in Major League Baseball—towers above the field like a half-inflated hot air balloon. With its construction taking place roughly around the same time the Rogers Centre was attempting the first "functional" retractable roof, Tropicana Field would have to settle for the "dome" feel like in Houston, Minneapolis, and Seattle, which, unbeknownst to everyone, would become a thing of the past by the time a Tampa Bay team would actually play in it. Not open to the night sky—as an open air ballpark would be—or with a steel-truss-woven, retractable roof, Tropicana Field has a ceiling idiosyncrasy no longer found anyplace else. Current radio play-by-play broadcaster for the Rays Dave Wills describes the roof's effect on the players: "The dome plays differently day versus night. It's a white colored, Teflon that you can still see—when it's daytime—the sun shining on top of it. At night, it's a little different when it comes to watching the baseball up against it from a standpoint of lights and everything like that. I think our lighting system at Tropicana Field is very good. I spent a lot of time with the White Sox before I came to Tropicana Field, and when I would watch Devil Rays games on TV, I thought the place was dark and drab and played brutal on television, but then I went in there for my first interview and the lights weren't even on. It looked brighter in person than on TV. Playing with that light-colored roof, you're not used to following the baseball. Most of these new domes are darker-colored domes. It's not as bad as it was at the Metrodome or maybe the Kingdome, but you really have to keep your eye on the baseball when it's up against the dome on pop-ups. It's tough, especially for infielders, who seem to have the toughest times for opposing teams. They're accustomed to taking their eye off the ball to find out where they are, and then they have a tough time of picking the ball back up under the roof." While fielders struggle trying to find a red seam on a white ball soaring across a white backdrop, it's likely they prefer the optical challenge to fielding a grounder at "the Trop." Charlie Slowes describes the uniqueness of the infield: "When I was hired by the Rays, I was actually hired in September of 1997, and, when I flew in for a press conference, they introduced us in the press box at Tropicana Field. There was no baseball field in place, yet. They didn't have grass down because they weren't using it for baseball. They had to figure out what kind of field it was going to be, and they eventually went with artificial field turf with infield dirt, which no one had done in a long, long time. The players initially didn't like that because you'd get a true hop off the grass and then they'd get a different hop off the dirt, so these balls were like rockets coming at them. Since there was cement under the dirt, they couldn't keep it soft. When you water something, the water underneath helps keep it soft. It would just dry out so quickly because they were in a facility that had air conditioning on 100% of the time. They didn't like that, but they've never gone away from it. They've put down new versions of artificial turf, but they still have a dirt infield so it looks more to the fans like a real field. That's what they were going for."

Though the patent for the term "home field advantage" probably belongs to some pigskin broadcaster from the late nineteenth century, one could make the case for Tropicana Field as its "term photo" in the dictionary. Dave Wills explains, "For the other teams coming into town for the first time, there's no other place in Major League Baseball where they can have an experience like they do when they come to Tropicana Field. It takes maybe a game—game and a half—for them to get acclimated to the roof. Get acclimated to the turf and the dirt. It should really seriously be a home field advantage for the Tampa Bay Rays. They have Astroturf in only one other field. If you're not in the American League East, what we've noticed is there are a lot of teams that are grouped with the Tampa/Toronto combination on their schedule. The Rays have adjusted, obviously within the first couple of games of any particular year, and have been able to use that to their advantage by winning close to 50 games per year at home the last handful of seasons. Any team that wins 50 games at home, you're doing what you need to do to play in the postseason. That's one of the reasons why the Rays have been to the postseason four of the last six years." Playing into the Rays' success is their having been accustomed to the unique roof above them and all the ground rules that come with its structural nuances.

A FOUR-RING CIRCUS

Being Major League Baseball's only fixed roof facility, Tropicana Field and its unique dome shape bring with them catwalks, or in Tampa Bay lingo, "rings," which stand high, watching over the field like a stagehand in an opera house. Like a group of teamsters "on break" playing a pickup game inside a crate-filled warehouse, certain rules had to be made inside Tropicana Field for when the ball would come into contact with these rings. Dave Wills explains both the schematics and the rule book "appendix T" at "the Trop": "The highest catwalk is the A ring. Then it goes down to the B ring, the C ring, and the D ring. The C ring and the D ring really only come into play during home runs. If you hit the C ring or the D ring in the outfield, it's a home run. I think that rule came into play right after one of the first few games. Frank Thomas of the White Sox hit one of them, and I don't think they were really clear on what they were supposed to do. I think the umpire decided, 'If that ball was going to be a home run, it should be a home run.' The C ring and the D ring are the two lowest catwalks at Tropicana Field. Now, if it hits the A ring or B ring in foul territory, it's a dead ball. If it hits the A ring or B ring in fair territory, the ball's in play, so you have to play caroms off the rings. John McDonald, when he was with the Toronto Blue Jays, made an incredible catch on a ball that went up there in one of the rings and rattled around for a little bit before it came down and he made the catch. We've also seen times where it gets up there and gets stuck and it's a double. One day, it almost cost us a chance of winning the division late in 2010 against the Twins when Michael Cuddyer popped one up against Joaquin Benoit. Jason Bartlett was getting ready to make the catch. It hit the ring and fell in and they scored a run to beat us. We've said many times over the past few years, when this team was the Devil Rays and they were losing 100 games a year, those things were cute, but they're not going to be so cute if they cost the Rays a chance to get into the postseason. You shouldn't be playing Major League Baseball popping things up and hitting things. That's what happens when you're playing wiffle ball in your front lawn. For a while then in the '10 postseason, MLB management said any time the ball would hit the rings, it would be a do over. A do over is something you shouldn't be having in Major League Baseball either. That's stuff for your backyard. It's kind of funny to see when things happen. When a ball does hit the ring on the infield, it's always kind of funny to see the reaction of the umpires and the opposing players, coaches, and managers. To see how closely they paid attention to the ground rules and read up on them as well." Unless Major League Baseball allows for the world's largest broomstick to be used to poke truant fly balls from the rings, the front yard style of baseball may just have to stay in Tampa until the Rays find a new home.

NEW NAME, NEW UNIFORM, NEW STADIUM . . . WELL, SORT OF

For the first 10 years of their existence, the Tampa Bay "Devil" Rays averaged 97 losses a season, including three 100-loss seasons. In fact, the club's one shining success occurred in 2004 when a low-for-them 91-loss record was good enough to emerge from the American League East cellar. With an average attendance plummeting from the inaugural season's 30,000 plus to just over 13,000, the "Devil" Rays were over a million lower than the league's average. To stimulate good rapport with the fans, the team, in November 2007 and under the relatively new ownership of Stuart Sternberg, cast out the "Devil" and changed their name to simply the "Rays." The team's uniform went from green to navy blue, and, in an attempt to take away what Charlie Slowes refers to as a "cavernous feel" inside the Trop, many unused seats were removed to make way for fan amenities that would, hopefully, induce fans to come to the ballpark. Slowes notes, "They've done everything they could possibly do to bring that place up to modern standards. It was built with small concourses with no view of the ballpark. It was like you were in a tunnel when you were going to get food. You used to have to go down to a different level to get across from left field to right field. They changed that last year by removing the Center Field Restaurant." Dave Wills describes other measures that were taken to "top the Trop": "The Rays tank was just put in there in 2007. It's become a fan favorite at the ballpark. When Sternberg's ownership group took over, they cleaned up every corner of that particular ballpark. Now they have an area in left field for kids. They have a bunch of carnival-like games, a batting cage, areas to go get your baseball card picture taken or make your own uniform. There are attendants now inside the bathroom to make sure they stay clean. There's a couple of areas where fans can mingle now. This past year (2013), we introduced 'the Porch' out in the outfield. At U.S. Cellular Field's 'Victory Level,' you could start from home plate and walk around and you could still keep an eye on the field while you get something to eat or drink. There's those social areas where you could gather in the outfield. The big concourse out there by the scoreboard and video boards. Our ownership group noticed that, so this past offseason, they spent a few million dollars on a thing they call 'Rays 360.' There's a walkway behind the seats in right and left that bring you out to 'the Porch' in center field. It's right behind the batter's eye, and 200 people can gather to watch the game from there, have a few beers, and just chill out. It's for the 'twentysomethings' that probably get a little antsy sitting in their seats for nine innings. Now they can all go out, get together, and have a couple of cold ones. Really, it's become one of the more popular places around Tropicana Field. Even [on] our minuscule attendance days, that area is still crowded. It's really become a hit." Perhaps the biggest "hit" the Rays had given their fans was the tutelage of manager Joe Maddon.

OCTOBER 19, 2008: A RAYS CATWALK DOWN MEMORY LANE

Wearing his "Buddy Holly-esque" thick-framed glasses, 2008 Manager of the Year Joe Maddon completed a 62-game swing for the Tampa Bay Rays with an American League East title and an improbable "worst to first" one-year turnaround. Dave Wills notes, "In 2008, I think we knew we were making strides under new ownership with manager Joe Maddon. I think everybody thought '08 would be the year we might make a run at .500. We got off to a pretty good start and jumped into first place. We had a little bit of a hiccup right before the All-Star break where we lost seven straight, and then, right after the break, we got back into first place and hung around there. There were so many magical moments there in the 2008 regular season. Then we get into the playoffs, and we beat the Chicago White Sox in four games. Then we advanced, obviously, to take on the Red Sox." As if the defending World Series champs needed any kind of antagonist backstory set up for this American League Championship Series, many of the "Cowboyed up" players on this Boston team of '08 had not only crawled out of a 1–3 hole the previous year to defeat the Cleveland Indians in the 2007 American League Championship Series, but also made an unprecedented comeback from a 0–3 deficit to defeat the New York Yankees in 2004 en route to the team's first title in 86 years. Commenting on the 2008 matchup, Dave Wills adds, "The Red Sox kind of reinvented baseball in 2004 when they won the World Series. They won it again in 2007. We're battling them in 2008. We have a brawl with them at Fenway Park, and now we're playing them in the American League Championship Series. We lost the first game, and then we just destroyed them in the next three. We beat 'em up pretty good in the first two at Fenway. Now we get the chance to possibly clinch at Fenway and we have a 7–0 lead and lose it. I just remember when we were walking out of Fenway Park, my broadcast partner Andy Freed said to me he thought we lost our chance of going to the World Series because of losing that game 5, and I said, 'You know what? There's just something about this team that this story's not supposed to end that way.' We come home and lose game 6 and now here's game 7. The place is packed. Close to 40,000 people there at Tropicana Field, and the place was rocking."

Considering the Red Sox's playoff mystique since the '04 season, many Rays fans had butterflies in their stomachs once the series went to a winner-take-all, decisive game 7. Wills comments, "You go back to September 20th of 2008, we're playing the Twins and getting a chance to clinch our first ever postseason birth. That was probably a more relaxing day because you figured, 'Well, if we didn't get it done today, we'll get it done tomorrow,' but there was no tomorrow in game 7. It was they do or die. On that particular day, waking up that morning, my wife looked at me and said, 'I can't believe the Rays are doing this to us,' but game 7's are the ultimate. It's going to be great. I remember Andy getting to the park all nervous and upset that we're playing a game 7. I actually played him Kurt Russell's speech from *Miracle,* so it got him in a better mood. Then we have our daily bantering with Joe Maddon. Joe told us he's already envisioning himself standing on the third base line at Citizens Bank Park for game 3 of the World Series. We ask, 'But we open at home. Why are you envisioning that?' Maddon goes, 'Well, because I've already stood on our line. Now I'm envisioning myself standing on *their* line.' So, after we walked out of that room, Andy said, 'I feel better. After watching the 'Miracle' speech and talking to Joe, I feel better.' We knew what happened the year before in Cleveland. While we were tested a bit, we were still a relatively young group—kind of like Cleveland was—but we came home. I thought we had a pretty good chance with James Shields on the mound in game 6. James gave up a home run to Jason Varitek, and that game got away from us. Now we've got Matt Garza throwing in game 7, and, while Garza has incredible stuff, he can blow up at any minute. He gives up that first inning home run to Pedroia, and we're like, 'Uh oh. This isn't going to be pretty.' This might be one of those games where the Red Sox came back against the Yankees. It might be a huge blowout, but Garza settled down, and our bats did just enough like they seemed to do all year long. We come back and end up winning the game 3-1. David Price goes on in the eighth to get the final two outs in that frame. Then, in the ninth, on the ground ball by Jed Lowrie to Akinori Iwamura, he takes it to the bag himself and we get out of the game. On the broadcast, I said, 'This improbable season has another chapter to it. The Rays are going to the World Series.'"

On their first ever trip to the postseason, the '08 Rays made it to the World Series, where, though they lost in five games to the Philadelphia Phillies, they proved to fans that the season was no fluke, and the team returned to the playoffs three out of the next five seasons. Signing off on the Rays' first ever American League pennant, Dave Wills adds, "What I remember most about that was obviously just the way the crowd was going nuts. What I remember seeing in person and I saw later on in highlights, some people were just soaking it all in. They were just stunned, and then there were others who were high fiving and cheering. People were crossing the aisles of sections to go and hug people. That moment was just incredible because the Red Sox had always been kind of the bully to the Tampa Bay Rays and then to do it on a night where 90 percent of the crowd was Rays fans. You've got to remember, back in '05 and '06, and even in '07, the only time that place would be filled up would be when we would play the Red Sox or the Yankees, and, most of that time, in the first couple of years in that turnaround, it was still 50–60 percent Red Sox or Yankees fans, and, honestly, the Rays would be somewhat outnumbered. It was just incredible for that game 7, where I would say it was about 85-90% Rays fans, and to be able to beat them in game 7 at our place, it was just a magical moment, and, to this day, it still gives me some goosebumps thinking back to that incredible night."

While Joe Maddon and his "Buddy Holly" frames will be taking in "fresh" air at 1060 West Addison Street in Chicago (Cubs) for the '15 season, the Rays, thanks to the hitting of Evan Longoria, Ben Zobrist, and Yunel Escobar; the pitching of Alex Cobb, Chris Archer, and Drew Smyly; and the "home turf" advantage of Tropicana Field, will more likely be changing the filters in the Rays tank for many postseason runs to come.

· 27 ·

Turner Field: Atlanta Braves

I think it's just like playing in a normal, average ballpark for players. It may be unique in that it's very easy to adapt to because there are no particular factors that come into play.

—Jim Powell, Atlanta Braves radio play-by-play broadcaster

Even though the Cincinnati Reds wear the mantle for being Major League Baseball's original paid organization, and the Philadelphia Phillies wear one as well for the longest tenured one-city/one-name organization, the Atlanta Braves could probably settle for "most-named" organization. One of the original eight of the National League, the Atlanta Braves, with a history spanning three cities, started out as the Boston Red Caps. After so many names that the trademark and copyright offices finally gave up, the name "Braves" finally took shape, even though the team location couldn't. In 1952, after over three-quarters of a century in Boston, the team moved westward, curving around Lake Michigan and settling in Milwaukee under the same name. Though their residence in Milwaukee hardly resembled the 76-year marathon in Boston, the Braves acquired some talent in the City of Festivals that would change the face of the organization. Slugger Henry "Hank" Aaron and pitcher Warren Spahn led the 1957 Milwaukee Braves to the team's second-ever World Series title. While the fans of Milwaukee were ecstatic about a championship, their enthusiasm soon wilted after the team's back-to-back pennant runs of 1957 and 1958. Giving the longest two weeks' notice in history, the Braves, after letting their lease run out, finally moved to Atlanta, where, with their nearest neighbor being the St. Louis Cardinals, they controlled the baseball market for the entire southeastern corner of the country. As part of the southern hospitality the city offered its newly arriving guests, Atlanta Fulton County Stadium was built in anticipation of the Braves and their southeastward trek.

While the proverbial helium leaked out of the inaugural balloons for a season awaiting the Braves, Atlanta Fulton County Stadium housed a very fortunate Atlanta Crackers team of the International League. Finally, on April 12, 1966, the Braves were officially in Atlanta, playing before 51,000 fans, which, considering the paltry numbers of their last year in Milwaukee, must have seemed like half a season's worth. While at Atlanta Fulton County Stadium the Braves won the team's third World Series title, Hank Aaron passed Babe Ruth on the all-time home runs list, and general manager John Schuerholz and team manager Bobby Cox began a string of successes which, according to Atlanta Braves radio play-by-play broadcaster Jim Powell, is "unprecedented and likely never to be repeated by any team in any sport." After 30 seasons the Braves once again moved, in 1997—this time, within the same zip code—to their current yet originally unexpected home of Turner Field. Unlike the franchise-enticing Atlanta Fulton County Stadium, Turner Field's original design and purpose were not specifically intended for Atlanta Braves baseball.

A year before the Braves played ball there, Turner Field was a different kind of sports facility. Jim Powell comments, "Turner Field truly is unique in that it would be the only stadium in Major League Baseball that was converted from a different kind of stadium. It was actually built for the 1996 Olympics, and, interestingly, it wasn't even used for Olympic baseball. They built a massive stadium for the Olympics' opening ceremonies, track and field, and then they cut off part of the stands and the wall out in the outfield. They lopped off 35,000 seats, and they did a great job of converting it into a baseball stadium. It is a very nice baseball stadium, but, because it was built for track and field, it actually has a little bit more foul territory than most of the brand new ballparks where they're pushing the stands closer and closer to the foul lines." While 85,000 seats would have been a great market research tool to test the popularity of the Braves versus the NFL's Atlanta Falcons, the team put better use to it once the lederhosen-clad crowds had made their way back "over the pond" after the summer of '96, reducing the official capacity to just below 50,000. Jim Powell adds, "Obviously, that opened up a gaping hole in this massive complex. They used some of that space to give it more of a baseball feel by converting that outfield area into sort of a grand entryway into Turner Field and a big fan plaza level where people walk around. You've got restaurants and misters. You've got monument grove where Hank Aaron, Warren Spahn, and others are recognized." While open concourses and views beyond center field weren't in the cards for the "cookie-cutter" Atlanta Fulton County Stadium, neither was the 81-game-spanning home run derby on the slate at Turner Field.

Being built practically in the same parking lot as its "launching pad" predecessor Atlanta Fulton County Stadium, Turner Field's 1,057 foot altitude could reasonably be expected to have the same kind of effect as far as home run power goes. Powell explains, "Growing up, all the talk at Atlanta Fulton County Stadium was about altitude. In my experience, since Turner Field's been open, I've never heard anybody talk about altitude. It's funny how Atlanta Fulton County Stadium was all about the launching pad, and, now, Turner Field, which plays almost completely neutral, is slightly depressed in home runs compared to the average Major League stadium. Runs scored almost exactly average. It doesn't add or subtract offense at Turner Field, and, because of that, you never hear anything about launching pads, altitude, and things like that, which makes me wonder maybe there wasn't so much a launching pad and altitude effect at Atlanta Fulton County Stadium as there was a Hank Aaron effect. Maybe people wanted to take away from or explain Hank Aaron's prolific ability to hit home runs by adding in some other factors that made it easier to understand. There have been some great sluggers playing in Turner Field, and there's never talk about altitude and the ball launching." Reinforcing Powell's theory, Aaron hit 195 home runs at County Stadium in his 12 seasons in Milwaukee, a yearly average of 16.25. However, supporting the other side of the coin, Aaron averaged 21.11 long balls a year inside Atlanta Fulton County Stadium during the *latter* half of his career. Where Aaron left off, Braves outfielder Dale Murphy picked up. From 1976 until his unexpected trade to the Philadelphia Phillies in the middle of the '90 season, Dale "the Murph" Murphy had his own "effect" at Atlanta Fulton County Stadium, hitting 371 home runs for the Braves and winning back-to-back National League Most Valuable Player awards during the '82 and '83 seasons.

Because of the higher-elevated Coors Field and Chase Field, the "launching pad" tag never stuck in the team's transition to Turner Field; however, that doesn't mean the home run power of Aaron and Murphy didn't stick around. Between 1999 and 2007, either Chipper Jones, Andruw Jones, or both Chipper Jones *and* Andruw Jones ('00) led the team in home runs in all but two seasons ('03 and '04). Still, a 50 plus home run output by players like Andruw Jones ('05) wasn't exactly "in the cards" when Turner Field was being developed. Jim Powell adds, "I think they set out to try and build much more of a neutral type of stadium, probably—at least in some part—because of the offensive reputation of Atlanta Fulton County Stadium, and they succeeded. The hitters will complain they lose home runs in the alleys because the dimensions are fairly deep. Talking to players who have played in both stadiums, the ball doesn't carry well. They felt the ball travelled much more easily at Fulton County than it does at Turner Field. It's pretty symmetrical. It's a pretty fair ballpark and it plays that way. I don't think there's a big adjustment at Turner Field for the players. It's not like the Braves have to go out and find ground ball pitchers because the ball jets out or they have to find particular types of players. There is a need for more speed because one can't hit many home runs. It plays so fair. Literally. The last time I checked the ballpark effects, it was exactly on average for runs scored. That's offense—one iota—in either direction." Going over from a "cookie-cutter," molded outfield to the 380- and 385-foot alleys in left and right center, the Braves, over the years, have needed speedy outfielders patrolling an area once tread by 200- and 400-meter relay-winning gold medalist Michael Johnson. Andruw Jones, while leading the way behind the plate during his years in an Atlanta Braves uniform, also won 10 straight gold glove awards in that "fair" Turner outfield.

Perhaps one factor swaying the gold glove voters was Jones's handicap playing at Turner Field, especially during night games, when, as recording artist Vicki Lawrence would say "the lights went out in Georgia." Jim Powell explains, "One thing I would say about Turner Field that is unique and something the players have to adjust to is there are no lights in the outfield. As a consequence, all the lighting is foul pole to foul pole. Fly balls, especially at dusk, are easily lost because the players are only getting light on one side of the baseball. Pitchers, oftentimes, have trouble seeing the catcher's signals. When they're putting down fingers, they can't see because there's no light behind the pitcher. The light is all around the catcher, so they will paint their fingernails or get up two or three times, grab some chalk off the base line, and get their fingers white so they're more easily seen by the pitcher. It's more of a factor for outfielders trying to find pop-ups and fly balls, especially at dusk. Once the lights take full effect, it really isn't a problem, but, at dusk, because there are no outfield lights, it can be an issue." No lights are needed to guide fans to one of Turner Field's more unique amenities, the Atlanta Braves Museum and Hall of Fame, a shrine to one of the greatest baseball runs ever.

THE 1991 ATLANTA BRAVES . . . AND
THE REST, AS THEY SAY, IS HISTORY

From 1991 to 2004, the Atlanta Braves won 14 straight National League West/East Division titles, a feat that has never occurred in the history of any other major sport. The men behind this remarkably consistent success were Braves general manager John Schuerholz, manager Bobby Cox, and a team of scouts who deserve to be enshrined in not only the Braves Hall of Fame but Major League Baseball's as well. Powell comments, "The Braves Museum and Hall of Fame is actually located inside the stadium. The scouts are recognized, and the Braves rich history of being the longest continuously operated franchise in Major League Baseball. In terms of the scouts, I would say Paul Snyder is one of the greatest in the history of the game. He's been with the Braves for a long time and is still around. He brought a certain culture to the scouting department with the Braves. Then John Schuerholz came to the ball club right as the team was about to turn around. Bobby Cox, who had done a lot of scouting and building of the farm system himself, came down to the field. In '91, Schuerholz was the general manager. He came from Kansas City, which also was very adept in scouting and had a pitching and defense type culture. Schuerholz made a couple of shrewd acquisitions with Sid Bream, Rafael Belliard, and Terry Pendleton. The Glavine's and the Avery's, Pete Smith, and people like John Smoltz were coming up in pitching and defense. It turned into a formula that worked for the Braves for 14 consecutive division titles. Scouting was right in the middle of that as well, as that philosophical change of 'You know what? We're developing a lot of great, young pitchers. We'd better put some defense with them as well." As part of their unmatched 14 consecutive division titles, the Braves won five National League Pennants and finally won it all in 1995, the team's third World Series title in its 140-year existence.

OCTOBER 11, 2010: BOBBY COX WALKS BACK INTO THE DUGOUT ONE FINAL TIME

With a managerial career touching five decades, former Braves manager and hall of famer Bobby Cox was known not only for his success from the dugout but for his trips out of it as well. Along with 2,504 wins as a manager with both the Braves and a Toronto Blue Jays team he brought to within one win of the World Series in 1985, Cox holds the Major League record for managerial ejections, 156. Although such a number, along with the uprooted base bags and kicked over dirt, won't be regarded in Cooperstown with the same admiration as being the fourth winningest manager in Major League history, Cox's ejections reflected his support of Braves players. Former Braves broadcaster Pete Van Wieren said of Cox, "Things you know playing for Bobby Cox, you know that Bobby always has your back." Toward the end of the '09 season, Cox extended his contract for one final year as the Braves' skipper. Though not by way of a division title, which had been the Atlanta norm under Cox, in 2010 the Braves made the playoffs for the 15th time in 20 seasons, earning a date with the eventual World Series champion San Francisco Giants for the Division Series. Down two games to one, the Braves hosted the Giants for game 4 on October 11, 2010, which ended up being the final curtain call for Bobby Cox's successful career. Jim Powell recalls what was for him the most memorable game as a Braves broadcaster inside Turner Field: "The Braves lost to the Giants 3-2, and that was Bobby Cox's last game. I'll never forget the game for a lot of different reasons. It was a very tightly contested Division Series. It was only the second time that the first four games of a postseason series were all decided by one run. There were some big moments throughout the series. Obviously, we all knew it was the swan song for number six. A beloved figure in the history of the game—period—much less the Braves. The Braves led 1–0 and Derek Lowe was carrying a no-hitter into the sixth inning. It was a great crowd and just a tremendous atmosphere. I just remember, when you're growing up, you're always dreaming—just like the players dream—of playing in game 7 of the World Series. You dream of calling game 7 of the World Series. I've never called a World Series game, but that game felt like a game 7. Just hanging on every pitch. Cody Ross's homer was the first hit for the Giants. Tied the ballgame at 1–1. The Braves reclaimed the lead 2–1, and then the bullpen gave it up late and the Braves lost 3–2. It was more than just the atmosphere and the fact that it was a decisive playoff game. It was also Bobby Cox's last game, and I saw something that I doubt I'll ever see again. The Braves lost the game, and we couldn't believe it. They had such a good team and magic with Bobby's last season, especially at Turner Field. A lot of late inning comebacks, and you just felt like this was a team of destiny. Suddenly, the season was over, and the Giants start to celebrate on the field. The fans don't leave because it was Bobby's last game. They started to cheer. They're calling for Bobby, and, eventually, Bobby comes onto the field. I'll never forget watching. The San Francisco Giants stopped their on-field celebration, turned, and stood there on the field, applauding and recognizing Bobby Cox. It was just a moment I can't imagine will ever be replicated, and, for that, it was the most memorable game I've ever called. I've worked in every single stadium in Major League Baseball—both the American and National League—and I've never seen a moment like that. To see Bobby standing there, docking his cap and dabbing at his eyes while the fans are going crazy. A Major League team that just won an incredibly tight playoff series, looking to cut loose—like they all do—and they stop and just celebrate—with the Atlanta fans—the career of Bobby Cox. I'd like to go back and listen to the tape. I would imagine there were long periods of time where we just couldn't talk. I don't really remember anything else about what was going on in the broadcast. I just remember watching and the emotions I felt. It certainly was the greatest day in my broadcast career."

While the umpires at Turner Field probably have not worn out their shoulders throwing an extended finger to the Braves' dugout since 2010, a competitive spirit representative of that of Bobby Cox still resides in the team clubhouse. John Schuerholz may have moved up the ladder to team president, but his involvement with team scouting continues to bear the fruits of All-Star caliber pitchers like Julio Teheran, Mike Minor, and Craig Kimbrel, and hitters like Freddie Freeman and Jason Heyward, making an invitation to the postseason practically a standing one.

· 28 ·

U.S. Cellular Field: Chicago White Sox

Our park can hold a candle to anybody's ballpark. It's terrific in every respect.

—Ken "Hawk" Harrelson, Chicago White Sox
TV play-by-play broadcaster

*W*hile disgruntled, goat-toting tavern owners were putting curses on their crosstown neighbor Chicago Cubs, the Chicago White Sox were 25 years into their own curse, placed on them, so to speak, in 1921 by baseball's first ever commissioner, Kenesaw Mountain Landis. The eight Chicago "Black Sox" of 1919, having accepted money from mob-connected figures like Arnold "the Big Bankroll" Rothstein to throw their World Series against the Cincinnati Reds, were banned from baseball. Among the members of the team acquitted by jurors but indicted by Landis was would-have-been hall of fame outfielder "Shoeless" Joe Jackson. In his 1,332 games as a professional, prior to being banned by Landis, Jackson batted an astonishing .356 while collecting 1,772 hits. The White Sox did not return to the World Series for almost four decades, when they lost to the exodus-embarked Los Angeles Dodgers four games to two. Another 24 years passed before the White Sox again came close to the fall classic, but in the 1983 American League Championship Series, Chicago fell short to the eventual World Series champion Baltimore Orioles three games to one. Inside their home of "old" Comiskey Park, the White Sox won only one World Series, beating the New York Giants two years prior to the team's "sitting in conference with a bunch of crooked players and gamblers where the ways and means of throwing games are discussed." Finally, after 80 years and almost as many uniform changes at the hands of former team owner Bill Veeck, "old" Comiskey Park gave way to "new" Comiskey Park. On April 18, 1991, before a sold-out crowd of 42,000 plus fans, the White Sox were trounced in their new park's inaugural game, 16–0, by Cecil Fielder and the Detroit Tigers.

TOO SOON?

With the construction of the new ballpark beginning only 711 days prior to that first "game" against the Detroit Tigers, there were naturally some architectural and design questions once the 42,000 fans started barreling through "new" Comiskey Park's turnstiles. Having been at the park from day one, White Sox TV broadcaster Ken "Hawk" Harrelson comments on the park's original design: "It was okay when they originally built 'new' Comiskey Park, but then there were some design flaws in there that were pretty obvious. I'm not an architect. Most people aren't, but they were able to spot them in a hurry. In the upper deck, they had the entries and the exits in the bottom, so when you came in, if you were in the upper deck, you had to walk all the way up the stairs and then all the way down. Then they redid the stadium. It cost them a lot of money, and they put the entrances/exits in the middle, whereas you would only have to walk halfway up or halfway down, so to speak." After the '01 and '02 seasons, the first two renovations of the ballpark occurred, costing the team $13 million. The biggest change was the addition of an ivy-draped, two-tiered batter's eye and an extended concourse level beyond the center-field wall. With a $68 million check from the U.S. Cellular Corporation for naming rights to the ballpark burning a hole in their pockets, the White Sox resumed renovations after the '03 season, costing the team a further $48 million. The largest of these costs was for the addition of LED "ribbon" boards around the club level and the subtraction of the top six rows of the stadium's upper deck. After the '05 season, phase five of the park's renovation changed the color of the seats throughout the ballpark to green and added a scout seating area behind home plate. Another proverbial cashed trust fund check or two later, the team was finally done renovating. Though the phrase "they did it right the *second* time" won't be catching fire with Hallmark in its line of congratulatory greeting cards, "Hawk" can best put a stamp on the seven-year, $100 million plus renovations to a ballpark, the original cost of which was only $50 million more, with the words, "All in all, our ballpark is just tremendous."

With Chicago's most expensive version ever of *Extreme Home Makeover* taking the better part of a decade, one can logically expect some changes were made to the field itself. To make room for the relocated bullpens and the new bullpen-themed bar, the fences down the left- and right-field lines were brought in from 347 to 330 feet, a pull hitter's dream come true. Interestingly, the change didn't really affect the White Sox as a team, as they remained third in baseball in home runs, with virtually no change from 2001 (214) to 2002 (217). However, the man "Hawk" Harrelson nicknamed "the Big Hurt," two-time American League MVP and hall of fame first baseman Frank Thomas, in his first two full seasons after the fences came in, hit 70 home runs, only 17 of which happened on the road. Aside from Thomas's poke-friendly, 17-foot gift, no drastic changes occurred, dimension wise, as a result of the renovations, with left center extending out a mere two feet and right center coming in only three. While newly designed ballparks like Oriole Park at Camden Yards were the main inspiration for the White Sox shattering so many savings jars from 2001 to 2012, U.S. Cellular Field itself became the standard for many of the subsequent ballparks in one particular area. U.S. Cellular Field's one constant over its 24-year existence has been its playing surface. In fact, the infield dirt was brought over from the "old" Comiskey Park and placed in "new" Comiskey when the park opened. The name by which the White Sox have stood over the past 75 seasons for their grounds-keeping has been Bossard. Harrelson explains, "There's only perfect conditions on our field because we have Roger Bossard, 'the Sod Father.' He's the best. He's built the field on many of the new stadiums and stadiums all over the world. We have the best playing surface in baseball. You can tie us, but you can't beat us in that regard. We're as good as it gets, so that makes it great for the players as well." Bossard took over for his father Gene, who was the head groundskeeper for the White Sox for 43 years. The Sod Father's drainage system, developed specifically for U.S. Cellular Field when it opened in 1991, has been copied and used in two-thirds of the league's ballparks today, all or most of which opened after U.S. Cellular Field.

Perhaps U.S. Cellular's most defining feature "taken in" by the fans would be the ballpark's various culinary contributions. Harrelson notes, "As far as a fan coming to the ballpark for the first time, the first thing that gets you is the aroma. We were voted the best food in Major League Baseball, so you're going to have the aroma. It's like going to a NASCAR race. A lot of people who have never been to a NASCAR race don't understand that there are more elements to it than just watching the cars run. There's obviously the visual, there's the audio, and then there's the unique smell to it. The same thing goes true with U.S. Cellular Field." With Major League Baseball's greatest eats available to them, the fans can likely appreciate another of the conditions resulting from the renovations, which is more seating room. Harrelson notes, "We have plenty of room in our seats, which is a big thing for the fans. I think what Jerry Reinsdorf did in the final analysis talking with the Illinois Sports Commission was they decided—especially during the renovation—they were going to go quality rather than quantity. A lot of parks, unfortunately, have gone for quantity. More seats, more seats, more seats. So they cut them down a couple of inches on each side. In a lot of the parks, especially if it's a big person, they have a very uncomfortable time." Another gift from U.S. Cellular Field to the fans is the angling of the seats to the pitcher's mound. Speaking on other stadiums and their spectatorial configuration, Harrelson notes, "Even in the right-field/left-field area, a lot of seats are not pointed towards home plate. They're pointed straight out, so if you're sitting in left field, you have to look over your right shoulder, and, from right field, you have to look over your left shoulder at what's going on with the pitcher and the hitter." Though the renovations, which cost nine figures, left U.S. Cellular Field almost 2,000 seats shorter than the original park design, the 40,000 plus that remained are arguably among the most comfortable in baseball.

"THE GOOD GUYS" RETURN TO GLORY

During the ballpark's first year, the White Sox played a "turn back the clock" game against the Milwaukee Brewers, the first in Major League Baseball in which the teams wore uniforms of yesteryear. The White Sox's choice was the black uniforms from 1917, the last year the team had ever won a World Series. The new uniform prompted "Hawk" to reach into his bottomless bag of nicknames and come up with "the Good Guys" for the team, which eventually led to the team slogan "Good Guys Wear Black." In the first 14 seasons at their new home, the Good Guys only qualified for the postseason twice, winning a collective two games between the series. Going into the '05 season, the White Sox had lost their two biggest sluggers, Magglio Ordonez and Carlos Lee, to free agency and their team leader, Frank Thomas, to injury, but the team had gained Jermaine Dye, Scott Podsednik, A.J. Pierzynski, and Orlando "El Duque" Hernandez, all of whom would become quite instrumental once October baseball rolled around. The White Sox heralded the American League's best regular season record, but it was their nearly impeccable postseason run (11–1) that returned championship glory to the Windy City for the first time in 88 years. Having swept a Red Sox team who had, just one year before, ended their own octogenarian drought, the White Sox eliminated the Los Angeles Angels (of Anaheim) in five games to set up the team's first World Series appearance in 46 years. The series was a short one, especially for the Houston Astros, who, though led by the pitching mastery of Roger Clemens, Andy Pettitte, and Roy Oswalt, were swept by the Good Guys thanks to late home runs by Geoff Blum and Podsednik (walk-off in game 2), stellar pitching by imported pitchers like Jose Contreras and Freddy Garcia, and a .438 batting average by series MVP Jermaine Dye. Part of this celebratory pileup of Good Guys at Houston's Minute Maid Park on October 26, 2005, was "Hawk"

Harrelson's all-time favorite White Sox player, Mark Buehrle, who on more than one occasion brought tears to the veteran broadcaster's eyes. On July 23, 2009, against the Tampa Bay Rays, Harrelson's weren't the only eyes that watered inside the confines of U.S. Cellular Field.

A SPECIAL WIN FOR A "SPECIAL GUY"

In his 12 seasons with the White Sox, Mark Buehrle gathered up 161 wins and 1,396 strikeouts while facing 10,317 batters over 390 games. Of the 10,317, only 27 faced Buehrle on that midsummer's day in 2009 at U.S. Cellular Field. Using 116 pitches, Buehrle dominated the defending American League Champion Tampa Bay Rays, throwing first pitch strikes to 19 of the 27 batters he faced. While the distribution of outs was fairly balanced (11 groundouts, 10 fly outs, and 6 strikeouts), it was the 25th of the night that made the collective heart inside Buehrle and the 28,036 fans in attendance skip a beat. Tampa Bay right fielder Gabe Kapler led off the top of the ninth with perhaps the loudest out in perfect game history, flying out to deep left center field and the White Sox's DeWayne Wise. Harrelson recalls the moment: "DeWayne Wise's catch was the greatest catch I've ever seen under memorable circumstances. It would have been a great catch anytime during a regular season game, but for a perfect game, to make that catch in the ninth inning, was phenomenal. The last thing I do as an announcer—before the pitch is made—is I check the outfield. That's just a habit of mine I've had my whole life. As a baseball player, you check your outfielders where you know where they are. As a base runner, you check your outfielders where you know where they are. DeWayne always played shallow. The shallowest center fielder of anybody in the American League, and when Gabe Kapler hit the ball, I'm thinking, 'Shit! He's not going to be able to get there.' Well, he kicked it in high gear about halfway there, jumped up, hit the wall, bobbled the ball, recovered it coming down, and made the catch." Luckily, the network couldn't pick up Harrelson's thoughts, thus avoiding an FCC fine; however, "Hawk's" call on the field, "DeWayne Wise makes the catch! What a play by Wise! Mercy!" helped soak in the moment for those tuning in to the game on TV. Two quiet outs later, Mark Buerhle had himself the 18th perfect game in Major League history. Looking back on this Good Guy's masterpiece, Harrelson says, "I've been in this game all or parts of seven decades, so I've seen a lot of stuff, but the most memorable game for me was Mark Buehrle's perfect game. It was mainly because of Mark. He reminds me so much of one of the great team-mates I had and that was (Jim) Catfish Hunter. They were about the same size. They had about the same kind of stuff. Great personalities. Great teammates.

Nothing negative about either one of those guys. When a guy like that goes out and does what he does with the stuff that he had, and he pitched a perfect game, I just cried because Buehrle is such a special guy. You have special guys. You've got Derek Jeter in New York. You had Cal Ripken. You had George Brett. You had special guys in the game who don't come along very often. Mark Buerhle was one of those guys. When you get a guy like that, especially if he's on your team, I feel like he's like a son. Those are things that you just do as a person who is a lifer—like I am—in baseball. If it had been Sammy Smith or Jimmy Jones who threw the perfect game, I'd have gone up after the game and said, 'Nice going, buddy,' and that'd be it."

While Good Guys like Mark Buehrle, Frank Thomas, and Jermaine Dye have either changed team uniforms, retired, or been enshrined in Cooperstown, new names like Chris Sale, Dayan Viciedo, and 2014 American League Rookie of the Year Jose Abreu, as well as familiar faces like Paul Konerko and Alexei Ramirez, fill the roster to make sure it's not another 88 years before the fireworks once again ignite behind Bill Veeck's historic clock in straightaway center and the confetti streams down from whatever's left of U.S. Cellular Field's upper deck.

· 29 ·

Wrigley Field: Chicago Cubs

I think the unique part of Wrigley is that it really is a slice of the early 20th century. There are only two places in all of baseball where you can get that. One is Fenway Park and the other is Wrigley.

—Len Kasper, Chicago Cubs TV play-by-play broadcaster

The word "Chicago" brings many names to mind: Bad (Bad) Leroy Brown, Michael Jordan, Oprah, Al Capone, and perhaps more infamously, Steve Bartman, whose name has become symbolic of the fruitlessness of baseball that has taken place on the North Side of Chicago for the past century. Chicago was founded in 1833, and though that predated organized baseball in the Windy City by 18 years, many would argue that 1833 was also the last time the Chicago Cubs won a World Series. With Boston breaking its "curse of the Babe" after 86 years in 2004, and the Cubs' crosstown neighbor White Sox also ending an octogenarian drought of their own (88 years) in 2005, the Cubs have now gone over 106 years without a team championship. While that's a record for a team in *any* sport, the 1908 title itself is riddled with controversy to this day. Though the Cubs dominated the Detroit Tigers in that year's fall classic, it's the road to the National League pennant that is most talked about today among historians and baseball writers alike. The Cubs had ousted the New York Giants, thanks in great part to perhaps the most infamously decided game in baseball history two weeks before. Giants' rookie first baseman Fred Merkle's not stepping on the second base bag on a seemingly game-winning hit by shortstop Al Bridwell—coupled with a subsequent call by the umpire ten hours later and from the comfort of his hotel room—gave the Cubs new life in their pennant race, as the Giants were never credited with the win. A 4–2 victory over John McGraw's men 15 days later had the Cubs fleeing for their lives out of New York and back to Detroit, where they won the second of their back-to-back world titles. If the term "back to back" ever took a physical form, one might make the case for the '07–'08 Cubs, as the team could look for decades in each direction without a glimpse of a World Series championship.

Perhaps referred to in the Chicago and New York communities as the Fred Merkle of the 21st century, former Chicago resident Steve Bartman committed a baseball spectator's cardinal sin by interfering with home outfielder Moises Alou's attempted catch in foul territory during game 6 of the 2003 National League Championship Series. With the Cubs shutting out the Marlins, and just five outs away from clinching the team's first pennant in almost 60 years, Bartman's interference led to a Lemony Snicket–worthy "series of unfortunate events" for the Cubs, headlined by third baseman Aramis Ramirez's error on a ball that could have started an inning-ending double play. The Marlins scored eight times in the eighth frame and went on to win game 6, 8–3, inside the now-not-so-friendly confines of Wrigley. Bartman had to be escorted out of the stadium by police once television replays and cell phone relays had fingered him as the culprit for this monumental collapse by the Cubbies. To this day, more than a decade later, Bartman has not returned to Wrigley Field. While Steve Bartman has taken the lion's share of the blame for the Cubs' failure to reach the World Series, his story is just one in a series of misfortunes over the past 106 years that have precluded the team from winning their third title.

Former Cubs fan William "Billy Goat" Sianis, along with his "plus one" companion goat, were asked to leave Wrigley during the 1945 World Series. On his way out, Sianis was said to have proclaimed, "The Cubs ain't gonna win no more." Manifesting Sianis's prediction, the Cubs went on to lose the series to the Detroit Tigers, and the "curse of the goat" began. In 1969, with the Cubs leading the Mets in the division late in the season, a black cat appeared in a game at Shea Stadium between the Cubs and Mets. The cat, an obvious symbol of bad luck, circled Cubs third baseman Ron Santo—who was standing on deck—and then vanished. The Cubs eventually lost the division to the "amazing" Mets, who went on to win the team's first ever title against the Orioles. The Cubs' bad luck inside Shea extended to other teams, as Red Sox first baseman Bill Buckner misfielded an easy groundout by the Mets' Mookie Wilson in the historic game 6 of the 1986 World Series. Buckner was wearing the batting glove from his days with the Cubs under his fielding glove, indulging the superstitious hearts of curse of the goat theorists. Despite all the misfortune and broken hearts, fan attendance at Wrigley surpassed the three million mark for eight straight seasons following Bartman's infamous catch. Though it's debatable whether the Cubs are actually cursed or not, the team's loyal fans have continued coming through the turnstiles at Wrigley for more than a century now, a trend on the north side of Chicago that will likely never change.

THAT OLD NEIGHBORHOOD FEEL

Opened on April 23, 1914, Wrigley Field is located in the Lakeview community of Chicago, and though it was built more than a century ago, the parcel of land on which the stadium sits leaves no room for expansion unless the direction is up or down. While the close-knit network of neighborhoods, restaurants, and businesses surrounding Wrigley make it seem like a pressurized atom that bursts 41,000 blue-and-white particles on a daily basis, many would argue it's part of the stadium's charm rather than the unfortunate hand it has been dealt. Chicago Cubs play-by-play broadcaster Len Kasper describes his unique daily Wrigley Field experience: "The great thing about Wrigley is it's like Central Park is in New York. Chicago's a bustling, busy, huge city, and, for a broadcaster, I walk into the ballpark for a 1:20 start around 9:30–9:45. The park is empty and all you can hear are the sounds of the city. I've jogged to Central Park a million times, and it's the same deal here. You're in the middle of this oasis. If you just look around, you feel like you're in a very rural area, but, if you listen, you understand that you're in a big urban environment. As we get closer to first pitch, as the gates open and batting practice starts, the sounds of the city—the L train going by, car horns honking—those get drowned out by the crack of the bat, the sound of the crowd, and, for the next four hours or so, the focus is really on that small parcel of land. Then when the game ends, fans file out and you start to hear the sounds of the city again. It's, to me, the way Major League Baseball was meant to be played, and if I go to the '30s, '40s and '50s, that's where all the ballparks were was downtown. I think about my favorite ballparks—Wrigley, Fenway, AT&T Park, Yankee Stadium—they're all in their own neighborhood. They're all part of a big city, and that's very special. To me, it's really a link to the past." The club owners have made sure this "link to the past" stays *within* the ballpark as well. Kasper adds, "The fun thing about the friendly confines is that there are fans who come here who have been around for a while and they haven't been to the ballpark since the '60s, and it looks exactly the same. They have preserved the feel and the vibe of this ballpark as well as any in the history of the game. The vines. The ivy. That's been there since 1937, as has the scoreboard. Really the only significant change in the ballpark since 1937 has been the addition of lights." The lights almost seem like a formality, as Wrigley hosts a way above average number of day games, due to its location within an actual neighborhood, in which restrictions allow for just 30 night games of the team's scheduled 81. The league standard is almost twice that. It's debatable whether or not the Cubs have that much of a disadvantage due to their unusual scheduling times; regardless, once players have been wearing a Cubs uniform for more than a season, the disadvantage falls to the visitors no matter what time the game starts at Wrigley Field.

BASEBALL'S GROUND RULES, APPENDIX W: WRIGLEY FIELD

Without question, the most unique feature of Wrigley Field's playing dimensions is the labyrinth of ivy draping the outfield walls. The term "friendly confines," referring to this horticultural presence on the field, is usually an oxymoron to those not acclimated to Wrigley. Len Kasper notes, "The ivy, the bricks, and the angles of the wells in left and right cause a problem for outfielders who have never played at Wrigley. In a lot of ballparks, an outfielder can steal a home run away, but, at Wrigley, there are baskets overhanging the field, which also can pose a problem. Occasionally, you'll get a line drive that hits the bottom of the basket, so playing the angles out there is different."

Adopting a set of rules that seems more suited for a sandlot pickup game than a Major League contest, Wrigley's one-of-a-kind ivy and the guidelines that come with it add a little more padding to the umpire calling the game's back pocket. Kasper continues, "There are a lot of things you need to know about the ground rules at the ballpark. A ball will get lost in the ivy, and I've seen a fielder reach in and not pick it up, and, once you reach in, it's a live ball and the umpires will not stop play." Needless to say, outfielders in a Cubs uniform learn to run with their arms extended, either to concede a ground rule double or audition for the sausage races on their next trip to Milwaukee. The ivy is just one of several features that put Wrigley Field at the peak of baseball's learning curve.

With a nickname like the Windy City, Chicago's weather definitely comes into play during Cubs games. Wrigley is located just a mile from Lake Michigan, and the wind can be coming or going, which drastically changes the way the ball plays. Len Kasper notes, "I think I can very easily claim that the conditions not only in the weather but of the physical characteristics of the ballpark have as much an impact on the game and on the players as any ballpark in baseball. We spend a significant amount of time every day on our broadcast in the first few innings talking about the weather conditions. The wind is always a factor. Even when there's no wind, that's noteworthy at Wrigley Field. When the wind blows in, it can play as the biggest ballpark in the game, and the wind blows in about 65 percent of the time. When the wind blows *out*, it's the best home run park in the history of *ever*." Though the wind may determine whether the game's a pitcher's duel or a slugfest, Wrigley Field's limited real estate tends to weigh in on a player's preparation before, or in the case of a rain delay, *during* the nine-inning contest. Kasper notes, "The tunnel from the visiting clubhouse to the dugout takes about a minute and a half to two minutes to navigate, so it's not the most convenient part for visiting players as opposed to Miller Park in Milwaukee, where the clubhouse is about five steps from the dugout. Batting cages are actually in the outfield. When the Cubs pinch hitters want to take some swings, they have to come into the middle of the tiny clubhouse and take them off a tee. There are a lot of little things that kind of add up over the course of time, and you realize it takes you a while to get used to playing at the ballpark. I've talked to players with the Cubs and they all say it takes about a full season to really understand and get used to all the day games and all the quirks of the ballpark." As far as Cubs outfielders are concerned, a full season may *still* not be enough prep time.

Along with presiding as judge "can I get it or not" with ivy-entangled fly balls, outfielders inside Wrigley have to take into account the brick façade that encompasses the playing field. The ball has a tendency to carom more and in unexpected directions off the wall, as opposed to what happens with the soft-landing-providing walls at pretty much every other ballpark in baseball. Considering this hard landing as a player, green means stop—rather than go—when chasing down deep fly balls. Adding to the mayhem are the recessed areas in both left and right field, referred to in Wrigley as "wells." Any misjudgments by an outfielder when it comes to the wells or the caroming effect of the bricks will often lead to a triple, or, in rarer circumstances, an inside-the-park home run. As if all this isn't enough, the right fielder has to battle the sun as well. Kasper claims, "I think playing right field is the toughest spot in any ballpark with the sun and the wind. Fortunately, the Cubs have Billy Williams as senior advisor, who played a lot of games out there and is a wonderful resource for all of our outfielders. He knows playing that position probably better than anyone on the planet." Cubs former right fielder Nate Schierholtz had a little bit more prep time than others when coming over to Wrigley Field. Kasper explains, "Nate Schierholtz was in his second year and I thought he made a very quick adjustment. One of the reasons is Nate played right field at AT&T Park in San Francisco. I think if there's one comparable ballpark, it is that one because of the wind and the funky, quirky angles of the outfield. If you come from San Francisco, Wrigley probably isn't quite as drastic as it would be coming from a lot of other ballparks." Though AT&T Park hasn't adopted *all* of Wrigley's traditions—as the Giants have already won three World Series titles since the park opened in April 2000, and the Cubs have yet to capture one inside their century-old home—the Cubs have still made some noteworthy playoff runs in recent years, including the '07 and '08 seasons.

JUNE 29, 2007: WHO SAYS
JUNE BASEBALL CAN'T BE DRAMATIC?

When Lou Piniella took over as manager of the Chicago Cubs in 2007, his reputation arrived at O'Hare International three flights before he did. Arguably one of the most explosive personalities in managerial history, Piniella came to Chicago with a World Series title ('90 Reds) and the winningest season in American League history ('01 Mariners) already on his resume. With the Cubs finishing third or worse in the three seasons that followed the state of Florida's offering Steve Bartman sanctuary, the '07 Cubs were sizing up to make it a fourth, coming into June 29's contest against the division leader Milwaukee Brewers already trailing them by six and a half games. Coming to the defense of the Cubs' slow start, Len Kasper comments, "The team had gotten off to kind of a middling start, adjusting to a new manager. No question a very talented team. The first two and a half months, you really have to get locked in." With the game being a weekday matinee (of course), the Brewers came out in the first inning showing why they were in first place, scoring all five of their runs in the introductory frame. The Cubs chipped away at the deficit with two runs in the fourth and one in the seventh, but up two runs and calling on their closer, Francisco Cordero, Milwaukee looked to be leaving the ballpark up seven and a half games to their cross-lake rival. Kasper adds, "It's late June, so it's still early enough to say you have a fighting chance. As big a game as it could be in June, that was the case." After two one-out singles and a sacrifice fly brought the Cubs to within one run, Aramis Ramirez came to the plate as the potential winning run. About his most memorable game as a Cubs broadcaster thus far Len Kasper recalls, "Aramis Ramirez comes to the plate. Cordero throws a first pitch slider to Ramirez and he hit a game-winning, two-run homer. For that date—that early in the season—it really was one of the most incredible moments I've ever witnessed. The crowd went absolutely crazy. It felt like a World Series game. Because it was a first pitch, it was such a surprise that my call was not really a broadcaster's call as much as it almost was a fan's call. I screamed, 'A drive. Deep left center. Cubs win.' My voice cracked. It really was the turning point of that season, and I think, to the fans, it was such an incredible moment. We had won many more later that year and obviously throughout 2008 when the Cubs won 97 games, but, for me, in my first nine years with the Cubs, that's the moment that stands out more than any other. Just the incredible atmosphere and the reaction. Obviously, the players mobbing Ramirez at home plate. I just remember total bedlam in the bleachers where the ball ended up landing. Everybody just lost their mind. That's the beauty of Wrigley. It was one of those 'anything can happen' type moments the day where it *did* happen." The Cubs eventually overtook the Brewers for the division title and returned, once again, to the postseason. Even though there wasn't a goat, cat, or Bartman to blame for the team's sweep by the Arizona Diamondbacks in the 2007 National League Division Series, or by the Los Angeles Dodgers in 2008, the Cubs faithful were, are, and always will be "blue" with bated breath for that third World Series title to take its victory lap around the friendly confines of Wrigley Field, laying Chicago's baseball ghosts to rest for good.

Yankee Stadium: New York Yankees

Yankee Stadium: "It's enormous. It looks like 'old' Yankee Stadium, but it's bigger and more modern."—John Sterling
Photo courtesy of AFP & Getty Images

When the place is filled and you're looking out from your broadcast booth, it's this marvelous, majestic, beautiful place with enormous concourses and everything is just perfect.

—John Sterling, New York Yankees radio
play-by-play broadcaster

Other new ballparks are great in their own way, but the stadium seems so large and expansive and important. The size and breadth of the place signifies it houses something big and significant.

—Michael Kay, New York Yankees TV
play-by-play broadcaster

$\mathcal{N}$o other team in any of the four major sports has won more championships than the New York Yankees, who hold 27 titles. In fact, the closest team to the Yankees is the St. Louis Cardinals, whose 11 championships are still less than half those of "the Bronx Bombers." With dynasties spread throughout the team's 112-year history, it's hard to imagine it took the Yankees more than 20 years to win their first title. If one were to trace the animosity of Orioles fans toward Yankee fans back to its roots, it may have originated sometime around 1903, when the team was purchased from Baltimore and moved to Hilltop Park in Manhattan. Inspired by the high setting in which they would begin to play their games, the Yankees' original team name was the "Highlanders," which stuck in New York for 10 years. Finally, in 1913, after moving in to share roommate duties with fellow New York ball club the Giants at the Polo Grounds, the name "Yankees" emerged, and while the team was eventually evicted from the Polo Grounds, the name would never change. With a century-spanning storyline better reserved for movies starring Gary Cooper and Broadway plays financed by the sale of the greatest slugger in baseball history, the Yankees won 26 championships in a stadium they were practically forced to call home, but a home is what they made it. Starting in the '20s, after the Yankees purchased George Herman Ruth, better known as "the Babe," from Boston for the stretchiest $125,000 in history, the Yankees boasted several dynasties, which bore the fruits of World Series championships for the Bronx. Ruth's squad, also known as "Murderer's Row," was the first Yankee dynasty. Considering Ruth's 659 home runs, 1,978 RBIs, and 2,518 hits in a Yankees uniform, it's hard to imagine needing any added help to win four titles. Ruth's teammate, Lou Gehrig, the "Iron Horse," aside from hitting 493 home runs, knocking in 1,995 runs, and "one upping" his left-handed counterpart with three additional titles in pinstripes (Ruth also had three with Boston), played in 2,130 consecutive games, a streak that would not be eclipsed for almost 60 years. As was the case with Yankee eras in the

20th century, the torch was passed from one Yankee great to the next. Gehrig, who retired from baseball after developing the disease that would both kill and be named after him, passed this torch to "Joltin" Joe DiMaggio, who, despite missing three years while serving in the U.S. military, won three American League MVPs and nine World Series titles and accumulated a 56-game hitting streak, a record that to this day many see as the least likely to be broken with respect to hitting. Where DiMaggio left off, Mickey "the Mick" Mantle picked up. Arguably the most beloved personality in all of baseball, Mantle was, according to former player/manager Johnny Mize, "the greatest baseball machine God ever put on the face of the earth." Reinforcing Mize's praise of Mantle, the switch-hitting slugger won batting's triple crown in 1956 and three American League MVP awards, and appeared in 16 All-Star games. The Mick also led the Yankees to 12 World Series, winning seven of them. Along with Mantle were teammates Billy Martin, Whitey Ford, Roger Maris, and Yogi Berra, to name a few. Berra's 10 World Series rings as a player are unmatched in Yankee *or* baseball history.

While the Yankees were going through their longest World Series drought since winning the first one, the new face of team ownership emerged in the form of George Steinbrenner. Colorfully referred to as "the Boss," Steinbrenner got right to work, signing Oakland A's ace Jim "Catfish" Hunter to a $2.85-million-a-year salary in 1974. Between 1974 and 1975 a previously unheard of renovation took place at the ballpark, costing $160 million, which adjusted for today's inflation would be over $660 million. After the opening of this "new" Yankee Stadium, the Yankees won the pennant but fell short in the 1976 World Series to Pete Rose, Johnny Bench, and "the Big Red Machine" Cincinnati Reds. Opening his wallet once more, Steinbrenner acquired outfielder Reggie Jackson to support then-manager Billy Martin's hitting lineup, which included Thurman Munson, Chris Chambliss, and Graig Nettles. Despite a grudge match between Steinbrenner and Martin that would have the manager rehired more times than a struggling actor on the ABC network, the Yankees won back-to-back World Series in '77 and '78, an era referred to in the Empire State as "the Bronx Zoo." Having been bested by the Los Angeles Dodgers in the strike-overshadowed 1981 season, the Yankees did not return to the fall classic for another 15 years. Starting in 1996, under the watchful eye of new manager Joe Torre, a team consisting of pitchers David Cone, Andy Pettitte, Orlando "El Duque" Hernandez, and all-time saves leader Mariano Rivera, as well as hitters like Derek Jeter, Bernie Williams, Tino Martinez, and Paul O'Neill, won four of the next five World Series, including a '98 season in which the team won 125 total games; the most ever in baseball history. Eventually nicknamed "the Evil Empire" by rival Boston Red Sox president/CEO Larry Lucchino, the team won two more pennants and reached the playoffs for the 11th consecutive season by the mid-2000s, when rumors of a new stadium surfaced. With such a storied past, it took the mayor of "the Big Apple" himself, Michael Bloomberg, to announce the venue that would replace Yankee Stadium. At an estimated cost of $800 million, the *new* "new" Yankee Stadium was to be built for the '09 season just across the street from the team's (then) current address. With construction that would last over two years, including a backlogged $50,000 hiccup due to a David Ortiz jersey being mixed into the concrete by construction worker and Red Sox fan Gino Castignoli, the Empire took the field in their more than half a billion dollars over budget home of Yankee Stadium on April 16, 2009. Despite besting the whoopee cushion by $49,998 for world's most expensive prank, Castignoli most likely wasn't offered a ticket for opening day.

YANKEE STADIUM: IN A WORD . . . *MAJESTIC*

When you put over a billion dollars into anything, especially a baseball stadium, you can expect it to stand above all others, and that appears to be true of Yankee Stadium. When asked what one would see when walking into the new Yankee Stadium, the radio voice of the Yankees, John Sterling, who hasn't missed a single game in his broadcasting career, replied, "You see this unbelievably magnificent, majestic ballpark. It's enormous. They have so many levels of seats and so much advertising. It's such a great sight. It's great for the fans. It looks like 'old' Yankee Stadium, but it's bigger and more modern. The odd thing is the space the ballpark takes up is enormous, yet it seats only 48,000 because they have bigger seats, wider rows, and bigger concourses." Yankees broadcaster Michael Kay, who has worked both TV and radio for the team and is the current lead on the team's Y.E.S. Network, describes the new ballpark in a way similar to that of his former broadcast partner: "I just think there is a certain majesty about the ballpark. I feel they were able to transfer the unique feel from across the street. You walk inside and you feel as if you are in a place that's important. There is a gravitas to it." The "majesty" and "gravitas" of the "new" Yankee Stadium has very much to do with the fact that at 500,000 square feet, it is roughly 60 percent larger than its timeless predecessor, which begs the question "Then why less seating?" The answer is (1) the new stadium's seats are up to two inches wider than the old ballpark's; (2) the leg room between rows is almost 10 inches greater than it was at "old" Yankee Stadium; and most of all (3) the park's 56 private luxury suites, 37 more than "old" Yankee Stadium. John Sterling notes, "Look how much smaller seating it is than the 'old' Yankee Stadium. It's that way for creature comfort and for all the suites. The suites are magnificent. I know that because when they play football or hockey, I usually take my two boys to the football and hockey games, and I'll stay in the suite, and, boy, *that's* the way to fly." Aside from the suites, which may seem to the fans in the bleachers to be like the top floor of New York's Waldorf Astoria, the team nearly doubled the width of the concourses in the new ballpark, going from 17 to 32 feet. With all this leg room, food amenities, and wistfulness for the life of "the folks in the suites," it may be difficult for fans to remember they're there to watch an actual baseball game. One tradition in particular that has carried over from the "old" Yankee Stadium, regardless of the smaller capacity, is what is referred to by John Sterling as the "bleacher creature roll call," which starts with the first pitch of the game. As the fans call out—one by one—to the Yankees administering their defensive duties, it is the "duty" of each player, as he is prompted by the fans, to signal some form of recognition. Sometimes, depending on a player's propensity to draw things out, he will let the chants continue, which is why it's a good thing the six-syllable Jarrod Saltalamacchia never donned a Yankee uniform.

"Creature comfort" is one thing, but the player's comfort is (forgive the pun) "a whole 'nother ballpark." Regarded as arguably the best in baseball, the "new" Yankee Stadium's team clubhouses are unmatched. John Sterling adds, "The Yankee clubhouse could be broken up into condos, it's so enormous. It has every feature you'd ever want, and the visiting clubhouse is really great, too. The batting cages are right there. When you go into the dugout, *bang*, you run into a batting cage. How great is that?" Compared to the extensive walk from the dugout at Wrigley Field and the subterranean sewer encounters of O.co Coliseum, to a visiting player, Yankee Stadium must seem like a three-day vacation wrapped around nine hours of baseball that couldn't possibly be done any quicker.

SOME THINGS JUST NEVER CHANGE

Before Mayor John Lindsay and the city of New York purchased "old" Yankee Stadium and agreed to make some long overdue renovations, the stadium's outfield dimensions were, as John Sterling would say, "ludicrous." When the "old" Yankee Stadium was built in 1923, straightaway center field, also known at the time as "Death Valley," extended 491 feet from home plate, which by today's standards would probably see a home run every several years. The right-field and left-field fences, however, were only 295 and 281 feet, respectively, from home plate, which in hitter's terms translates to "pull your swing or lift more weights." In 1932 the team found a better use for the center-field real estate, adding a "monument" to former manager Miller

Huggins. As Yankee greatness increased, so did the number of monuments, which created the term "Monument Valley," a tribute to Yankees past right in the middle of the deepest playing field imaginable. Eventually the dimensions were brought in some, but still to a depth to which only the most powerful players like Mickey Mantle could hit. Sterling notes, "The *old* 'old' Yankee Stadium was ridiculous. It was the worst ballpark for a right-handed hitter. Imagine what DiMaggio would have done if he was in a normal ballpark. There, the left-field foul pole was 301 feet, but it went around, and, before you know it, it was 402. Then in left center, it was 457 and dead center was 461. Ludicrous. Who knows why they did that? Over the years, when they had the 'new' Yankee Stadium in '76, they gradually brought them in." Monument Valley was eventually corralled off and was not a literal pinball chase for outfielders like Mantle and DiMaggio. In the '70s, with the city's wallet calling the shots, the dimensions of the old Yankee Stadium came in to their final resting place of 318 and 314 feet to left and right field, 408 feet to straightaway center, and 399 and 385 feet to left and right center field, respectively.

Although with the new stadium's copious acreage of allotted real estate the team could place the real Death Valley in straightaway center, the Yankees decided to keep the new park's dimensions exactly the same as they had been in "old" Yankee Stadium. Sterling adds, "The dimensions are basically the same to the last Yankee Stadium. Left center is still 399, but the ball carries well. It's a good hitting ballpark, and I'm a believer in good hitting ballparks. Look at how when they built Seattle (Safeco) and Citi Field (Mets). Now they have to move in the fences. Detroit was ludicrous when they first built it. Comerica Park after Tiger Stadium, one of the great hitting ballparks. I think fans want to see the action and the runs, so if I built a ballpark, it would have short distances and high walls so you'd have doubles and triples off the walls. Yankee Stadium is not a great triples park but pretty good. If you have a fast guy who hits a ball in the gap and it goes to the wall, he'll get a triple." Seeing as how one doesn't get nicknames like "Sultan of Swat," "Yankee Clipper," or "the Bronx Bombers" by running three-quarters of the base paths, fans have to settle for the more than occasional home run trot when taking in a game at the only site in baseball known unmistakably as "the Stadium."

When it comes to hitters and pitchers, depending on which you ask, Yankee Stadium's most unique feature on the field—the porch in right—is an enemy or a godsend. Reflecting on this proverbial "double agent," Michael Kay notes, "The most unique feature of this big park is the short right-field porch. The original Yankee Stadium also played short to the porch in right and this is the same deal. I think visiting pitchers, as well as Yankee pitchers, are very aware of the wall and how it plays short out there. You never want a 'righty' batter to go the other way, and you certainly don't want a lefty batter to pull the ball. It spooks some players and has defeated others, especially fly ball pitchers. I have seen visiting pitchers throw their head back in utter disgust as balls they thought would be caught end up carrying over the wall." When asked how a pitcher would try to approach playing in Yankee Stadium, John Sterling simply answers, "Keep the ball down." He adds, "One thing about the American League East, all the ballparks outside of Tampa—which is okay—are great hitting ballparks. Camden Yards, Fenway Park, Yankee Stadium, and Rogers Centre. It's very tough pitching in the American League East for that reason because you play 18 or 19 games against each team. Some pitchers are comfortable on a certain mound and certain aren't. Good pitching will always stop good hitting. There never was a ballpark that was more of a band box than Ebbets Field. That doesn't mean they didn't have good pitching and they weren't low scoring games in those days. It has to do with how good the pitcher is." From 2009 to 2011 Yankees starter C. C. Sabathia, carrying over from his magical second-half pitching run of 2008 with the Milwaukee Brewers, taught Yankee fans how to stop good hitting, winning 59 games (19.67 a year), striking out 624 batters, and hoisting a three-year average ERA of 3.18. When using the phrase "how good a pitcher is," an obvious candidate will always be New York Yankees closer Mariano Rivera, whose 652 regular season and 42 postseason saves are both all-time records for relievers. In the final five seasons of his 19-year career, Rivera, pitching in the "new" Yankee Stadium, recorded 44 saves three times, and during the stadium's inaugural year he posted his fourth lowest ERA ever (1.76).

BACK TO BUSINESS IN '09

One year before Joe Torre took over duties as Yankees manager, the team had made their first postseason appearance in 14 years. The '95 postseason was a short-lived one, as the Seattle Mariners, with Ken Griffey Jr., Randy Johnson, and Edgar Martinez, disposed of their pinstripe opponent on a walk-off, game 5 win in the Division Series. In 1996 Joe Torre brought the American League East title back to the Bronx with rookie shortstop Derek Jeter; young pitcher Andy Pettitte; and a cast of traveled veterans like Paul O'Neill, Cecil Fielder, and third baseman Wade Boggs, who had played for the Yankees' rival Boston Red Sox for most of his career. With a supporting cast of Jim Leyritz, Bernie Williams, and (then) set-up man Mariano Rivera, the Yankees mowed through the Texas Rangers and Baltimore Orioles en route to the World Series against the defending world champion Atlanta Braves. After falling behind 0–2 at home in the first two games, the Yankees won four straight thanks to clutch hitting, pitching, and on Joe Torre's part, managing. This formula continued for the Yankees over the next 11 seasons. Team general manager Brian Cashman found the best free agent pitcher/batter/reliever, etc., and offered them a large contract, and the Yankees RSVPed to their seemingly annual trip to the fall classic. The Yankees, between 1996 and 2003, went to six World Series, winning four. In fact, beginning with the 125-win '98 season, Joe Torre's team won nine straight division titles. Unfortunately, much of that period was overshadowed by Bobby Cox and his 14 straight division-title-winning Atlanta Braves. While the Yankees did not win the American League East in 2007, their streak of consecutive trips to the postseason reached 13. As the "midge-aided" Cleveland Indians eliminated relief pitcher Joba Chamberlain and the Yankees in four games in the 2007 American League Division Series, so ended Joe Torre's 12-year reign with the team. Already having managed the Mets, Braves, and Cardinals before becoming the Yankee "skipper," Torre, much like the team he was headed to had done back in 1958, left New York for Los Angeles, where he led the Dodgers to the National League Championship Series two straight years before retiring a season later. Soon thereafter Torre was inducted into the hall of fame.

With the "new" Yankee Stadium beginning to rise across the street, the '08 season was the swan song for "the House That Ruth Built." The Torreless Yankees did not qualify for the postseason that year, the team's first 162-game season since 1993. While another "Joe" was leading the team, another "George" was building a Yankee house, and Brian Cashman, as always, was filling it with imported talent. With the arms of tandem C. C. Sabathia and A. J. Burnett coming from Milwaukee and Toronto and the bats of Johnny Damon, Mark Teixeira, and Jerry Hairston coming over from Boston, Los Angeles (Angels), and Cincinnati, the '09 Yankees sported a league best 103–59 record heading into the playoffs. One theme so prevalent during the '09 Yankees postseason run was "the core four," which consisted of the only remaining members of the previous world champion Yankees lineup of 2000: Derek Jeter, Jorge Posada, Andy Pettitte, and Mariano Rivera. While the "fresher legged" imports were earning their checks via walk-off home runs, game-tying home runs, and American League Championship Series MVP awards (Sabathia), the core four were living up to their postseason name, as Jeter's .344 batting average, Pettitte's three wins to add to his 19 for the postseason (record), and Rivera's five saves to add to his 42 (another record) propelled the Yankees back to being one win away from their 27th World Series title. In game 6 of the World Series, Andy Pettitte got his fourth win, thanks to six RBIs by eventual World Series MVP Hideki Matsui. Though not in a save situation, Rivera closed out the final inning, and joining his "core" companions, the team celebrated—like it had all those times at the "old" Yankee Stadium—with Sinatra's "New York, New York" serenading a pile of pinstriped bodies on the pitcher's mound.

AFTER "THE BOSS" AND THE "CORE FOUR"

The year following the Yankees' successful christening of their new home, team owner George Steinbrenner passed away, turning the duties over to his son, Hank, and while the championship banners weren't lifted over the next few seasons, pinstripe glory was making room for itself in the halls of Cooperstown, starting with Mariano "Mo" Rivera. In September 2011 Rivera cemented himself into the role of "greatest closer ever" by passing Trevor Hoffman's 601 career saves. Rivera extended the summit another 50 saves before planting his flag at the 652 mark. In Rivera's final appearance in September 2013, he received a visit to the mound from teammates Derek Jeter and Andy Pettitte, who "pulled" Rivera in Michael Kay's "close second" most memorable game as a broadcaster in the "new" Yankee Stadium. Kay notes, "When Jeter and Andy Pettitte took him out of the game, Rivera broke down in tears on the mound. The park was louder that night than even the 2009 World Series."

Michael Kay's most memorable game at the "new" Yankee Stadium perhaps explains why a closer closing out his storied and statistically unprecedented career may summon more noise and love from the "bleacher creatures" than a World Series championship. Derek Jeter, the Yankees "Captain," a title observed with great reverence in the Bronx, played his entire 20-year career in pinstripes. Jeter's .310 lifetime batting average doesn't even include his 200 postseason hits, the most in Major League history. In fact, the only person close to Jeter's postseason hits mark is former teammate Bernie Williams, who is still 72 short of "the Captain." With 3,465 career hits, good enough to make Jeter sixth on the all-time list, number 3,000 will always stay with Michael Kay, who, when asked what his most memorable game was at "the Stadium," replied, "It would have to be Jeter's 3,000th hit game against the Rays where he was 5 for 5 and got the game winning hit as well as hitting a home run for his 3,000th, which I called history with an exclamation point." Jeter, after that afternoon in July 2011, added another 457 hits over the next few seasons before his final game at Yankee Stadium on September 25, 2014, against the Baltimore Orioles. In the team's home finale—Jeter's final game in pinstripes—the Captain doubled in his first at bat, knocking in Brett Gardner for the Yankees' first run of the game. The Yankees carried a three-run lead into the top of the ninth, where anytime would have been suitable to pull Jeter from shortstop and allow him the barrage of "curtain calls" from the Yankee faithful. Orioles center fielder Adam Jones put to rest any photo opportunities for tipped caps from the dugout (at least for the time being) by belting a two-run blast off Yankees closer David Robertson. A Steve Pearce home run with Jeter still posted at shortstop ensured the emotionally conflicted crowd they would see one more at bat from number 2. One Jose Pirela single and Brett Gardner sacrifice bunt later, pinch runner Antoan Richardson stood on second base, poised for the potential game-winning run as Jeter walked up to the plate one final time at Yankee Stadium. On the first pitch from Baltimore reliever Evan Meek, Jeter lined a single to right, scoring Richardson and winning the game for the Yankees. Rounding first, Jeter stopped as Richardson beat the throw home, and raised his arms, which would soon be lowered by a mob of teammates both present *and* past. Among the throng of hugs Jeter received were those from his "core four," former manager Joe Torre and former teammates Bernie Williams, Andy Pettitte, and Tino Martinez. Sterling describes Jeter's universe-aligning final Yankee Stadium at bat: "It certainly was like it had been scripted. I mean how great was it that he got the game-winning hit in the bottom of the ninth inning? David Robertson had to give up two home runs—good for three runs—to bring about the tie. That's the end of the movie when Jeter lined that base hit." Taking a page from Michael Kay, with the Yankees all-time leader in hits (3,465), doubles (544), stolen bases (358), at bats (11,195), and games played (2,747) "walking off" before walking into the home dugout one final time, it took a majestic-sized venue like Yankee Stadium to hold *that* big of an exclamation point.

· 31 ·

This Was a Parking Lot, Now
It's Turned into an Outfield

$\mathcal{W}$hen interviewing broadcasters who have been calling games for two-thirds of their lives, especially in the "post–Camden Yards" era, there's a good chance they used to call a different booth their home, most of the time in the same city. Many of the broadcasters I interviewed had a close-up view of the evolution of ballpark development and construction in general, from the "cookie cutters" to the domes. While Fenway Park and Wrigley Field stand as the senior partners for the firm of "Cathedrals, Coliseums, and Associates," outside of Oakland, Kansas City, and the greater Los Angeles area, the trend in new park construction has gone from "stadiums" to "ballparks" as the setting for America's pastime. Although a good percentage of these former homes of today's teams have gone by the wayside via implosion, or, in the case of the once great Houston Astrodome, pure abandonment, their stories live on in the memories of not only these long-tenured broadcasters but the fans who attended the games as well.

"OLD" YANKEE STADIUM

While outside of the Bronx, Yankees haters and Ted Williams/Ty Cobb enthusiasts alike may prefer to use the phrase "the Ruth *that* house built," the "old" Yankee Stadium stood for 85 years, housing 26 World Series champions over that time. The amount of success achieved in the stadium's first 40 years was so great, only last names were necessary to identify players (Ruth, Gehrig, DiMaggio, Mantle). Under the leadership of managers Miller Huggins, Joe McCarthy, Casey Stengel, and Ralph Houk, the Yankees won a combined 20 World Series and 26 American League pennants. The "old" Yankee Sta-

223

dium was such a monument to the game that even broadcasters and players from other teams couldn't help but soak in its "majesty." Longtime Chicago White Sox broadcaster and former Red Sox player Ken "Hawk" Harrelson states, "The first time I walked into old Yankee Stadium, I cried, because here I was from Savannah, Georgia. Babe Ruth, Lou Gehrig, Mickey Mantle, Joe DiMaggio. It's overwhelming." Joe Castiglione, the voice for the past 32 seasons of the Yankees' sworn rival, the Boston Red Sox, recalls, "The original Yankee Stadium was where I saw my first game as a kid. The first game I ever went to was September 1953. It was Jerry Coleman day when Jerry came back from Korea. I always told Jerry about that." Around the time Jerry Coleman, who won four World Series championships in a Yankees uniform, was sharpening his skills as a Yankees broadcaster, "old" Yankee Stadium was undergoing a renovation so drastic, people would call the building with the exact same mailing address "new" Yankee Stadium. Two years and (adjusted for today's inflation) $600 million later, the "house that Ruth built" was a far cry from its former self. A site that once held 80,000 plus fans was reduced to 57,000, and an outfield that had spanned as deep as 487 feet in 1923 eventually came in as "shallow" as 408 feet from home plate. Still, just like its former incarnation, Yankee Stadium reopened itself in 1976 as a contender, with the team winning the American League pennant before being swept by "the Big Red Machine" Cincinnati Reds in the World Series. The following season, a fall-classic-suited nickname emerged for the Yankees as their outfield import, Reggie "Mr. October" Jackson, along with Yankees favorites Thurman Munson and Chris Chambliss, led the team to two straight titles, in 1977 and 1978. Soon afterward the pennant-less shadow once again cast itself over the Bronx landmark, not to be lifted until 1996, when new skipper Joe Torre made the team championship relevant, and he kept it that way for the next 12 years, winning four World Series titles and six American League pennants. Having arrived in the Yankees' broadcast booth in 1989 and 1992, respectively, John Sterling and Michael Kay, two of the Yankees' leading voices on the radio and TV today, were both present at so many great moments inside the "old" Yankee Stadium that when asked to think of his most memorable game, Sterling replied, "Oh, that would be absolutely impossible." Kay, who worked in the New York area for the *Post* and the *Daily News*, like Sterling, has been with the Yankees since the '89 season. Describing the feeling he got from the "old" Yankee Stadium, Kay says, "The thing about the old park was you actually felt you were walking in the footsteps of greatness. All the championships that had taken place and all the all-time greats that had played there could be felt. Curt Schilling once called it 'aura and mystique.' You could feel it." Kay was able to "feel," firsthand, a few championships of his own, broadcasting for the

Yankees on WABC Radio during the team's 1996, 1998, 1999, and 2000 World Series titles. Despite all the playing and replaying of Frank Sinatra's "New York, New York" to a pinstriped pile ending baseball's year in late October, Michael Kay's most memorable game from "old" Yankee Stadium took place on July 1, 2004, against (who else but) the Boston Red Sox. Kay recalls, "Derek Jeter made a head first dive into the stands to catch a foul ball and had to leave the game bloodied and bruised. The game had an ebb and flow to it that was nail biting and eventually finished with a John Flaherty walk off hit." Jeter's head-first dive not only ended the Red Sox half of the 12th inning but also sent the team captain to the hospital for X-rays. After Manny Ramirez's second home run of the game in the top of the 13th put the Red Sox on top 4–3, Flaherty, pinch hitting, doubled in Miguel Cairo—who had already tied the game with his own double—for the game's winning run. The catch was one of many that make "the Captain's" career highlight reel longer than a senate hearing on CNN.

Known in the Bronx community as "Pa Pinstripe," John Sterling has not missed a game in his career as the Yankees' lead radio broadcaster. Coming over from the Atlanta Braves, Sterling broadcast from the booth of the "old" Yankee Stadium for 20 years before moving across to the team's new ballpark of the same name. Having been witness to six World Series appearances, two perfect games (David Wells '98, David Cone '99), and 10 American League East division titles in "old" Yankee Stadium, John Sterling, when asked to pick a most memorable game, responds, "There are too many games. It's very tough for me to pick out individual games. I hate to say this, but they blend in." Fortunately from a writer's standpoint, Sterling picked a game with a backstory worthy of the silver screen: October 26, 1996, game 6 of the 1996 World Series against the defending champion Atlanta Braves. One off-the-field element to note about the '96 season was manager Joe Torre's two brothers, Frank and Rocco; the latter passed away on June 21 from a heart attack and the former, coincidentally, was in need of a heart transplant during his brother's first trip to the World Series. Calling the 1996 World Series, Sterling and the entire Yankees community were well aware of Frank Torre's condition. Frank received the transplant just in time for "game 6 of '96." Pa Pinstripe recalls the night, saying, "In the final game of the 1996 World Series, we got back from Atlanta winning three games to two. We went down there 0–2, and the three games were phenomenal. In between, Joe Torre's brother, Frank, received his heart replacement. *He got a heart, and he was alive, and he could listen to the game!* That Saturday, they beat Atlanta and won the World Series for the first time in a number of years. There was so much in it that it was phenomenal." Under any other circumstances, one might consider it difficult to come up with a "close second," but in the case of the never-truant John Sterling and the New York Yankees, one other game in particular didn't "blend in" with the rest: October 16, 2003, game 7 of the American League Championship Series against the Boston Red Sox. Pitting arguably the two greatest pitchers in Red Sox history—Pedro Martinez and former "BoSox" ace Roger Clemens—against each other, game 7 of the 2003 ALCS was defined by the long ball. With Clemens giving up home runs to Trot Nixon and Kevin Millar, the odds were stacked against the Yankees' chances for a return to an unprecedented 39th fall classic. Fortunately for the Bronx Bombers, Red Sox manager Grady Little kept his ace in one batter too long, as Yankees catcher Jorge Posada's double scored Bernie Williams and Hideki Matsui to tie the game. Fast-forward three scoreless innings by Mariano Rivera to the bottom of the 11th inning, and Yankees third baseman Aaron Boone—who earlier had come in as a pinch runner—took Red Sox reliever Tim Wakefield's knuckleball into the left-field bleachers for a walk-off, pennant-clinching home run. The broadcast on Fox that night ended with the image of a "winking" Babe Ruth.

Current Los Angeles Dodgers TV/radio broadcaster Charley Steiner called Boone's walk-off home run during his three-year stint with the Yankees before switching coasts to follow his lifelong dream of calling Dodgers baseball. Steiner, a native of New York, grew up at a time when the Yankees seemed to be the only thing happening in baseball. As a member of the Yankees organization, Charley was reminded of this history, literally, every morning when he showed up for work. Steiner notes, "For me, absolutely personally and selfishly, when I first got there to Yankee Stadium in 2002, I was given a parking space in the player's lot. Each space had a number, and so here I am coming to Yankee Stadium for the first time as a Yankee announcer and they point me to my parking space and it's number 61. This is good. This is karmic convergence. For me, that may be the most sentimental memory I have of the old place." Signing off on "old" Yankee Stadium in a way only he could, Charley Steiner states, "The old stadium was not really the old stadium. It was kinda the refurbished old stadium. It used to be the house that Ruth built. This was the house that Mayor Lindsay *re*built. It was old. It was creaky. It was rusty. It was all of the things that make old things wonderful. I loved going to Yankee Stadium. All the men and women—whether it was the security guys, the clubhouse guys, the folks in the kitchen, whatever—they were all same folks who had been there for 100 years, so there was a familiarity and a continuity about it. One man's creaky is another man's historic. For that, I loved it, and it was *The Yankees*. At the end of the day, it was *The Yankees*."

"OLD" COMISKEY PARK

Before "new" Comiskey Park opened for the '91 season, "old" Comiskey Park lived up to its name, as it was two years senior to both Tiger Stadium and Fenway Park. Over its 80-year history, "old" Comiskey Park hosted many of baseball's biggest memories, including the first ever All-Star Game in 1933 and three World Series, only one of which was won by the home team Chicago White Sox, against the New York Giants in 1917. Perhaps the most lasting memory of the White Sox in their old home, unfortunately, is the "Black Sox" scandal of 1919, which banished would-have-been hall of fame players like "Shoeless" Joe Jackson and Eddie Cicotte from professional baseball for life. Ken "Hawk" Harrelson of the White Sox broadcast team played with the Red Sox for a good part of his career and has lasting memories of Comiskey Park on the field as well as in the booth. Harrelson states, "When I played there against the White Sox, I realized what a tough park it was to hit in, not because of the dimensions so much—which were big—but because the White Sox always had great pitching. If you go in there for a four game series and you come out of there and have won two, you've done something, because you were going to face four good pitchers." Among these excellent pitchers were Red Faber, Ted Lyons, and Ed Walsh. Not to be

"Old" Comiskey Park: "When I played there against the White Sox, I realized what a tough park it was to hit in, not because of the dimensions so much, but because the White Sox always had great pitching."—Ken "Hawk" Harrelson
Photo courtesy of Ron Vesely

excluded from the "honorable mention" list are hitters Luke Appling, Nellie Fox, and recent hall of fame inductee Frank Thomas. Eventually the wear and tear began to show at "old" Comiskey Park, which was also a perk for some like current Tampa Bay Rays radio broadcaster Dave Wills, who once worked for the White Sox at their former home. Wills states, "Everything at 'old' Comiskey Park for me was as a fan or as a reporter. When I was a young kid just getting out of college, I covered some games at 'old' Comiskey Park but never as a play-by-play announcer. It's kinda funny. I've been to so many games as a fan at 'old' Comiskey Park, I probably even know it better than 'the Trop.' Back in the late '70s as a fan, you'd walk around and see the cutouts in the wall of chicken wire, and you could go sit at a picnic table area and watch the game from the field level in the outfield. That was always kinda neat." Eventually, "old" Comiskey Park made way for "new" Comiskey Park, which, judging by the $100 million plus in renovations the White Sox organization had to shell out to finally "get it right," couldn't have been built any faster. Former White Sox broadcaster Wayne Hagin, who saw former team general manager Roland Hemond literally kiss "old" Comiskey Park goodbye on its final day, recalls the team's first day at the "new" Comiskey Park: "Old Comiskey Park was the oldest ballpark in the big leagues, so when we came up to open up the brand new stadium, people who drove up and parked their cars to go into this new structure, it was almost like they went to a funeral for the old one and the casket was still open. Part of right field was still existent and it really bothered the White Sox fans to come to the new one and go, 'Oh, look at the old one.' The remains were still there because they hadn't completely knocked it down. It was really strange." One other "remain" of "old" Comiskey Park was the site where home plate once stood, which is cemented into the parking lot of (now named) U.S. Cellular Field. As if the open casket that once was the White Sox home didn't upset the fans enough, the results on former White Sox owner Bill Veeck's scoreboard—also an import from "old" Comiskey—likely drove the nail home. Wayne Hagin adds, "In all those 80 years of the ballpark, the '90 season was the only year that they had gone without being shut out, and the very first game of the 'new' Comiskey Park was a shut out, 16–0 by Detroit, and Carlton Fisk said, 'Those are the gods of the 'old' Comiskey speaking to us.'" Eventually, in 2005, the gods spoke again, as the White Sox ended their 88-year title-less drought inside their constantly upgrading stadium, which, when considering the bill, will have to suffice the city another 90 years before a replacement is built to create another "open casket."

TIGER STADIUM

Opening within a few years of "old" Comiskey Park, Wrigley Field, and Fenway Park, Tiger Stadium, named after the team who takes its field every day, saw as much success over its 88-year history as the other three parks combined. Ironically, none of Detroit's World Series glory was ever boasted by the Tigers' own Tyrus Raymond Cobb, arguably the greatest player to ever put on a baseball uniform. After Cobb moved on from the game, the team won its first World Series title, in 1935, and a second 10 years down the road, both thanks to "Hammerin'" Hank Greenberg. A whole generation later, Detroit's second most famous Tiger, Al Kaline, led the team to another title, and 16 years later Kirk Gibson, Alan Trammell, and Lou Whitaker hoisted the World Series glory once again for the Motor City. Growing up in between these periods of Tigers success was current lead radio broadcaster for the team, Dan Dickerson, who remembers Tiger Stadium as a fan, saying, "I think it was that traditional walk into the ballpark, completely opposite of Comerica. You could not see the field until you walked up that ramp in the upper deck or the concourse in the lower deck; the little aisle way. *Then* you saw the field. I always loved that. You walk out and are just like, 'Ah! We're back at a ball game again.' It was a pretty cool sight. I've got a couple of pictures I took of that field just walking down the aisle way into the ballpark. My perspective really was more from a fan's perspective. God bless my parents. When I got my license, they would let me hop in the car, drive down, and pay $1.50 to sit in the centerfield bleachers. That was in the '70s and those teams weren't very good, but I would just sit down there in the stands and enjoy watching the game." Perhaps the most unique feature of Tiger Stadium was the overhanging upper deck in right field, a design emulated in such new ballparks as Citi Field and Globe Life Park in Arlington. Dickerson continues, "As time went on, I realized maybe the best seat in the house was in the right-field upper deck. The front seat was up 10 feet in front of the wall down below. That was a true overhang. They talk about Texas having the overhang as kind of a nod to Tiger Stadium, but it's set behind the lower deck. In foul territory, right across from the upper deck overhang, were some seats that were really out over the field. No matter how small a crowd might be, there was always somebody in that seat right down there in the corner because you look out, and there was nothing below you but foul territory. You really felt like you were in theater seating overlooking the field. Unbelievable vantage point. That turned out to be maybe my favorite seat of the last few years I would go to games at Tiger Stadium. Just a gorgeous view and a great seat, the likes of which we'll never see again." Aside from the overhanging upper deck, the broadcast booth itself was probably the most unique seat at Tiger Stadium. Currently the lead play-by-play radio broadcaster of the Seattle Mariners, Rick Rizzs spent three seasons as a Tigers broadcaster. Rizzs recalls the excitement of calling games from inside the close proximity of the Tigers broadcast booth: "When Tiger Stadium was built in 1912, there wasn't any radio, so, at some point, they needed a press box for the writers. They were up on top and we broadcasters were way down below. They stuck us underneath the upper deck, and we were so close to home plate. We were right there—maybe 80 feet away—and we could hear everything. It was kind of dangerous at times because those foul balls would come back into the booth, and you had to be alert. In our visiting booth, it was a little bit toward the third base side, so we had to be careful of left-handed hitters. In Ernie Harwell's booth, which, eventually, I occupied, you had to be ready for the right-handed hitters. Ernie had a net, and, when I went to Detroit to try to replace Ernie in 1992, I took down the net. I thought, 'You know? I'm going to work without a net,' but, after the first few ball games, I said, 'I'm putting the net back up,' because those baseballs were flying back. I said, 'I could see fine through this net. There's more right-handed hitters than left-handed hitters.' I think that's one of the things that stood out for us as a broadcaster." For Rizzs, the other thing that stood out was an element unsurprising in a building nearly 100 years old. Signing off on Tiger Stadium, Rick Rizzs continues, "Just walking into the ballpark, it was the history of Tiger Stadium. That thick grass on the infield that Sparky Anderson liked for Alan Trammell and Lou Whitaker, and everybody else. The feel of it. The double tiered upper decks with the posts. I remember their seats with an obstructed view. There was a seat right behind a post out in left field. I sat in it one time after a ball game. It was the charm, the history, and the tradition that I loved about Tiger Stadium, and the players that you know played in there that created that history and were a part of that ballpark. Ty Cobb. *Ty Cobb* played there. Babe Ruth, Lou Gehrig, Harry Heilmann, Hank Greenberg, Charlie Gehringer. You name all the greats. Al Kaline, Willie Horton, the great team of the '68 Tigers that won the World Series. That's what I liked about Tiger Stadium. The ghosts were still there. You could still see those guys out there. That's what I love about the old ballparks. We don't have many left. I love the history of the game. Always have, always will, and that was the fun part about walking into Tiger Stadium."

SHEA STADIUM

Having moved out of their temporary home of the famed Polo Grounds after a two-year stint, the New York Mets, one of baseball's newest teams, found their new home of Shea Stadium, which would see twice as many world

Shea Stadium: "Every bit the home to me that the apartment was where I grew up." —
Howie Rose
Photo courtesy of the New York Mets

championships as the Brooklyn Dodgers' Ebbets Field. The first, the "Amazing" Mets of '69, defeated the mighty Baltimore Orioles as a decided underdog, leaving the city reeling to this day from their improbable first championship. Another 17 years later and against American League Cy Young and MVP winner Roger Clemens, the '86 Mets—Mookie Wilson in particular—got the best of the Boston Red Sox and the infamously gaffing first baseman Bill Buckner, beleaguering the "curse of the Babe" a further 18 years. Off the diamond but still in the park, Shea Stadium was host to one of the biggest musical events in U.S. history, when The Beatles played before 55,600 fans on August 15, 1965, setting a "pop" concert record for attendance and revenue. Though not John, Paul, George, and Ringo, the '74–'75 New York Yankees "squatted" in Shea for two full seasons as their home was undergoing a renovation for the ages. Eventually, after 45 seasons, Shea Stadium closed its doors, giving way to the heavily discussed Citi Field, a ballpark whose construction took place right before the eyes of Mets fans attending games in Shea, making the old stadium seem like Henry VIII's next-to-be beheaded wife. Shea Stadium left behind it a quality not found in many ballparks. Current Philadelphia Phillies broadcaster Tom McCarthy not only broadcast inside Shea for a short while but also attended games there during his youth. McCarthy recalls his impression walking into Shea Stadium: "When I was a kid—even when I was doing the games—when I used to come out of the tunnel or walk into the press box at Shea Stadium, the first thing that I would look at was the big old scoreboard in right center field. That, to me, was a throwback to the old days. They updated it as the years went on, but it still had that same feel of the '60s. The first thing I would look at when I would come through the tunnel as a kid was the starting lineup that would go up the left side for the visitors and the right side for the Mets. It was just numbers and their position, so you kinda had to know the numbers of the players to know whether 41 was in the nine hole or whether 17 or Felix Millan was at second base or whether 7 was at first base for Ed Kranepool. It got even better in the '80s. Whether 8 was behind the plate batting cleanup, whether 17 was at first base batting third or 4 was in the leadoff spot. Was it a left-hander, and, did that mean that 1 was in the leadoff spot in center field? That, to me, is something that I will always remember."

As fortuitous as historical events can (or can't) be at times, the '08 season—the swan song for Shea Stadium—came to a close with the Mets competing for a playoff spot. Former Mets broadcaster Wayne Hagin recalls what was his most memorable game during his one year at Shea Stadium: "Johan Santana, on the Saturday before the final game of the year, they had to beat the Florida Marlins. He shut them out that day, and he did it on one knee. I think he pitched on three days rest that day, and he showed his guts and his guile because he had signed as a free agent, and he had delivered. He won 16 games that year, but he left so many games with leads. He should have easily won 20 something games and should have been the Cy Young award winner in 2008. He did everything he was supposed to do. He lived up to it. Here's a guy who came from Venezuela and had never been in the big scene, big lights, and all that because he had been in Minnesota, and he accepted it. He enjoyed it, and he walked out there and pitched the game of his life for the New York Mets when they needed him most. The year before, the final game of the year was pitched by Tom Glavine, who had been much heralded. He gave up seven runs in the first inning of that final game and they lost. Here they are knowing that they have to win on that Saturday at Shea and he delivered. Then we found out after the game that he was going to have immediate surgery on his knee, so he pitched on a bum knee and pitched the game of his life for the New York Mets. That's the game I remember because he gave them every hope the next day that they would make up for the loss the year before. This was their turn and they're closing out Shea and they're going to go out in style. He gave them every bit of hope on that Saturday when he pitched his heart out. He was remarkable." Sadly, the Mets had to win *two* games that weekend, and Santana's gem was the last win for the Mets in Shea

Stadium, as they lost the next day to the Florida Marlins. Riding home from the soon-to-be landmarked home of the Mets, Hagin remembers the Mets fans' feedback: "In 2008, when they lost that last game, it's about an hour later, and I'm taking the subway back into Manhattan where I lived. Those fans. I don't know if it was the adults or the kids who had more foul language talking about the Mets and their demise that day. I don't know who had the saltier vocabulary; the adults that had their kids or the kids who had their adults. They were so embroiled with the Mets losing that day. So mad. Those trains were unbelievable to hear."

Before the stereotype-laced New York subway ride home, Hagin, on the air, had turned the postgame show over to longtime Mets radio broadcaster, and above all fan, Howie Rose. Hagin notes, "Howie had been down on the field for the post-game ceremony as the public address announcer. When he came back to the booth, I asked him to sit down and say goodbye to Shea on the air. He did a beautiful, out of the blue, and very tearful goodbye to Shea Stadium. Ad libbing the whole thing. It meant so much for him. Here I am; the new guy. It's my first year in New York. What am I saying goodbye to Shea Stadium for when I can have Howie Rose come in and do it? It was our final segment on the post-game show and because I had asked him to do it, that's why he was so appreciative." When asked several years after the final broadcast what he takes from Shea Stadium, Rose answers, "I take from it my childhood, my adolescence, my adulthood, my profession, my avocation, and, frankly, my heart. It was every bit the home to me that the apartment was where I grew up. So when people like to belittle—whether it's Shea Stadium or any old ballpark that's reached the end of the line—I take exception to that because the memories were the beauty really. The aesthetic splendor is in the memories, not so much the edifice. For me, there's just a lifetime of memories associated directly with Shea Stadium. I get very emotional and somewhat protective about not only the events that happened there but my memories of having been associated with it, either directly in the stands as a fan or in the broadcast booth as an announcer who is honored to be a part of the lineage of the three announcers who were there at the beginning with the Mets: Bob Murphy, Lindsey Nelson, and Ralph Kiner; announcers who I grew up listening to and watching. So I take from Shea Stadium everything. Shea Stadium is with me everywhere I go in baseball and in my career."

"OLD" BUSCH STADIUM

For 40 seasons the St. Louis Cardinals, having moved out of their home of Sportsman's Park, made downtown St. Louis the premiere setting for sports in their colossal home of "old" Busch Stadium. During their time in the "not quite cookie-cutter" confines of "old" Busch Stadium, the Cardinals went to six World Series, winning two championships, as well as eleven division titles and eight appearances in the National League Championship Series. "Old" Busch Stadium was also host to Cardinals first baseman Mark McGwire's home run campaign of '98, including the night of September 8, 1998, when McGwire's 62nd round-tripper of the season passed Yankee Roger Maris's single-season record, which had stood for 37 years. Sharing its home with the occasional St. Louis football team, "old" Busch Stadium was retrofitted and had its infield and outfield surface altered so many times, had they still been alive, Lewis and Clark would have trekked right past it on their way back from the west and not even known. Still, one thing that was left unchanged in "old" Busch Stadium was the results in the standings, as the St. Louis Cardinals closed out their old home with two deep runs in the postseason, including the 2004 World Series against the "curse of the Babe"–breaking Boston Red Sox. Sitting in the broadcast booth for game 4 of the eventual Red Sox sweep in 2004, former Cardinals broadcaster Wayne Hagin recalls what "old" Busch Stadium, and with it St. Louis, resembled: "If you want to typify what Busch Stadium meant, it represents the Midwest. It represents a place. That hospitable aspect. The graciousness. That's the flavor. That's the people of the Midwest. 2004 comes around and it's the Cardinals and the Red Sox in the World Series. The Red Sox sweep after they beat the Yankees four straight after being down three games to none. What typified Busch Stadium, and what typifies the new Busch Stadium today is the people and how courteous they are. How gracious they are. It embodies the Midwest spirit. Red Sox fans, sensing the kill, couldn't go to the first two games at Fenway, but they could get tickets to a bigger Busch Stadium for the World Series in games 3 and 4. The fourth game being the finale. There were Bostonians who flew to St. Louis in the event they won the World Series, but they couldn't get tickets to the game. The game's over. The Red Sox sweep. They beat the Cardinals on their field and the celebration begins on the field. When all of the despondent Cardinal fans are leaving, there are Boston fans outside, standing in the street. They have no tickets. They're just jumping for joy. They've got all the Red Sox shirts, jerseys, hats, and all that. Ushers who work at the gates at the old Busch Stadium said, 'You want to go in and see your team?' They hadn't won a World Series in 86 years. 'You want to go see it? Go ahead and go in.' You tell me what franchise or what ballpark in America would have done that. Nobody knows that unless you were there."

EBBETS FIELD

Opened on April 9, 1913, Ebbets Field, named after team owner Charles Ebbets *by* Charles Ebbets, stood for over four decades as the home of the Brooklyn Dodgers. A team that had undergone more name changes than songwriter John Cougar Mellencamp, the Brooklyn Dodgers won two pennants inside Ebbets Field playing as the Brooklyn Robins. Finally, after the proverbial soul searching was complete, Brooklyn's team name once again became the Dodgers, who would go on to seven more World Series, and finally, in 1955, beat the mighty New York Yankees for the organization's first title in its 71-year existence. Aside from the postseason, Ebbets Field was host to perhaps the biggest breakthrough in the history of major sports, when Brooklyn Dodgers first baseman Jackie Robinson broke the color barrier, becoming the first African American player to compete on a Major League level, in 1947. Robinson earned the Rookie of the Year award and not only went on to win the 1949 National League Most Valuable Player award, but six years later also helped the Dodgers to their only title in Brooklyn. Two of today's hall of fame baseball broadcasters—Vin Scully and Eric Nadel—had different perspectives at Ebbets Field, Scully as a broadcaster and Nadel as a young fan. Recalling his first impression of Ebbets Field as a six-year-old child, Nadel says, "When you go to your first baseball game, you walk out through the entryway and all you see is green. You've just been watching everything on black and white TV and had no idea. In Brooklyn, we didn't play on grass. We played in schoolyards that were pavement. We played on little league fields that were dirt. There wasn't a blade of grass on them, and you go to Ebbets Field, and it's this emerald green lawn. It's just overwhelming. At six years old, I went to four games. I remember exactly where I sat at all four games. I remember the first game I went to, Hank Aaron hit a couple of home runs for the Braves. He batted second. He was incredibly skinny. I'll never forget. I asked my dad how he could hit a ball that far as skinny as he is. We sat out in the bleachers in left field one time. Twice we sat behind home plate, and then on Gil Hodges night—Gil was our neighbor—my dad got tickets from one of his patients right behind the Dodgers dugout. Twi-night doubleheader and I dressed in my Dodgers uniform. I could see them wheel this boat out on the field to give to Hodges. I'll never forget how enormous the right-field scoreboard looked to a six-year-old kid. It was as big as a skyscraper."

Coming into his 65th season as a baseball broadcaster, Vin Scully's career began inside the booth at Ebbets Field. Reflecting on a building that was demolished more than 50 years ago, Scully states, "Ebbets Field is where I broke in as a young broadcaster. Ebbets Field was a double deck grandstand from dead center all the way around to the right-field foul pole. However, right field itself was backed up by a concave, concrete wall. Then on top of the concrete wall was a wire screen, so there were no fans in right field. It was a very intimate ballpark. The modern-day park—it seems to me—the crowds are almost like wallpaper. You hear them, but you don't really see any individual. In Ebbets Field, you were extremely aware of many of the people that came to the game. People like Hilda Chester, who was certainly famous as a great fan. I'm not sure where she worked, but, whatever she did, she used most of her money to be at the ballpark. She was certainly not a lady of great means, but you were aware of her. We also drew crowds of 8 to 9,000 a lot of the time, so it was quiet, and you were aware of individual voices. Compare that, of course, to the Los Angeles Coliseum, where we had 93,000 for big ball games including the World Series. The roar was intense, incredible, and thrilling, but you were not aware of individual fans. The same goes with Dodger Stadium. I had eight years of broadcasting at Ebbets Field, so it became my home away from home. I was as young as many of the Dodger players were, so I felt, indeed, like I was part of the family thanks to the O'Malley family who treated me so well." The owner of the team in the '50s—a decade when the Brooklyn Dodgers went to four World Series—Walter O'Malley sought a new home for his "family," which was not met well with New York City power broker Robert Moses. A site for a new stadium was not granted, and O'Malley loaded his family into the proverbial station wagon and headed west to Los Angeles. Though Ebbets Field was demolished shortly thereafter, its design lives once again in New York, outside the Mets' Citi Field.

POLO GROUNDS

Long before computer software and the term "point-O" were invented, one of baseball's most famous stadiums, the Polo Grounds, had a few "point-somethings" before reaching its final destination of Coogans Bluff in Manhattan. While it may have seemed like a halfway house for New York teams like the Yankees and the Mets, the Polo Grounds stood from 1911 to 1957 as the home of the New York Giants. During the team's 47-season stay there, the Polo Grounds hosted 13 World Series, with the home team Giants winning four. The Polo Grounds also introduced the world to arguably the greatest all-around player baseball has ever seen, Willie Mays, who during the 1954 World Series showed the world who was the master of the domain of the Polo Grounds center field. Current San Francisco Giants lead play-by-play radio broadcaster and longtime fan of Mays Jon Miller, who never actually graced the confines of the Polo Grounds, describes Mays's defensive play, otherwise known in baseball history as "the Catch," in game 1 of the 1954 World Series against the Cleveland Indians: "483 feet to straight-away center gave incredible amounts of field for Mays to cover. He always thought he would catch it. What he was most proud of was holding the runners. He wanted to make sure the guy at second didn't tag up and score. The throw went all the way back in to home plate. That was the best part of the play for him." Having received a yearbook from his dad during his first game as a kid, Jon Miller saw a photograph of the Polo Grounds while sit-ting in the San Francisco Giants' home of Candlestick Park. Miller confesses to having been "fascinated with it," saying, "The upper deck overhung the field by a considerable amount. The outfield fence did not curve in. It kept going straight out. If you didn't pull the ball, it kept going. There was still an extra notch then it was recessed in dead center and there were stairways to either side. There were windows out there where people could see out to the field." Boston Red Sox play-by-play radio broadcaster Joe Castiglione describes his experience inside the Polo Grounds as an attending fan: "It was very uncomfortable and certainly had great character." Another familiar voice of baseball spent his childhood in the Polo Grounds as well. Hall of fame broadcaster Vin Scully, who eventually worked in the Polo Grounds, describes his "full-circle" experience: "As a real youngster, long before I got into the business, I grew up, literally and figuratively, in the bleachers of the old Polo Grounds in New York. I was one of the fans hollering and cheering and rooting for players. That was a horseshoe stadium. I grew up in the bleachers and also in the upper deck in left and right field. In those days, being so young, my eyes were riveted on the players. My first game, if I had to guess, I was probably 11 or 12—somewhere in that area—and sit-ting in the bleachers, which would put you about 425 feet from home plate. I would sit there, and I would have this dream of someday broadcasting or writing—either one—and I would look at the horseshoe press box, which was suspended from the upper deck directly behind home plate. I would sit out there in center field and dream of, one day, being up in that press box. Because I've been greatly blessed, that dream came to fruition, and I wound up sitting in the press box, broadcasting, looking out at the bleachers, think-ing and remembering what it was like sitting out there. So, in one sense, the Polo Grounds, which was actually horseshoe in dimensions, and the way the ballpark played out was full circle for me to go from the bleachers to the press box." Scully and his Brooklyn Dodgers, much like the Giants, left New York after the 1957 season for the Golden State, California. The Dodgers went to Los Angeles and the Giants to San Francisco, where to this day the teams still represent one of the largest rivalries in all of Major League Baseball.

ATLANTA FULTON COUNTY STADIUM

Built to entice the Braves from their seemingly interim home of Milwaukee County Stadium, Atlanta Fulton County Stadium welcomed its new tenants on April 12, 1966, and they remained there for exactly 30 years. One of the imports to come down to Atlanta with the Braves was Hank Aaron, and he brought with him the second half of his home run record chase of Babe Ruth. On April 8, 1974, Aaron surpassed "the Babe" in what legendary broadcaster Vin Scully refers to as "maybe the single most important play" he has ever called in his career. Scully comments, "I love the roar of the crowd, all the way back to that eight-year-old kid crawling underneath the radio. The night that I described Henry Aaron breaking Babe Ruth's record, I let the crowd roar—as I always do—because I love it. Just listening to it, but it also gives me a chance to think and catch my breath a little bit. So when Henry Aaron hit his home run, I said, 'What an incredible moment. A black man is being honored in the Deep South for breaking the record of a white icon.' I've had a few of those. The few and far between, but I've been highly honored to have a small plot in each of them." Despite their record-breaking slugger leading the charge, the Atlanta Braves of the late '70s weren't exactly chasing other things. Like pennants. Current play-by-play radio broadcaster of the Atlanta Braves Jim Powell describes Atlanta Fulton County Stadium: "For the most part, my experience with Atlanta Fulton County Stadium was much more as a fan growing up and falling in love with baseball. The Braves were not very good when I was growing up. I turned 10 years old in 1975, and they would lose virtually every year. Every day at Fulton County in those days was a souvenir day. If there was a foul ball, as long as you had any speed at all, you could run the three sections over to get it because there weren't any fans out there. It was just totally different than your experience at Turner Field, where they win every year and the fans pack the place. I remember we'd look in the paper to see when Phil Niekro would be pitching, because that would be the only time the Braves would have any possibility of winning. We'd go sit in the upper deck, watch batting practice, and see if 'Knucksie' could pitch and hit his way past the opposition that day." The Braves weren't always justifying empty seats with their position in the standings. Thanks to the leadership of hall of fame-worthy Bobby Cox, the Braves began an unprecedented run of 14 straight division titles, almost half of which took place at Atlanta Fulton County Stadium. With the streak beginning in the Braves' "worst to first" '91 season, it was the '93 season in which they literally "caught fire." Jim Powell notes, "They had the famous fire at Atlanta Fulton County Stadium on the same day Fred McGriff joined the team. The Braves were trailing the Giants by nine and a half games, and the press box caught on fire. Mark Lemke has a great picture of him and Jeff Blauser, who was a noted prankster. The fire department hosed down the field with the fire raging in the background in the press box, and Lemke and Blauser have this funny look on their face like they're ready to go out and play baseball. That's another moment all Braves fans know about Atlanta Fulton County Stadium; the fire in the last few years. The Braves caught fire shortly thereafter, mostly because of Fred McGriff." The Braves eventually overtook the San Francisco Giants, on the final day of the season.

Three years later Atlanta Fulton County Stadium was playing its swan song, with its tenants the defending World Series champions. The Braves qualified for the World Series again in 1996, facing American League Rookie of the Year Derek Jeter and his New York Yankees. Thanks to 19-year-old Andruw Jones, the Braves returned to their last home stand ever at Atlanta Fulton County Stadium with a chance to close it out as back-to-back champions. New York Yankees radio broadcaster John Sterling, who by that time was broadcasting opposite his former Atlanta Braves, describes the middle games of the series: "Games 3-4-5 in Fulton County are three of my greatest memories. George Steinbrenner came into Joe Torre's office either after game 1 or before game 2 and Torre said, 'We're all fouled up from having too much time off. We'll probably lose tonight, but don't worry. We'll go to Atlanta and win all three. That's my town,' and they won all three. The first game they won, it was a kick going back. In the first game, David Cone pitched great and Bernie Williams had a great game. Now, the second game, they were down 6–0 in the sixth inning and scored three runs, and in the eighth inning, Jim Leyritz hit a three-run home run off Mark Wohlers to tie the game and the Yankees won it in the 10th. Then the next game was the game where Andy Pettitte outdueled John Smoltz 1–0. It's 2–2 in the series. Yanks have a 1–0 lead, and the Braves had two runners on base and two out and Luis Polonia was up. John Wetteland couldn't get rid of him. He fouled off pitch after pitch after pitch after pitch, and Jose Cardenal, the outfield coach, figured Polonia's not going to get around on Wetteland's fastball, even though he was hitting ropes. He moved Paul O'Neill—who had a bad leg—over a little bit to right center. Sure enough, Polonia hit a long drive to right center and O'Neill went back. He was 6'5", and reached out and caught it to end the game. If the ball goes off his glove, the two runs walk home and the Braves win 2–1 and they're up 3–2 with Maddux and Glavine ready to pitch. I'm standing in Atlanta with my wife and Paul O'Neill and his wife after the game, and I said to him, 'Hey. Did you have that all the way?' and he said, 'No. I didn't think I was going to catch it.' Then we go back to New York. There's a day off between the fifth and sixth game. Joe Torre's brother, Frank, gets a new heart, and then the Yankees win the World Series. That was a magical year." Although that was not the send-off to Atlanta Fulton County Stadium the Braves fans would have hoped for, the team continued its 14-year run, returning to the World Series again in 1999 to face, once again, the New York Yankees, and as in 1996, they lost four straight games to the eventual champion "Bombers."

CLEVELAND MUNICIPAL STADIUM

Known throughout the Cleveland community as "the Mistake by the Lake," Cleveland Municipal Stadium, formerly known as Lakefront Stadium, was the home of the Cleveland Indians for the better part of 64 seasons. For 13 years the Indians, due to large empty seat numbers, played their weekday games at League Park and only weekend and holiday games at Lakefront. In defense of the absent fans, Lakefront Stadium was built because Cleveland was hoping to host the 1932 Olympic games. The city lost the bid to Los Angeles, leaving an army of empty, wooden seats and even fewer splinter-free fans. With a set of working lights in place and a better product on the field, Lakefront Stadium hosted all of the team's home games and changed its name to Cleveland Municipal Stadium. Soon afterward the Indians, thanks to Lou Boudreau, and more notably, pitchers Bob Lemon, Bob Feller, and Gene Bearden, won their second World Series championship, in 1948 against the Boston Braves. After the Indians' glory days, Cleveland Municipal Stadium once again turned into a bleacher ghost town. Colorado Rockies play-by-play broadcaster Jack Corrigan, who grew up a fan in Cleveland, notes a feature of the old Indians' home: "In August and maybe occasionally into early September, it could be the most humid place in the world sitting right on the lake, and the air would get in there and just stagnate. It could be really tough in that regard. Plus they have a bug—some people call them midges—in Lake Erie. In Cleveland, they're often called Canadian Soldiers because they come across the lake and invade. They only live for about 48 hours, but they are a major nuisance for the time they are there. It even happened in one of the playoff series against the Yankees at Jacobs Field—now Progressive Field—so you can imagine being a mile closer to Lake Erie, like the old stadium. It sat right on the water. We broadcast a game in the spring when the weather was warmer but Lake Erie's water temperature was still awfully cold. The game ended up being called because of a heavy fog bank that rolled in off the lake and just sat over the stadium. Bobby Bonds was the hitting coach for the Indians and he hit fungoes to Dwight Evans of the Red Sox to try and show the umpires that the game could resume. Whether he could or not, Evans didn't catch a single one. Since it was a legal game at that point—and the Red Sox were ahead—we all thought Evans was told not to catch anything in order to get the win. The incomparable 'Oil Can Boyd,' after the game, said, 'Well, that's what they get for building a stadium next to the ocean." Another broadcaster who used to call Cleveland Municipal Stadium his home is lead radio play-by-play man for the Boston Red Sox, Joe Castiglione, who describes his broadcasting roots in Cleveland, saying, "I saw so many games at old Cleveland Stadium. It certainly didn't have a lot of charm. The Lakefront was special for me personally. It had meaning to me because my kids all saw their first games there. I started my broadcast career there. I worked in Cleveland 12 years and I saw hundreds of games. We had a great location. We were very close to home plate. We could hear the umpire. In fact—I'll never forget—one time, our farm director got thrown out by the home plate umpire for barking at him from one of the broadcast booths." Corrigan, whose Cleveland roots go back to when *he* was the size of a Canadian Soldier, describes his transition from bleachers to booth at Cleveland Municipal Stadium: "It's really where I had learned to be a broadcaster, because the Indians, during my time growing up in the '60s and early '70s, weren't very good. You could go to that ballpark, go to that upper deck, and have an entire section to yourself. My buddy, Joe Coreno, and I would carry an old portable reel-to-reel tape recorder and we'd do play by play. It cost us a buck to get in or we had two free tickets from the old Cleveland Press 'Straight A Student' promotion. Those memories were often better than the games. I watched Ted Williams hit a homer in his final game in Cleveland sitting with my dad. That was pretty cool. My dad tapped me on the knee as Williams was rounding the bases and just said, 'That's a hitter.' Didn't say anything else, but it stuck. For me, a kid growing up in Cleveland and getting a chance to do the Indians, it was beyond belief. My very first Major League game—Opening Day in 1985—was at Tiger Stadium with Sparky Anderson and Detroit, right after they had won the 1984 World Series. It was phenomenal. Then to come and be in the place where you watched the Browns and you watched the Indians all those years and to be in the booth with the great Joe Tait, the Basketball Hall of Fame announcer who was my partner. It was a remarkable experience. The stadium was a dump but it was *our* dump for Clevelanders. It was a shame they couldn't win in that building for such a long time. For all the great things at Jacobs Field/Progressive Field, for an older group of Clevelanders, there's always going to be that special pull to the old lady on the lakefront."

ASTRODOME

Opened in April 1965, Houston's Astrodome has been referred to in many circles as the "Eighth Wonder of the World," and for good reason. Standing 18 stories above the ground, the Astrodome, baseball's very first indoor stadium, held six levels of cushioned seats that wrapped around the entire ballpark. Per-

Houston Astrodome: "A mold breaker. Something that was completely revolutionary at the time." — Bill Brown
Photo courtesy of the Houston Astros

haps the main reason Houston was granted the Houston Colt .45's franchise in 1962 was the approved building of the Astrodome. The dome was such an influence over the franchise that when its name was changed to Astrodome, so was the team's. Longtime TV play-by-play broadcaster for the Astros Bill Brown describes the marvel that is the Astrodome: "It was a mold breaker. It was something that was completely revolutionary at the time. The idea of having an indoor, air conditioned stadium. I was told by Mickey Herskowitz—who's written 50 some odd books and has been a long-time Houston sportswriter—if a person from Houston went to Europe in 1965 or 1966 and somebody in Europe asked where he was from, he would say, 'Houston,' and they'd say, 'Oh. The Astrodome.' So this really stamps the city of Houston for this architectural marvel that was known worldwide and gave it an identity." Aside from its massive structure, the *indoor* aspect of the Astrodome eventually gave it another identity on the field. Bill Brown continues, "In the beginning, it had a normal grass field, but then, because the grass died, 'Astroturf' had to be developed, and this was something that really happened on the fly. Initially, the panels of the roof allowed the sun to come streaming in, and, when they first started playing games there, they quickly found out that nobody could see the baseball with the sunlight just streaming in through these roof panels. Fly balls and pop-ups were not being caught because players lost it in the sun, so something had to be done because it would have made a farce of the game. What was done was they painted the panels of the roof and that blocked out the sun's rays. Unfortunately, when that happened, it meant the grass didn't get any sun on it, so the grass died. Now the field became more of a dirt field, and they were actually painting the dirt green to make it look like grass to get through the season. Then they decided, 'This won't ever work,' and that's about the time that Astroturf was developed. They were kind of working on that when the dome was built, but it wasn't considered to be ready yet. They just put their full court press on and got it perfected and they tested it out. They brought the players there in the winter time, and they brought some football players over from the University of Houston because they had to play football in there, too. The players okayed it, so that was the beginning of Astroturf. That became the template for outdoor stadiums at that point." While inside the Astrodome, the Astros qualified for the playoffs six times, including two National League Championship Series appearances. The Houston Astros have had many great players, including Jeff Bagwell, Craig Biggio, Mike Scott, Don Wilson, and J. R. Richard, but one "temporary" Astro's express made its stop in Houston from 1980 to 1988. Nolan Ryan, baseball's all-time strikeout leader, threw a record seven no-hitters during his career, but only one with the Astros. Ryan finished his career with the Texas Rangers, from 1989 to 1993. With the trend for domed stadiums deferring to retractable roofs, the Astrodome soon became dated, and the Astros played their final game there on October 9, 1999, making way for the team's new home, Minute Maid Park. Though replaced, the Astrodome has still not "walked the line" of other former baseball structures that have been imploded or demolished. It still stands today, but for how long?

METRODOME

In 1982, after spending two decades in the Minor League turned Major League ballpark Metropolitan Stadium, the Minnesota Twins moved out of the cold Aprils and Septembers and into their indoor quarters of the Metrodome. A multipurpose facility, the Metrodome hosted the Twins until 2009 and the NFL's Minnesota Vikings until 2013. While playing in the confines of their air-conditioned Metrodome, the Twins went to the playoffs six times, including three trips to the American League Championship Series and two

Metrodome: "A great multi-purpose facility, but it never really served one tenant particularly well."—Dick Bremer
Photo courtesy of Brace Hemmelgarn, Minnesota Twins

World Series titles, in 1987 and 1991, thanks to hitters like Kent Hrbek and Kirby Puckett and pitchers like Jack Morris and Bert Blyleven. Despite the team's success, the Metrodome had its unique, troublesome "qualities," like a white-coated roof and a rock-hard playing surface, plaguing outfielders and infielders alike. Its name was actually the Hubert H. Humphrey Metrodome, and Minnesotans, perhaps voicing their objections to the playing conditions in it, nicknamed the Metrodome "the Humpty Dump." Adding to the baseball ground rule book, the right-field wall of the Metrodome, otherwise known as the "Hefty Bag," featured a 7-foot padded wall, towered over by a 16-foot, plastic wall extension, which held seats for football games. The plastic, tarped-off area above the wall, also known as "the Baggie," was considered still in play, so balls bouncing off and back onto the field were live balls, and anything above "the Baggie" was a home run. Despite the stadium's design quirks, the Twins were able to achieve success in the late '80s, early '90s, and on into the 21st century. Despite the team's appearance in the 2002 American League Championship Series, there were still rumors that they would be relocated. Luckily, those rumors were squashed, and a new facility was announced and built for the team in 2010, thus ending the Twins' 28-year run inside the

Metrodome. Twins TV play-by-play broadcaster Dick Bremer looks back on the Metrodome, saying, "Minnesota had been the land of vice presidents and Super Bowl runner-ups until 1987 and a group of guys who opened up the Metrodome in 1982 as the worst team in the major leagues. They lost 102 games the first year at the Metrodome, and, five years later, that core group won the area's first world championship since the Lakers did it before moving to Los Angeles. The Metrodome will always hold a special place—even though it's no longer there—in the hearts and minds of sports fans in the upper Midwest. It was, to say the least, a very unique environment [in] which to watch a sporting event, whether it was a World Series baseball game or a Super Bowl. The Vikings played there for over 30 years, and the Metrodome hosted a couple of Super Bowls. It was a great multipurpose facility, but it never really served one tenant particularly well. The record will show, even though it was not at all a good baseball stadium or ballpark, the Twins were the local team that was able to win a championship there."

LOS ANGELES COLISEUM

Serving as perhaps the largest "halfway house" in history, the Los Angeles Coliseum was the home of the Los Angeles Dodgers for five seasons; once there, the Dodgers resumed a trend they had just begun back in Brooklyn: winning. Just four years after their triumph over the New York Yankees and the team's first ever World Series title, the Los Angeles Dodgers, awaiting their home on another side of the valley, beat the Chicago White Sox in the 1959 World Series. Dodgers hall of fame broadcaster Vin Scully, who came as part of the "package deal" with the team, describes his brief residence in the site that once hosted the 1932 Olympics: "When I finally came out to Los Angeles, we had left the small confines. The noisy but very warm Ebbets Field. We came out to Los Angeles and the first thing I learned is Los Angeles County is something like 490 square miles. I remembered Gertrude Stein, who said about Oakland, 'There's no *there* there,' and I wondered where the 'there' was in Los Angeles. Well, the Coliseum became our home. That would be from 1958 through 1961. So, while we were working in the Coliseum, the transistor radio came upon the scene, and, all of a sudden, I not only had the confidence of having eight years under my belt, but I found that I would talk directly to the crowd in the Coliseum and I would get reactions from the crowd. I had the crowd singing happy birthday to an umpire, and because of the transistor radio, we had a wonderful rapport with the fans. Not one on one, of course, but it was close in the sense that I was talking directly to them. Let's face it, the Coliseum was pretty impersonal. It was built for track and field and football, not for baseball, but still, it was a temporary home because while we worked in the Coliseum, we were fully aware of the fact that they were building our future home to be known as Dodger Stadium. So it was temporary, and, yet, it had a good warm feeling because of the transistor radio." Scully and the Dodgers moved over to the San Gabriel Mountains and Chavez Ravine in 1962, where they remain today, having gone to another eight World Series and won four of them (1963, 1965, 1981, 1988), making the Ravine the Dodgers' "there."

ARLINGTON STADIUM

As was the case in many of the cities in the '60s and '70s that lured franchises, Texas's Turnpike Stadium, a Minor League facility, quickly became a Major League ballpark and even more by the time it was demolished in 1994. Opened in 1965, Turnpike Stadium hosted the Texas Spurs, a Double A Minor League team, and held a Minor League seating capacity. At the time, Arlington's mayor, Tom Vandergriff, got to work on luring a Major League team to the area. With the Washington Senators version 2.0 giving a poor offering in the seats and the standings, Turnpike Stadium, which eventually took on the name Arlington Stadium, soon became the Senators' home, on April 21, 1972, as the team became the Texas Rangers. Hall of fame radio play-by-play Rangers broadcaster Eric Nadel describes Arlington Stadium's unique configurations: "The old stadium was a Minor League stadium. When the club (Senators) moved, it only had about 15,000 seats. They put in 18,000 bleacher seats. There were more seats in fair territory in that stadium when the Rangers moved and started playing there than there were in foul territory. They subsequently built a small upper deck. I tell you, personally, the 15,000 seats were all great seats." One feature of today's home of the Rangers, Globe Life Park in Arlington, is what fans refer to as the "jet stream," in which wind shot into the ballpark and back out before a change of climate shifted its direction. Arlington Stadium was built with the playing surface sunk 40 feet below the parking lot level. The "jet stream" had had no such effect in the Rangers' old home. Nadel explains, "That ballpark was the reverse. It was set up the same way, had the same wind, but it didn't have a high enough structure to cause the wind to shoot back out. It was an impossible home run park to hit the ball to right field. It literally drove Jeff Burroughs out of town." While hitters like Rafael Palmeiro, Ivan "Pudge" Rodriguez, and Juan Gonzalez didn't follow Burroughs, they, along with later Rangers like Will Clark, Rusty Greer, and manager Johnny Oates, found a way to win in their new ballpark, taking the American League West division title in 1996, 1998, and 1999.

QUALCOMM STADIUM

With the NFL's San Diego Chargers already having a two-year head start to break it in, Qualcomm Stadium, formerly known as Jack Murphy Stadium, welcomed the city's newest addition, the San Diego Padres, in April 1969. Holding football-stadium-sized crowds at times, Qualcomm Stadium housed its Padres for 35 seasons, during 10 of which the building was the 1,500-pound gorilla in the room as former team owner John Moores battled the city to get a new downtown ballpark for the team approved. Eventually former team president Larry Lucchino's original dream came to fruition, and the Padres moved into their new home of Petco Park. Though no World Series rings were presented or championship banners hoisted within Qualcomm Stadium, the Padres did manage to win two National League pennants during their stay in Mission Valley. Perhaps one of the most important games for baseball itself occurred at Qualcomm on September 28, 1988, with the Los Angeles Dodgers, and more important, Orel Hershiser, in town. Hershiser was nine innings shy of tying former Dodger Don Drysdale's consecutive scoreless innings pitched streak when he took the mound. With the score tied at 0–0 after nine innings, Hershiser, having tied the record, pitched the 10th as well. He broke Drysdale's record, but the game was still going. Padres play-by-play radio broadcaster Ted Leitner describes this historic night in baseball through his "multitasking" perspective: "I not only called the game but did the sports there on channel 8 for 25 years. What I would do all those years would be do the five o'clock news at the studio and then drive to the ballpark, get ready for the game, and then I would step out and do a 6:30 sports live on the mini-cam and then get done with that, and then, at a quarter of 7:00, go back to the booth and do the game. I also did the 11 o'clock news, so that game, which went 16 Innings as I recall, after Hershiser had broken the record, I had to leave, left, went back and did the 11 o'clock sports. The game was still going on. I get back in my car, I drive back, and I finish up the broadcast." Leitner also covers local university San Diego State's college football and basketball broadcasts. Luckily, neither of *those* teams was playing the night Hershiser broke Drysdale's scoreless inning streak.

KINGDOME

Though the city of Seattle played the role of the proverbial toddler whose pacifier had been yanked from its mouth when its Major League team, the Pilots, moved to Milwaukee after just one season in 1969, it got a second chance in April 1977 under the name Mariners and beneath the white canopy of the Kingdome. For 22 seasons the team played in the Kingdome, which saw more tiles fall from the ceiling than Mariners playoff appearances. One playoff run in particular, coupled with a decomposing roof, pushed the Mariners to their home today of Safeco Field. Seattle Mariners play-by-play radio broadcaster Rick Rizzs describes the year that put Seattle on baseball's map: "The Kingdome wasn't much of a ballpark, but it was our park. We loved it. We made it our home, and, for a long time, we struggled on the field, so we struggled in attendance; but, in 1995, people discovered this franchise, and it wasn't until late in the season. On August 1, the Mariners were 13 games out of first with two months to play. The Mariners started winning. Ken Griffey, Jr. came back in the middle part of August. Junior shattered his wrist on May 26 making a catch on a fly ball hit by Kevin Bass of the Orioles. He slammed into the wall in right center field and broke his wrist. They put in a plate with about eight screws, so he was gone for three months, and I'm thinking, 'How in the world is this ball club going to hang in there?' Well, Richie Amaral and Alex Diaz went out and played good defense in center field. Edgar Martinez hit .400 when Junior was gone. Jay Buhner was the heart and soul of that ball club and stepped up. Mike Blowers driving in runs, hitting home runs. Dan Wilson, Randy Johnson, everybody picked up the slack, but they were still 13 games back. Now, Junior came back and the Mariners started winning. The Angels started losing. They lost Gary DiSarcina, and we ended up in a one-game playoff. All of a sudden now, in the one-game playoff, it was Randy Johnson against Mark Langston, who we made the trade for with the Montreal Expos to get Randy Johnson, Brian Holman, and Gene Harris back in 1989. That Kingdome was so loud, I thought the fans were going to blow the concrete roof off its structure. It was so loud, you couldn't even hear yourself think. For that stretch in 1995, the Kingdome became the greatest place in the world to play. It was our ballpark. It was our team that was doing the unthinkable, coming back from 13 games behind in only two months to tie the Angels and then beat them in the one-game playoff. Randy Johnson outpitched Mark Langston. Luis Sojo got the big hit. The broken bat double down the right-field line where everybody scored. 'Here comes Blowers, here comes Tino, here comes Joey. Throw home gets by and Cora scores. Here comes Sojo and Sojo scores. Everybody scores!' That broke up a 1–0 ball game and made it 5–0. They went on to win 9–1. For that glorious run in 1995, the Kingdome was the greatest place in the world for these guys to play because the fans were just unbelievable." Later that postseason, the Mariners beat the New York Yankees in the Division Series on Edgar Martinez's two-run double, another play that almost made the fans "blow the concrete roof off its structure."

RIVERFRONT STADIUM

In June 1970, after nearly 60 years in their old home of Crosley Field, the Cincinnati Reds moved into arguably the most successful "cookie cutter" of them all, Riverfront Stadium. The team played for 32 years inside Riverfront and introduced the baseball world to "the Big Red Machine" practically right out of the gates from its christening. With a hitting lineup of Johnny Bench, Tony Perez, Joe Morgan, Dave Concepcion, Pete Rose, George Foster, Cesar Geronimo, and Ken Griffey Sr., as well as six starting pitchers with 10 wins or more, the '75 Reds are arguably the greatest team ever assembled outside of the Bronx. Beating the Boston Red Sox in one of baseball's most exciting World Series, "the Big Red Machine" got right back to work the following season and swept Billy Martin's New York Yankees in the 1976 World Series. Hall of fame radio broadcaster Marty Brennaman, who started his career with the Reds at just the right time, describes Riverfront Stadium during that era: "That ballpark housed Reds teams that were, without question, the most fruitful period in the history of that franchise. You had a ball club in 1975

Riverfront Stadium: "That ballpark housed Reds teams that were, without question, the most fruitful period in the history of that franchise." —Marty Brennaman
Photo courtesy of the Cincinnati Reds

and 1976 that, quite honestly, many people feel may well be the greatest team in the history of baseball; if not, then in the top two or three. You had Pete Rose, who broke Ty Cobb's all-time hit record. You had Tom Browning, who pitched a perfect game. Riverfront Stadium was a ballpark that, when it opened, was probably ahead of its time because of the man who was president/general manager of the club, Bob Howsam. He realized that speed was an integral part of the success of any team at that time in Major League Baseball. He had a field constructed that was Astroturf with the exception of the mound, home plate, and around each base, and that was a radical change. He realized speed was the name of the game, and he built that team in the early '70s around guys who could run and steal bases and force the defense to make mistakes by taking the extra base, and it worked. I was a big fan of Astroturf, and then, over the years, I realized that it was detrimental to the game and the people playing the game. Fortunately, when the new ballparks came around, starting with Camden Yards, everything was natural turf." The Reds returned to World Series glory in 1990 when the "Nasty Boys," under the direction of Lou Piniella, swept the defending World Series champion Oakland Athletics. Around the turn of the century word came down the wire that a new stadium was to be built. Rather than wait it out like many of the other teams with new parks on the horizon, the Cincinnati Reds prepped both the players and the fans for their new digs, about to be built right next door. Describing Riverfront Stadium's brief makeover, Marty Brennaman notes, "When Great American Ball Park was being built, they did away with the Astroturf at Riverfront. They took the stands down from the left-field foul pole to the right-field foul pole, and, ironically, it became a ballpark. It had features that were unique to that park. Fences that were not very high, and a guy could go above the wall and steal home runs, and it was really a neat looking ballpark when they had to close it and go to the next place and finally implode it." Signing off on Riverfront Stadium, Brennaman adds, "It was a park that, in the years it was there, was the finest period in the history of that franchise. While I thoroughly enjoy the modern amenities that we have at Great American Ball Park, and all the things that go into making a new ballpark very appealing and amenable to not only the fans but to the people who work in it, nothing will replace Riverfront for the excitement those teams generated in the years they played there."

THREE RIVERS STADIUM

Manifesting its name, Three Rivers Stadium, the former 30-year home of the Pittsburgh Pirates as well as the NFL's Pittsburgh Steelers, sat along the banks of the confluence of the Ohio, Allegheny, and Monongahela rivers near downtown Pittsburgh. Another of the "cookie-cutter" stadiums, Three Rivers hosted two World Series championship Pirates teams ('71 and '79), featuring players like Roberto Clemente, Willie Stargell, and Dave Parker. Current Pirates play-by-play TV and radio broadcaster Greg Brown recalls his youth growing up around Three Rivers Stadium and these successful Pirates teams: "I grew up a Pirates fan, so, for me, Three Rivers Stadium was my mecca. Pittsburgh was Oz to me. I grew up in a small town in Pennsylvania, so I went as a fan for the first time to my first Major League Baseball game. It holds a very special place in my heart. That's where I grew up watching the team, and they were the team of the '70s. The Pirates were the powerhouse. They won National League East titles seemingly every year. Maybe a half dozen. They won their World Series in 1971 there. They won it in 1979. It was the 'We Are Family' team. Those years, for Pittsburgh fans, are near and dear to their hearts. The winning years. There are also some horrific, horrible years. The mid-'80s brought the drug trials. Pirates players and players throughout baseball had to come to Pittsburgh to the federal court and testify. It was the time the Galbreath family sold the team. It looked as though they were going to leave." Not only did the team not leave, but they were able to put a winning product back on the field and fans back in the seats. Greg Brown notes, "I remember having been in the marketing department in the early '80s. We had a vice president of marketing say to the salespeople, 'We will never draw two million people in this city, so just get used to it. Set your sights lower.' They drew over two million in back-to-back years in the early '90s." Thanks to hitters like Barry Bonds, Bobby Bonilla, and Andy Van Slyke, the Pirates played for the National League pennant three straight times in the early '90s. Greg Brown moved his office from the marketing department to the broadcast booth, and he describes Pirates baseball at that time: "It was different baseball then. It was 'cookie cutter' with the artificial turf. It was a faster game. Baseball itself was different, especially in the National League East. Other than Chicago, everybody played on artificial turf. It became almost different when you came to a natural grass place like Chicago or San Francisco. It was almost weird because we got so used to the pace and the speed of the game. There were fewer bad hops for the infielders. Outfielders had to play back on balls because the ball would bounce back over their heads. It was a different game." As different as it was on the field, Three Rivers Stadium was more distinct in the stands. Brown continues, "Three Rivers Stadium was great for the Steelers. It was intimidating for opposing teams. The decibel level was beyond belief. The Pirates played in a football stadium. What they needed was their own ballpark, and that's what they got finally when they got PNC Park." With the club's new home rising, time wound down for Three Rivers Stadium. The final game there was played on October 1, 2000, a game that remains in Greg Brown's memory. The "Jolly Roger raiser" recalls Three Rivers' swan song, saying, "John Wehner, a Pittsburgh kid, was a utility player, not a home run hitter. Gene Lamont put him in the lineup the last game ever at Three Rivers Stadium in 2000. In front of almost 60,000 fans. The team was down a couple of runs to the Chicago Cubs. John Wehner, not only was he in the starting lineup—which is a rarity because he's a utility guy—but he hits a three-run homer. Wehner will tell you it's easily the greatest moment of his life as a baseball player. Imagine a Pirates fan—a kid growing up in Pittsburgh—who beat the odds to become a baseball player. To be in that game. In that moment. It brought the house down. You can't write this script. He had a total of four home runs in his career and that was one of them. The last home run ever hit in the history of Three Rivers Stadium was hit by John Wehner, a Pittsburgher. That's the greatest moment in my broadcasting career."

The Pirates lost the game 10–9, and Wehner later joined Brown in the broadcast booth. On February 11, 2001, Three Rivers Stadium followed the road of so many of yesterday's ballparks and was imploded. Greg Brown signs off on his "mecca," saying, "I made certain I was there on Mount Washington in the early morning hours when they imploded Three Rivers Stadium. I wanted to see it because that was my place. That was my playground."

VETERANS STADIUM

While it took almost 19 years from proposal to completion, Veterans Stadium lasted almost twice that long as the home of the same-name, same-city Philadelphia Phillies. Opened in 1971, Veterans Stadium, much like its twins in nearby Pittsburgh and Cincinnati, was of the "cookie-cutter" mold. Like its brothers, Veterans Stadium was able to enjoy postseason success early in its existence. The Phillies went to the National League Championship Series three straight seasons, losing to Cincinnati's "Big Red Machine" once and the Dodgers twice. Two years later, with familiar former opponent Pete Rose now on *their* side, the Phillies—thanks to hitters like Mike Schmidt, Manny Trillo, and Bake McBride, and pitchers Steve Carlton and Dick Ruthven— were able to finally capture the franchise's first World Series title. The Phillies returned to the World Series three years later as centenarians and lost to the Baltimore Orioles in five games. Ten years down the road and with familiar opponents Darren Daulton and Lenny Dykstra now donning Phillies colors, Philadelphia lost to the Toronto Blue Jays and Joe Carter's walk-off heroics in the 1993 World Series. That was the last time Veterans Stadium saw any Major League postseason action before the team opened up Citizens Bank Park in 2004. Phillies play-by-play TV broadcaster Tom McCarthy, who attended "the Vet" as both a fan and an employee, sheds some light on the team's home of more than three decades, saying, "The one thing I felt about 'the Vet' is even though—settingwise and landscapewise—it wasn't the prettiest place to me, it was emblematic of the city of Philadelphia. It was everything that the blue-collar worker of Philadelphia always represented. It was a work horse. It hosted concerts, football, and baseball, and, when you needed it to rise to the occasion, whether it be the 1980 playoffs, the 1993 playoffs, or even the 1983 playoffs, it was there, because it was loud. It was energetic. It was able to put in as many people from Philadelphia as possible, which gave them an advantage, because they were as loud as anything. When it was sold out, it was definitely a home field advantage. They were able to use this place that was a 'cookie cutter' to their advantage when it came to the postseason."

MILE HIGH STADIUM

The Colorado Rockies were introduced to baseball in 1993 as part of the league's expansion, which also included the Florida Marlins. Considering the geography, weather, and population of the team's host city, Denver, expectations couldn't have been lower for eventual fan turnout. Former Colorado Rockies play-by-play radio broadcaster Wayne Hagin, who opened the franchise from the booth, describes how Colorado proved the baseball world wrong: "People have to remember that Denver, when it was awarded the franchise, they had a storied Minor League history with the Denver Bears and then of course, the Denver Zephyrs. That's what put baseball on the map in Colorado. People who were in the know and certainly trying to make things happen for Colorado to have a franchise actually registered 1.7 million as the possible attendance that first year. They based all those figures on the studies, their research, all of the things they thought would probably be pretty close to accurate. They missed by almost 3 million. That's an incredible story. They fell 17,000 shy of 4.5 million people that year. You'd have to average between 57 and 58,000 a game. For them to draw that many people—which will be a record that will never be broken—I think maybe part of it was the football mentality of the Broncos, where people went to every game because they were used to going to every game. If there was a game played at that stadium, off they went and they just fell in love with baseball. It was a very hot baseball area; much more so than people thought. Every team can draw per region, especially those in the Midwest like St. Louis, Kansas City, Minnesota, but nobody could draw like the Rockies did from Nebraska, Kansas, and Wyoming. A high percentage of season ticket holders actually came from Grand

Junction. Grand Junction is completely on the other side of the Rockies. You have to drive through the mountains to get to Denver." The Rockies' record attendance numbers got off to a good start, as a record opening-day crowd of 80,227 fans showed up on April 9, 1993, to watch their new team take the field against the Montreal Expos. Hagin recalls the game, saying, "It was amazing how people fell in love on that first day—80,227—no one's ever going to forget that day. What was special about it was the first batter was Eric Young. He leads off the game with a 3–2 count against Kent Bottenfield of the Montreal Expos and 80,227 people in the stands. The fans didn't know a thing about Eric Young. They just knew that he was their Rockies leadoff hitter. He was a part of their fabric, and they cheered so wildly. He hit a 3–2 pitch for a home run that just made it over the left-field wall. I mean it barely made it, and John Vander Wal and Larry Walker were in the outfield for Montreal that day. Both would soon become Rockies within the next year, and both of them said the ground shook so hard they couldn't believe it. That's what the Broncos used as a home field advantage all those years. This deafening roar at the stadium. We felt it that day. I remember on the broadcast when he hit the home run, I said, 'And the snow on Pike's Peak is falling off with the decibel level of Mile High Stadium.' Now nobody could write that because nobody could ever expect that to happen. That just came out of my mouth because I was a native Coloradan. I was born in Denver, and I knew what that sound meant and they cheered so wildly. The Broncos fans are unbelievable. They're loud just to be loud. At Coors Field, it is built where the sound can certainly have an effect, but I don't know if you could ever compare it to Mile High. That thing was unbelievably loud. They quit cheering when the final out was finally done. They cheered the entire game. The Rockies did not have a single shutout at home that year, but they took an 11–0 lead to the ninth inning. They ultimately won it 11–4, so it gave us a brief glimpse into what was going to happen with Rockies baseball. It was always going to be offensive-minded, especially at Mile High. To be a part of that first game, it was much more than anybody could even anticipate. It was much bigger than we ever expected." While Coors Field isn't exactly pushing the 4.5 million fan mark, Mile High Stadium, although short-lived from a baseball standpoint, left its mark before ceding the path to its inspired successor. Hagin signs off on the Rockies' interim home, saying, "It was an event for these people—not just a game—for 81 games. It was an event they didn't want to miss."

SPORTSMAN'S PARK

While many of the "cookie-cutter" stadium tenants of the '60s, '70s, and '80s were intersport roommates with the city's NFL franchises, the St. Louis

Browns shared their home of Sportsman's Park with fellow baseball team the St. Louis Cardinals for 33 years. The Sportsman's Park in which the Browns and Cardinals played was the city's third constructional offering to the Browns, two previous attempts having been prone to fire damage. While National Geographic won't likely be doing a documentary on the cohabitation of two Major League ball clubs, the St. Louis Browns and Cardinals are a clear-cut example of "dominant and recessive" long after the gene cycle has run its course. The Browns only qualified for one World Series while in St. Louis, which occurred in 1944 against (who else but) the St. Louis Cardinals. All six games were played at Sportsman's Park version 3.0, with the Cardinals taking "home" the glory in game 6. The Browns moved to Baltimore after 1953, but the Cardinals stayed put, winning seven World Series titles and 10 National League pennants in the house they "crashed." Not only did the Cardinals take over Sportsman's Park, they renamed it Busch Stadium after new team owner August Busch. Eventually a "new" Busch Stadium was built, where the Cardinals remained for nearly 40 years. Having grown up in the Midwest, Kansas City Royals hall of fame radio play-by-play broadcaster Denny Matthews looks back on his youth inside Sportsman's Park, saying, "When I was a kid, we would go to St. Louis once a summer to the old Sportsman's Park. It was a neat ballpark. I've always been fascinated by stadiums. I was probably 12 or 14 years old. I had one of those little Brownie cameras. I took a bunch of pictures of Sportsman's Park and I've got a bunch of pictures of Comiskey Park because you knew that was going to be gone before long. Major League stadiums just kind of fascinated me, along with—obviously—the game, and I'm glad I took a bunch of pictures of Sportsman's Park. It was neat. Everything is bigger when you're a kid. More impactful. If you go back to that same place 25 years later, it's the same place, you look and say, 'My God. It shrunk. I remember this place as being a lot bigger.' That's because you were seven years old. Everything is bigger when you're seven years old. The grass is greener, and the players are bigger and better. Your perspective is just turned inside out, which is kind of cool in a way."

MILWAUKEE COUNTY STADIUM

Home to the Milwaukee Braves, Milwaukee Brewers, and at one time the NFL's Green Bay Packers, Milwaukee County Stadium was literally built on a dump, paving the way for one-liners to be used throughout its existence. Though the Braves—the team lured to the city from Boston by the building of Milwaukee County Stadium—stayed there only 13 seasons, they have still seen more championship glory than the Brewers, who took over as tenants from 1970 to 1999. In 1957, thanks to hall of fame slugger Henry Aaron and pitchers Warren Spahn and Lew Burdette—who had three of the four wins for Milwaukee—the Braves beat Mickey Mantle, Whitey Ford, and the New York Yankees in seven games, winning the franchise's second title. The team's third was won in Atlanta 38 years later. The Brewers' only success in Milwaukee County Stadium occurred in the early '80s, when the team won back-to-back division titles, making it as far as the seventh game of the World Series before losing to their Midwest neighbor St. Louis Cardinals. Former Milwaukee Brewers and current Atlanta Braves radio play-by-play broadcaster Jim Powell, who came in to work for the team during the twilight years of Milwaukee County Stadium, looks back on the team's former home, saying, "It was a stadium they built in the '50s looking to lure a team in. Ultimately, the St. Louis Browns, along with the Boston Braves, were both interested. They built it with less than 30,000 seats, but they built it so it could be expanded. It worked because the Milwaukee Braves did so well and the Green Bay Packers played there. They continued to expand it. By the time I worked there, it was up over 50,000. It's a rarity now with stadiums, but, back in those days, it was a little more common for football and baseball teams to share the same stadium. There was a lot of people in Milwaukee who remembered County Stadium as much for Packers games as the Braves or the Brewers. They could barely squeeze a football field into County Stadium the way it was configured. In a football game, guys would score a touchdown, run through the end zone, and disappear into a dugout. I remember the antiquated press box. They remodeled it at one point, but it had catwalks like a lot of the stadiums of that era. It's hard to imagine playing in a place like that for 50 years now that we've seen places like Miller Park, Turner Field, and today's other great stadiums."

As with many of yesterday's ballparks turned into today's parking lots, fans attending Milwaukee County Stadium witnessed the team's future home of Miller Park being constructed beyond the center-field bleachers. While many fans prefer the nostalgia, it's arguable, in Milwaukee, that many more were looking forward to the indoor comfort of a climate-controlled Miller Park. The Aarons, Spahns, and Burdettes may have moved on, but one key figure in Milwaukee baseball history has transitioned from County Stadium to Miller Park: Bernie Brewer. Powell adds, "The key feature that most people would remember from County Stadium would be the big beer stein Bernie Brewer would slide down into. He became the most unique mascot in baseball at that time, so the Brewers were well known for Bernie Brewer and his beer stein." Bernie Brewer, inside Miller Park today, does his home run antics down a more modernized slide, and thanks to players like Ryan Braun, Carlos Gomez, and Jonathan Lucroy, on a more frequent basis, giving hope to Brewers fans that their new home will have a championship caliber team.

RFK STADIUM

Though RFK Stadium was better known for the great Washington Redskins teams that have come through, its original design was not for football. Before the Redskins moved in, RFK was the home of baseball's Washington Senators, who left for Texas before the '72 season to become the Rangers. Baseball did not return to Washington until it was imported from Canada via the Montreal Expos in 2005. Radio play-by-play broadcaster for the Nationals Charlie Slowes describes the "circle of life" that was baseball in the nation's capital: "RFK was built for baseball. It's a round, 'cookie-cutter' type stadium from the '60s and it was a multipurpose stadium for baseball and football where the stands were really more designed for baseball. It only held 51,000 or so for football, so it was really small for an NFL stadium. The smallest for years. The Redskins had a waiting list of people wanting tickets that would be like 45–50,000. They used to say, 'We could sell 100,000 tickets.' The Redskins had this small, loud stadium that was their home field advantage. They hadn't had baseball there for 33 years except for the occasional Cracker Jack All Star Game or old-timers game. Some event to promote baseball in the hopes of one day getting a team." When DC was awarded the team, all the baseball-less years of RFK began to show. Slowes notes, "The stands used to move. The first base and third base field-level seats would be angled obviously for baseball, and they'd square them up to be parallel for football. All the wheels and mechanisms not being moved for so long basically rotted out. They couldn't move it anymore, so they basically had to rip everything out of the lower bowl at RFK for baseball and redo it for the Nationals before the '05 season. The clubhouses were shoebox small. The amenities were worse than old Tiger Stadium or Wrigley Field or spring training parks that were old or out of date places. That was the biggest adjustment. Normal amenities were not there. The field itself was in great condition. The ballpark played big. It was a symmetrical ballpark so the dimensions and height of the fence were the same all the way around foul pole to foul pole. It was an easy park to learn to play and great for broadcasting."

With the players adjusted from their former home of Olympic Stadium in Montreal, the more important factor was how the fans would respond to their new team, especially considering that the lack of fans was what drove the city's teams away in both 1960 and 1971. Slowes notes, "One of the great things about RFK stadium was the third base stands. Since they were mobile and on rollers, the fans could make them move up and down. They would stand up and jump, and the third base side stands would rock. The place was so loud, even without a sellout crowd. The noise level was unbelievable. In a way, they fell in love with playing there right away and they had a tremendous first half of their first season. Right there, it really cemented baseball in DC. I think a level that they never had with the Senators because the Senators didn't really draw crowds. If you go look at the history of attendance in the Major Leagues, team by team, in the '60s, teams didn't draw like they do now. You didn't have a lot of 30,000 plus crowds. It was common to have 10 to 15,000 fans on a weeknight. The Nationals averaged 33 to 34,000 that first year in 2005." While the Nationals only played in RFK three seasons before moving to their new home of Nationals Park, the team won the hearts of fans on their very first day, especially those who had endured the 33-year void of baseball in the DC area. Easily his most memorable game at RFK Stadium, Charlie Slowes recalls, "They opened against Arizona April 14. Sellout crowd. I will never forget, from our booth at RFK Stadium, which was kind of hanging from the upper deck—you had to go through a catwalk to get to this area— you could see people out the back of our booth coming into the park when the gates opened and see kids running in. See their parents, or their grand-parents, or their uncles. The faces of the adults were more amazing than the kids. To see baseball on that field again. You would see tears streaming down people's faces. Then Livan Hernandez pitches. He's shutting out Arizona into the ninth inning. He gives up a three-run homer to Chad Tracy. They were up 5–0 and Chad Cordero comes in to get the last out. If you talked to Vinny Castilla, who played on some pretty good teams. Livan Hernandez won a World Series. Players who played in that game. Brian Schneider. Jose Vidro. I could list all of them. They will tell you that was one of the greatest days of their career. President Bush came into the clubhouse before the game, hung out with them for 15 minutes, took pictures with the players, warmed up with Brian Schneider in the batting cage, and then came out and threw the first pitch. The crowd that night. The noise in the stadium. The reaction to everything was unbelievable. It meant a lot to people who were old enough to remember the Senators. If anyone remembered baseball at RFK, to actually see it again at RFK might have meant more to them than walking into a new stadium right then."

JARRY PARK

New York has Central Park. Montreal has Jarry Park. The French-Canadian city was awarded an expansion baseball franchise to begin playing during the '69 season, which, considering that no ground breaking had really begun, made 1968 a busy year in "Le Belle Province." Former Montreal Expos hall of fame radio play-by-play broadcaster Dave Van Horne looks back on the team's first home, saying, "Jarry Park was quite a facility and actually the founding of that location and the building of the stands to form this 28,000 seat ballpark saved the franchise before it even began. There was talk on the eve of the 1969 season of moving that franchise quickly, under the cover of darkness, to somewhere like perhaps Buffalo, New York. That was no secret. They were looking at other locations because they felt that, while Montreal was awarded the franchise, they couldn't find a place to play until finally they came up with Jarry Park, which, by the way, is a huge municipal park. It would be like in New York having no baseball facility, getting a franchise, and saying, 'All right. We've got to go into Central Park, and, in the corner, we'll build this little ballpark.' That's exactly what happened in Montreal. Jarry Park is the name of this huge civic park. Then the ballpark was also named Jarry Park because that's where it was located. The name Jarry Park was there long before Major League Baseball. It had facilities for softball and tennis and soccer in particular. A swimming pool. Everything else. It was a large park and then in this little corner of the park, there were these little 1,500 to 1,800 cement block seats behind home plate and a diamond where they played baseball—not softball—and that's the location that finally saved the franchise for Montreal." While Major League Baseball isn't making any plans to add a third New York franchise to the city and place it in the corner of Central Park, it sure worked—at least for nearly a decade—for our neighbors to the north.

CANDLESTICK PARK

Opened two years after the Giants set up shop in the City by the Bay, Candlestick Park was the home of the San Francisco Giants for 40 years. Unfortunately for Giants fans, it also became the home of the NFL's San Francisco 49ers. Accommodating football crowds, Candlestick Park increased its seating by another 11,000 once the 49ers became roommates. Giants hall of fame radio play-by-play broadcaster Jon Miller discusses what once was Candlestick Park: "When I first went to it, it was a baseball park built for the Giants and you could see the East Bay on a clear day. From the upper deck, you could see ships on the dry dock over at Hunters Point Shipyard. Then they enclosed it, and it became 49ers stadium, so any aspect of the ballpark that was nice as a baseball park disappeared." Candlestick Park saw two World Series (1962 and 1989) and three National League Championship Series (1971, 1987, and 1989). The team's return to success happened in their current home of AT&T Park, where the Giants have now won three of the last five World Series (2010, 2012, and 2014). Signing off on Candlestick Park, Jon Miller states, "When I came back to do Giants games, it was very exciting for me just because that is where I've grown up, but the feel of it and the look of it was not very similar by that time to what I remembered as a kid. In the end, Candlestick was not a pleasant ballpark. The weather was often terrible, but I think Candlestick was more memorable for the players who played there and the great things that occurred there than anything about the ballpark itself. The fond memories of Candlestick from a baseball standpoint had to do with Willie Mays. Always at the top of that list. Willie McCovey, Orlando Cepeda, Juan Marichal, and, later on, Jack Clark, Will Clark, and Kevin Mitchell. Mike Krukow winning 20 games. Barry Bonds arriving. Those are the kind of things that will be remembered fondly about Candlestick Park."

METROPOLITAN STADIUM

Having come full circle in 2010 from the franchise's first home game on April 21, 1961, the Minnesota Twins returned to the outdoor "comfort" of professional baseball in the upper Midwest. The team's original home of 20 years, Metropolitan Stadium was preferred to the Hubert H. Humphrey Metrodome, even in the harsher climate infamously found in the Land of 10,000 Lakes. Having grown up in the region, Minnesota Twins play-by-play TV broadcaster Dick Bremer recalls his childhood at Metropolitan: "Generally we went once a year to Metropolitan Stadium and that was, without question, the highlight of my summer. I remember going as a kid, and it sounds like a cliché, but it was very true. I remember I watched games from there on television, but when I first got to my seats in the upper deck and I saw the emerald green grass, it almost took my breath away. A lot of people will talk about that experience. The first time you actually go to a big league ballpark, you see the grass, and I guess that's what sticks out the most. The ballpark, of course, is one thing, but the players—to be able to see Harmon Killebrew and Bob Allison in person—that was just a wonderful thing for a little kid to experience. To be able to go there and see the ballpark, hear the organ music, see the players, the whole experience. As a kid, I got rained on and rained out at the outdoor ballpark, but that didn't discourage me from believing that the game was meant to be played outside. I never got a chance to broadcast baseball there. Ironically, the only broadcasts I did from Metropolitan Stadium were a few Viking preseason games that I did the last couple of years they played there, but I never got to do a baseball game there, and that's one of my great regrets." Out in the fresh Minnesota air, the Twins went to one World Series (1965) and two American League Championship Series (1969, 1970). Like a concerned mother staring out the kitchen window, certain parties pushed to bring the Twins inside, paving the way for the team's home of the

Metrodome. Dick Bremer adds, "Both the Vikings and the Twins played at Metropolitan Stadium. At the Vikings' behest, the Twins kind of got dragged indoors because the Vikings felt they needed a new indoor facility. As most people know, Decembers can be a little harsh in this climate, so the Vikings kind of twisted some arms and got the Twins to move indoors. It was a very sterile, unappealing reaction that most fans got from the very first time they walked into the Metrodome. For the Twins and the baseball fans of this area, it was quite an adjustment to make. I think it's fair to say the adjustment, some people weren't willing to make. There were fans who, during the entire time the Metrodome was up, said, 'I went there once. I decided I would never go back there again.' It was an awful experience, not so much for football—because it was built for football—but to try to play baseball in there was really an affront to everyone and everything that was beautiful about the game." Returning baseball to the rain outs, snow delays, and heat-lamp-laced concourses found at the Twins' new home of Target Field, Minnesota fans can lift their boycott and enjoy baseball the way they once did at Metropolitan Stadium.

SHIBE PARK/CONNIE MACK STADIUM

Back when the Phillies weren't the only team in town, Philadelphia was home to Shibe Park, better known as Connie Mack Stadium. Built in 1909, Shibe Park was originally the home of the Philadelphia Athletics, who not only inherited the Phillies as roommates (in 1938) but also the NFL's Eagles (in 1940) before the latter crashed Franklin Field. Before moving to Kansas City after the '54 season, the Athletics not only won five World Series titles, but they also named their home after the team's greatly beloved owner. The Phillies playoff success, however, came with only one World Series appearance, a loss to the New York Yankees in 1950. Shibe Park exhibited one of the most unique playing field configurations of all time. The park's square block structure rose high above the first and third base lines, but the field itself extended with the park, making both the infield *and* the outfield an enormous diamond shape. The original distance to dead center field at Shibe Park was 515 feet from home plate, besting even "old" Yankee Stadium and the Polo Grounds. Eventually the Phillies moved on to Veterans Stadium, in 1971. Miami Marlins hall of fame radio play-by-play broadcaster Dave Van Horne describes his first impressions of baseball as a youngster at Shibe Park: "I grew up in the Lehigh Valley in eastern Pennsylvania. We had a very strong radio signal out of Philadelphia, so I listened to the Philadelphia broadcasts through both the Philadelphia A's and the Philadelphia Phillies games when I was growing up. The ones I paid closest attention to were people like By Saam, Gene Kelley, and the broadcasters in that era from the '50s and leading up to the '60s. When I was growing up and going to see Major League Baseball at Shibe Park in Philadelphia, there were people that I heard when I was a youngster. I had no idea at that time that I would wind up spending my lifetime as a baseball broadcaster, so I wasn't listening with a particularly critical ear. I was listening with the ear of a fan, and I just enjoyed listening to the games at night either in the bedroom or out back on the patio and listening to those wonderful voices that described the baseball game. It was a real thrill to listen to those broadcasters for several seasons before I actually got to go to Shibe Park and see them. When I first walked into Shibe Park, it was overwhelming because all of the things the broadcasters had described and talked about came to life right before my eyes. It made a strong impression on me as a youngster." Today, Dave Van Horne helps Marlins Park "come to life" for the youngsters of south Florida.

SUN LIFE STADIUM

Back in the early '90s, when Miami and Wayne Huizenga were battling the city of Tampa Bay for "prettier girl" honors in the expansion baseball sweepstakes, the Florida Marlins played in a home that would take on so many names, the engineering department voted to make the park entrance one giant dry erase board. Before "the good years," the Marlins played in what was known as Joe Robbie Stadium. Later, during the 10-year span in which the sign outside read "Pro Players Stadium," the Marlins won both of their World Series titles, in 1997 and 2003, to the chagrin of two of baseball's longest tenured franchises, the Indians and the Yankees. Marlins hall of fame radio play-by-play broadcaster Dave Van Horne, who was in the booth during a magical 2003 run that was fueled by Marlins hitting, pitching, and Chicago Cubs fan Steve Bartman, signs off on the team's former home, saying, "It was never a baseball stadium. It was always a football stadium. It was reconfigured for baseball. Awkwardly. It was never a good facility for baseball, although those that followed the Marlins in 1997 and saw that first world championship and those who, in 2003, followed the Marlins to that second world championship there would argue. There were a lot of bad seats because they were configured for football. The outfield wall was temporary. The dimensions were very different. It was just never a good baseball facility. One of the main reasons, other than the configuration of a football field to baseball, was the weather. There were so many delays. Not so many rainouts as one might think in Miami, but a lot of rain delays during the course of a home stand. Day after day, batting practice would have to be postponed because of late afternoon showers which seemed to strike from mid to late June all the way through July into late August, so that was a real pain. The ballpark itself didn't have the facilities that a lot of the parks have for continued work by players during rain delays. They had a few batting cages, but that was about it. It was never designed for baseball. Everything was kind of put together just to get by in baseball for a few years and they wound up playing there until the '12 season. From 1993 to 2012. It had its moments as a baseball facility because of the caliber of the teams on the field, but it was never a good baseball facility." Sun Life Stadium, though "not a good facility for baseball," still saw two world championships, Al Leiter's no-hitter, and Ken Griffey Jr.'s 600th home run, over its 19-season lifetime.

KANSAS CITY MUNICIPAL STADIUM

Built 32 years before a Major League team would ever even play there, Kansas City Municipal Stadium housed some of baseball's greatest players. Unfortunately these players' stats will always be recognized alongside and not within the annals of Major League Baseball. Before the Athletics took residence in 1955, Municipal Stadium had been the home of the Negro League's famous Kansas City Monarchs, as well as the Minor League's Kansas City Blues. After the A's had had their feel of Kansas City Municipal for 13 seasons, the team moved westward to Oakland. One year later Kansas City was awarded a franchise that would be named the Royals. Having been with the team since day one, Royals hall of fame radio play-by-play broadcaster Denny Matthews describes the team's temporary home of four years before their current residence of Kauffman Stadium: "When I started in 1969, of course, we were in the old ballpark in Kansas City. The first four years of Royals history, we played in Municipal Stadium in Kansas City, where the A's had played, the Minor League team, and the Negro League team. It was a very typical, old look stadium like Tiger Stadium and all the other old ones that were built in the '20s, '30s, and '40s." One thing that stood out from Kansas City Municipal—as could be expected from having a team owner like Charlie O. Finley footing the bill—was its amenities, which would likely be found in no other ballpark, like a zoo. Despite its quirks, Kansas City Municipal stood for over 50 years and was able to keep professional baseball in the City of Fountains.

OLYMPIC STADIUM

While Jarry Park was the site that saved the Montreal Expos franchise from being awarded "behind the scenes" to Buffalo, Olympic Stadium was what kept the Expos in town, at least for a while. Built for the 1976 Olympic games, Olympic Stadium became the Expos' new home. Olympic Stadium's retractable roof design predated that of Toronto's Rogers Centre by 12 years; however, the concept never really worked out. Instead of being separated into panels, Olympic Stadium's roof looked more like the world's largest soda can lid, opened and closed by a series of cables connected to a large, outside tower. Eventually the stadium became domed and the retractable roof idea was scrapped. Former Montreal Expos hall of fame radio play-by-play broadcaster Dave Van Horne describes his years inside the broadcast booth at Olympic Stadium: "I would agree—from an architectural stand point—it was quite a facility. From a baseball ballpark standpoint, it never worked. It was in the middle of a residential area in the east end of Montreal. It wasn't surrounded by bars, restaurants, hotels, and facilities for fans. Olympic Stadium was it. One of its most convenient assets for the fans was the fact that the Montreal metro system went right into the stadium. From wherever you were on the island of Montreal, if you had access to the metro system, you were able to ride right to Olympic Stadium, but it was never a good baseball facility. They played for eight seasons in Jarry Park, which seated 28,000 and they moved into Olympic Stadium in 1977, and, by 1979, the farm system had produced such a wealth of talent that the Expos were contenders for the first time. They started to fill that stadium for several years—drew well over two million fans a year—and it was a different place. When it was filled, there were 40,000 plus enjoying their team. A good team. With a contending team on the field, it was very exciting to be in there; but, except for those years, a brief emergence as a contender in the early '90s—1994 specifically—it was not a good ballpark. The retractable roof idea never worked and it became an open stadium with terrible sight lines because of the sun. Television producers hated to go in there because, if it was a day game, the sun created a crazy configuration of shadows due to the configuration of the stadium itself. It was loud when there was a crowd in there. The crowd noise would be absolutely deafening, and when there wasn't a crowd in there, it was not a good, warm facility. It was cold early in the season because it took so long for the dampness of the winter snows and ice to come out of the stadium and out of the cement. The stadium was basically a cement structure. It wasn't terribly comfortable either, so, except for those years where they were contenders, it never worked and that's why the consortium group that had the team in the '80s and '90s tried to put together an effort to get a downtown, retractable roof ballpark built be-cause Olympic Stadium just wasn't working. That effort to get that downtown ballpark built went down in 1994 with the players' strike. At the same time, Montreal had the best record in baseball. A terrific team on the field, and the rug was pulled out from under that team, and that was the last 'hoorah' for the

Montreal franchise. It was very painful because I think everybody knew from the time the team's original owner Charles Bronfman put the team up for sale. It took over two years to sell the team. Nobody stepped up to keep the team in Montreal. Charles had to practically give the team away to the consortium to keep it in Montreal, and, from the time he put the team up for sale until their last breath in Montreal, it was a struggle. Everyone remembered the last few years, as I referred to it in the past, 'the downward spiral' of that franchise began, really, when Charles put the team up for sale. They were never able to recover. He was an excellent owner who believed in the development of players and the farm system. He gave the farm system and development people a lot of resources to do that and that farm system produced. There was nothing like it in the '70s. It became a model for all of baseball, and it continued on through the '70s and on into the '80s, and they put terrific teams on the field. The bulk of those players were produced by the farm system, and when his ownership ended, the franchise was in trouble." The downward spiral concluded with the Expos crossing the border to become the Washington Nationals in the spring of 2005.

MEMORIAL STADIUM

Memorial Stadium in Baltimore may well be the only mixed-use facility in sports in which the baseball team "won the argument." Built in 1954 to house the imported St. Louis Browns, who upon moving were immediately known as the Baltimore Orioles, Memorial Stadium came to host the NFL's Colts as well for over 20 years. Instead of configuring the stadium for football—as so many stadiums, like Candlestick Park, had done in the past—Memorial held its ground, and the Colts eventually moved out after the '83 season. San Francisco Giants hall of fame radio play-by-play broadcaster Jon Miller, who spent 13 years as the lead for the Orioles, describes the site that housed the Orioles for nearly 40 years: "Memorial Stadium, number one, was in a beautiful setting. It was in a neighborhood—sort of like a tree-lined street—just beyond the outfield of the ballpark. You'd have the scoreboard and then, out behind the scoreboard, you could see these houses, and they were beautiful houses. It was just a beautiful setting. I always remember Joe Morgan, when we started working together in 1990, said the ballpark where he always wanted to play in the American League when he was a National Leaguer was not Fenway so much as it was Memorial Stadium because 'Memorial Stadium was the ballpark that had so many great teams.' The Orioles were the preeminent team in the American League—not the Yankees—from the mid-'60s into the '80s. They had a winning team year after year. Brooks Robinson, Frank Robinson,

Jim Palmer, Mike Cuellar, Dave McNally, Earl Weaver the manager. The Orioles were good every year and that's the park where they played. That was the thing that Joe wanted to experience." From 1969 to 1979 the Orioles won six division titles, four American League pennants, and one World Series title (1970), yet the seats of Memorial Stadium remained unfilled. Jon Miller adds, "In Memorial Stadium, the attendance was never good. They had a hard time drawing more than 1.2 million. That was the biggest they could get. The first year I did Major League Baseball was with Oakland in 1974. We played the Orioles in the playoffs. These were the two best teams in the game year after year. We had matchups of Jim Palmer versus Vida Blue, Catfish Hunter facing Dave McNally, but we didn't sell out any games that postseason against the Orioles in the best of five. We went to Baltimore for game 3 and they drew 24,000 on a Tuesday and 29,000 the next day for the final game. The Orioles had been good year after year, winning the division over and over again. They had four 20-game winners one year and they drew 930,000. This was just the way it was. The Orioles had a terrible time drawing a crowd. In 1979 they extended the fan base and the team got really good. They started calling it 'Oriole magic.' The Orioles could be trailing through the night, but then there was that 'Oriole magic' that would happen. Then the Baltimore cab driver, 'Wild' Bill Hagy came on the scene. He had his big cowboy hat and he was in the upper deck. He would get the people in his section to do this Oriole cheer 'O-R-I-O. . .' and he would spell it out like he was doing the YMCA. It was really exciting to hear 40-50,000 people all doing this cheer. That really changed the experience. They drew nearly 1,700,000 that year. I moved to Baltimore in 1983 and I remember just being flabbergasted. The team had a workout before opening day at Memorial Stadium. Then we got in buses and went down to the inner harbor. There was this little amphitheater area, and there were 50,000 people down there lining the inner harbor. I remember being struck by it. They lost the year before. They didn't make it to the postseason, and, yet, here the fans were 50,000 strong. They loved these guys. It was as if they had won. The fact they made this incredible comeback was enough apparently. They got to that last game against all odds. They won the World Series my first year there and they drew 2.2 million, which, at that time, seemed phenomenal."

Although he broadcast for an Oakland A's championship team in 1974, an Orioles World Series champion in 1983, and three San Francisco Giants World Series champions in 2010, 2012, and 2014, one of Jon Miller's most memorable nights as a broadcaster occurred in 1988, with the Orioles entering the ballpark with a 1–23 record. Miller notes, "They had the '88 season where they lost the first 21 games of the season, which is an all-time worst start of any team in any season. The thing that really stood out and became one of the great nights for me in any ballpark was while this losing streak was going on, people started calling this morning disc jockey, Bob Rivers, and would say, 'The Orioles are losing these games and they're making jokes out of them. The nighttime shows. Johnny Carson and Arsenio Hall. They're the butt of all these jokes nationally, and I feel bad for them because I still love the team. I think there's a lot of people like me. I just want to tell them that I still am behind them and don't get too down. This is going to end.' This became a grassroots promotion for the Monday night game with Texas. Rivers got so many calls, and it just took on a life of its own. Bob dubbed it 'fantastic fans night.' The team saw what was happening at the ticket office and we started talking about it on the air. By this time, they had finally won a game and lost the last two on the road trip. They were 1–23. It sounded worse than 0–21. They were 1–23 and there were 50,000 people there in the ballpark, which, by itself, was immediately something beyond anything I'd ever seen. When you have a bad team, people sort of ignore you. Your park is mostly empty, and here were 50,000 people doing Oriole cheers. They went out and they beat Texas and they killed them. It was as if they had been winning all along. The first hitter of the game hit a pop-up to Cal, and I remember saying, 'Here's the pitch, the swing, and a high pop-up.' The crowd just went nuts. 'Cal's under it and he's got it,' and the crowd was going crazy, as if this were game 7 of the World Series. No team could ever have felt more appreciated and loved than the Orioles that night. There's an old cliché that the fans' support helped the club win. I thought that was the one night that I could point to and say, 'That actually happened.' I always remember that as one of my most memorable nights in any ballpark just because of the circumstances that said, 'This can't happen,' and yet, it did happen."

With the agreement set for the team's future home of Camden Yards, the last thing for the Orioles to do for Memorial Stadium was sign off, with a little help from Dr. Charles Steinberg. Jon Miller describes the "cinematic" night: "They played the final game and brought back all these former players from all the years of Oriole baseball beginning in 1954. They didn't tell anybody what they were going to do. So the game ended, and the music from *Field of Dreams* started playing. All of a sudden, Brooks Robinson pops up out of the dugout in his old number 5 Oriole uniform with a glove. He runs over to third base, and the people just go nuts. Then Frank Robinson pops out and he runs out to right field. People are not just delirious now with cheering, but a lot of them are emotional. People started crying. One by one, all these great Orioles from the past, and it kept on going and going. There was never an announcement made at anytime. They showed the guy in the dugout on the big screen and they had his name on the screen as the next guy popped out of the dugout. Brooks Robinson at third base. Later, Doug DeCinces went out to third base with him. Louie Aparicio went out to shortstop and Mark Belanger went out to shortstop. Ultimately, Cal went to shortstop. There were all these different eras of Orioles. Jim Palmer went to the pitcher's mound. All these great Orioles pitchers from different years went out to the mound. Dennis Martinez, who was still a very fine pitcher for the Montreal Expos, came back. Boog Powell went to first base. Jim Gentile was at first base. Lee May came back. It was an incredible ceremony. Not any announcements. Nothing. Just the players coming out one by one with this music playing. I thought it was one of the great ways to capture the great memories the people had. It wasn't that the ballpark itself was particularly special or there was any one thing about it that made it unique over any other. It wasn't like it had a 37-foot-high wall in left field or Babe Ruth used to hit home runs into those seats in right field. It was these guys. Dr. Steinberg seemed to understand that and it was beautiful."

Although the world has said "good-bye" to these ballparks—whether by a kiss or a submitted "no" vote—these edifices, in spirit, haven't made their farewell rounds. Like the open casket of "old" Comiskey or the unused "eighth wonder of the world," these former settings will linger not only inside the hearts of the broadcasters who called countless games there, but with the fans who attended them as well. Many of the stadiums may be parking lots now, but the memories, the "ghosts," and the history seep deeper into the ground on which they stood than any tar or cement ever could.

• 32 •

A Seance from the Booth

$\mathcal{T}$he beautiful part of talking to broadcasters whose voices will live on is that they, too, have listened to broadcasters whose voices have lived on. Baseball broadcasters, much like the sport they call, pass the torch, and a new set of voices take over. While not sitting in the same booth as many of the predecessors for whom they hold such mighty regard, today's broadcasters, growing up, felt as if they were right next to these living legends. They told them a story, which at times may have seemed as scripted as tales featuring Roy Rogers or Sam Spade from the golden age of radio. Thanks to these voices of yesterday, the voices of today "caught a bug" and decided their answer to the question "What do you want to be when *you* grow up?" Years from now, the answer to that same question will be inspired by the broadcasters of today. The following are the voices of yesterday who still linger in the hearts and memories of today's broadcasters.

JACK BUCK

Famous for his call "Go crazy, folks! Go crazy!" after Ozzie Smith's pennant-clinching walk-off home run in the 1985 National League Championship Series, as well as for saying "I don't believe what I just saw" about Kirk Gibson's walk-off home run in game 1 of the 1988 World Series, Jack Buck is regarded as one of the greatest, most inspiring, and most selfless broadcasters in baseball history. Working in the Cardinals broadcast booth alongside the legendary voices of Milo Hamilton, Harry Caray, Buddy Blattner, and Joe Garagiola, Jack Buck took over the reins after his broadcasting partner of 16 years, Harry Caray, was fired by the Cardinals in 1969. Buck went on for another 30 plus years as the voice of the Cardinals, signing off a team win with his irreplaceable "That's a winner." Jack's son Joe Buck is the lead on Fox TV's coverage of the World Series, and in 2011, after David Freese's walk-off solo home run forced perhaps the most improbable game 7 in World Series history, Joe channeled his father—albeit briefly—by closing the broadcast with "And we will see you tomorrow night."

Jack Buck was as wholesome, sincere, and kind as any Midwest person is personified to be. He was beyond that. He was a remarkable, funny person. If you had the chance to spend one moment with him, your whole day was just a blessing, and he gave you that time. People don't realize that Jack Buck would walk up to the newest rookie on the opposing team and introduce himself. They already knew who he was. That rookie would then do every show that Jack would ever want to have. He would go on the field and do his pregame show, and, by introducing himself, the next time he saw the guy, he never forgot a name. He walked up to that kid and said, "Hey, can I get you on the pregame show?" He was a master at that, but he was so personable. After games, when the lights were out and he had finished the postgame show, he'd walk out, and people would stand out there from Iowa, Kansas, Missouri, Arkansas, Texas, or wherever they listened to KMOX. They never got a glimpse of Jack before the game, but those who knew where to stand when he walked out, they would stand, and he'd come out, and he'd see a kid. He would sign his scorecard up in the booth and he would give it to a kid that day. Every night, he would hand that over to a kid. When he walked into the "old" Busch Stadium, he'd look over and see a family wandering, and he'd say, "Hey. You guys need some tickets?" and he'd give his four tickets to that family. In my opinion—and I've had this shared with me by many in the business—he understood, more than any other broadcaster in the history of the game, the ambassadorship of being a baseball announcer for a team, for a city, and for a region, and he did it better than anyone I've ever seen in my life. Jack would go into the community. He'd do the police luncheon every year because he loved the police and what they meant to his city. He took pride in his city, and that's what every announcer needs to do. What an amazing guy.

—Wayne Hagin, former St. Louis Cardinals
radio play-by-play broadcaster

There's not a game day that passes without my thoughts briefly turning to the late, great hall of famers, Harry Caray and Jack Buck. As a kid growing up in the 1950s and '60s in western Illinois, I would listen nightly to Harry and Jack call St. Louis Cardinals baseball on 50,000 watt juggernaut, 1120 AM, KMOX-Radio in St. Louis. I'd turn on my transistor radio 30 minutes prior to the game to listen to the "Dug-

out Show," and then would listen through the ballgame and finally the wrap-up show which included the "Star of the Game," an interview with one of the players. The two hall of famers had differing styles. Harry was the cheerleader, excitement booming from his voice on every Cardinals hit or run, while disappointment rang out with every rally snuffed out, or error made that led to an opponent's run. Jack was more controlled, and his professionalism is what stood out to me. Excited when the Cardinals scored, but always willing to give the other team credit on nice plays. Still one of the all-time best at game calling. Both of their game descriptions were influential to me growing up; and, I believe I've borrowed a little from both to use in my own broadcast style. To this day, one of my most memorable professional highlights was back in 1998, the Diamondbacks inaugural season, Jack Buck had me on his "dugout interview." I had probably listened to thousands of his dugout interviews over the years growing up, and then, some 35–40 years later to be a guest on the show, Wow! Harry Caray and Jack Buck were the reason I told my parents, when I was only 8 years old, that when I grew up I wanted to be a big league baseball broadcaster.

—Greg Schulte, Arizona Diamondbacks radio
play-by-play broadcaster

I grew up in Missouri listening to Jack Buck and Harry Caray. Jack Buck's style was—to me—something to try to not copy but to get close to. It was a target to shoot for. He's obviously a great broadcaster. Winner of the Ford C. Frick award and in the hall of fame. He just had so many terrific moments and honors in his career, not only in baseball but in football as well. I admired him as a broadcaster. I thought his style was just so easy. He was an easy listen. He didn't try to impress you with his knowledge or vocabulary, but just to tell you what was going on. It was such an easy fit. He was an artist at making it seem simple; but then, when I got into the broadcasting fraternity and got to know him and saw what a great guy he was, it just reinforced everything for me to shoot for as a broadcaster. Not only to be good at the craft of broadcasting but to be approachable and responsible and try for charity work. All the things that he did really wrapped it up in a total package for me. I thought he was just a great human being. Occasionally, he would interview me for his pre-game radio show, and this was a big honor. Somebody I really respected highly as a kid growing up. To be able to be interviewed by Jack Buck, it was almost hard to get the words out when he was asking the questions. Sometimes, in my head, if I'm doing a game, I will say something, and I will think, "That's Jack Buck. That sounds exactly like Jack Buck." I'm not trying to do it. It just comes out that way. It gives me pause, but I think—after listening to hundreds of games broadcast by an individual—it's probably natural to absorb some of that.

—Bill Brown, Houston Astros TV play-by-play broadcaster

I grew up in Savannah, Georgia, and the only Major League team we could get was KMOX out of St. Louis. I grew up listening to Jack Buck and Harry Caray, but my favorite was Jack. I used to love Jack Buck. I'd go to sleep every night listening to the St. Louis Cardinals play. We had a very small house. My mom was a single parent, and she would make 56 bucks a week. My bedroom was about as big as this room [Cactus League press box] right here, so I'd get in my bed, and I had my baseball. I had to put some socks into the screen windows because they had holes in them. If I didn't put socks in there, the mosquitoes would come in. My mom bought me a fan because we didn't have any air conditioning. So I'd put my fan on, and I'd put my sock in the screen. I had my baseball and I would throw it up for two or three hours, listening to the St. Louis Cardinals. Ironically, the Cardinals were never my favorite team even though I grew up listening to them.

—Ken "Hawk" Harrelson, Chicago White Sox TV
play-by-play broadcaster

Working with Jack Buck—one of the greatest announcers that there has ever been behind the microphone—and having a chance to be part of his craft. Just what he did daily. To be around him to ask questions—to work with him—that was a big deal to me, and, being a kid from St. Louis and having a chance to just take in and sit next to and work with Jack was a thrill. I try to take a piece of every guy I've ever listened to, whether it be hockey, basketball, baseball, whatever the sport; Jack was the guy that always stood out to me. Being from St. Louis, you turned on the radio and you heard that voice. "It's time for baseball." I loved the sport, so that's the guy I grew up listening to and had a chance to work with, so it made it a tremendous experience.

—Dan McLaughlin, St. Louis Cardinals TV
play-by-play broadcaster

ERNIE HARWELL

Having spent 55 years in a broadcast booth, Ernie Harwell was the inspiration and mentor for many of today's baseball voices. Being the radio voice behind Alan Trammell and Lou Whitaker, arguably the greatest shortstop/ second baseman combo in the history of the game, Harwell's call "It's two for the price of one" sounded perhaps just as many times as his home run call "That one is *long* gone." During his 42 years in a very unique broadcast booth at Tiger Stadium, Harwell called two World Series champion Detroit Tigers teams, in 1968 and 1984, before retiring in 2002. Calling a game is one thing, but Ernie Harwell showed the broadcasting world, both inside and outside of the booth, what a legend he truly was.

> *Ernie was a mentor to me. I got to know Ernie when I worked in Cleveland. We heard him across the lake, and my first year doing Cleveland Indians baseball in 1979, I met him for the first time. He was always so kind and we became very good friends. Even after he retired, I'd go to see him at his home in Novi, Michigan. Just a warm, giving, Christian guy. A very dear friend. He had a wonderful life.*
>
> —Joe Castiglione, Boston Red Sox radio
> play-by-play broadcaster

> *Ernie Harwell was a really important person in my life. I listened to tapes at a very young age when I was just starting out. He always had great things to say and encouraging words. I loved the way he called the game. I felt that was kind of my style off the field as well. Ernie was such a great man. He was a man of faith. He was the first one—once I got into professional baseball as an announcer at the age of 22—that I connected with. He's the one that helped me realize that you can be a man of faith. You can be a family man. You can have a strong family and be a strong husband and father and work in this game, which is a very demanding schedule. That was a pretty big crossroad for me. To be able to see that and see how he excelled at his job. He was the first person who called me when I got the Brewers job, and it was my first Major League job. When I got back to the hotel and there was a phone call, it was Ernie Harwell. He was the first person to welcome me to the big leagues. I'll never forget that. He was a great man.*
>
> —Brian Anderson, Milwaukee Brewers TV
> play-by-play broadcaster

> *My hero growing up was Ernie Harwell. There's a statue of Ernie outside of Comerica Park. He not only was my idol growing up and the reason I got into this business but he became a mentor and a friend very late in his life and early on in my broadcasting career. Ernie was my guy, and he gave me so much great advice; not really advice he actually told me. It was more advice about how he acted and I just watched. I think every broadcaster will probably have a good Ernie Harwell story to tell. As great a broadcaster as he was—and will live on as one of the greatest of all time—he might have been the greatest human being I have ever met.*
>
> —Len Kasper, Chicago Cubs TV play-by-play broadcaster

> *I listened to Ernie Harwell a lot growing up because the Tigers game broadcasts would boom across the lake. On CKLW, I think. If you*

were in my part of the Midwest, Ernie was THE baseball guy. Ernie was such a wonderful gentleman. I think the thing that so many of us liked about Ernie was his brevity. He was the guy that taught me that it's okay to just let the game sounds go for a little while. You don't have to fill every moment.

—Jack Corrigan, Colorado Rockies
radio play-by-play broadcaster

I got advice from Ernie Harwell when I first took the job. The Tigers were off to a 9–23 start and we were in Minnesota and I said, 'How do you do this every day when your team stinks?' This was my first year. I just remember he said, 'You might see something you've never seen before. You might see a great game between two bad teams, or you might see a great individual performance.' Simple advice, but a great reminder of why we love the game. That advice served me very well in the years that followed, when the Tigers had their worst three year run in franchise history (320 losses). I loved the way he would always give both teams a good call. He'd give a better call for the home team, but didn't get down when the other team did something good. You have to acknowledge it. You get more excited for the home team, obviously, but you give both teams a good call when something good happens. I always liked that about him. I liked the fact that it was very comforting to just turn on the radio and hear him. He was engaged. The energy was always good. He had stories to tell. I think we're a little different in that regard. I'm a numbers guy. I love statistics. It's one of the things that drew me into the game. Listening to him was always a great reminder that stats are fine, but the people behind the numbers are also important. He was always so good at that. People loved hearing the story behind the person, and he'd always blend it seamlessly into the broadcast. He had an enormous impact.

—Dan Dickerson, Detroit Tigers radio play-by-play broadcaster

MEL ALLEN AND RED BARBER

The original two winners of the Ford C. Frick award for excellence in broadcasting, Mel Allen and Red Barber shared more than just awards; they shared a booth as well. Mel Allen was the voice of the New York Yankees during the team's most fruitful period from 1939 to 1964, calling games for 21 American League pennant winners and 15 World Series champions. Red Barber, before working alongside Allen in the Bronx, broadcast across town for the Brooklyn Dodgers from 1939 to 1953 and had a front-row seat to Jackie Robinson's breaking of the color barrier in 1947. During the 1955 World Series, Barber's former team finally got the best of his current team, but order was restored in New York the following year. Eventually the Dodgers moved west, but Allen and Barber continued as what is thought of today as arguably the greatest broadcasting duo in the history of the game.

> *When Mel Allen and Red Barber were doing the Yankees games, I really felt those guys were my friends growing up. Red Barber used to sign on and say, "Hi, friends. Red Barber here," and Mel was super friendly. "Hello there, everybody." I say hello to everybody and so long to everybody as an homage to him. That's my opening and my closing on every broadcast.*

> —Eric Nadel, Texas Rangers radio play-by-play broadcaster

> *When I was nine years old, I knew I was going on the air. I got very lucky. When I grew up, there were three teams in New York. I listened to Mel Allen, Russ Hodges, Red Barber, and then Vin Scully. I listened to 'em all, and you take a little bit from everyone and then you get on the air and then your own personality comes out. Mel Allen was my hero and then I got to be friends with him later on in life.*

> —John Sterling, New York Yankees
> radio play-by-play broadcaster

> *My inspiration was Mel Allen, who I still think is the greatest of all time. The one I emulated.*

> —Joe Castiglione, Boston Red Sox
> radio play-by-play broadcaster

> *When I was about eight years old, I wrote a composition for the good nuns in grammar school saying that I wanted to be a sports announcer, and, at those times, no one thought of being a sports announcer. The boys wanted to be policemen, firemen, soldiers, doctors and the girls wanted to be ballet dancers, nurses, teachers, and singers, and here's this one little red-headed kid saying he wanted to be a sports announcer. Well, in those days, we did not have baseball broadcasts on the radio. The one thing that I had was listening to college football games, and in listening to college football games, I listened to great voices like Ted Husing and Bill Stern and then I heard Red Barber and then I heard Mel Allen, so it wasn't one announcer, it was a whole group. When I eventually began as a professional announcer, certainly Red Barber had the greatest influence on me to the degree he was almost like a father because he cared and he really wanted me to succeed, which meant he would be critical and he would praise whenever he felt it was worthy. He was very fair. Very*

just. That was a tremendous influence. I worked shoulder to shoulder with Red from 1950 through 1953, and then I worked a lot of World Series with Mel.

—Vin Scully, Los Angeles Dodgers
radio play-by-play broadcaster

I was too young to remember Mel Allen, but, once I got the radio job 23 years ago, Mel would occasionally pull me aside and give me bits of advice when he was around for Old Timer's Day. The best advice he ever gave me was to stop broadcasting and just make believe you are telling your mom what's going on in the game. Talk to her and don't make it seem as if you're talking to all the people who are really listening. This will make it seem as if you're talking to all of them individually.

—Michael Kay, New York Yankees
TV play-by-play broadcaster

BOB MURPHY AND LINDSEY NELSON

Two of the three original broadcasters for the New York Mets, Bob Murphy and Lindsey Nelson worked alongside each other for 17 years, during which the two called the "Amazing" Mets' first-ever championship, in 1969. Nelson moved on to San Francisco after the 1979 season, but Murphy called Boston Red Sox first baseman Bill Buckner's gaffe of Mookie Wilson's grounder, losing game 6 of the 1986 World Series. While in the booth together, Murphy and Nelson had a "complementary" broadcasting relationship, one that is still spoken of years later.

Bob Murphy was the guy for me. Bob used to do the television and radio with Lindsey Nelson and Ralph Kiner of the Mets. I remember when he was relegated to just radio duty, I was younger, and I didn't understand it. I was disappointed because my understanding of the game of baseball was what I watched on television. I was reintroduced to radio when I went off to college because I couldn't get the Mets games on TV. I could get them on the radio, and that's where I sort of rediscovered Bob Murphy and said, "Okay." He was the right choice to go over to radio because he paints the picture better than most people that are in the game at this point. When I first met him, he wasn't a big guy. I'm about six foot three, and, at the time, I was about 340 pounds. I introduced myself, and I was doing an interview with him for Phillies radio. I told him he was the guy I listened to all the time when I was growing up, and he said, "Thomas, I'm happy I didn't stunt your growth while I was broadcasting." Bob Murphy was the guy whose voice still rings in my head. He was casual when he would call different things going on, and I could always tell when there was a home run because of the peak in his voice. I can still feel that and hear that in my head

—Tom McCarthy, Philadelphia Phillies
TV play-by-play broadcaster

When the Mets came in, Lindsey Nelson and Bob Murphy were my guys. Lindsey had all these folksy, country expressions, and I loved listening to those guys. The Mets were so bad, but those guys were always in such a good mood. They were so happy. They were so cheerful to be at the ballpark, and they did such a good job of bringing up their players.

—Eric Nadel, Texas Rangers radio play-by-play broadcaster

I grew up in New York. I listened to Lindsey Nelson and Bob Murphy on the Mets games. I would probably think I was inspired by them once I had the bug that I thought this was something that I wanted to do. There's probably a little of each of them in what I do and how I do it. Came to meet them later on. It was a big thrill. Getting to do games with Bob Murphy in New York. It was on my transistor radio under my pillow when I was supposed to be sleeping when I was a little kid. That was a big circle for me, from my transistor radio to the seat next to me in a Major League booth.

—Charlie Slowes, Washington Nationals
radio play-by-play broadcaster

Bob, Lindsey, and Ralph were a part of my life seven months out of the year for a long, long time. I actually have the seat that I used to sit in inside the broadcast booth at Shea Stadium, which had been Bob Murphy's before mine. I remember asking Murph's wife—because Murph had long since passed on—if she would have any problem with me taking that chair. If she wanted it, that was hers, but she was so generous to say, "I'm so happy it means so much to you. You take it." That's kind of a museum piece to me. It's battered but it just means the world to me. It sits in my office.

—Howie Rose, New York Mets radio play-by-play broadcaster

HARRY CARAY

Usually it's the players who are referred to as "journeymen" late in their careers, but in the field of broadcasting, Harry Caray was one of baseball's most beloved journeymen. Broadcasting for four different teams over 52 years, Harry Caray stayed in the Midwest for all but one of them. Perhaps best known for the Cubs broadcasts in the 15 twilight years of his career, Caray started down the river with the St. Louis Cardinals, working with hall of famers Joe Garagiola and Jack Buck. After being fired by the team in 1969, Caray broadcast for one season with the Oakland A's before returning to the Midwest for the next 25 years, broadcasting for the White Sox for 10 and then for the Cubs. Caray, much like former broadcasting partner Jack Buck, has literally left his legacy with the game of baseball, being father to the late Atlanta Braves broadcaster Skip Caray and grandfather to Chip Caray, also of the Braves. Caray's enthusiasm for his team spoke volumes. His leading of the seventh inning stretch and "Take me out to the ballgame" is something that is often copied but never replicated in the Windy City.

> *Obviously, for me, growing up on the South Side of Chicago, Harry Caray was my guy, He was a guy, who, even if he was broadcasting bad teams, was still having the time of his life. That's one of the things I've tried to incorporate in my broadcasts. I like that he had fan connectivity. To broadcast from the bleachers in center field always seemed kind of fun. Harry, to me, was the guy who looked like he was having a blast. He conveyed that to the fans, and I think the fans are saying, "Hey, if this guy's having this much fun at the ballpark, why can't we?" That's one of the things I try to do in our broadcasts; make it sound like there's no better place to be at that particular moment. Harry was a guy I've tried to emulate, and it's been a lot of fun, and what I do beats working for a living.*

> —Dave Wills, Tampa Bay Rays radio play-by-play broadcaster

> *I will suffice to say Harry Caray was Chicago Cubs baseball. He made it so special to be at Wrigley Field and to do games and be alongside him. That's a guy who probably did his best work in St. Louis. He did remarkable work on the south side of Chicago with the White Sox for 10 years, and then probably wasn't at his best in Wrigley, but it meant so much to be there and to see him alongside you. You felt like you belonged. "Wow! There's Harry Caray." Here I am, five feet away, doing my game back to Colorado, and there's Harry and that made you feel good.*

> —Wayne Hagin, former Colorado Rockies radio play-by-play broadcaster

> *There's a caricature of Harry—kind of a famous drawing of him—that's right above our broadcast booth. A tradition he started on the South Side with the White Sox and he brought to Wrigley Field back in the '80s*

was conducting and singing the seventh inning stretch from the home broadcast booth. It continues on to this day with celebrity guest singers. I would say probably half, if not more, of the singers, at some point, say, "This one is for Harry." There are constant daily reminders of his presence. I think that's a unique part of the experience at Wrigley Field. There's no question about it. We talk about Harry almost every single day with the seventh inning stretch. I don't think there's a better way to honor one of the all time greats than to continue to do that every single day.

—Len Kasper, Chicago Cubs TV play-by-play broadcaster

HARRY KALAS

Working in the broadcast booth, literally until his death in 2009, Harry Kalas was the voice of Philadelphia Phillies baseball for the better part of four decades. He broadcast for the Phillies beginning in 1971, and the team won two titles during his time in the booth; the second was against the Tampa Bay Rays just months before Kalas's death. Working on the opposing broadcast for the 2008 World Series was Harry's son, Todd Kalas. Broadcasting players like Steve Carlton, Mike Schmidt, and Pete Rose, Kalas called six no-hitters in his 43-year career, as well as Mike Schmidt's 500th career home run and Pete Rose's National League record-setting 3,631st hit, passing the St. Louis Cardinals' Stan Musial. Kalas's signature home run call "outta here" will live in the memories of Phillies and baseball fans alike for many generations to come.

Todd Kalas had a chance to sit in with his dad for an inning while we were in Philadelphia. It was obviously a special moment for Todd and his father because his father then passed away the very next year. Obviously, it's got to be an incredible moment to be able to do anything with your dad. If your dad was a fireman, you became a fireman. If your dad was a plumber, you became a plumber. To be able to work together had to be an incredible moment and I know it was for Todd. As a matter of fact, Todd will still do some things to honor his father. A fan designed a tie that recognized Harry's talents and Todd wears that on the day his father passed every year. We have a Miami "all white out" trip with the Rays where Todd will wear his dad's white shoes on that particular day. Despite the fact that you're rooting for two different teams, it was an incredible, special moment that they were able to be together for that series.

—Dave Wills, Tampa Bay Rays radio play-by-play broadcaster

It was neat to see Harry sort of soak in the fact that the Rays and the Phillies were facing each other because Todd was there. Even though he was just doing some interviews and pre- and post-game stuff for the Rays, he was still there, and he was still getting a chance to be a part of this with his father, and that was really cool. On top of that, I got a chance to stand in the booth while Harry and Wheels (Chris Wheeler) called the final out of the World Series. Just to watch the field. To see his call and see Wheels' reaction. They had never called the final out of the World Series because in '80, they weren't allowed to do it. The national people did the TV and the radio. In '83, they got knocked out by the Orioles in the World Series, so they didn't get a chance to call the final out. The same with the Blue Jays in '93, so this was his final moment. His last chance to call a World Series championship for the Phillies. It was the perfect setting for the greatest voice in Phillies history and arguably one of the greatest sports figures in Philadelphia history. To call the last out of the 2008 World Series. It was a big deal for him to call and be a part of that. He died in April the next year. It seems somewhat symbolic that was the last great moment he got a chance to call.

—Tom McCarthy, Philadelphia Phillies
TV play-by-play broadcaster

DAVE NIEHAUS

Calling games for the team since day one, hall of fame broadcaster Dave Niehaus the lead radio voice of the Seattle Mariners for 33 years. Beloved by not only the Mariners community but that of Seattle as well, Niehaus broadcast professional baseball for over 40 years, starting with the California Angels. Niehaus is credited for two of baseball's most famous nicknames, "A-Rod" (Alex Rodriguez) and "the Kid" (Ken Griffey Jr.). His signature call "My oh my" is one for which Niehaus is well known, but for Seattle, the broadcaster's call for Edgar Martinez's walk-off hit, otherwise known as "the double," will forever resonate with Mariners fans.

What stays with me about Dave Niehaus was his complete love and joy of the game of baseball. He loved broadcasting baseball games. He loved being the conduit between the fan, the players, and what was going on. Nobody—no one—did a better job of setting up the atmosphere and excitement of a play. What separates the great announcers from the good announcers is Dave Niehaus never ever missed a great call. He was always there, and, not only did he set it up, but he came through with the call. That is going to be remembered for the ages. When Edgar hit the double, the biggest hit in our history, in game 5 of the Division Series against the Yankees at the Kingdome, Joey Cora was on at third base. Joey hit a bunt single and Junior had a single up the middle. So Junior was on first, Joey was on at third, and Dave said, "The Mariners would love a line drive into the gap right here. Cora would score, and with Junior's speed, he can score from first base and win it." Sure enough, on the very next pitch, Edgar hits the line drive down the left-field line off Jack McDowell on a fork ball. It's a story in itself, and, of course, Cora scored easily and Junior came flying around third base, and Dave said, "They're gonna wave him in, and the throw will be late, and the Mariners will play for the American League Championship. I don't believe it. My oh my. It just continues." The Mariners won over the Yankees. Sitting next to him, it was one of the greatest thrills of my life, and, during that moment, my job, as the number two announcer, was to get out of his way and let Dave do his thing, because I knew he was. So I took off my headphones and I said, "I'll get a chance to come in here at the right time." Dave's calling the play, and I'm jumping up and down as Junior's rounding third and Dave came up with that beautiful call. The one that we remember now and forever. He was right on with everything. That's what I remember about Dave. The other thing is all the great, old announcers, they were wonderful storytellers. They had all these great experiences of wherever it was they grew up. For Dave, it was Princeton, Indiana. He would come up with stuff from back in the day and incorporate it into his play by play, but, also, his experiences of 10 years working with the Angels. Working with Buddy Blattner, Dick Enberg, Don Drysdale, and then becoming the number one guy at the start of the franchise with the Mariners. All the players, managers that he really got to know. He was so close with all the managers and coaches, but it really was the stories that he told. The unique ability to relay that story. A lot of people can tell stories, but it's like they're reading it out of a book. This guy has lived it and made you feel it. The number one goal of any broadcaster is can you put the fan in the front row and have them see the game on the radio? Because, if we do our jobs right, radio is a visual medium. You can see the game on the radio if you're a baseball fan. You can have an idea of where the ball's hit, where the runners are, what's going on, how close is it going to be, and nobody was better than Dave Niehaus at doing that. He was so respectful. He allowed me to do my job. I tried my best for years to complement him, but he was just one of the best in the business. He's in the hall of fame, and I think that says all you need to know about Dave Niehaus. I loved the guy. He was great to me, and I will always remember that. I miss him like crazy, and, to this day, I still think Dave's going to walk into that booth. Come in, slam his scorebook on the desk, and say, "All right. Let's play some baseball."

—Rick Rizzs, Seattle Mariners radio play-by-play broadcaster

JERRY COLEMAN

Not too many broadcasters can claim to have played in six World Series and won four in their playing career. Of the ones who can, only one—though he'd never say it himself—could claim to have actively served and fought for the United States in two major wars (World War II, Korea) before sitting behind the microphone. Jerry Coleman, former second baseman of the New York Yankees—after playing baseball for nine seasons and serving as a fighter pilot in the Air Force—became a broadcaster for the New York Yankees before coming over to the San Diego Padres. Coleman spent seven decades around the game and will forever be remembered in both the Padres and Yankees communities not only for his voice, but also for his heart and humility.

> *It wasn't Jerry's way of doing a game. It was just him. There will never be one like him in all of sports. There's never been one like him in baseball. There isn't anybody who's left—when he was playing—to fight in the war twice. We were in Milwaukee. There was a quiz on the scoreboard. "Who was the only Major League player to leave and fight in combat twice?" I nudged Jerry and said, "Look at that. Who is that?" He said, "I don't know." He really didn't. I said, "It's you," and he said, "Oh." That was Jerry Coleman. They removed his ego at birth. Everybody thought he was a hero except him. He would always tell me, "The only heroes were the guys who came back in coffins. They're heroes. I'm not." I said, "No. If you and your guys didn't do their job, others would have died and come back in coffins, and that, to me and everybody else, is a hero. That's why people consider you as they do." That's the only disagreement we had in 35 years. What a relationship. I had never met anyone like him in my life and I never will. I had no relationship in comparison to my father as I had with Jerry. He was brother, father, professor, everything to me. His broadcasting? Garvey's home run in '84. We're down 2–0 to the Chicago Cubs. We came from Chicago, lost both games to a great Cubs team. We're down and we're going, "Third game. It's over," and Garvey hits the home run. Jerry's call is the most replayed clip and the biggest one play in Padres history. That was the least of what he was. The most unassuming guy of all time. I've had to sit on the planes and on the bus and had to get dental tools out. "Tell me about this. Tell me about that." He would tell me these stories with a proviso, "When I'm alive, don't tell these stories. I ain't no hero," so I've been telling them since he's been gone. The guy was 89, and yet, I'm in shock that it was too soon. It never occurred to us that he'd be gone, ever. I thought he'd outlive us all.*

—Ted Leitner, San Diego Padres radio play-by-play broadcaster

NAT ALLBRIGHT

It is the duty of a radio broadcaster to paint a picture for those who are not there to see the event in person. In the case of radio broadcaster Nat Allbright, he, too, painted the picture, only he, too, was not there in person to see it for himself. Hired by then Brooklyn Dodgers owner Walter O'Malley, Nat Allbright, from a studio in Virginia, received the information about Brooklyn Dodgers baseball games via Morse code and re-created them into a radio broadcast. Allbright not only did this for baseball, but when the Dodgers moved west to Los Angeles, he re-created games that were never played, including an All-Star game during the strike season of '81. Allbright's improvisation garnered so much attention, he made a business of his craft and re-created sports' greatest moments with his customers injected right into the action. Allbright's broadcasts reached destinations the Brooklyn Dodgers' live broadcasts couldn't, including the home of a young, future hall of fame broadcaster, the Cincinnati Reds' own Marty Brennaman.

> *I listened to a guy who re-created Brooklyn Dodger games. His name was Nat Allbright. I listened to him in the '50s and had no idea what re-creation was. That term meant nothing to me. If I listened to a baseball game, I assumed the guy was there. He was not. He was in a studio in northern Virginia, broadcasting Brooklyn Dodger games, and he was sensational. I was not even a Dodger fan. He was so good, and had such an impact on me in those years—to plant the seed that I was not even aware of—and I discovered later in life that this is what I wanted to do. When I went into the hall of fame, he was still alive and living in Arlington, Virginia. I called him on the telephone and I told him, "I just felt like you need to know the impression that you made upon me as a kid growing up in Virginia and how it affected me greatly in my decision later in life to do what I'm doing." He was very appreciative. I think he was emotionally taken by it. I would hope that a young guy maybe one day would pick up the phone and call me and tell me the same thing.*

> —Marty Brennaman, Cincinnati Reds
> radio play-by-play broadcaster

JOE NUXHALL

Having pitched in a Major League game at the age of 15, Joe Nuxhall spent nearly his entire life with the Cincinnati Reds, so much so that the address of the team's home of Great American Ball Park, was dedicated to him. After returning to the same club for which he had pitched as a 15 year old, Nuxhall played another 16 seasons in a Reds uniform before turning his voice talents toward the team's broadcast booth. A few years after he took his seat behind the microphone, Nuxhall's partner and future hall of fame broadcaster Marty Brennaman came in, and the two made history.

> *We worked together 31 years. There's never been a broadcast team in the history of this game that's ever worked that long. Nobody's done that and nobody ever will again because guys just don't stay together that long. We had an incredible relationship. We knew each other so well that he could stop a sentence in the middle of it and I would finish it and put the period on it, and, conversely, he could do the same thing with me. He referred to us like an old married couple, and, in many ways, we were. I don't think that you could know a guy any better than I got to know him and he got to know me. We had a great affection for one another. We had a great run.*

> —Marty Brennaman, Cincinnati Reds radio play-by-play broadcaster

CHUCK THOMPSON AND BILL O'DONNELL

Years before the Orioles came to Baltimore in the form of the St. Louis Browns, hall of fame broadcaster Chuck Thompson was already planting baseball's seed in Charm City. Once referred to as "the voice of God in Baltimore," Thompson was eventually joined by his longtime broadcast partner, Bill O'Donnell, in 1966, which was the year the Orioles won their first World Series. The team went to four more World Series with Thompson and O'Donnell behind the microphone together (1969, 1970, 1971, 1979), winning it all again in 1970. O'Donnell died of cancer after the '82 season, and Thompson, with a heavy heart, broadcast the Orioles to their third World Series title the following year (1983).

> *I was born and raised in Virginia and listened to a lot of baseball. Primarily in Baltimore. Chuck Thompson and Bill O'Donnell—I thought—made as fine a broadcast team as there was in the history of the game.*

> —Marty Brennaman, Cincinnati Reds radio play-by-play broadcaster

PHIL "THE SCOOTER" RIZZUTO

Though he is probably referred to in the Bronx as "the other Yankee short-stop," Phil "the Scooter" Rizzuto made a larger imprint on the franchise from the booth. In 13 seasons as the Yankees shortstop, Rizzuto was on seven World Series championship teams and nine American League pennant winners. Rizzuto, along with broadcasting partners Jerry Coleman, Bill White, and Frank Messer—all of whom he referred to by their last names rather than their first—were the voice of many more pennant- and championship-winning teams, up until "the Scooter's" swan song, the '96 season, ending with the New York Yankees as World Series champions. Rizzuto's catch-phrase "Holy cow" is regarded as one of the most recognizable calls in baseball history.

> *I've always said there were four male voices heard in my house when I grew up: my father, Phil Rizzuto, Bill White, and Frank Messer. I would listen to those three Yankee announcers as much as my parents would allow as I was growing up. Their camaraderie and knowledge of the game made me feel part of it, and, by the time I was nine years old, all I wanted to be was like them, announcer of the Yankees. It was kind of a blast to be in the booth where Mel Allen and Phil Rizzuto had announced.*

—Michael Kay, New York Yankees
TV play-by-play broadcaster

BILL KING

If there ever was an "iron man" of broadcasting, it was Bill King. Not only did King broadcast the Oakland A's for 25 years, which included the team's three straight trips to the World Series from 1988 to 1990, but he also worked games for the Oakland Raiders for 27 years, calling their three championships ('76, '80, '83), and for the Golden State Warriors for 21 years, including the team's '74–75 championship season. Bringing much excitement to the game with his signature call "Holy Toledo," King broadcast some of the A's most memorable moments, including Rickey Henderson's breaking of Lou Brock's all-time stolen base record and Scott Hatteberg's walk-off home run to win an American League record 20th straight game for the A's in 2002.

> *The winning streak was a whole chapter in the book "Holy Toledo."*
> *Bill was an iconic figure in the Bay Area. Part of the reason I wrote*

that chapter was to try to illustrate to people how gracious Bill was to me in the fact that he elected to stay on vacation when a lot of people in our business—because of their egos or insecurity—would have said, "I'm working those games because something incredible might happen and I need to be there." It was so fitting that he came back and did the 20th game because Hatteberg's call was an immortal moment and was the punctuation of the movie. I wasn't listening to the game. I was at home watching it on ESPN. The only thing I can say about that game and about Bill was there were so many of his calls from that game in the movie. In doing the research for the book, I listened to a lot of the calls from the game. Here is a man who was 74 years old at the time. The A's blew this huge lead with Tim Hudson pitching and it was a long game that lasted forever, and, yet, when that moment came, Bill was there to capture it perfectly. He had this remarkable ability to rise to the occasion. When the game was on the line and you needed someone to put the drama clearly into focus, he was the guy you wanted on the air. He really did capture that at that moment and did it perfectly with the perfect pitch. The perfect level of excitement. Yet, he was totally clear. You could understand everything that he was saying. That call was not only the punctuation to the movie but maybe the punctuation of Bill's career because it was probably the last really huge call that he had that was really noteworthy. There were a lot of really good calls after that but that's the one most people remember and it was immortalized in bottle openers and Scott Hatteberg and Bill King bobbleheads. All kinds of places in the Bay Area where you can hear it. So the call itself has taken on a life of its own. Even Art Howe, who was the manager of the club, said that every once in a while, he'll push the button on the Bill King bobblehead just to hear that call. Just to hear Bill's voice and remember Bill because that's how much Bill meant to Art.

—Ken Korach, Oakland A's radio play-by-play broadcaster

TOM CHEEK

Known as "the Voice of the Toronto Blue Jays," Tom Cheek broadcast for the team beginning on day one and would do so for another 27 and a half years before a brain tumor surfaced and eventually took his life. Having broadcast for the back-to-back World Series champion Toronto Blue Jays in 1992–1993, Cheek's most famous call, "Touch 'em all, Joe," was made about only the second walk-off home run in baseball history to end a World Series, as Toronto's Joe Carter's three-run shot ended the night for Philadelphia closer Mitch Williams and the season for the '93 Phillies.

Without question, without hesitation, without even a thought, Tom Cheek was a massive influence on me growing up and even past being grown up. He was the original voice of the Blue Jays. April 7, 1977, was the first game they ever played, and he was the broadcaster that day. He did 4,036 consecutive regular season games, also working All-Star games, spring training, and all those postseasons. Not just the postseasons the Blue Jays played. They used to broadcast across Canada postseason games from our broadcast crew and Tom would do those, so he worked all those games in a row. Never missed a day of work until June of 2004 when his father passed away. He went to be with his family, and then, a week later, he was back and they found a brain tumor that would kill him 18 months later. He had everything. He had the voice, the knowledge, the passion. He had fun. He was from the Florida pan- handle, so he had the kind of homespun, folksy turn of phrase. Stuff like "He took him to powder river" and that sort of thing. He was incredible, and he was a constant. I got to work with him for the last two and a half years of his career, and he wound up being a real huge teacher, mentor, and champion for me. I can't say enough of the opportunity to get to know someone who was that iconic figure that you're growing up thinking of as this larger than life guy. He was larger than life in real life, too. There's no one who is over 35 in Toronto for whom Tom Cheek was not just the voice of baseball but the voice of summer. He's in the hall of fame now, which is wonderful. He should have been in before he passed away. Some of his stuff comes out in my call. I know it does, and there's nothing I can do about it. I learned how to broadcast baseball from Tom Cheek when I was seven years old, all the way up until I was sitting in the booth beside him and learning even more from him.

—Mike Wilner, Toronto Blue Jays
radio play-by-play broadcaster

MIKE HEGAN

Perhaps the only broadcaster in history to ever call and play in the same game, former voice of the Cleveland Indians Mike Hegan had more than 50 years of baseball under his belt by the time he called his final game in 2012, a game he was called back to after retiring in 2011. Hegan, who played in two World Series (1964, 1972) and called two World Series (1995, 1997), was behind the microphone for the Indians during the team's record-setting 455-game sell-out streak from June 5, 1995, to April 4, 2001, and was in on many unforgettable broadcasts, including the Indians' 12-run rally against the '01 Seattle Mariners. Had the Mariners not relinquished the lead, their season would have eventually ended with 117 wins, which would have been the most in baseball history.

> *Mike Hegan was tremendous in the booth. I'll always be grateful to him because he was a good friend to me and helped me a ton when I was transitioning to Cleveland from their Triple A club in Buffalo. It was sad when they learned of his passing in December of 2013 because it brought back a lot of memories. He was an ex-player and had that great ex-player perspective. I think he was a real treasure for Indians fans. He and Tom Hamilton were a tremendous team. They were fun to listen to. It was just enjoyable to listen to them every night. People will always remember him. Part of that is his dad, Jim played for the team. He grew up and went to high school in Cleveland, so there were some roots there and then he spent more than two decades in the booth after playing. When you talk about him, to most people, he was just a friendly guy and he was able to convey that on the air. When you listened to him, you just thought you were listening to this friendly guy talking baseball, who had a pretty good career that he would never talk about but had great stories from that career. He was great at sharing stories and breaking down the game pretty darn well.*
>
> —Jim Rosenhaus, Cleveland Indians
> radio play-by-play broadcaster

ERNIE JOHNSON SR., PETE VAN WIEREN AND SKIP CARAY

Broadcasting from the Deep South of Atlanta from the late '70s into this century, the Georgia Radio hall of fame trio of Ernie Johnson Sr., Skip Caray, and Pete Van Wieren were the voices behind a Braves team that went from worst to first in '91 and began a string of successes that will likely never be repeated in baseball. Caray, son of hall of fame broadcaster and beloved baseball "character," Harry Caray, passed the Caray family broadcasting torch to his son Chip, who also works Braves games as well as Fox and TBS. Johnson Sr., Caray, and Van Wieren will be remembered for years to come as the voices of Braves baseball during the Bobby Cox years.

> *In Atlanta, we were blessed with Ernie Johnson Sr., Skip Caray, and Pete Van Wieren. I don't know how none of these three have been recognized with a Ford C. Frick award. They worked together for a long, long time. You could tell they were such great friends and they were such complementary broadcasters. Skip with the humor and the wit and the zingers, and, also, there was nobody better at calling a big moment than*

Skip Caray. I remember as a kid listening to him do Atlanta Hawks games, too. He was phenomenal as an NBA radio announcer, which a lot of people don't realize. Pete Van Wieren was aptly named the professor. He was the guy in the broadcast who had all these facts. All the information to make sure they stayed on task like a truly consummate professional broadcaster. Then you had Ernie Johnson, Sr., who was like grandpa. He's the guy that took a broadcast and made it comfortable like you were sitting in your rocking chair, sipping cold lemonade on a suffocating, humid, Georgia summer day. The three of those together? I can't single out any one of them without the other two. It was like the sum of their parts was greater than any individual by far. I literally grew up to those guys. I learned a lot of the baseball I know from those guys and have no doubt that, subconsciously, all three of them are represented in every one of the Braves broadcasts I participate in. They can't help but influence me because they were my inspiration. They made it seem like it was so much fun to do baseball that when I was 12 years old and thinking, "What do I want to do someday," the first premise became "I want to get into baseball games free." Then I started trying to figure out what kind of job allows you to get into baseball games for free. Eventually, I focused on the broadcasters because—for one—they didn't change, unlike managers, who change all the time. Those three made it seem like they were having so much fun. It seemed like literally the greatest job you could possibly have. From day one, I was always simply pursuing a play-by-play job in Major League Baseball, and it was because of those three: Ernie Johnson Sr., Pete Van Wieren, and Skip Caray. All three deserve to be recognized in Cooperstown. They were that good.

—Jim Powell, Atlanta Braves radio play-by-play broadcaster

HERB CARNEAL

Broadcasting baseball in the upper Midwest for nearly five decades, Herb Carneal reached even the ears of fellow hall of famer Denny Matthews growing up. In the booth for the Minnesota Twins two World Series championships of 1987 and 1991, Carneal's voice was behind the greatest figures in team history, including Harmon Killebrew, Tony Oliva, Kent Hrbek, Jack Morris, Bert Blyleven, and Kirby Puckett. During his time with the club, Carneal broadcast four Twins no-hitters, by Jack Kralick, Dean Chance, Scott Erickson, and Eric Milton, as well as seven Twins players, including Rod Carew, Gary Ward, and Kirby Puckett, hitting for the cycle. Bringing baseball to fans' ears for over half a century, Carneal will be remembered as a baseball fixture in the Minnesota community for many years to come.

I grew up in Minnesota primarily, so I listened to Herb Carneal, and later, was able to not only work with him but work next to him in the booth and was able to call him a friend. That meant a great deal to me.

—Dick Bremer, Minnesota Twins TV play-by-play broadcaster

BOB PRINCE

Known throughout baseball as "the Gunner," Bob Prince was the voice behind Pirates baseball for nearly three decades. A witness to two World Series–winning Pirate teams, including the Bill Mazeroski–led team of '60, Prince's signature call "You can kiss it goodbye" is still remembered in the Pirates community nearly 30 years after the hall of famer's death, which occurred after a short-lived return to the broadcast booth in 1985.

To this day, being a broadcaster who is now third on the list, as far as tenure, behind Lanny Frattare and Bob Prince, people speak of Prince almost in reverent terms. He was larger than life not only on the air but off the air. From what I understand, he would often go into a restaurant or bar and just pick up the tab and was obviously very gracious with his time and money. Somehow, he endeared himself to the community, and they felt like, when they listened to Bob Prince—he was professionally known as "The Gunner"—they were listening to a friend. I try myself to think in those terms as well when I do a game. From what I hear, people said it was like you were sitting in a bar with Bob Prince and he was describing the game. I got to know him toward the end of his life when Rick Starr and Chris Cross were the general manager and program director at KDKA. Steve Greenberg was the vice president of marketing and I was his assistant. Starr and Cross came to us with a crazy idea one spring in '85. They wanted to know our opinion if they could bring Bob Prince back to do some games on the air. I can recall vividly the excitement that I had and the shock when I heard them make the suggestion. Then we had to go to Joe L. Brown—then the interim general manager—for permission because he was the GM when Prince was fired in the mid-'70s. So they brought him back. Unfortunately, he became ill after just one night. It was a cold rainy night. He did an inning against the Chicago Cubs. The players came back during his play-by-play. It was magical, but then he contracted pneumonia. He had been recovering from throat cancer and he passed away. I know for a fact that the Pirates did not bring him back as a charity case. The team was struggling. It was just a bad time. They thought it would be a good idea to bring him back for excitement.

—Greg Brown, Pittsburgh Pirates
TV/radio play-by-play broadcaster

RUSS HODGES

The voice behind the New York Giants' Bobby Thomson's "shot heard around the world" for the 1951 National League pennant, Russ Hodges is the definition of a broadcaster whose voice truly transcends time itself. Hodges's call is regarded by Oakland A's lead radio broadcaster Ken Korach as "the most famous call in the history of baseball." Having worked alongside long-time New York Yankees broadcaster Mel Allen, Hodges went on to broadcast New York Giants baseball and be the voice behind such memorable players as Bobby Thomson, Willie Mays, and Juan Marichal. Much like Vin Scully, the voice of his crosstown rival Brooklyn Dodgers, Hodges accompanied the team westward, where his voice backed Giants players like Willie McCovey and Orlando Cepeda. Hodges's call of Thomson's "shot" is immortalized in film, books, and sports arenas even beyond the game of baseball.

> *I love music as much as sports. I was taken to Broadway and I fell in love with it. There was a show called* Gentlemen Prefer Blondes. *It was a good show that made Carol Channing a star. They had a nice ballad in there called (singing) "Bye-bye baby. Don't forget that you're my baby." I went to the show, heard that song, and then Russ Hodges, when a home run was hit, would say, "It's bye-bye baby in the left-field stands," so if Brian Roberts ever hits a home run, I'm gonna say, "Bye-bye Brian."*
>
> —John Sterling, New York Yankees radio play-by-play
> broadcaster

LON SIMMONS

Famous for his home run call "Tell it good-bye," hall of fame broadcaster Lon Simmons has made his career in the Bay Area of San Francisco/Oakland. Beginning his broadcasting career with the cross-country-traveled Giants in 1958, Simmons worked alongside another hall of famer, Russ Hodges, for the better part of 12 years. Having also broadcast for champion 49ers teams in the '80s, Simmons skipped over the bay to Oakland, where he called A's games from 1981 to 1995, including the team's three straight World Series appearances from 1988 to 1990 and championship in 1989. Simmons took the Bay Bridge back over to San Francisco to close out his career with the Giants, retiring after the team's 2002 National League pennant-winning season.

In '72 and '73, Lon and Bill Thompson were the Giants broadcast-ers. There was a game Bill had laryngitis. Lon did the whole game by himself. It was just so entertaining. In the final game at Candlestick Park, Bill Thompson came on the broadcast for an inning and did play-by-play. That was really fun. Lon and Bill Thompson—old friends and broadcast partners—one last time on the air. Then Lon, in the post-game ceremony, is getting a huge ovation from the huge crowd when he was introduced. I always felt that went a long way to getting Lon into the hall of fame. The fact that a former broadcaster was so beloved in the area where he worked that he got an ovation that lasted two or three minutes. He kept asking the crowd to stop so he could proceed. I thought that said it all as to how good he was because that's the kind of ovation that only goes to a great former player. That was one of my last memories of not only a great player but a great broadcaster at Candlestick, provided by the fans themselves.

—Jon Miller, San Francisco Giants
radio play-by-play broadcaster

RICHIE ASHBURN

Having played outfield for the Phillies most of his career, Richie Ashburn, after having accumulated 2,574 hits and countless defensive honors over 15 years, turned his talents toward the broadcast booth. Spending 35 years behind the mic for the Philadelphia Phillies, Ashburn, referred to as "His Whiteness," broadcast alongside hall of famer Harry Kalas for 27 years, until the day he died in 1997. Honoring "Whitey" Ashburn's contributions both on the field and in the booth, the Phillies named the main concourse area at Citizens Bank Park "Ashburn Alley" and the booth the "Richie 'Whitey' Ashburn Broadcast Booth."

Richie was a really well-loved broadcaster in Philly. Hall of famer. People loved him. We were on the road in New York at the Grand Central Hyatt, where we all stayed for years. He passed away on the floor above me, and I felt that was a little bit strange. Then we went to Shea Stadium that night. That's the team that Richie Ashburn played for after he played for the Phillies. Richie wore number 1, and he went to the University of Nebraska, and the day that he passed, we go and play the Mets that night and we beat them. The guy who knocked in the winning run was Kevin Jordan, who went to the University of Nebraska. He had maybe a 10–pitch at bat, and we won the game

1–0 against the Mets. I thought how ironic it was that the night Richie passed—the flags were at half mast, and it was all about the mourning of Richie—and we won 1–0, Richie's number, and the guy who knocked in the winning run played at the University of Nebraska. It was eerie. The baseball gods were there. Obviously, so was Richie, and he set that moment up himself. That was his way of saying goodbye to the people. It was pretty spectacular. That's one of the small handful of moments in my 37 years that I've actually felt the baseball gods of the game. What a really inspirational guy he was and a good broadcaster. I'll never forget going to his service. They bused us over as a team. There were 10,000 people at the service. They lined this park for miles. That told me right there how loved he was.

—Rex "Hud" Hudler, Kansas City Royals
TV play-by-play broadcaster

Much as the presence of "Whitey" Ashburn was felt at Shea Stadium on the day he passed, the same is true for many of baseball's voices who have passed on. While their faces and likenesses are immortalized in caricatures, bronze statues, and stadium mailing addresses, the voices are what persist the most for these broadcasters, ensuring their "on the air" light is forever glowing in the hearts and minds of the fans, players, and broadcast partners they've left behind.

· 33 ·

Living Legends

$\mathcal{T}$he beautiful thing about sports broadcasters is their longevity, not only behind the microphone but in life itself. Some of the broadcasters that today's hall of famers listened to early in life are either still behind the microphone or retired from a lengthy career. Iconic figures that today's broadcasters emulated once they had decided "what they wanted to do when they grow up" can look back and know exactly what they did or said to make today's voices "catch the bug" to be a voice over the radio and on TV. Years from now, tomorrow's broadcasters will hold the same level of regard for yesterday's broadcasters, passing a torch as inextinguishable as the game itself.

VIN SCULLY

Broadcasting Dodgers baseball since 1950, Vin Scully's 65 years in the booth are as unprecedented as they are insurmountable. Aside from the postseason appearances that the networks brought him in to broadcast, Scully's Dodgers have been to the fall classic 13 times, winning six titles ('55, '59, '63, '65, '81, '88) with him calling the final out, including Johnny Podres's complete game shutout of the Dodgers' nemesis New York Yankees in game 7 of the 1955 World Series for the club's first championship. The Dodgers have qualified for the postseason 23 times during Scully's career, including 20 division titles. Scully has called 19 no-hitters, including three perfect games (Larsen '56, Koufax '65, Martinez '91), as well as Hank Aaron's record-breaking 715th home run in 1974 and Barry Bonds's record 71st, 72nd, and 73rd home runs in 2001. Scully's signature "It's time for Dodgers baseball" is a staple in the Los Angeles community.

Vinny had a great effect. When I was a kid, Scully did the Dodgers, but they were the enemy. He was more like Maury Wills or Don Drysdale to me. As I got older, I realized how good Vinny was and came to appreciate him. I heard an entire Dodger game once. I felt like I knew everything going on. Anecdotes about the players. The whole thing was just so entertaining and fun to listen to, and that was the point.

—Jon Miller, San Francisco Giants
radio play-by-play broadcaster

Vin Scully was obviously a tremendous influence, although no one can ever be like Vin Scully.

—Brian Anderson, Milwaukee Brewers
TV play-by-play broadcaster

The greatest announcer of all time always will be Vin Scully. There's nobody like him and never will be, and he's a better man than he is a broadcaster, which says so much about Vin. I could see him on national baseball broadcasts, or some NFL game or golf tournament, but it wasn't until I came to the National League West with the Rockies that I actually had the chance to meet him. The interaction, the friendship with him, has been a major highlight of my time in Denver.

—Jack Corrigan, Colorado Rockies
radio play-by-play broadcaster

Vin Scully is the single greatest broadcaster who ever lived, and he's a better person than he is a broadcaster. After the nationwide search, the Colorado Rockies picked me. I was so honored. It was one of four offers I got in three days in November of '92. I was offered the Baltimore job with Jon Miller, the Red Sox job, the Angels job, and the Rockies job all within three days. I selected the Rockies because I felt my heart was right to go to Colorado. That's where I was born and raised and I wanted to be the first. Jack Buck and Vin Scully were the two guys I asked, "What would you do?" To each man's credit, they said, "Take Colorado. Put the initial footprints in the broadcast sand, and everyone will follow you." That was good enough for me.

—Wayne Hagin, former Colorado Rockies
radio play-by-play broadcaster

I'm old enough that my first game that my dad took me to was to Ebbets Field. I was a Brooklyn Dodgers fan because, where I grew up, that's what people did and who people were. They were Brooklyn Dodgers fans. My first memory was when the '55 Dodgers finally beat the Yankees. Johnny Podres shut 'em out 2-0, and, at the age of six, everybody around me—grown-ups and neighbors—were crying. "Grown-ups should not be crying when they're happy," I thought. It made no sense to me. Suddenly, I caught this passion about this team that had won a baseball game, not just any game, the World Series. I was six years old and I didn't quite understand the enormity of it all. So the next year, in 1956, I started listening to the radio and I could hear Brooklyn Dodgers games, and I would hear this young announcer named Vin Scully, who was 26 at the time. I was planted in front of that radio like the RCA Victor dog in front of a big speaker. I would just sit there and listen, and I would hear the crowd. I'd hear the crack of the bat. I'd hear the selling of peanuts, popcorn, cracker jacks, programs, and then I heard this voice. The umbrella of it all was Vin. So I'm listening and I'm just enthralled. He's got me. I might as well have been in a seatbelt. I couldn't move. When I was seven years old, I knew what I wanted to be when I grew up. I wanted to be the announcer for the Dodgers. Unfortunately, when I was eight, they moved away, but the broadcasting bug had bitten me but good. It was Vin who bit me, and after the Dodgers left, I would listen to the Yankees and Mel Allen and later to the Mets with Lindsey Nelson. At night, I'd have the old A.M. radio pick up through the static KDKA in Pittsburgh with Bob Prince, or I'd listen to Harry Caray with Jack Buck on KMOX in St. Louis before Harry went to Chicago. I knew when I was seven what I wanted to be, and then it was just a matter of "Could I get there?" I never had a "plan B." This was all I was going to do, and, if it didn't work out, it's a fair observation and a fair conclusion that you and I would not be talking today. I get to work with Vin every day and we have become friends. A guy that I grew up thinking, "He's the best that's ever done it," and nothing has changed my mind about that. It's one of those "Please don't pinch me. I might wake up." In a word, it's Scully.

—Charley Steiner, Los Angeles Dodgers
TV/radio play-by-play broadcaster

MILO HAMILTON

Broadcasting in five different cities and for seven different clubs over a 59-year career, Milo Hamilton, at 87 years of age, is one of the most influential broadcasters in the history of the game. Though being the voice of only one championship team ('79 Pirates) in his career, Hamilton was in the booth for 11 no-hitters, Barry Bonds's record-tying 70th home run in 2001, Hank Aaron's record 715th home run in 1974, Nolan Ryan's 4,000th strikeout in 1985, and most recently, Craig Biggio's 3,000th hit in 2007. Recipient of the Ford C. Frick award in 1992, Hamilton spent the final 28 seasons of his career in Houston, where in 2005 he called "Killer B" Chris Burke's walk-off, National League Division Series clinching home run against the Atlanta Braves, which to this day is among the most memorable moments in the Houston Astros' 52-year history. Hamilton retired after the '12 season, having called more than 4,000 Major League games.

> *After I got my career started and was working a 1,000-watt radio station in North Carolina, Milo Hamilton was a great influence on me. He was doing the Atlanta Braves games. Later, we became friends. He had a great impact on my life as a broadcaster.*
>
> —Marty Brennaman, Cincinnati Reds
> radio play-by-play broadcaster

> *My inspiration probably was two-fold: Milo Hamilton and Lanny Frattare. They were calling the games when I was growing up. I impersonated them. Milo and Lanny were the guys that were my heroes. When I came here to Pittsburgh in later years and actually met them, I remember how nervous I was—shaking in my shoes—because they were almost like gods to me. They were my inspirations plural.*
>
> —Greg Brown, Pittsburgh Pirates
> TV/radio play-by-play broadcaster

> *I grew up in Texas—three hours from a Major League facility—so I got my baseball through the radio and my formative years—preteen and teenage—from two guys. The voice of the Astros, Milo Hamilton, who's in the hall of fame and then a guy that not many people know of outside of Texas, Mark Holtz. He was really one of the legends. A great play-by-play guy who passed away tragically. Those two guys were really strong influences for me when I was at the age that I was a baseball player in high school and college. So I used to announce the games and do play-by-play in the dugout and things of that nature, and I would always imitate those two.*
>
> —Brian Anderson, Milwaukee Brewers
> TV play-by-play broadcaster

> *When the Braves moved to Atlanta, I got to hear Milo Hamilton broadcast the Braves games on a fairly regular basis. Of course, being born and raised and working on the East Coast, I think the one that probably had the most profound effect on me as a broadcaster was Milo Hamilton. I just enjoyed his delivery, his pace of games and the way he would weave in stories and the color aspect of baseball broadcasting. He had a big impact during the early years of my career when I began broadcasting the minor leagues.*
>
> —Dave Van Horne, Miami Marlins
> radio play-by-play broadcaster

JOE GARAGIOLA

Calling baseball games in various capacities for 58 years, 1991 Ford C. Frick award recipient Joe Garagiola Sr. filled the airwaves with his wit, knowledge, and personality on both local and national levels. Working shoulder to shoulder with Jack Buck and Harry Caray in St. Louis, Garagiola then went on to broadcast the Yankees alongside another future Ford C. Frick recipient, Red Barber, before being hired by NBC to do national games with even more Ford C. Frick winners, Curt Gowdy and Vin Scully. Beyond baseball, Garagiola occasionally hosted *The Tonight Show*, filling in for the legendary Johnny Carson and appeared as a panelist on NBC's *Today Show*. The broadcasts for which Garagiola is perhaps best remembered are the All-Star games and World Series the hall of famer called alongside Scully; however, Garagiola's favorite moment in baseball was when his son, Joe Garagiola Jr.—then general manager of the Arizona Diamondbacks—won the club's first World Series championship in 2001.

> *Joe Garagiola's style was he didn't want to come right out and say, "This guy did this." He wanted to have a sense of entertainment telling you. He had one of the best views of Willie Mays's catch. I'm still kind of fascinated by it. One of my great thrills as a broadcaster was when he was doing "Game of the Week." Vin Scully's kid was getting married, and I was hired to work with Garagiola. I was very excited to have this chance to work with him. He said, "You're the play-by-play man, so you're in charge. It's my job to work around you." I said, "I think you could be in charge and I could work around you." When he got the Ford C. Frick award, I sent a telegram telling him working with him was such a great thrill.*

> —Jon Miller, San Francisco Giants,
> radio play-by-play broadcaster

MARV ALBERT

Sometimes the basketball world spills over into the baseball world, at least in the field of broadcasting. Colorado Rockies radio play-by-play broadcaster Jack Corrigan's biggest influence was Joe Tait, whom Corrigan listened to announcing Cavaliers basketball growing up in Cleveland. Miami Marlins radio play-by-play broadcaster and hall of famer Dave Van Horne was strongly influenced by the University of Kentucky's Cawood Ledford, who broadcast basketball and football for the school for nearly four decades. When it comes to the hardwood, perhaps the most recognized voice over the past 40 years has been former New York Knicks lead play-by-play broadcaster Marv Albert. Winner of more awards than *Ben-Hur*, *Titanic*, and *Gone with the Wind* combined, Albert has left his broadcasting footprint in both football and basketball, on both college and professional levels, as well as hockey, boxing, and tennis. Albert is known to do Major League Baseball pregame and postgame shows on occasion, and it is his pace and energy that make him an inspiration for various baseball broadcasters today.

> *I grew up in New York, so you had a lot of choices. I listened to everything. I listened to Lindsey Nelson and Bob Murphy on the Mets games. Marv Albert was doing everything else in New York. The Knicks. The Rangers. Later on, when I did the NBA for a year, I got to know Marv Albert pretty well. Coincidentally, when my first son was born and I missed the game, it was Kenny Albert who filled in for me on the radio. Another circle of life. His son filled in while my son was coming into the world.*

> —Charlie Slowes, Washington Nationals
> radio play-by-play broadcaster

> *My biggest broadcast inspiration was Marv Albert. It's ironic that baseball is the one sport he never really did full time. Just here and there. I knew I wanted to be a broadcaster from about age 12 or so and Marv was the central figure. I became the president of his fan club when I was 13, and he wrote the foreword to my book. He was the biggest influence on my career. He ended up bringing me into Madison Square Garden to work as his backup with the New York Rangers, so I was lucky enough to be there in '94 when they won the cup. Marv and I actually shared the play-by-play of the final game, when he did two periods and I did one. It was the confluence of any number of different dreams that I had as a kid, so I would certainly say Marv would be my overall broadcast idol, even to this day.*

> —Howie Rose, New York Mets radio play-by-play broadcaster

· 34 ·

Signing Off

$\mathcal{A}$fter 43 interviews with 33 broadcasters discussing 60 stadiums, I might be expected to "have a few stories." Not to disappoint, I have several. When I started off with this project—once I had grasped the notion that I wanted to interview the actual broadcasters themselves—I got to daydreaming quite a bit. "Hey, wouldn't it be great to talk with Jon Miller about AT&T Park?" and "How awesome would it be to discuss both 'new' and 'old' Yankee Stadiums with John Sterling?" and finally, "What if I got to speak with Vin Scully about *anything*?" After I got a few agents and friends "in the business" interested in this concept for the book, I just could never figure out how to get that first foot in the door. Being from Las Vegas, I'm a four-hour drive from the nearest team. Scrambling for ideas one day, I was reading the *Review Journal*, Vegas's main newspaper. Opening up a section, I saw a picture of the Oakland A's Ken Korach accompanying an article for his recently released book, *Holy Toledo: Lessons from Bill King, Renaissance Man of the Mic*. Reading the article, I discovered that he, too, is a resident of the Las Vegas valley. I also learned that Ken used to announce for UNLV, just like a friend of the family. One phone call, two passed-along e-mails, and an appointment later, I was sitting across from him in a Henderson, Nevada, public library. After we completed our interview, Ken asked me, "Are you going to do this with all 30 teams?" I remember how daunting the question seemed at the time, but also how resolute I was, responding "Yes," albeit with a cracking voice. Though Ken didn't have any "digits" to pass along for me to do the same process with other broadcasters, he did offer up what turned out to be a great piece of advice: Cactus League; Phoenix; springtime.

What an experience spring training is. If you love baseball, my advice would be to travel to the Sonoran Desert or central Florida during February

301

and March. Half of baseball's teams play in facilities that make most Minor League ballparks green with envy, and all within a radius of about 50 miles. My first day, I had what is still my favorite interview, Eric Nadel of the Texas Rangers. He and I spoke in the actual seats at the Rangers' spring training stadium in Surprise, Arizona. We sat above a section but were close enough that the couple below us could practically hear every word. I noticed them "half turning" their heads every so often and kept thinking, "I sure hope we're not bothering these two." After the interview was over and Nadel walked away, the couple approached me and said, "We enjoyed your interview. We're Rangers fans. We recognized Mr. Nadel's voice immediately. When does your book come out?" To this day, I regret not having taken down the couple's contact info, or at least giving them mine. I can only hope they pick up a copy someday so my conscience can finally be cleared.

Aside from being a great story that I have told at least a couple dozen times preparing this book, Nadel's interview opened up a mammoth-sized door for me. While I was speaking with Nadel, he mentioned Ebbets Field as a kid and gave me a perspective I wasn't even planning on when preparing for these interviews. These broadcasters, too, were fans of the game. Their insight extends beyond the booth, all the way back to their first game as a child. Broadcasters like Vin Scully, Denny Matthews, Joe Castiglione, and Dave Van Horne shared experiences of attending stadiums like the Polo Grounds, Shibe Park, and Sportsman's Park. Needless to say, I was very fortunate to have interviewed Nadel so early in the process. The hall of fame broadcaster was also my first taste of "broadcaster networking," as a special "plug" from Nadel to fellow hall of famer Jon Miller resulted in my meeting with Miller by the end of the week. I remember typing Miller's name into my interview software on my computer. I paused for a split second just to take in this surreal moment. Here I was speaking with someone I had watched almost every Sunday night during the baseball season for 20 years. It was at this point that my mind-set went from "if" the book gets a publishing deal to "when."

Having already checked off one of my "what ifs" by speaking with Jon Miller, the interviews kept coming, mostly via phone. Feeling lucky, I decided to go after the Yankees. I already knew I was going to make my annual drive to Angel Stadium of Anaheim to watch my beloved Yankees face the Los Angeles Angels, so I decided to "reach for the stars" on this particular trip. Unbelievably, after a couple of e-mails I was speaking with *the* John Sterling and scheduling an interview. He actually told me I'd be doing *him* a favor by meeting with him since he'd be getting to the stadium so early. Here I was in the first stadium I had ever set foot in, almost 30 years before, looking over to my right to a digital clock set to eastern standard time and sitting straight across from the voice of my favorite team. The World Series ring Sterling was wearing was bigger than the candy ring pops I buy for my four-year-old daughter. Sterling shared his love for music, and channeling the late Russ Hodges, sang "Bye-bye baby," and said, "If Brian Roberts hits a home run, I'll say, 'Bye-bye Brian'." That night Brian Roberts hit the go-ahead home run in the ninth inning, which proved to be the game winner. After my interview with Mr. Sterling—holding my press credential—I felt like Charlie with the golden ticket. Walking into the press dining room, I found Michael Kay, another Yankees broadcaster I had imagined myself interviewing in the daydream phase of this project. Resolute, I gave Kay the spiel and we exchanged contacts. From that point on, I felt that everything was gravy as far as the book was concerned. I soon got an agent, and shortly afterward, I got the book deal.

Things were going very well; Jon Miller himself volunteered to help with the Camden Yards chapter of the book. This was an added bonus because Miller was the team's lead voice the night Cal Ripken Jr. passed Lou Gehrig's record of consecutive games played. The same thing happened when I couldn't lock down an interview with an Angels broadcaster. There I was, sitting with the PR rep for the Royals (Rex Hudler's current team), and I asked if "Hud" was available for an interview. A phone call and several text messages later, the TV voice of the Angels during their championship season was discussing the 2002 World Series game 6 and the Rally Monkey with me. "Hud" and Miller provided as good memories as I could have ever hoped for from the Angels and Orioles current broadcasters. That's just the way this project went. Everything just found a way to fall into place.

Nearly two months after I thought I was done with the interview process, I get a phone call from none other than Vin Scully himself. This was, as Charley Steiner would say, the "pinch me" moment of the book. Not only was I able to conduct a 30-minute interview with Scully, I was able to send his regards to New York Mets lead radio voice Howie Rose when I called him immediately afterward. As Mel Allen would say, "How about that?" My third "what if" was checked off before I even had a chance to prepare myself for it. I found it incredible that Scully could speak about Hilda Chester, whom he probably hadn't heard from in decades, as if he'd just seen her the day before. The moments of the past year are far more than I could count, much less describe in enough detail, when signing off on this book. It was great to tour the country, virtually, from the Phoenix Valley and my own home. The regions covered by these broadcasters: Rick Rizzs in the Pacific Northwest, Dave Van Horne in south Florida, Joe Castiglione in New England, Dick Bremer in the upper Midwest, Mike Wilner "north of the border." I was able to gather an impression of these broadcasters' roots just from my 30-minute encounters with them: Marty Brennaman's Virginia-bred hospitality, Greg Brown's "inner child" coming out in his voice and recollections of Three

Rivers Stadium, Ted Leitner's forthcoming account of San Diego politics mixed with baseball, Charlie Slowes's New York lingo following him to the nation's capital, Charley Steiner's wit and brevity suiting him for a career on the other side of the hills in Hollywood if he ever leaves his craft of broadcasting Dodgers baseball. Finally, being a Yankees fan and listening to the "other dugout's" side of many of my least favorite memories: Greg Schulte discussing game 7 of the 2001 World Series, Jim Rosenhaus describing "the Bug Game" in Cleveland during the 2007 playoffs, Dan Dickerson's retelling of Kenny Rogers's unforeseen mastery of the Yankees in the 2006 Division Series, and most of all Joe Castiglione's revisiting of game 4 of the 2004 American League Championship Series. Seeing how much happiness these moments brought these broadcasters and their teams' fans was almost like receiving some sort of closure, a "one's loss is another's gain" type of thing. I feel this closing chapter of the book would need another several pages to do justice to the abundance of hospitality I have received from these 33 broadcasters. I would have never imagined people I had listened to and watched growing up could be so giving of their time and words. Meeting them, for me, was better than meeting the players, which I did in a few cases. Looking back on this experience on which I have spent, without regret, one year of my life, I may have to relisten to the audio from time to time to assure myself it all really *did* happen. To quote Chicago White Sox broadcaster Ken "Hawk" Harrelson—whom I listened to on WGN growing up and got a chance to meet in person—the best way for me to close the book would be to say, "It's been a great ride."

Bibliography

AT&T PARK

www.baseball-almanac.com/managers/manager_wins_top_100.html
www.baseball-reference.com/managers/mcgrajo.01.shtml
www.sportsecyclopedia.com/nl/nygiantsb/nygiants.html
www.baseball-reference.com/players/o/ottmel.shtml
www.ballparksofbaseball.com/nl/AT&TPark.htm
www.sportsecyclopedia.com/nl/sfgiants/sfgiants.html
www.baseball-reference.com/teams/SFG

ANGEL STADIUM OF ANAHEIM

www.baseballpilgrimages.com
www.losangeles.angels.mlb.com/ana/history/timeline.jsp
www.baseball-almanac.com/teams/anah.shtml
www.baseball-almanac.com/teams/anahatte.shtml
www.losangeles.angels.mlb.com/ana/ballpark/directions/index.jsp
www.blogs.ocweekly.com/navelgazing/2010/angels_rally_monkey_creator_
    rip.htm
www.angelswmblog.blogspot.com/2008/02/47-june-6-2000-rally-monkey-
    debuts.html
www.baseball-reference.com/postseason/2002
www.miscbaseball.wordpress.com/2011/08/28/16-1994.northridge-earth-
    quake-little-league-and-the-big-a-stadium.htm

305

BUSCH STADIUM

www.stlouis-mo.gov/visit&play/stlouis-history.com
www.stlouis.cardinals.mlb.com/stl/history/timeline.jsp
www.baseball-reference.com/bullpen/St._Louis_Browns
www.baseball-almanac.com/teams/cards.shtml
www.mlb.mlb.com/mlb/history/postseason/mlb_ws.jsp?feature=club_
    champs
www.gamedayr.com/sports/mlb/mlb-teams-most-world-series-appearances
www.stlouis.cardinals.mlb.com/stl/history/postseason_results.jsp
www.ballparksofbaseball.com/2000-09attendance.htm
www.ballparksofbaseball.com/2010presentattendance.htm
www.stlouis.cardinals.mlb.com/stl/ballpark/facts/index.jsp
www.stlouis.cardinals.mlb.com/stl/ballpark/ballpark_village.jsp
www.ballparksofbaseball.com/past/BuschStadium.htm
www.ballparksofbaseball.com/nl/BuschStadium.htm
www.weather.com/weather/wxclimatology/monthly/graph/USM00787
www.weatherspark.com/averages/31697/7/st-louis-missouri-united-states
www.mlb.mlb.com/stats/sortable
www.espn.go.com/mlb/stats/parkfactor/_/year/2011
www.scores.espn.go.com/mlb/playbyplay?gameid=311027124
www.stlouis.cardinals.mlb.com/stl/history/postseason_results.jsp

CHASE FIELD

www.weather.com/weather/wxclimatology/monthly/graph/USAZ0166
www.ballparksofbaseball.com/nl/chasefield.htm
www.springtrainingonline.com/features/history-3.htm
www.businessweek.com/stories/1999-03-29/jerry-colangelo-the-man-
    whos-bringing-baseball-to-the-desert
www.baseball-reference.com/players/j/johnsra05.shtml?redir
www.baseball-reference.com/players/w/webbr01.shtml?redir
www.baseball-reference.com/players/s/schilcu01.shtml?redir
www.baseball-reference.com/postseason/2001_WS.shtml

CITI FIELD

www.baseball-almanac.com/mgrtmnym.shtml
www.baseball-reference.com/managers/stengca01.shtml

www.history.com/this-day-in-history/baseball-owners-allow-dodgers-and-giants-to-move
www.ballparksofbaseball.com/past/sheastadium.htm
www.ballparksofbaseball.com/nl/CitiField.htm
www.espn.go.com/mlb/stats/team/_/stat/pitching/year/2010/seasontype/2
www.espn.go.com/mlb/team/stats/batting/_/name/nym/year/2011/new-york-mets
www.infoplease.com/ipsa/A0112350.html

CITIZENS BANK PARK

www.espn.go.com/nfl/story_/id/7377416/philadelphia-eagles-fans-once-booed-santa-santa-joviel-63-year-old-frank-olivo-loves-philly-teams
www.mainlinetaxi.com/sportsinphiladelphia.asp
www.philadelphia.phillies.mlb.com/phi/story/ballparks.jsp
www.home.comcast.net/ghostsofthegridiron/stadiums.htm
www.pro-football-reference.com/teams/phi/playoffs.htm
www.baseball-reference.com/postseason/1983_WS.shtml
www.philadelphia.phillies.mlb.com/phi/ballpark/information/index.jsp?content=facts_figures
www.mentalfloss.com/article/30377/birth-phillie-phanatic
www.baseball-reference.com/players/m/myerrsbr01.shtml
www.baseball-reference.com/players/l/lidgebr01.shtml

COMERICA PARK

www.baseball-reference.com/players/c/cicoted01.shtml?redir
www.baseball-reference.com/players/c/cobbty01.shtml
www.espn.go.com/sportscentury/features/00014142.html
www.baseball-reference.com/players/g/greenha01.shtml
www.baseball-reference.com/players/k/kalinal01.shtml?redir
www.blog.detroitathletic.com/2012/09/09/looking-back-at-the-careers-of-trammell-and-whitaker
www.baseball-almanac.com/players/player.php?p=trammal01
www.ballparksofbaseball.com/al.comericapark.htm
www.ballparksofbaseball.com/past/tigerstadium.htm
www.baseball-reference.com/players/v/verlaju01.shtml?redir
www.baseball-reference.com/players/scherma01.shtml
www.baseball-reference.com/players/r/rogerke01.shtml?redir

www.baseball-reference.com/players/o/ordonma01.shtml?redir
www.baseball-reference.com/boxes/DET/DET200610140.shtml
www.baseball-reference.com/awards/triple_crowns.shtml
www.baseball-reference.com/players/c/cabremi01.shtml?redir
www.sports.espn.go.com/mlb/news/story?id=3141703

COORS FIELD

www.atlanta.braves.mlb.com/atl/ballpark/history.jsp
www.baseball-reference.com/players/event_hr.cgi?t=b&id=aaronha01
www.ballparksofbaseball.com/past/milehighstadium.htm
www.ballparksofbaseball.com/nl/CoorsField.htm
www.mlbreports.com/2012/07/14/humidor
www.espn.go.com/mlb/stats/team_/batting/year/2002/sort/homerun/or-
    der/true
www.baseball-reference.com/players/j/jimenub01.shtml?redir
www.baseball-reference.com/players/r/rosajo01.shtml?redir
www.baseball-almanac.com/teamstats/schedule.php?y=2007&t-Col
www.baseball-reference.com/boxes/col/col200710010.shtml
www.scores.espn.go.com/mlb/recap?gameid=271001127

DODGER STADIUM

www.losangeles.dodgers.mlb.com/la/histiry/timeline.jsp
www.losangeles.dodgers.mlb.com/la/history/postseason_results.jsp
www.baseball-almanac.com/ws/yr1955ws.shtml
www.maxmasonartist.com/content/dreamland-dodger-stadium-and-chavez-
    ravine
www.data.bls.gov/cgi-bin/apicalc.pl?cost1
www.walteromalley.com/stad_hist_index.php
www.baseball-reference.com/players/d/drysddo01.shtml
www.losangeles.dodgers.mlb.com/la/history/players.jsp
www.andrewclem.com/baseball/dodgerstadium.html
www.miscbaseball.wordpress.com/2009/08/13/the-scoreless-streaks-of-her-
    shiser-and-drysdale
www.baseball-reference.com/players/h/hershor01.shtml?redir
www.baseball-reference.com/boxes/LAN/LAN2006019180.shtml

FENWAY PARK

www.baseball-reference.com/teams/BOS

www.sportsdelve.wordpress.com/2011/09/24/mlb-from-worst-to-first-and-first-to-worst

www.msn.foxsports.com/mlb/story/postseason-schedule-results-playoffs-2013-red-sox-dodgers-tigers-braves-092713

www.espn.go.com/mlb/story/_/id/8302304/boston-red-sox-send-adrian-gonzalez-carl-crawford-los-angeles-dodgers-blockbuster-trade

www.cbsnews.com/news/red-sox-epic-collapse-one-for-the-record-books

www.usatoday.com/story/sports/mlb/redsox/2013/04/10/fenway-park-red-sox-record-sellout-streak-ends/2072633

www.baseball-reference.com/boxes/BOS/BOS200410170.shtml

www.baseball-reference.com/postseason/2004_ALCS.shtml

www.espn.go.com/blog/new-york/mets/post/_/id/36038/this-date-in-86-miracle-at-shea

www.baberuthcentral.com/babesimpact/legends/the-curse-of-the-bambino

www.baseball-reference.com/players/r/ruthba01.shtml

www.history.com/this-day-in-history/New-York-Yankees-announce-purchase-of-babe-ruth

www.redsoxdiehard.com/fenway/facts.html

www.boston.com/sports/baseball/redsox/2012/08/13/explaining-pesky-pole

www.fenwayfanatics.com/fenway-park/history

www.baseball-reference.com/boxes/BOS/BOS197810020.shtml

www.baseball-reference.com/boxes/BOS/BOS197510210.shtml

www.bleacherreport.com/articles/1154661-red-sox-vs-yankees-fenway-most-amazing-rivalry-the-bucky-dent-home-run

www.boston.redsox.mlb.com/bos/ballpark/information/index.jsp.content=history

www.eyewitnesstohistory.com/titanic.htm

www.nesn.com/2011/08/fenway-park-adds-green-monster-seats-red-sox-revamped-offense-leads-boston-to-alcs-in-2003

www.boston.redsox.mlb.com/bos/ballpark/information/index.jsp?content=facts

www.boston.redsox.mlb.com/bos/ballpark/information/index.jsp?content=history

GLOBE LIFE PARK IN ARLINGTON

www.thisgreatgame.com/1981-baseball-history.html
www.miscbaseball.wordpress.com/2009/06/03/kenny-rogers-perfect-game
www.baseball-almanac.com/boxscore/07281994.shtml
www.texas.rangers.mlb.com/tex/ballpark/special_events/halloffame.jsp
www.fangraphs.com/leaders.aspx?ps=all&stats
www.texas.rangers.mlb.com/tex/ballpark/information/index.jsp?content
　　=facts_figures
www.espn.go.com/blog/dallas/texas-rangers/post/_/id/4893409
www.baseball-almanac.com/teams/rang.shtml
www.baseball-reference.com/leagues/MLB/1994-standings.shtml
www.espn.go.com/mlb/story/_/page/caple-120829/montreal-expos-gone-
　　not-forgotten-amid-push-bring-mlb-back
www.baseball-almanac.com/yearly/yr1995a.shtml

GREAT AMERICAN BALL PARK

www.sportsecyclopedia.com/nl/cincyreds/reds.html
www.state.nj.us/about/baseball.html
www.cincinnati.reds.mlb.com/cin/hof/hof/index.jsp?/oc=hof_faq
www.geography.howstuffworks.com/united-states/geography-of-cincinnati.
　　htm
www.cincinnati.reds.mlb.com/cin/ballpark/information/index
www.cincinnati.reds.mlb.com/stats/sortable
www.scores.espn.go.com/mlb/recap?gameid=320928123
www.sports.yahoo.com/news/baileys-2nd-no-hitter-sends-015845587-mlb.
　　html
www.baseball-almanac.com/WS/WSmenu.shtml
www.baseball-almanac.com/WS/Yr1940ws.shtml
www.mlb.mlb.com/mlb/history/mlb_history_people.jsp?story=com_bio_7
www.bigstory.ap.org/article/hamiltons-run-chapmans-fastball-give-reds-
　　speed

KAUFFMAN STADIUM

www.baseball-reference.com/teams/OAK
www.ballparksofbaseball.com/al/kauffmanstadium.htm

www.ballparksofbaseball.com/past/KCMunicipal.htm
www.mlb.mlb.com/KC/ballpark/information/index.jsp?content=moreinfo
www.kansascity.royals.mlb.com/kc/ballpark/history.jsp
www.kansascity.royals.mlb.com/news/article.jsp
www.baseball-reference.com/players/s/santaer01.shtml
www.scores.espn.go.com/mlb/boxscore?gameid=330922107
www.baseball-reference.com/players/b/brettge01.shtml?redir
www.sports.espn.go.com/espn/espn2-5/story?page=moments/67
www.espn.go.com/mlb/player/_/id/6280/ervin-santana

MARLINS PARK

www.climatecentral.org/news/top-5-most-vulnerable-us-cities-to-hurri-
    canes/
www.miami.marlins.mlb.com/mia/history/timeline.jsp
www.realclearsports.com/lists/team_drop_offs/florida_marlins_1998.html
www.statista.com/statistics/203469/mlb-average-ticket-price-for-florida-
    marlins-games
www.baseball-almanac.com/teams/marlins3.shtml
www.ballparksofbaseball.com/nl/MarlinsPark.htm
www.baseball-reference.com/players/s/stantmi03.shtml
www.baseball-reference.com/players/f/fernajo02.shtml?redir
www.mets.nonohitters.com/pulled-during-a-no-hitter
www.scores.espn.go.com/mlb/boxscore?gameid=330929128
www.baseballpilgrimages.com/ballparks/no-hitters.html
www.bleacherreport.com/articles/425837-the-10-most-amazing-and-bi-
    zarre-no-hitters-of-all-time
www.baseball-reference.com/teams/MIA/2014.shtml

MILLER PARK

www.statesymbolusa.org/wisconsin/nicknamewisconsin.html
www.milwaukee.brewers.mlb.com/mil/fan_forum/racing_sausages.jsp
www.baseball-reference.com/players/y/yountro01.shtml
www.milwaukee.brewers.mlb.com/mil/history/timeline.jsp
www.milwaukee.brewers.mlb.com/mil/ticketing/all_inclusive_areas.jsp#ati
www.espn.go.com/mlb/stats/team/_/stat/batting/year/2007/sort/home
    runs/order/true

www.milwaukee.brewers.mlb.com/mil/history/postseason_results.jsp
www.baseball-reference.com/players/s/sabatc.01.shtml
www.baseball-reference.com/players/b/braunry02.shtml
www.baseball-almanac.com/teamstats/schedule.php?y=2008&T=ML4
www.realclearsports.com/lists/Top_10_blown_calls_baseball/don_den-
    kinger_the_call_1985_world_series_game_6.html
www.sbnation.com/2011/10/7/247555/brewers-vs-diamondbacks-game-
    5-brewers-diamondbacks

MINUTE MAID PARK

www.turnkeysolutions.com/corporateart/headline/the-ghosts-of-railroads-
    past
www.travelandleisure.com/travel-guide/houston/activities/union-station-at-
    minute-maid-park
www.houston.astros.mlb.com/hou/ballpark/information/index.jsp?content
    =facts_figures
www.baseball-fever.com/archive/index
www.hittrackeronline.com/historic.php?id=2005_6
www.scores.espn.go.com/mlb/boxscore?gameid-230701118
www.usatoday30.usatoday.com/sports/baseball/2008-08-20-bestseats-min-
    utemaid
www.sportingcharts.com/mlb/stats/team-home-runs-per-game/194
www.baseball-reference.com/players/b/biggicr01.shtml
www.baseball-reference.com/leaders/HBP_career.shtml
www.houston.astros.mlb.com/mlb/events/biggio3000

NATIONALS PARK

www.baseball-reference.com/bullpen/washington_senators
www.ballparksofbaseball.com/past/RFKStadium.htm
www.ballparksofbaseball.com/nl/NationalsPark.htm
www.baseball-reference.com/players/j/johnswa01.shtml?redir
www.ballparksofbaseball.com/past/GriffithStadium.htm
www.baseball-reference.com/players/s/strasst01.shtml
www.baseball-reference.com/players/h/harpebr03.shtml?redir
www.baseball-reference.com/players/z/zimmejo02.shtml
www.baseball-reference.com/postseason/2012_NLDS1.shtml

O.CO COLISEUM

www.baseballpilgrimages.com/american/oakland.html
www.baseball-reference.com/bullpen/Oakland_Coliseum
www.oakland.athletics.mlb.com/oak/history/ballparks.jsp
www.espn.go.com/classic/biography/s/Finley_Charles.html
www.baseball-statistics.com/Ballparks/Oak/
www.distance-cities.com/distance-kansas-city-mo-to-oakland-ca
www.ballparksofbaseball.com/al/ococoliseum.htm
www.pro-football-reference.com/bullpen/Oakland_Coliseum
www.espn.go.com/mlb/stats/team/_/stat/pitching/year/2013/split/33/
    league/al/sort/opponentavg/order/false
www.baseball-reference.com/players/c/chaveer01.shtml?redir
www.pro-football-reference.com/teams/rai/playoffs.htm
www.cbssports.com/mlb/eye-on-baseball/24606514/as-sign-lease-with-oco-
    coliseum-will-stay-put-for-10-years
www.espn.go.com/mlb/story/_/id/9393784/sewage-problem-puts-oakland-
    seattle-mariners-same-locker-room
www.baseball-reference.com/boxes/OAK/OAK201005090.shtml

ORIOLE PARK AT CAMDEN YARDS

www.baltimore.orioles.mlb.com/bal/history/timeline.jsp
www.ballparksofbaseball.com/past/MemorialStadium.htm
www.baltimore.orioles.mlb.com/bal/history/postseason_results.jsp
www.baseball-reference.com/teams/BAL2012.shtml
www.espn.go.com/mlb/stats/team/_/stat/batting/seasontype/2/sort/
    homeruns/order/true
www.espn.go.com/mlb/team/stats/pitching/_/name/bal/seasontype/2/bal-
    timore-orioles

PNC PARK

www.popularpittsburgh.com/pittsburgh-info/pittsburgh-history/threerivers.
    aspx
www.pittsburgh.pirates.mlb.com/pit/history/timeline5.jsp
www.ballparksofbaseball.com/past/ThreeRiversStadium.htm
www.biography.com/people/roberto-clemente-9250805

www.baseball-reference.com/players/c/clemero01.shtml
www.baseball-reference.com/players/player.phh?p=stennre01
www.scores.espn.go.com/mlb/playbyplay?gameid=331001123

PETCO PARK

www.seaworldentertainment.com/en/who-we-are/history
www.baseball-reference.com/teams/SDP
www.scores.espn.go.com/mlb/boxscore?gameid=240408125
www.boston.com/sports/baseball/redsox/gallery/larry_lucchino_through_
    the_years?pg=5
www.mlb.mlb.com/news/article.jsp?ymd=20121022&content_id=39980186
    &c_id=mlb
www.hittrackeronline.com/stadiums.php
www.baseball-reference.com/players/m/maybica01.shtml
www.baseball-reference.com/players/p/peavyja01.shtml?redir
www.baseballpilgrimages.com/national/sandiego.html

PROGRESSIVE FIELD

www.scores.espn.go.com/mlb/recap?gameid=270821103
www.cleveland.indians.mlb.com/cle/history/postseason_results.jsp
www.cleveland.about.com/od/cleveland/history/f/what-is-clevelands-nick-
    name.htm
www.clevelandindians.mlb.com/news/article
www.baseball-reference.com/teams/CLE/staff.shtml
www.espn.go.com/mlb/stats/team/_/stat/pitching/year/2013/league/al/
    sort/homeruns/type/expanded/order/true
www.waitingfornextyear.com/2013/uni-talk-eblock-c-or-script-i-red-or-
    blue-and-life-after-wahoo
www.baseball-reference.com/players/g/giambja01.shtml
www.fivethirtyeight.blogs.nytimes.com/2011/09/27/september-collapse-of-
    red-sox-could-be-worst-ever/?_php=true&_type=blogs&_r=0
www.sportingnews.com/mlb/story/2012-03-22/terry-francona-red-sox-
    yankees-world-series-announcer
www.baseball-almanac.com/teamstats/schedulephp?y=2013&t=CLE
www.baseball-reference.com/teams/CLE/2013.shtml
www.cleveland.com/tribe/index.ssf/2013/08/Cleveland_indians_drummer_
    john_adams

ROGERS CENTRE

www.ballparksofbaseball.com/past/ExhibitionStadium.htm
www.ballparksofbaseball.com/al/RogersCentre.htm
www.toronto.bluejays.mlb.com/tor/history/postseason_results.jsp
www.rogerscentre.com/fun/community_funfacts.jsp
www.aplussportsandmore-fanshop-baseballfield.com/Retractable-roof-ball-parks.html
www.answers.com/Q/What_material_is_used_on_baseball_warning_tracks
www.baseball-reference.com/players/d/davisra01.shtml
www.scores.espn.go.com/mlb/recap?gameid=320812114
www.baseball-almanac.com/teamstats/roster.php?y=1993&t=TOR
www.baseball-reference.com/players/h/hallaro01shtml?redir
www.baseball-reference.com/players/b/burnea.01.shtml?redir
www.scores.espn.go.com/mlb/recap?gameid=290512114
www.espn.go.com/mlb/team/roster/_/name/tor/toronto-blue-jays

SAFECO FIELD

www.baseball-reference.com/players/h/hernafe02.shtml?redir
www.baseball-reference.com/teams/SEA/2012.shtml
www.baseball-reference.com/teams/SEA/2001-schedule-scores.shtml
www.scores.espn.go.com/mlb/playbyplay?gameid-320821112
www.hittrackeronline.com/detail.php?id=2014_530_type=ballpark
www.seattletimes.com/html/mariners/2019323286_mariners03.html
www.newballpark.org/2013/01/02/bringing-in-the-fences
www.pikeplacefish.com
www.phrases.org.uk/bulletin_board/61/messages/663.html
www.ballparksofbaseball.com/al/SafecoField/htm
www.seattlemariners.mlb.com/sea/ballpark/information/index.jsp?

TARGET FIELD

www.thrillist.com/entertainment/minneapolis/minneapolis-vs-st-paul-which-city-reigns-supreme
www.espn.go.com/travel/stadium/_/s/mlb/id/9/target-field
www.baseball-reference.com/boxes/MIN/MIN201004120.shtml

www.online.wsj.com/news/articles/SB100014240527023040170457516576
    0977036190
www.minnesota.twins.mlb.com/min/ballpark/comparisons.jsp
www.baseball-reference.com/players/m/mauerjo01.shtml
www.baseball-almanac.com/hitting/hihrl.shtml
www.baseball-reference.com/players/t/thomeji01.shtml?redir
www.baseball-reference.com/players/event_hr.cgi?id=thomeji01
www.scores.espn.go.com/mlb/recap?gameid=30081709
www.espn.go.com/mlb/player/stats/_/id/288638/phil-hughes

TROPICANA FIELD

www.tampabay.rays.mlb.com/tb/history/tb_history_tampabay.jsp
www.mercurynews.com/ci_21840958/mark-purdy-giants-almost-left-san-
    francisco-tampa
www.ballparksofbaseball.com/al/TropField.htm
www.baseball-reference.com/boxes/TBA/TBA199803310.shtml
www.sports.espn.go.com/mlb/news/story?id=3101213
www.baseball-almanac.com/teams/rays3.shtml
www.tampabay.rays.mlb.com/tb/history/postseason_results.jsp
www.tampabay.rays.mlb.com/tb/history/year_by_year_results.jsp

TURNER FIELD

www.baseball-almanac.com/teams/brav.shtml
www.ballparksofbaseball.com/past/AtlantaStadium.htm
www.baseball-reference.com/bullpen/john_schuerholz
www.baseball-reference.com/players/event_hr.cgi?id=aaronha01
www.baseball-reference.com/players/a/aaronha01.shtml
www.baseball-reference.com/players/m/murphda05.shtml
www.mlb.mlb.com/stats/sortable
www.ballparksofbaseball.com/nl/turner%20field.htm
www.databaseolympics.com/players/playerpose.htm?ilkid=JohnsMIC01
www.baseball-reference.com/players/j/jonesan01.shtml?redir
www.baseballhall.org/hof/cox-bobby
www.atlantabraves.mlb.com/team/coach_staff_bio.jsp?coachorstaffid=
    112764&c_id=atl

www.atlanta.braves.mlb.com/atl/history/postseason_results.jsp
www.mlb.mlb.com/atl/history/year_by_year_results.jsp
www.atlanta.braves.mlb.com/team/roster_40man.jsp?c_id-atl

U.S. CELLULAR FIELD

www.baseball-almanac.com/WS/yr1919ws.shtml
www.baseball-almanac.com/players/player.php?p=jacksjo01
www.law2.umkc.edu/faculty/projects/ftrials/blacksox/rothsteinbio.html
www.baseball-reference.com/boxes/CHA/CHA199104180.shtml
www.chicago.whitesox.mlb.com/cws/history/postseason_results.jsp
www.chicago.whitesox.mlb.com/cws/history/uniforms.jsp
www.ballparksofbaseball.com/al/USCellularField.htm
www.articles.chicagotribune.com/2002-04-12/sports/0204120100_1_sox_
    fans_ivy_renovation
www.ballparks.com/baseball/american/comis2.htm
www.usatoday.com/story/sports/mlb/whitesox/2013/05/17/US-cellular-
    field-made-right-call-on-rehab/2210221
www.baseball-reference.com/players/event_hr.cgi?id=thomafr04&t=b
www.espn.go.com/mlb/stats/team/_/stat/batting/year/2002/sort/home
    runs/order/true
www.chicago.whitesox.mlb.com/cws/team/exe_bios/bossard_roger.html
www.chicagoist.com/2005/04/04/2005_baseball_preview.php
www.chicago.whitesox.mlb.com/cws/history/championship05.jsp
www.baseball-reference.com/players/b/buehrma01.shtml?redir
www.scores.espn.go.com/mlb/boxscore?gameid=290723104

WRIGLEY FIELD

www.encyclopedia.chicagohistory.org/pages/114.html
www.nytimes.com/2008/09/23/sports/baseball/23merkle.html?pagewanted
www.cubbiesbaseball.com/chicago-cubs-curses
www.chicago.cubs.mlb.com/chc/history/owners.jsp
www.baseball-reference.com/managers/pinielo01.shtml
www.scores.espn.go.com/mlb/boxscore?gameid=270629166
www.chicago.cubs.mlb.com/chc.history/year_by_year_results.jsp

YANKEE STADIUM

www.mlb.mlb.com/mlb/history/postseason/mlb_ws.jsp?feature=club=
    champs
www.ballparksofbaseball.com/al/YankeeStadium.htm
www.newyork.yankees.mlb.com/nyy/history/timeline1.jsp
www.baseball-reference.com/players/g/gehrilo01.shtml?redir
www.baseball-reference.com/players/r/ruthba01.shtml?redir
www.baseball-reference.com/players/d/dimagjo01.shtml
www.baseball-reference.com/players/m/mantlmi01.shtml
www.nytimes.com/2008/04/14/sports/baseball/14jersey.html?_r=0
www.ballparks.com/baseball/american/nyybpk.htm
www.newyork.yankees.mlb.com/nyy/ballpark/new_stadium_comparison.jsp
www.ballparksofbaseball.com/past/yankeestadium.htm
www.baseball-reference.com/players/s/sabatc.01.shtml?redir
www.baseball-reference.com/players/j/johnsra05.shtml?redir
www.baseball-almanac.com/teams/yank.shtml
www.baseball-reference.com/managers/torrejo01.shtml
www.espn.go.com/new-york/mlb/story/_/id/6993396/new-york-yankees-
    mariano-rivera-sets-mlb-mark-602nd-save
www.baseball-reference.com/players/j/jeterde01.shtml?redir
www.scores.espn.go.com/mlb/boxscore?gameid=340925110

THIS WAS A PARKING LOT, NOW IT'S TURNED INTO AN OUTFIELD

www.mlb.mlb.com/mlb/history/postseason/mlb_ws.jsp?feature=club_
    champs
www.baseball-almanac.com/mgrtmny.shtml
www.baseball-almanac.com/stadium/yankee_stadium.shtml
www.baseball-reference.com/teams/NYY/
www.baseball-reference.com/players/c/colemje01.shtml?redir
www.scores.espn.go.com/mlb/playbyplay?gameid=240701110
www.baseball-reference.com/postseason/2003_ALCS.shtml
www.ballparksofbaseball.com/past/comiskeypark.htm
www.baseball-reference.com/teams/CHW/leaders_pitch.shtml
www.maccafen.net/Gallery/SheaStadium/Shea.htm
www.ballparksofbaseball.com/past/SheaStadium.htm
www.stlouis.cardinals.mlb.com/stl/history/postseason_results.jsp

www.ballparksofbaseball.com/past/BuschStadium.htm
www.ballparksofbaseball.com/past/EbbetsField.htm
www.baseball-reference.com/teams/LAD/
www.baseball-reference.com/players/r/robinja02.shtml?redir
www.ballparksofbaseball.com/past/AtlantaStadium.htm
www.ballparksofbaseball.com/past/PoloGrounds.htm
www.baseball-reference.com/teams/SFG
www.baseball-reference.com/teams/CLE/1948.shtml
www.ballparksofbaseball.com/past/ClevelandMunicipal.htm
www.ballparksofbaseball.com/past/Astrodome.htm
www.baseball-almanac.com/teams/astr.shtml
www.baseball-reference.com/players/r/ryanno01.shtml?redir
www.baseball-reference.com/teams/HOU/
www.minnesota.twins.mlb.com/min/history/postseason_results.jsp
www.ballparksofbaseball.com/past/Metrodome.htm
www.startribune.com/sports/vikings/237514831.html
www.ballparksofbaseball.com/past/ArlingtonStadium.htm
www.baseball-almanac.com/teamstats/roster.php?y=1993&t=TEX
www.baseball-almanac.com/teams/rang.shtml
www.ballparksofbaseball.com/past/QualcommStadium.htm
www.truebluela.com/2013/9/28/4781638/orel-hershiser-mlb-record-score-
    less-streak-59-innings-don-drysdale
www.ballparksofbaseball.com/past/kingdome.htm
www.baseball-reference.com/boxes/SEA/SEA199510020.shtml
www.baseball-reference.com/teams/SEA/
www.ballparksofbaseball.com/past/RiverfrontStadium.htm
www.ballparksofbaseball.com/teams/CIN/1975.shtml
www.baseball-reference.com/teams/PIT/
www.ballparksofbaseball.com/past/ThreeRiversStadium.htm
www.baseball-almanac.com/teamstats/roster.php?y=1980&t=phi
www.baseball-reference.com/teams/PHI/1980.shtml
www.philadelphia.phillies.mlb.com/phi/history/postseason_results.jsp
www.ballparksofbaseball.com/past/VeteransStadium.htm
www.ballparksofbaseball.com/past/MileHighStadium.htm
www.ballparksofbaseball.com/past/SportsmansPark.htm
www.baseball-reference.com/teams/BAL/
www.stlouis.cardinals.mlb.com/Stl/history/postseason_results.jsp
www.ballparksofbaseball.com/past/CountyStadium.htm
www.milwaukee.brewers.mlb.com/mil/history/postseason_results.jsp
www.baseball-reference.com/postseason/1957_WS.shtml
www.ballparksofbaseball.com/past/JarryPark.htm

www.sanfrancisco.giants.com/sf/history/postseason_results.jsp
www.ballparksofbaseball.com/past/CandlestickPark.htm
www.minnesota.twins.mlb.com/min/history/postseason_results.jsp
www.ballparksofbaseball.com/past/MetropolitanStadium.htm
www.ballparksofbaseball.com/past/ShibePark.htm
www.philadelphia.phillies.mlb.com/phi/history/postseason_results.jsp
www.oakland.athletics.mlb.com/oak/history/postseason_results.jsp
www.ballparksofbaseball.com/past/SunLifeStadium.htm
www.baseball-almanac.com/teamstats/roster.php?y=2003&t=FLO
www.ballparksofbaseball.com/past/KCMunicipal.htm
www.ballparksofbaseball.com/past/OlympicStadium.htm
www.ballparksofbaseball.com/past/MemorialStadium.htm
www.baseball-reference.com/teams/BAL

A SEANCE FROM THE BOOTH

www.sportsecyclopedia.com/memorial/stl/buck.html
www.blod.detroitathletic.com/2012/07/13/harwells-signature-phrases-were-
    part-of-his-appeal-to-tigers-fans/
www.detroit.tigers.mlb.com/det/history/harwell/det_history_feature_har-
    well.jsp
www.history.com/this-day-in-history/baseball-hall-of-fame-announcer-red-
    barber-dies-at-84
www.baseball-reference.com/bullpen/Mel_Allen
www.nytimes.com/2004/08/04/sports/baseball/04murphy.html
www.nytimes.com/1995/06/12/obituaries/lindseynelson-76-broadcaster-
    for-mets-for-17-years-is-dead.html
www.sports.espn.go.com/mlb/news/story?id=4064793
www.baseball-almanac.com/players/player.php?p=colemje01
www.nytimes.com/2011/08/16/sports/baseball/nat-allbright-voice-of-dodg-
    ers-games-he-did-not-see-dies-at-87.html?_r=0
www.cincinnati.com/story/tvandmediablog/2014/06/09-joe-nuxhall-reds-
    crosley-field-st-louis-cardinals-stan-musial/10065127
www.sabr.org/bioproj/person/5e296015
www.americansportscastersonline.com/thompsonmemoriam.html
www.nytimes.com/2007/08/14/sports/baseball/14/cmd_rizzuto.html
www.oakland.athletics.mlb.com/oak/fan_forum/bill-king.jsp
www.philadelphia.phillies.mlb.com/phi/history/phi_history_ashburn.jsp
www.sabr.org/bioproj/person/cda44a76
www.m.indians.mlb.com/news/article/66195858

www.m.yankees.mlb.com/news/article/66195858
www.thisgreatgame.com/minnesota-twins-top-10-games.html
www.grhof.com/08%20CA%2077%20BRAVES%20Announcers.htm

LIVING LEGENDS

www.officialvinscully.com/broadcasting-highlights.php
www.voices.suntimes.com/sports/vin-scully-has-called-7-percent-of-all-
   mlb-no-hitters/
www.baseball-reference.com/teams/LAD/
www.losangeles.dodgers.mlb.com/la/history/postseason_results.jsp
www.houston.astros.mlb.com/mlb/news/tributes/milo_hamilton.jsp?c_
   id6702
www.blog.chron.com/ultimateastros/2012/09/26/milo-hamiltons-top-
   5-calls-from-aaron-to-biggio-watch-and-remember/
www.web.yesnetwork.com/news/article.jsp?ymd=20130220&context_
   id=418109216
www.usatoday.com/story/sports/columnist/hiestand-tv/2013/02/20/joe-
   garagiola-vin-scully-red-barber-nbc-today-show-westminster-kennel-club-
   dog-show-st-louis-cardinals/1932797
www.sfgate.com/giants/shea/article/lon-simmons-never-tells-giants-good-
   bye-4286644.php
www.cbssports.com/cbssports/team/malbert

Index

About the Author

Kirk McKnight is an American author specializing in interview-based sports books ranging from the diamonds of baseball to the hardwood floors of college basketball. A 2002 graduate of Brigham Young University's Marriott School of Business Management, Kirk studied screenwriting at the University of Nevada Las Vegas for one semester but subsequently molded his writing from fiction to nonfiction, with an emphasis on collegiate and professional sports. Kirk currently resides in Las Vegas, Nevada, with his wife Collette and daughter Adaira.